The New Mexicans

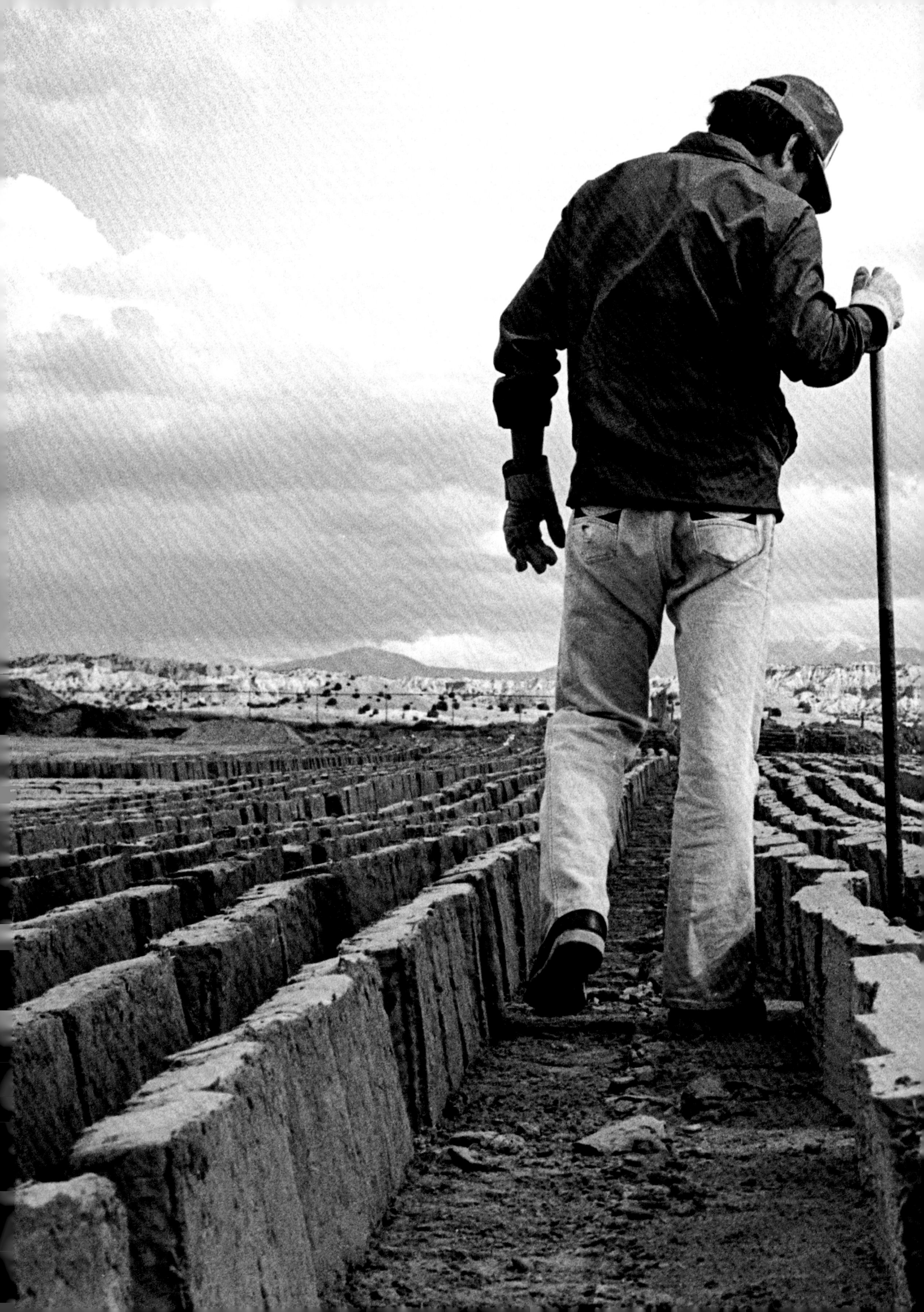

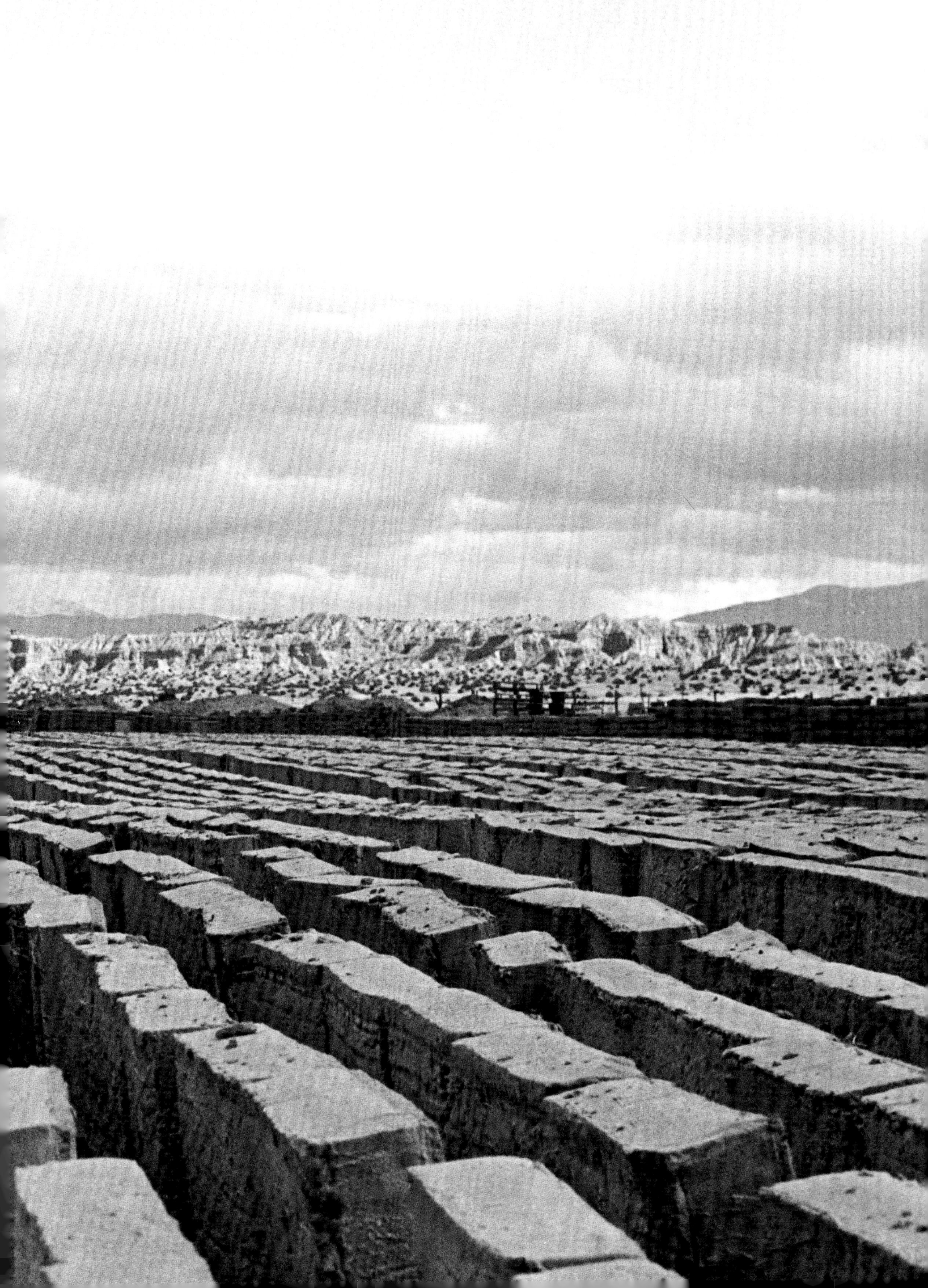

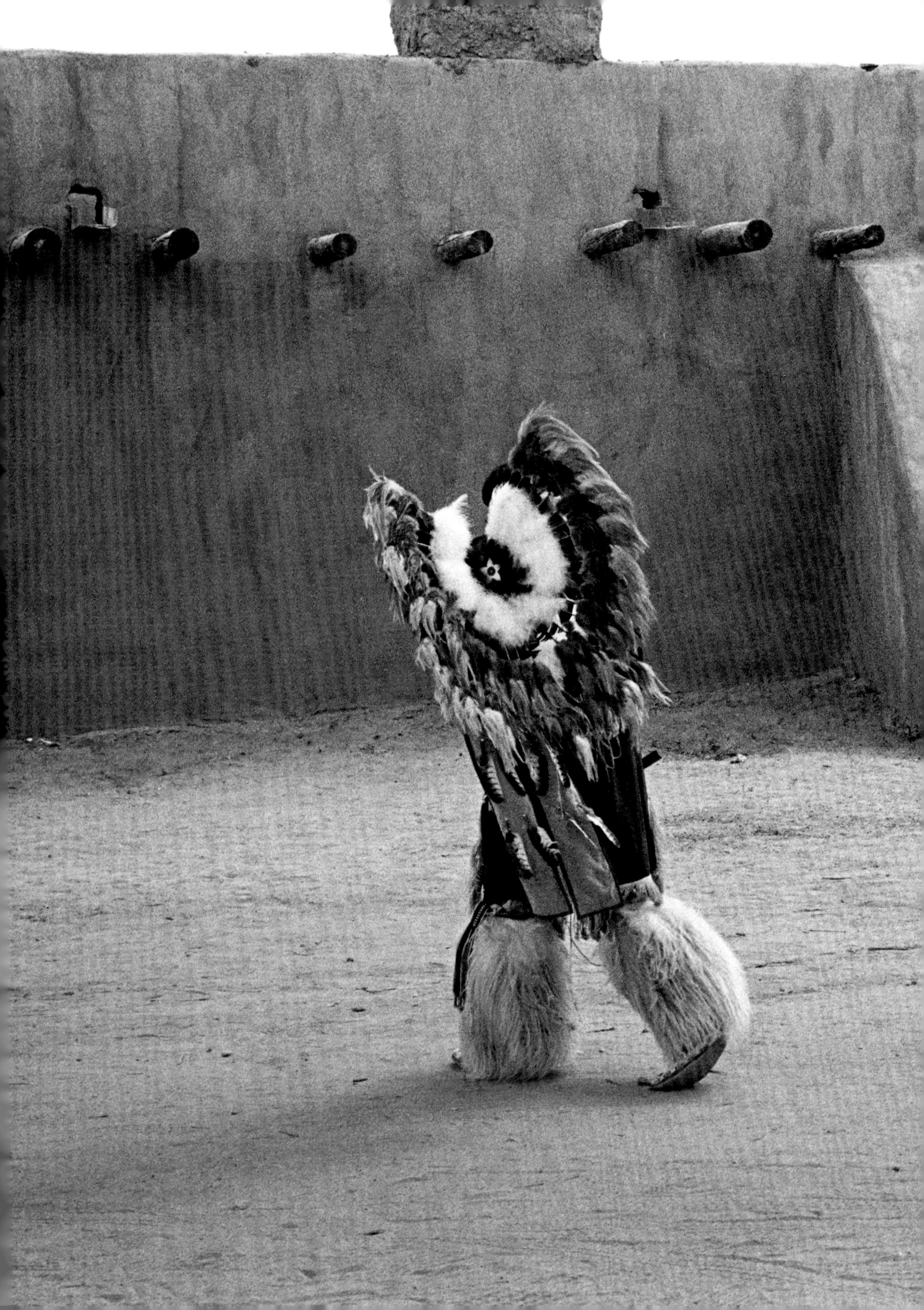

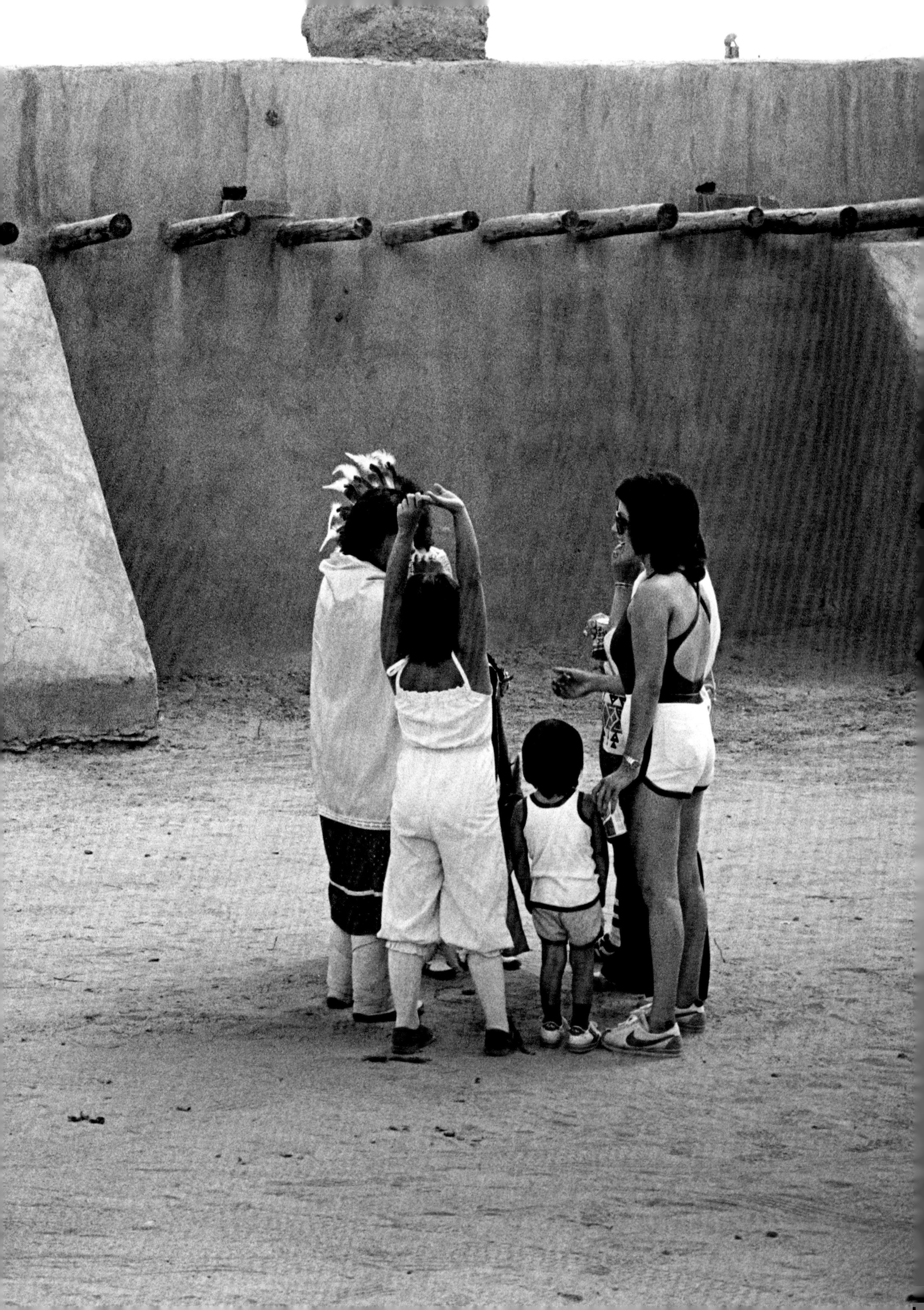

The New Mexicans
1981–83

Kevin Bubriski

Foreword by Bernard Plossu
Essay by Matthew J. Martinez

MUSEUM OF NEW MEXICO PRESS
SANTA FE

The Museum of New Mexico Press acknowledges the original peoples of New Mexico—Pueblo, Navajo, and Apache—who have deep connections to the land and have made impactful contributions to the state of New Mexico. We honor the land, all things living, and those who remain committed stewards of this beautiful landscape for future generations.

PAGES 2–3: Making adobe bricks at the mosque at Dar al Islam, Abiquiú, 1982.
PAGES 4–5: Comanche Dance, Feast Day, Ohkay Owingeh, 1982.
OVERLEAF: Chimayó, 1982.

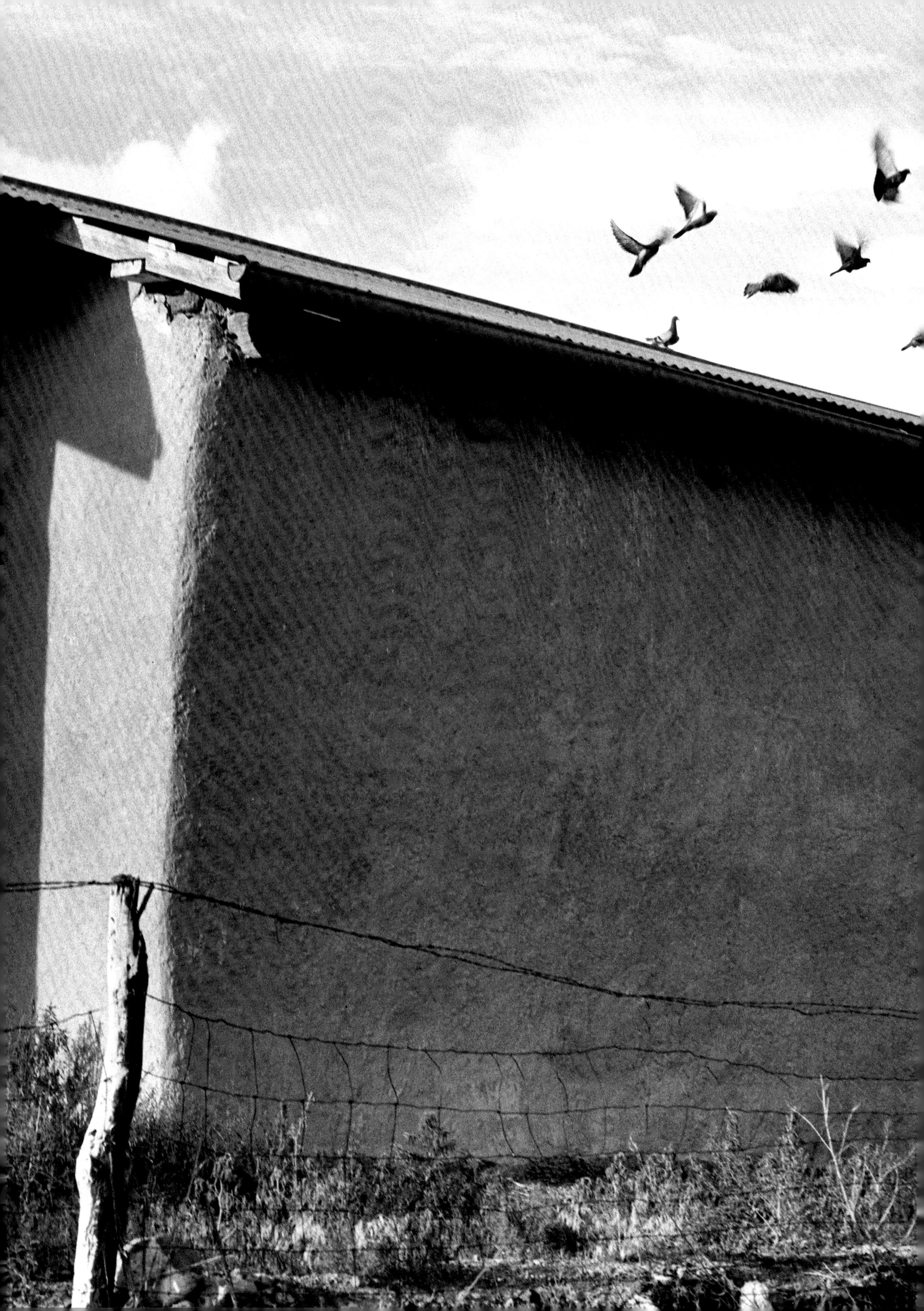

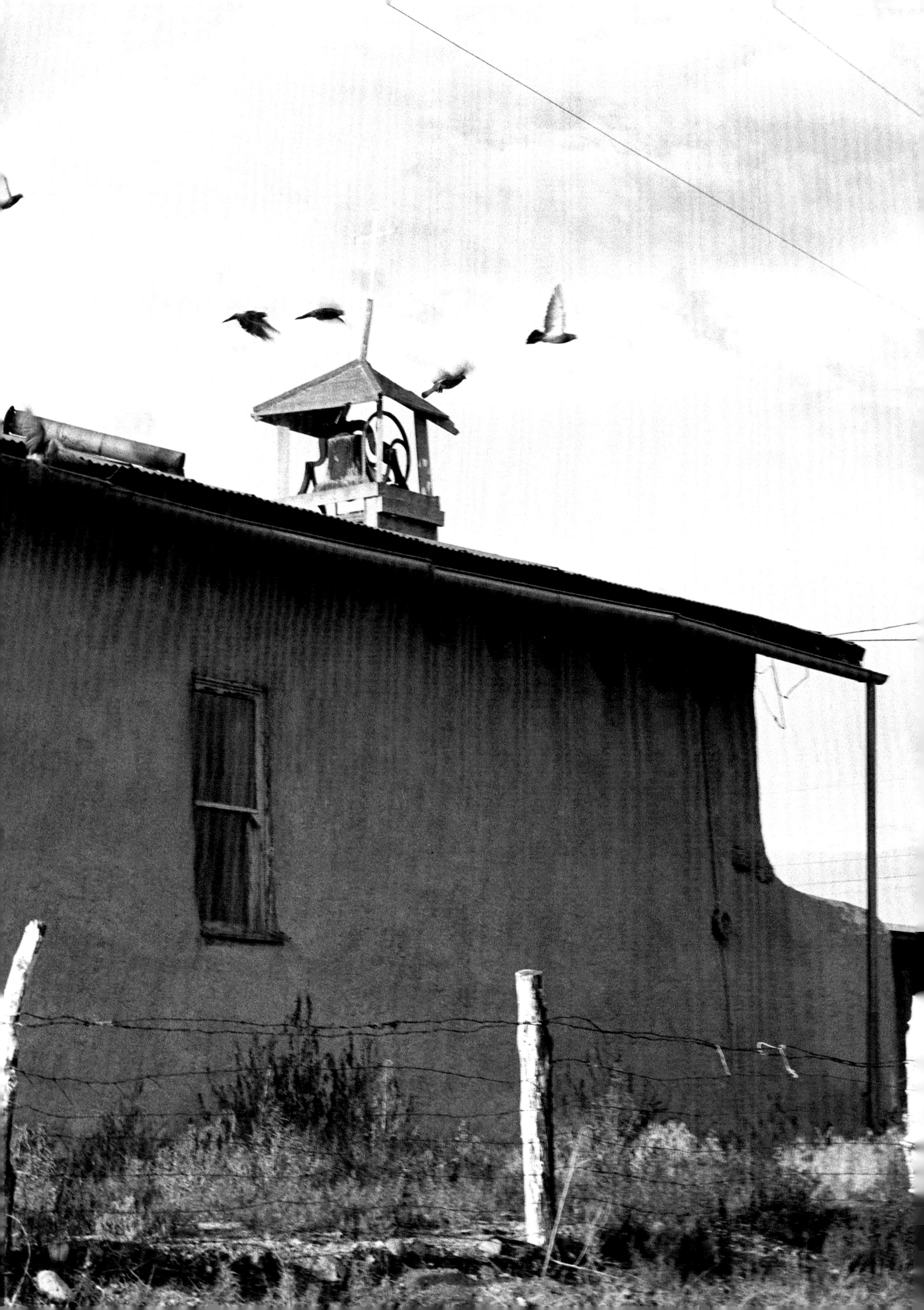

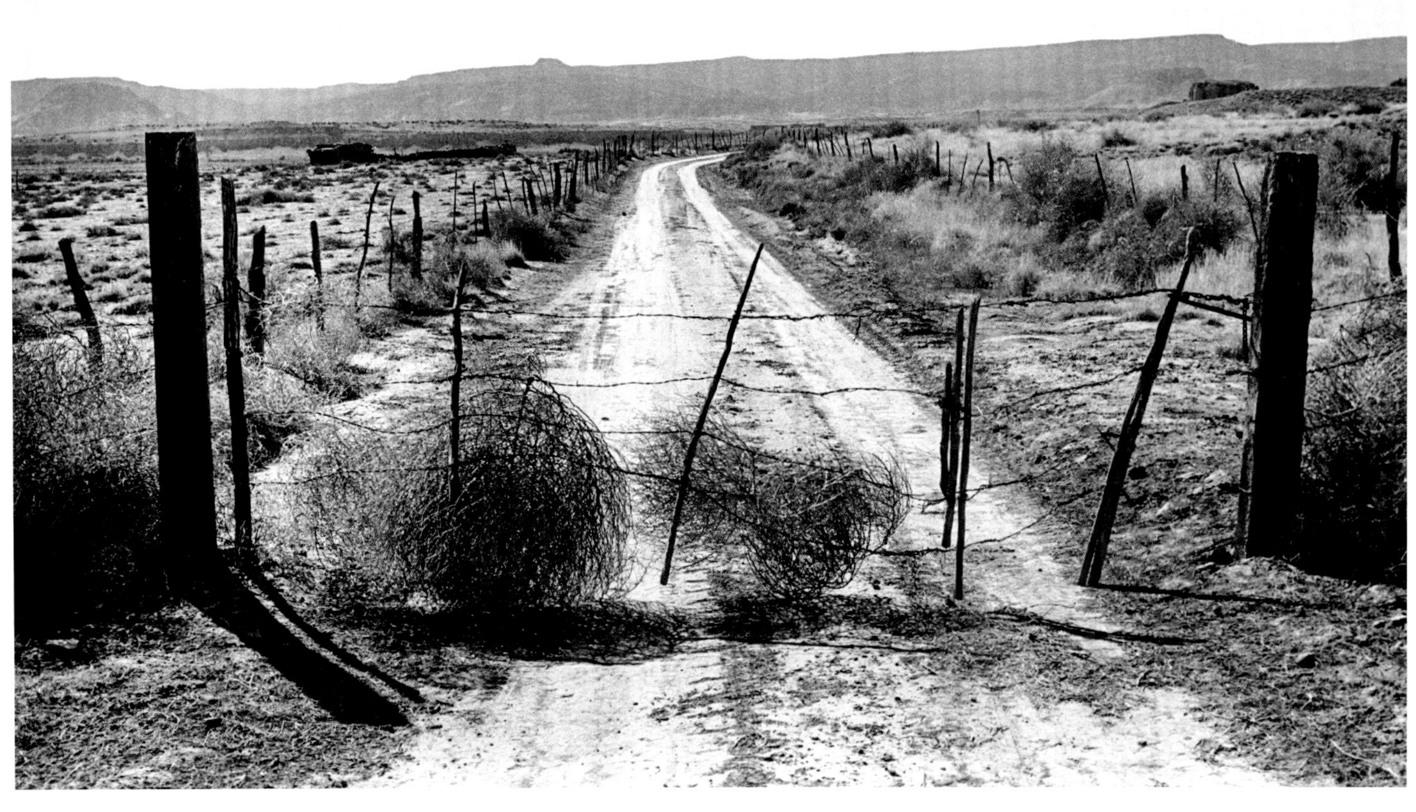

Coyote, 1982.

Foreword

Ready All the Time

One day, while living in New Mexico in the late 1970s and '80s, I met the young photographer Kevin Bubriski, who had moved to Santa Fe like so many of us, coming from elsewhere.

He showed me his prints of Nepal, and I knew right away that he was a true photographer. The evidence of good pictures is immediate.

Kevin stayed, like many of us, for years, captured by the passion of what is called, in this state, "the Land of Enchantment."

Many of us have spent years, even a lifetime, photographing the breathtaking landscapes of New Mexico. Bubriski reacted differently: he was concerned with the people, just as it had happened to him years before in Nepal. And little by little, he tried to capture the different lifestyles of this state, moving from south to north, from Albuquerque real to Santa Fe chic, and on up to Taos. He became what is called "a concerned photographer" of this land.

His pictures were done patiently along the years. Patience is one of the key qualities of good photographers: things happen visually to those who are ready all the time.

So: pictures of wild horses, of meaningful dances in Pueblos, of hip people bathing in the snow, of lowriders, of elegant people—men wearing ties—at social gatherings, of cowboys in rodeos, of musicians with guitars and accordions, of funerals, of runners, and portraits of all his fellow photographers. The list goes on.

But Kevin also wanted to see and photograph the Native people, those who were the original inhabitants of this land for centuries, the American Indians. That is not easy, as one has to be "accepted" to do this. His pictures were influenced by what he had done before in Nepal, and I can say his photographs of the Indian peoples of New Mexico have the same sincere quality and strength as those he had done before in Asia.

Kevin's pictures of Pueblo dances in this sense are remarkable.

For me, that was meaningful. It had also been my goal while living in the Southwest, after having photographed in the '70s tribes of African desert nomads, the Bororos and the Tuaregs, whose lifestyle was quite similar to that of the seminomadic Apaches or Navajos.

We are, our family of photographers, visual anthropologists. That is why I am a great admirer of Edward T. Hall, the distinguished anthropologist who was living in Santa Fe also in the 1980s, totally dedicated to the Southwest.

Thanks, Kevin, for all that you did visually in this strong land. You are concerned. You are sincere.

BERNARD PLOSSU
La Ciotat, France, February 2024

The New Mexicans

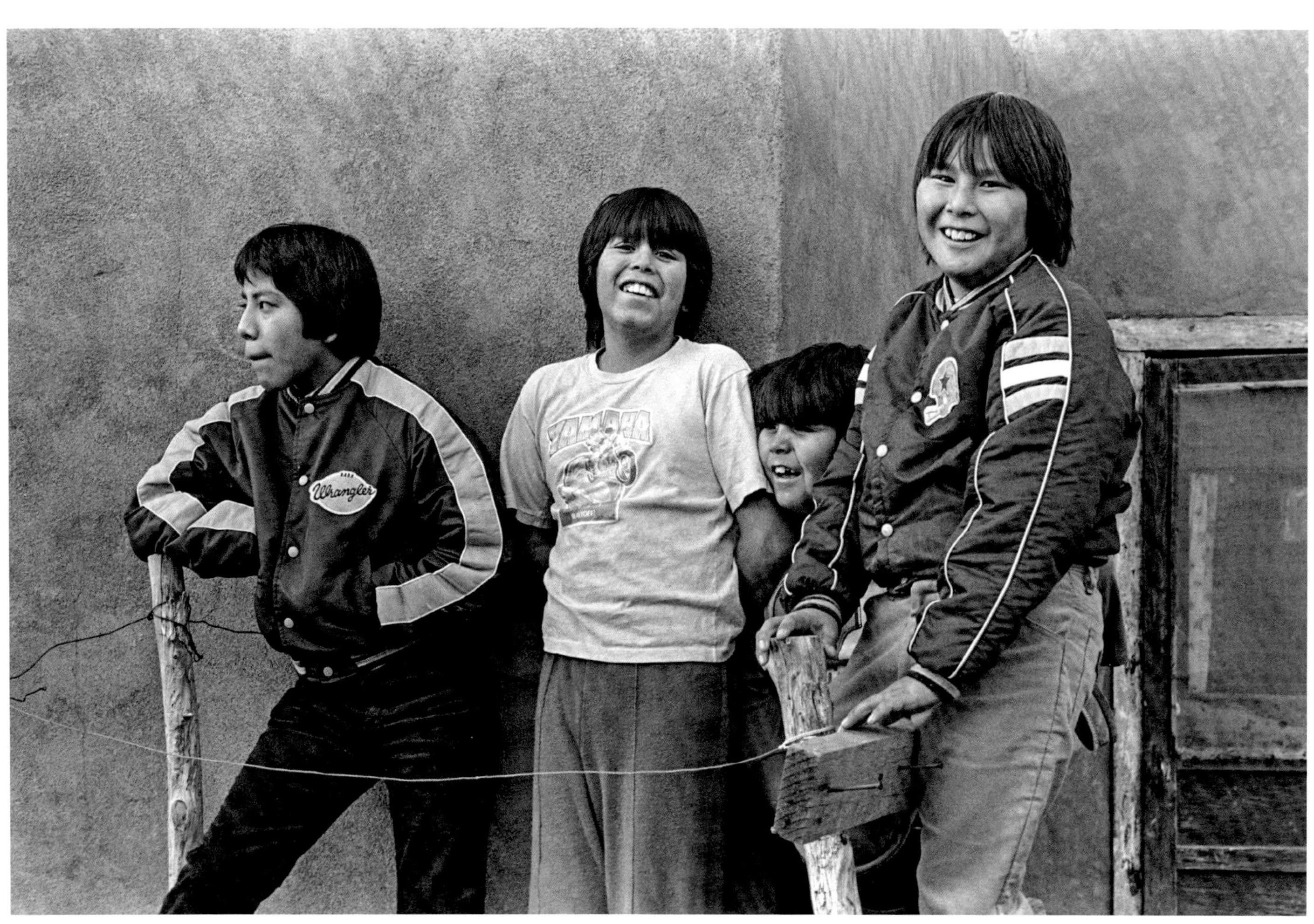

Ohkay Owingeh, 1982.

Framed and Unframed

A SPIRIT OF PLACE

MATTHEW J. MARTINEZ

As a child, I remember my father telling me stories of visitors traveling through Ohkay Owingeh in the summertime. My father and his sisters recalled how as children they used to sit in front of the church and wait for tourists to drive by so they could get paid to have their pictures taken. They would then walk across the street to the mercantile store to buy pocketfuls of penny candy. A nickel back in the late 1940s and early 1950s would purchase plenty of sugar goodies to spread among their brothers and sisters.

My father has since passed on, and I would do anything to see some of those old photographs of my father and his siblings as children. I imagine them stored in some dusty East Coast attic along with other "souvenirs" from a long-forgotten summer vacation to New Mexico. I continue to cherish and laugh about my family's stories and share them with my own son. This is how traditions remain alive. We as New Mexicans are the link to those who came before and those yet to be born—and photographs can be powerful agents in creating dynamic spaces of memory and continuity.

I've often wondered if visitors to New Mexico realize the impacts their photography—the taking of images—may have on future generations. The very act of taking a photo is extractive. But for New Mexicans, every extractive practice is balanced by the core value of reciprocity, deeply embedded within community relations and cultural traditions. As an example, when we gather clay and other materials to create a micaceous pot, we appropriately ask our Mother Earth, Nan Ochu Kwiyó, for permission. Among Tewa people, the deliberate act of sharing one's intentions in gathering and using clay is a central part of the process in creating a pottery bowl.

Photographing is no different. It falls in line with what it means to actively engage in reciprocity. How these images are taken and shared, often in intimate settings, can create and strengthen ongoing community relationships. A photograph can connect people and community values and, at the same time, interweave stories that define a community's rich histories. When the images travel out to the general public, they take on lives and interpretations of their own.

Historically, New Mexico's cultural traditions, peoples, and landscapes have inspired photographers and artists, and Indigenous peoples throughout the Southwest have been some of the most photographed and documented people in the United States. Kevin Bubriski's photographs of Pueblo dances and ceremonies are part of this long tradition of image making and image taking. With the publication of this book, they become an act of reciprocity, returning to the peoples and communities from which they originated.

Like the gathering of clay from Mother Earth, the framing of a subject to be photographed is an intentional act. Bubriski states that "with camera in hand, I have always let my curiosity lead my eye. Or maybe it's my eye that leads and triggers my curiosity." As a tangible artifact, one that physically holds that moment, a photo conveys a sense of proof of what actually happened. What is not included in the photograph, what lies outside the frame, is also a significant part of the framed image, informed by the viewer's experience and knowledge of a larger context. In viewing these black and white photos of Pueblo dances, one can feel the echoing beat of drumming at the plaza, smell the aroma of piñon and juniper smoke from the fireplaces, and hear the laughter of nearby children.

One of the many captivating images in *The New Mexicans* is of the late Joe Garcia as a young man, with his wife and daughter. Taken during the annual feast day at Ohkay Owingeh, this probably records a short break for the dancers, a moment to catch up on staying hydrated during a smoldering mid-June afternoon. Joe's daughter gladly partakes in sipping from a can of Shasta. Like many of these photographs, this image captures the innocence of this young Comanche dancer with his family. Later in life, Joe would become Governor of his tribe and a national force in Indian Country. As an act of reciprocity, these photographs will serve as deep personal records for the families who view them and will in turn spark memories of private moments and public gatherings.

Other extraordinary photographs are those of Native men incarcerated at the New Mexico State Penitentiary, holding their annual powwow along with friends and family members. These photos capture a time and intimate space where cultural traditions are practiced, despite being within a restricted system. Powwow traditions are often intertribal and centered on community and family relations. Perhaps influenced by the signing of the American Indian Religious Freedom Act just a few years earlier in 1978, Native men and their families created a healing space as seen through photographs of dance and song. As a return to basic liberties, the Act allowed American Indians to practice and express their traditional religious rites and cultural practices. Native traditions, both social and within village settings, often serve as a time on their own to express a way of life. What is compelling is the level of access Bubriski pursued with his camera in hand.

The 1980s were a pivotal time in this country and for New Mexicans, a time of transition, of vibrant and tumultuous social movements, a moment in which we stood on the brink of a new internet era that would change so much. Bubriski's photographs capture this moment. Although they are black and white, their shadows and light exude a vivid sense of everyday people and communities full of color and life—even when those people aren't included in the frame. The photograph of an abandoned Cadillac facing a pair of wooden crosses in Truchas sparks vivid memories and endless questions. An abandoned car may be an all-too-common sight in rural New Mexico, but the image grabs our attention and incites our curiosity. Who owned this vehicle? Did they have a family, and where did they travel in this boat-like car? What would have been playing on the radio? Did the car eventually become a shiny lowrider? Although seemingly abandoned on cinder blocks, this vehicle continues to have life through family memory and lore. Just ask any New Mexican about their most memorable road trip.

Photographs themselves can serve as vehicles, allowing us to revisit places and people and discover new truths. And a photograph can radically change how we think and feel. Kevin Bubriski's photographs in *The New Mexicans, 1981–83* remind us of a spirit and place we call New Mexico, and they show us who we were and are.

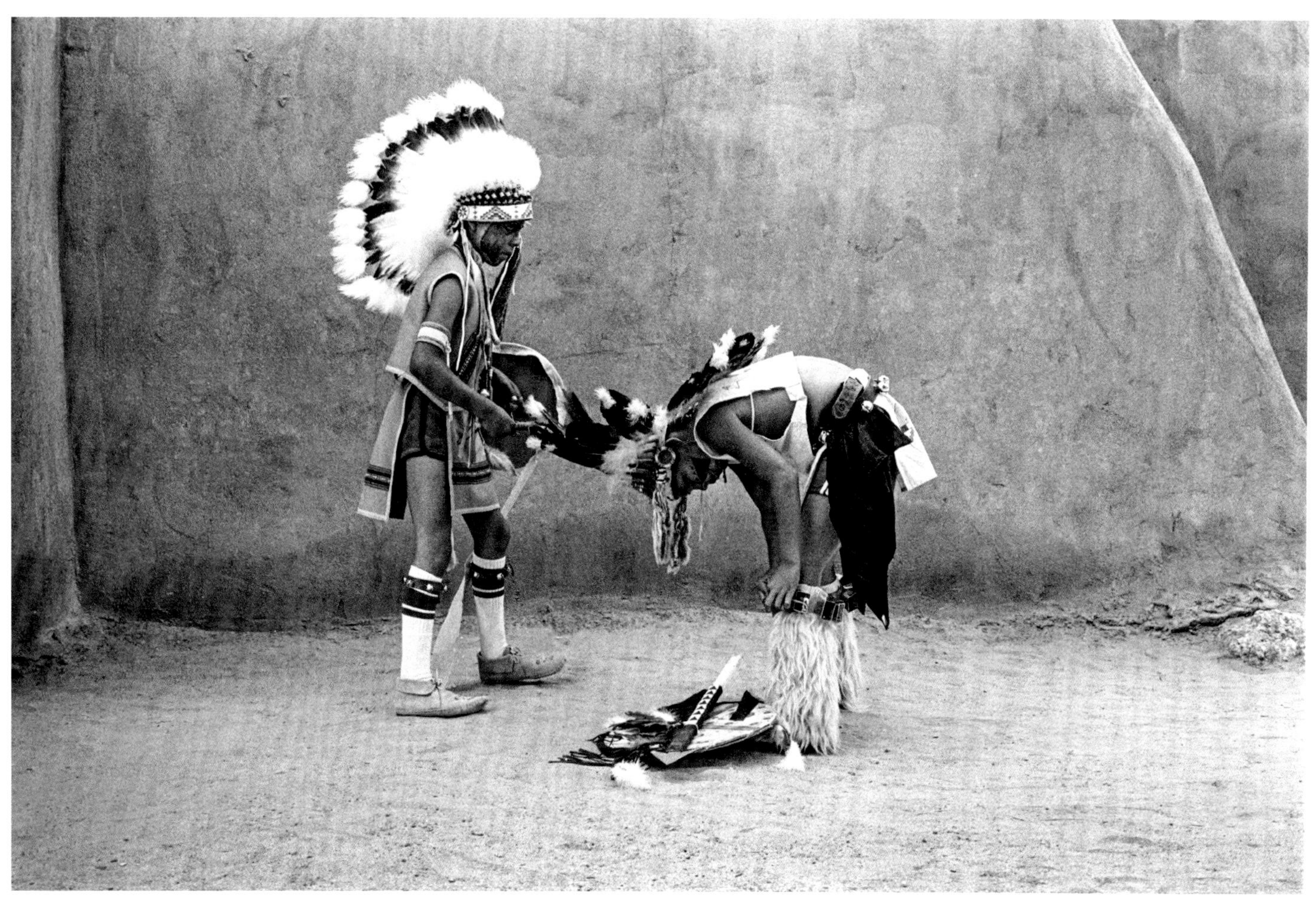

Comanche Dance, Feast Day, Ohkay Owingeh, 1982.

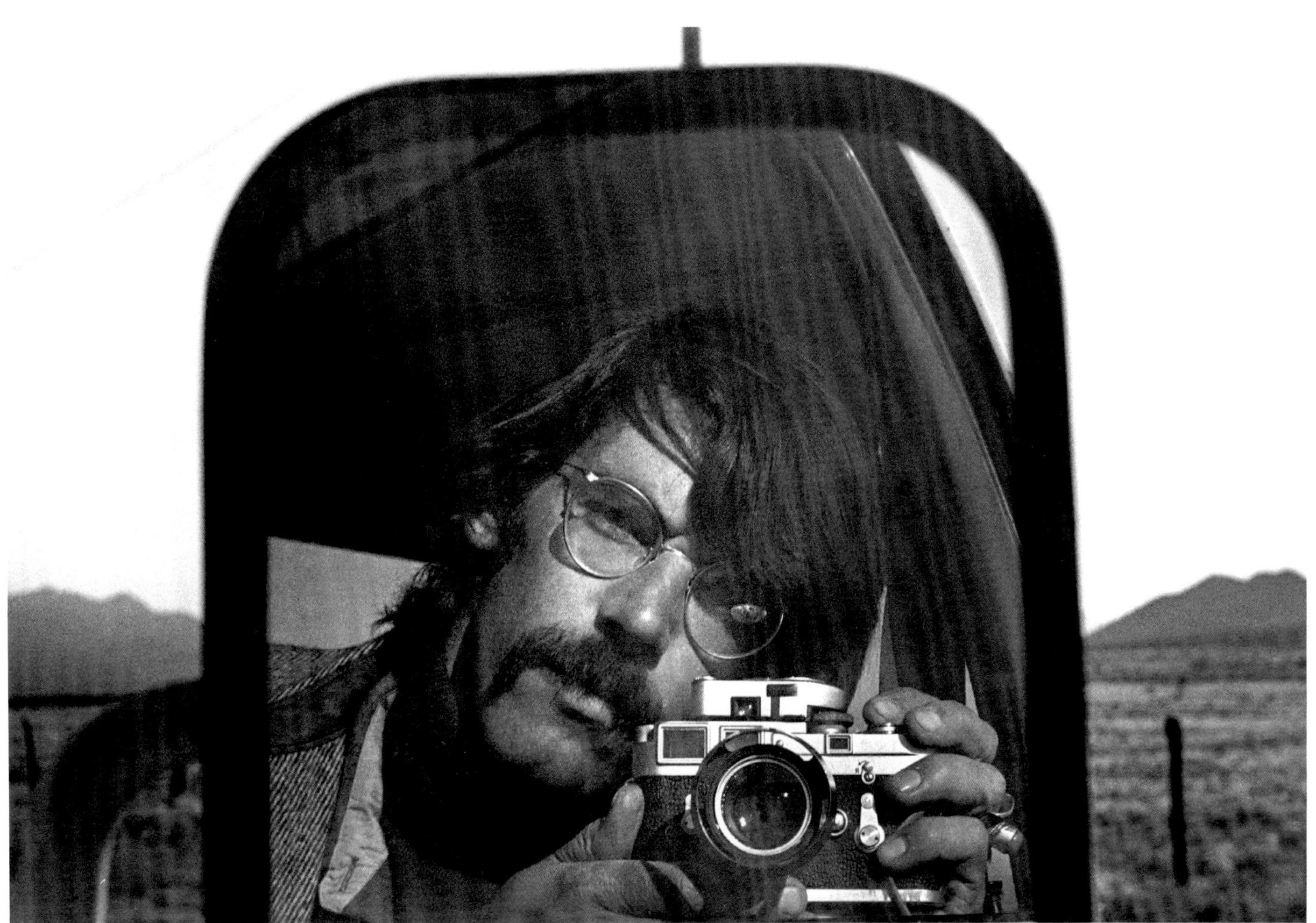

Self-portrait, Coyote, 1982.

The New Mexicans 1981–83

KEVIN BUBRISKI

I arrived in New Mexico in the first week of January 1981, after a nonstop solo drive from the Northeast to the Southwest. Just back a year from four years in the Peace Corps in Nepal, I had never had a driver's license and never driven before. My license was only a week old, and this was my first time in the driver's seat, alone in a car. On my first day out I traveled from northwestern Massachusetts to western Pennsylvania; day two to St. Louis; day three to Tulsa. The fourth and last day of my cross-country drive took me from Tulsa, Oklahoma, to Santa Fe, New Mexico. Somewhere around Amarillo I picked up a hitchhiker, who turned out to be a student at St. John's College in Santa Fe.

We arrived late at night at a simple, rough adobe house near Canyon Road that the hitchhiker was sharing with five other students. That night I distinctly remember the comforting smell of the woodstove's piñon smoke, which immediately put me at ease. The aroma reminded me of the pinewood fires of the family homes I had lived in a year earlier in Nepal's remote northwest mountain villages. I woke the next morning to brilliant sunshine and warm greetings from my hitchhiker's housemates.

After a few days enjoying the St. John's students' hospitality, I found a room to rent in Cheryl Brostrom's house on Abeyta Street, just off the Acequia Madre, Santa Fe's main irrigation ditch—a quiet and old residential neighborhood less than a mile east of the Plaza. I shared the kitchen with Cheryl and her grade-school-aged son for the next several months, along with Stephen Cooper, a massage student from Breckenridge, Texas; Pennsylvanian Paul Hudock, a cook at the Pink Adobe restaurant; and Houston, Texas, filmmaker Bruce "Pacho" Lane.

Having successfully made that four-day journey from Massachusetts to Santa Fe in the dead of winter, I now felt entirely comfortable with my old—and very used—pale blue little Renault. I made it a point to get in the car and explore the Santa Fe area. Compared to the Northeast, where I grew up, the winter sun of New Mexico was ever present and warm, the spaces wide, the people relaxed and open. Morning greetings from strangers in town felt normal and comfortable.

I had gone to Santa Fe to study filmmaking at the Anthropology Film Center on Upper Canyon Road. Richard Sorenson, director of the Human Studies Film Archives (HSFA) in the National Museum of Natural History, was building at the Smithsonian a cultural film archive on the Himalayas and other remote regions of the world. I had met Richard the year before in Kathmandu, and he liked the samples of my Nepal photography that I had on hand from my Peace Corps years. He suggested that I learn documentary film skills in Santa Fe and then come back to Washington to pursue possible collaborations. Months later, on hearing that funding for the Smithsonian's HSFA had dwindled and several programs had been cut, I stayed on in Santa Fe instead.

At the Anthropology Film Center, a school run by filmmaker Carroll Williams and anthropologist Joan Swayze Williams, there was just a handful of us learning the practice of 16-mm documentary filmmaking. The Film Center was a curious place, laid back and eccentric, where a pack of large, noisy, but gentle black-and-tan hound dogs outnumbered the students. Carroll, an avid motorcyclist, storyteller, and chain-smoker of unfiltered cigarettes (Camels or hand-rolled), introduced us to the finest documentary filmmaking equipment. We were shooting 16-mm film with everything from hand-wound Bolexes to state-of-the-art Arriflex and Eclair NPR cameras. We recorded sound with multiple microphones on high-fidelity Swiss Nagra tape recorders and spliced together our pieces of film and strips of sound with clear cellophane tape over the splicer's sprockets. My short documentary film for the class, *Chimayo Pilgrimage*, followed construction worker Leroy Perea on Holy Thursday as he walked with a forty-pound cross on his shoulder north from Santa Fe and up the Nambé Road to Chimayó. Leroy had injured his back at work. In penance and with prayers for healing, he walked alone on the empty road one day before the annual spectacle of huge Good Friday pilgrimage crowds making their way to the Santuario de Chimayó.

By late spring, classes were over, and I was working with Pacho Lane and his one-person film company Earthworm Films. We were making a film titled *Los Moros y los Cristianos* in Chimayó—a horseback drama of the Crusades and the battles between the Christians and Moors that was enacted along with a weekend parade and fiesta in the village. Before the film was finished, Pacho got called away to South America to work with documentary filmmaker Les Blank on *Burden of Dreams*, Blank's film portrait of Werner Herzog, who was then on location shooting *Fitzcaraldo* in the Amazonian jungles of Peru.

As summer ended, and with Pacho in Peru, I was fortunate to meet Michael Hausman, producer for the PBS Playhouse film *The Ballad of Gregorio Cortez*. The film was shooting locally, and Michael hired me on as still photographer for the production. I got to work directly and closely with director Robert Young and cinematographer Ray Villalobos, observing their ways of creating and imaging the film, and at times assisting with camera work. We were a traveling circus, a large cast of actors, horses, wranglers, set designers, costumers, lighting technicians, caterers, and local extras moving from locations in Santa Fe, Cerrillos, Chama, and Las Vegas, New Mexico, then up to Cortez, Colorado, and finally down to Gonzales, Texas. It's impossible to forget the excitement of riding atop a steam-engine train moving through the mountainous terrain of southern Colorado as we filmed a stampede of Texas Rangers on horseback in hot pursuit of the hero Gregorio Cortez, played by Edward James Olmos. Also memorable was the acrid, smokey atmosphere of the torch-carrying lynch mob assembled at night outside the prison doors—and then shooting inside the actual prison and courtroom in Gonzales, Texas, where the real Gregorio Cortez had been held and tried.

During my first months in Santa Fe, while still at the film school, I also met people at a Himalayan cultural center on Canyon Road. I got to know the director, Paljor Thondup, and on Saturdays Paljor, his friend Pema Rabgay, and I sometimes visited Synergia Ranch, with its collection of artists, theatrical folks, alternative-energy windmills, and early photovoltaic prototypes. Synergia's branch operations spanned the globe from the Hotel Vajra in Kathmandu to the ferro-concrete research vessel the *Heraclitus* to Biosphere 2 in Arizona. At Synergia, Paljor enjoyed practicing his superb marksmanship and made a name for himself by shooting a rattlesnake through the floorboards of a cabin at the ranch. Paljor, Pema, and I made a road trip up to Boulder and Denver to attend public presentations and a private audience with a Buddhist spiritual leader. Paljor's entrepreneurial nature meant that we traveled in a panel van filled with Himalayan carpets and staged pop-up sales and shows of the carpets at my brother's place in Golden and other locations. I did not see Paljor in later years, but I was delighted to hear that in the year before his death he published a memoir about his homeland and his work over many decades as a warrior for world peace.

Through Paljor Thondup I met Ricky Stevens, who worked fulltime for Continental Airlines. Ricky was away most of the time and was happy to have me caretake her condominium in the Llano Compound on East Palace Avenue for the next six months.

Contractor John Coffee hired me part-time to work on his construction and maintenance crew at the compound. After leaving Ricky's condo, I spent the following six months sharing an apartment at the upper end of East Palace Avenue with Kitty Leaken, staff photographer for the weekly *Santa Fe Reporter*. Kitty had endless energy, an exuberant smile, and an engaging spirit. Her apartment and yard were the scene of many lively gatherings.

French photographer Bernard Plossu responded immediately to my photographs from Nepal, and we became very good friends. I was invited to join him on many photo outings and spent time with his family in Eldorado, where Bernard often hosted guests from France, across Europe, and Africa. I also became the printer of his fine art photographs. Bernard had his camera with him always, and from him I learned to always have my camera with me as well. A bit like a rabbit, Bernard would jump into action with his one simple manual camera, with its one 50-mm fixed-focal-length lens. As Bernard would say, "50 mm—that's the way French painter Corot saw the world." As the printer of Bernard's photographs, I had a very close relationship with his work, knowing all of his contact sheets, absorbing his editing process, and coming to anticipate his critical eye. What was very special about Bernard was his large, enthusiastic spirit and his readiness to leap into action, to click the shutter and grab what he saw. He did take intentional photographic trips, but he was always alert to the moment wherever he was and felt there might be something to capture at anytime, anywhere.

Through Bernard's introduction I had my first photography exhibition at Nicholas Potter's bookstore just a block from the Santa Fe Plaza. And Bernard introduced me to many fellow photographers in Santa Fe: Pierre Mahaim, Walter Nelson, Mary Peck, Douglas Keats, Siegfried Halus, Nancy Sutor, Terry Husebye, Edward Ranney, and Paul Caponigro. In the spring of 1982, Bernard, Walter, Pierre, and I road-tripped out to San Francisco and back. In San Francisco we stayed with Tim Eaton, who became my first fine art photography dealer at his gallery, housed at the time in the San Francisco U-Haul headquarters building. In Berkeley we met with Arthur Ollman, who a decade later presented a large one-person show of my Nepal photographs at the Museum of Photographic Arts in San Diego, where he had become director. Arthur also wrote the introduction for my first book of photographs, *Portrait of Nepal*. Surprisingly, and as luck would have it, the book won first place in documentary photography in the 1993 Golden Light Awards for Photographic Book of the Year from the Maine Photographic Workshops—ahead of now-iconic books by Nan Goldin, Mary Ellen Mark, Danny Lyon, and Sebastião Salgado in that year's competition.

New Mexico has attracted photographers going back to the nineteenth century and photography's earliest technologies. It is the harsh and dramatic beauty of the landscape, the shifting, sharp-edged light, and the great diversity of peoples that draw us to the state. In the early 1980s one could bump into Elliot Porter, Paul Caponigro, Joan Myers, Edward Ranney, or William Clift at Grant Kalivoda's Camera & Darkroom store just off the Plaza. Two or three years earlier, one might also have met Laura Gilpin at the shop. When Gilpin died in 1979, her assistant Mary Peck took over the studio and became custodian of Gilpin's archive. Mary also continued her own large-format photographic work in the Everglades, the New Mexico desert, the temples of Greece, and the Himalayas of Bhutan. Living in Santa Fe among such photographers, it was inevitable that I would buy a 4×5-inch sheet-film view camera. I found numerous mentors around me: Ray Belcher, Doug Keats, Walter Nelson, Brad Bealmear, Arnie Trujillo, and others. Arnie and I camped near Chaco Canyon for a few blistering hot days in May of 1982 and had the pristine ruins to ourselves and our view cameras. Brad, Walter, Weston DeWalt, and Robert Reck generously loaned me their darkrooms during my years in New Mexico. I had freedom to do my own work, and in return, if something of theirs came along that needed darkroom work, I would do it. No money ever changed hands. It was always a comfortable barter.

Four-wheeling off-road drives with Walter Nelson in his Chevy Blazer got me into the magical light and beauty of remote desert landscapes. Walter always worked with the 8×10 view camera, taking his time under the black cloth to figure out his image composition on the ground glass. Another aspect of Walter's art was to draw with oil pastels or paint with oils the backdrops for his flower arrangements, which he would photograph with 8×10 color sheet film; he then very ambitiously made his own dye transfer prints. Walter also generously shared his Rodeo Road condo with me. He had converted the two-car garage into a luxuriously spacious darkroom, large enough for regular equipment as well as his Merz drum film processor and a super-sized enlarger for handling 8×10 negatives. I have a guilty memory of once mistakenly disconnecting the refrigerator outside the darkroom—

the refrigerator where Walter stored a large stash of Agfa's deliciously warm-toned Portriga Rapid photographic paper that he was keeping for the long term. I offer my forty-years-belated apology to Walter for spoiling that treasured stash of Portriga Rapid.

Soon after I finished my studies at the Anthropology Film Center and wrapped up the film jobs I worked on through the fall of 1981, I started to get freelance jobs in still photography. Making my own films seemed a remote possibility due to the exorbitant costs of 16-mm film production. I began to work from time to time with Wally Gordon on his magazine *Letter from Santa Fe* and traveled with him to political rallies and events and on the campaign trails of Toney Anaya, Jeff Bingaman, Bill Richardson, and Harrison "Jack" Schmitt. Wally was quick and intelligent and brought me into an immediate intimacy with the political figures that he followed.

In early August of 1982, I was hired at *The Santa Fe New Mexican*—"the West's oldest newspaper"—to fill in for two weeks while staff photographer Barbaraellen Koch was on her summer vacation. On my second or third day at *The New Mexican*, the managing editor assigned me to travel south of Santa Fe to Waldo, New Mexico, to cover the manhunt and search for clues after the murder of Father Reynaldo Rivera, a Franciscan priest at the Cathedral Basilica of Saint Francis of Assisi in Santa Fe. I haven't located those negatives, but I vividly recall photographing the many men in plain beige uniforms walking in tandem, combing the high desert landscape of La Bajada for evidence related to Fr. Rivera's murder. Not many days later, I was assigned to photograph Fr. Rivera's funeral. My editor was disappointed that I didn't get any aerial shots, like Brian Walski's images for the *Albuquerque Journal*, which he took from an upper-story window and that showed the magnitude of the long, solemn march from the Basilica through downtown Santa Fe to the cemetery. My images were, instead, all ground-level portraits of a grieving community. I wanted to be close to the faces of the mourners—and for the first time, my photographs went out by Associated Press wire to the national media.

The following early Saturday morning, I was driving through Santa Fe looking for things to photograph, still on hire for two weeks filling in for Barbaraellen Koch. I spotted a fellow who had run a long hose across the road out to a small triangular traffic island to water the grasses and flowers planted there. The sunlight beautifully caught the spray of water with energized backlighting. I pulled the car over, grabbed my camera, and asked the man with the hose for permission to take some photos. Not only was he happy to be photographed—he also invited me to his garden party later that afternoon. At that point he mentioned that he was Forrest Fenn, a name I recognized as a larger-than-life figure in the Santa Fe art world. The party was a fine event with plentiful drinks, attractive gardens, wandering musicians, and a collection of well-heeled guests from the worlds of art and politics, including former Texas governor and U.S. Treasury secretary John Connally and his wife. I was welcome to wander among the guests and photograph; a couple of days later a selection of the photos made it into *The New Mexican*.

From the apartment on East Palace, I moved in early fall of 1982 to Albuquerque to start employment as staff photographer at the new semiweekly newspaper *The New Mexico Sun*. My Santa Fe photography friends were wary of my move to Albuquerque, but this was my first full-time photography job, and I was stoked. Living in Albuquerque gave me a different perspective on Santa Fe and on New Mexico in general. At *The Sun* I was assigned several different stories each day and had to shoot the story, process the film, and make prints in short order to meet deadlines. I kept up with all the assignments and then spent all my free time delving deeper into the topics and places that I was becoming acquainted with.

Every day I put fifty to one hundred miles on my newly purchased but very old Chevy Nova, racing from one assignment to the next, rushing to the darkroom to process the film, quickly drying it with a hair dryer, printing the selections, fast drying the prints (the hair dryer again), and then getting them to the managing editor for approval and layout.

My new residence was a modest apartment in a quiet part of Albuquerque. The only neighbor I got to know lived in the unit above me—a gentle middle-aged fellow on parole after doing several years for armed robbery. I don't remember his name, but I do remember his remark that he noticed I always put the figure or subject of my photographs in the center of the image, as if the subject was in the crosshairs. He called this centered placement "the meatball." At the newspaper my photo editor, Anthony K. Roberts, was always criticizing me for having the subject of my photographs centered and looking straight into the lens. Tony didn't want that "meatball" placement.

Tony "Kal" Roberts, my boss at *The New Mexico Sun*, had won the Pulitzer Prize for Spot News Photography in 1974 for his coverage in a Los Angeles parking lot of a woman held at knifepoint by an assailant. The incident, recorded in a photographic series titled *Fatal Hollywood Drama*, ended when the alleged kidnapper was killed by a security officer's gunfire. Tony was a larger-than-life character, 6 feet 5 inches tall, who wore a black ten-gallon cowboy hat wrapped with a rattlesnake-skin band. His sharply pointed black cowboy boots with hard, thick heels clicked loudly on the concrete floor the moment he entered the building. Tony's work back in L.A. had included album covers and other promotional photographs for Johnny Cash, Waylon Jennings, Kris Kristofferson, and Tanya Tucker. In Albuquerque he drove a white Porsche and wore a sporty, white-with-red-racing-stripes Porsche nylon jacket—with a tall can of Coors tucked in each side pocket. It was great when Elray Deroin of Pawnee, Oklahoma, a member of the Otoe-Missouria Tribe, joined our photography staff. Elray's quiet and thoughtful demeanor was a perfect counterpoint to my own restlessness and Tony's flamboyant style. When *The New Mexico Sun* failed, Tony returned to his career as an actor in Hollywood, where back in 1965 he had co-starred with his wife, Gloria Neil, in *The Beach Girls and the Monster*.

In the early 1980s, Albuquerque was more large town than small city, especially as compared to the endless square mileage and large population the sprawling metropolis now encompasses. Unlike New York City, where one walks for miles through an incredible density of human presence, Albuquerque felt sparsely populated and sedate—and very laid back. New residential neighborhoods on the northern and eastern sides of the city stretched up toward the Sandia Mountains. They were comfortable and quiet, and not rich with visual surprise. My favorite part of the city was the South Valley. Here, there was a vibrant Chicano community, and the Rio Grande flowed through with its slow-moving waters, large cottonwoods, public spaces, and parks along its banks. The Rio always pulled me like a magnet to its shores, where fisherman sat patiently, families picnicked, folks walked their dogs, and young people gathered at San Gabriel Park.

As a photographer in New Mexico, I had always been attracted to public events—Santa Fe Indian Market, the burning of Zozobra, the Albuquerque International Balloon Fiesta—not only for the general spectacle but also for the numbers of people, distracted by the busy activities, who didn't notice one more camera on the scene. Although the crushing crowds at such events could end up being fruitless photographically, such gatherings sometimes presented a wealth of possibilities. For me, making a photograph was a question of deciding what to include and what to exclude, of telling a story with one or a series of photographs, or of happening upon the one or two moments of magic that might not tell a story at all but that pack a curious or captivating collection of visual information into the frame. Finding photographic compositions made up of the miscellaneous raw material of interlocking visual information around me often took precedence over storytelling.

With camera in hand, I have always let my curiosity lead my eye. Or maybe it's my eye that leads and triggers my curiosity. I think of Henri Cartier-Bresson's description of his process as a young man: to wander down a street, and then turn and walk the next street—a bit like hunting, a bit like a curious wandering feline. Lee Friedlander, another chronicler of social landscapes, titled one of his many books *Like a One-Eyed Cat*. That was me in New Mexico and elsewhere, always seeing what was possible photographically and catching real moments in which the composition was a serendipitous collision of curious visual elements.

Looking back today at the many photographs I made at ceremonial dances and on feast days at Ohkay Owingeh, Santa Clara, and Tesuque Pueblos, I try to recall the circumstances of my process. New Mexico photographers Gabriela Campos and Nathaniel Tetsuro Paolinelli, who are thirty or more years younger than I, told me how remarkable it was that I had permission to take those photographs, now that such photography is carefully restricted. As I look back, though, I don't remember any special permissions. My camera was overtly present and there for all to see; maybe not entirely welcome, but not objectionable either. In many of the images, the people being photographed are aware of me and acknowledge the camera. I feel fortunate to have been allowed to make these images, and I hope they are not now, forty years later, met with disapproval by anyone in the Pueblo communities.

It was through Steve Long, who worked in social services at the Pen, that I was given the opportunity to teach photography at the Penitentiary of New Mexico in Santa Fe. I brought my 4×5 view camera and Polaroid sheet film and worked directly with about a dozen young men at the prison. The tripod-mounted camera, large and bulky, with its black cloth thrown over the photographer's head to allow him to view the image on the ground glass, was a big curiosity for all. We worked cooperatively to make narrative tableau images. One person was the camera operator, another the director choosing placement of the subjects, and the young men in the role of subjects created their poses together. The barren outdoor landscape offered nothing other than prison walls, encircling fences, short desert grass, and the vast sky above.

One Saturday morning I was invited to photograph a weightlifting competition at the penitentiary. Bombay photographer Rahoul Contractor got a ride with me to the event. Afterward, at a diner back in Santa Fe for lunch, Rahoul enthusiastically described the tattoos of the competitors and imagined how such beautiful work might be preserved. Moments later, out of the blue at the lunch counter and with an odd nervous energy, Rahoul told me that he probably had AIDS. This was in 1982, early in the pandemic, before deaths had spiked and spiraled as they did in the following years and before a test for HIV had been developed. I later heard that, along with Rahoul's close family, several good friends in Santa Fe—including photographer Nancy Sutor and painter Barbara Erdman—helped to care for Rahoul before his death in Albuquerque in 1985.

On another Saturday, an all-day Indian Powwow was held at the state penitentiary. By this time I was familiar with many of the young men, and it was a thrill to see their faces light up at the sound of the drums and the presence of so many family members and friends from outside. Inmates from both the men's and women's sections of the prison were able to share lunch, many sitting together as private couples in the open space. My last visit to the prison was in 1983, on assignment to photograph the women's unit for *The New Mexico Sun*. I remember that I had remarkable freedom to be in the unit and to visit with the women in their individual rooms as well as in the large common sleeping areas. There was open consent from the women who posed for me, who appreciated the presence of the camera and held up portraits of their families and sweethearts. Once again my editor was critical of my images because the women were looking directly into the camera lens. For me, the portraits are powerful because of the direct and assertive eye contact, with each woman appearing proudly to present her authentic self.

At the *Albuquerque Journal*, news photographers Jim Fisher, Richard Pipes, and Brian Walski and videographer Miguel Gandert welcomed me to their occasional Sunday evening get-togethers at Jim's house. I was new to the world of photojournalism and welcomed their advice and stories, accompanied by beer and the great dinners Jim's wife would prepare. One Sunday our gathering was interrupted by a news alert. An inmate had escaped from the downtown Albuquerque detention center, jumping from an upper-story window. We all went to the scene. Richard Pipes got his shots immediately of an injured young man being carried to the ambulance. We then rushed to the *Albuquerque Journal* darkroom, where Richard "souped his film" (printed the best negative wet), struck a perfect print on the first sheet of resin-coated (RC) photo paper, and delivered the still-wet print to the night desk. Within the hour, the four of us were right back at Jim Fisher's place, cracking open fresh beers.

I met Marilyn Garcia in Albuquerque in 1982 while working at *The New Mexico Sun*. Marilyn was the graphic designer for magazines, brochures, and print media at the Meredith Corporation, where

The Sun had its offices. Through my time with Marilyn in Albuquerque, my connection with the community deepened. By January 1983, we were spending almost all of our free time together, heading out on short road trips around the area, up to Santa Fe to spend time with Bernard Plossu and his family and other friends, and hanging out with new friends in Albuquerque. Santa Fe was the place to go on the weekend, during free time, or occasionally on assignment. But many of our weekends were spent in Albuquerque or at Marilyn's Santa Ana Pueblo home with her family. Marilyn, her mother Mary, and her three brothers—Mark, Michael, and Marvin—were there for me with warmth, support, and friendship.

By the summer of 1983, I found myself emotionally torn between the deep friendships I was establishing in New Mexico and my longing to return to Nepal. It was a difficult choice and an uncomfortable decision, but I packed all my worldly belongings into a small U-Haul trailer, hitched it to my Chevy Nova, and with my brother Peter, who was visiting from New York, made the long drive back to the Northeast.

In New York I joined Archive, a respected photographic cooperative and agency under Lauren Stockbower's directorship. Within six months, in early 1984, I received a commission from the United Nations Development Program in Bangladesh. I also had established a working relationship with the filmmaker Robert Gardner at Harvard's Film Study Center, who sponsored my continued work in Nepal.

It was hard to leave Marilyn, her family, and so many other friends in New Mexico. Marilyn and her husband now live in Bernalillo, close to Santa Ana Pueblo, and she continues her fine graphic design work. Many of my other New Mexico friendships have continued and thrived these forty years and more. For all of us, these photographs and stories from the early 1980s are our shared blast from the past. Four decades later, my two years in New Mexico and the photographs that document them continue to haunt me with a deep nostalgia and a flood of memories.

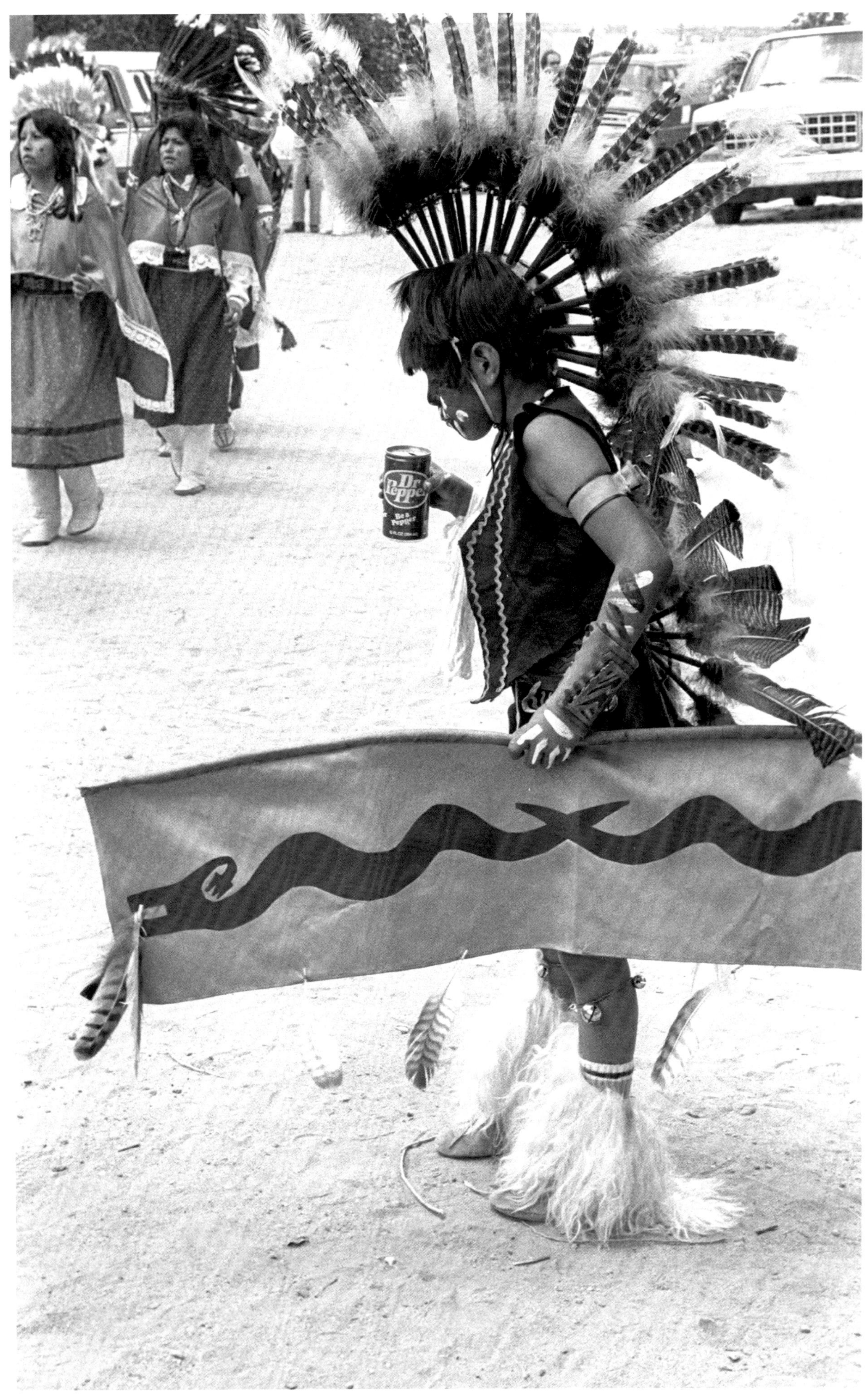

Comanche dancer, Feast Day, Ohkay Owingeh, 1982.

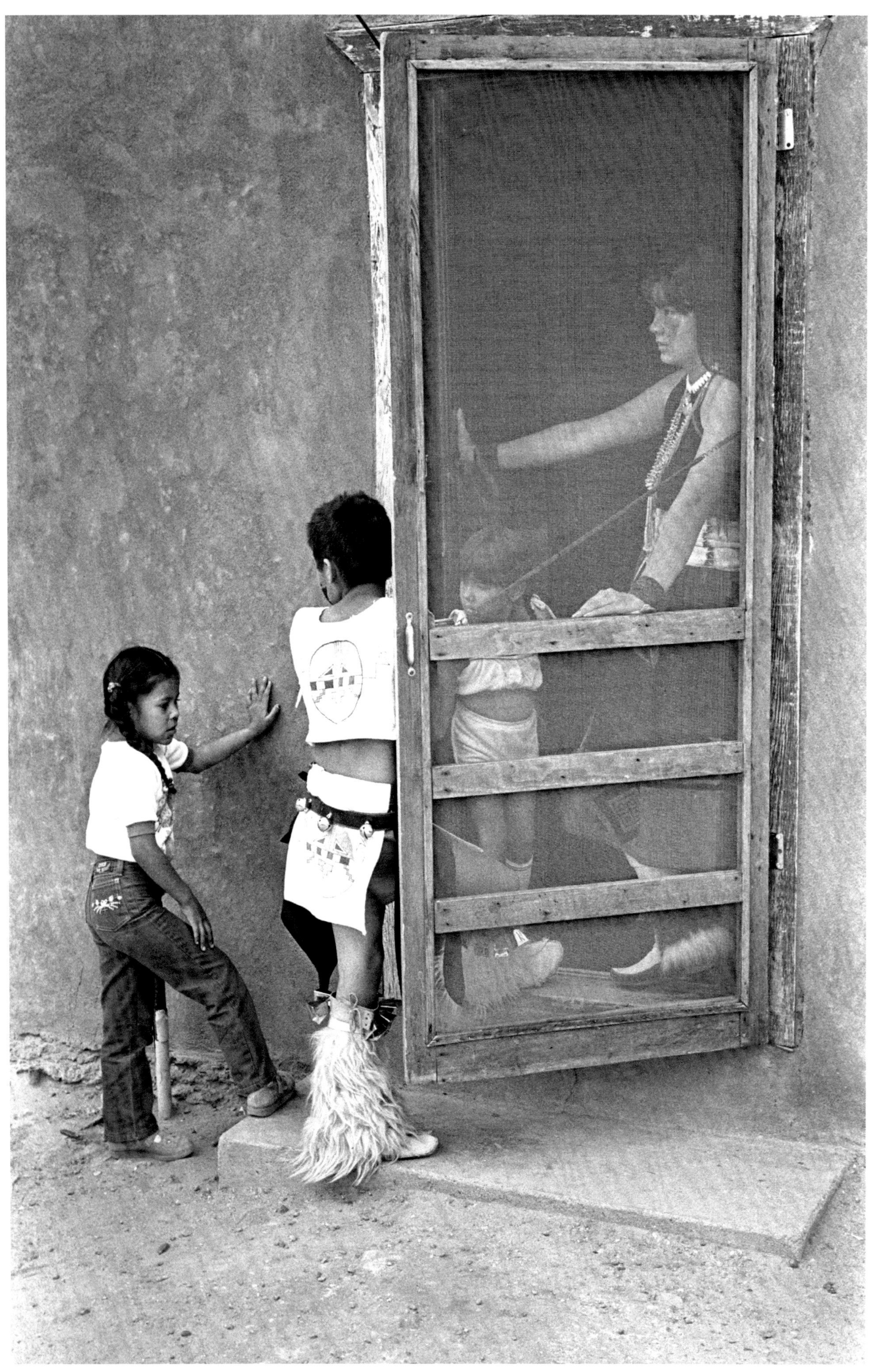

San Juan Feast Day, Ohkay Owingeh, 1982.

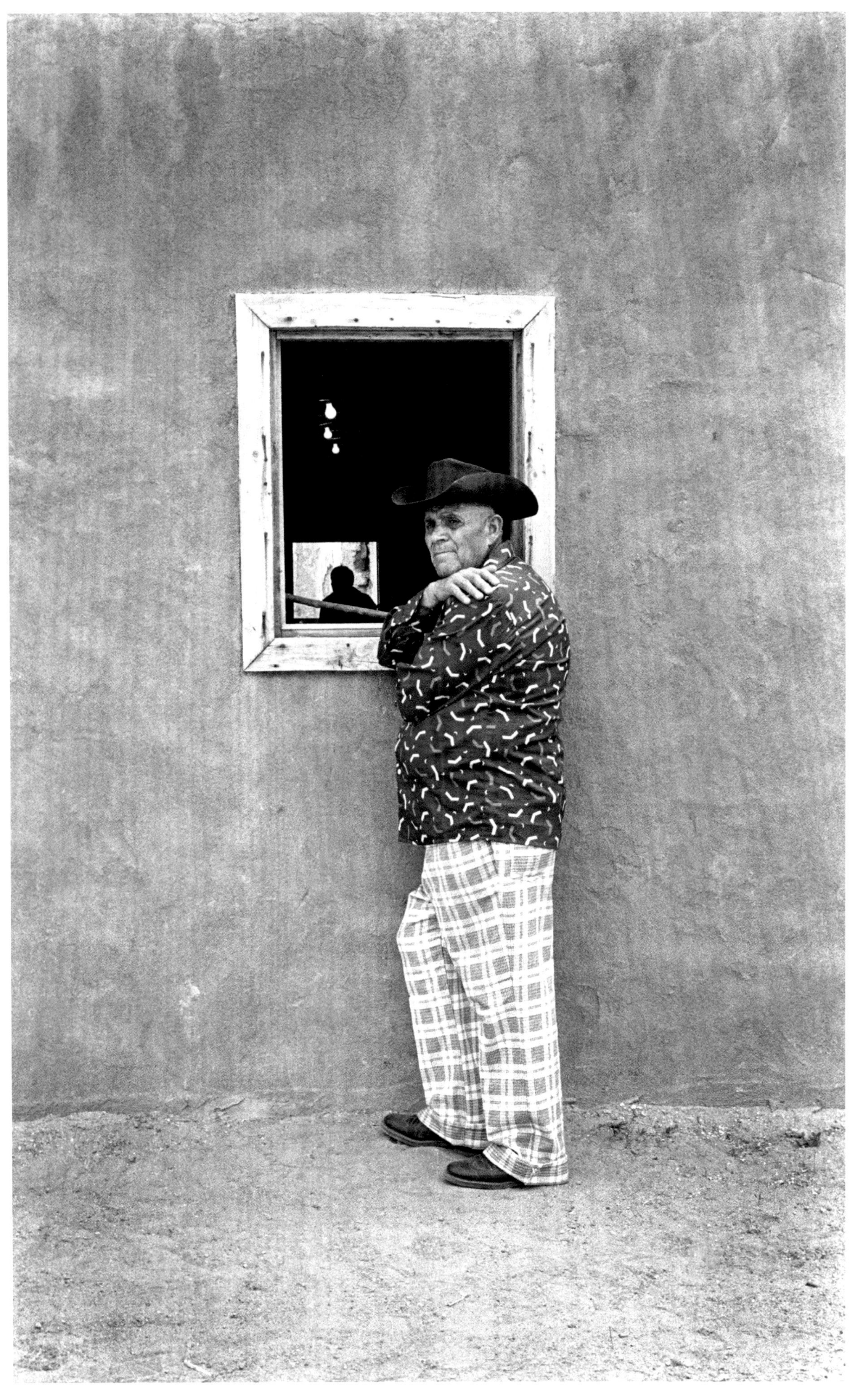

San Juan Feast Day, Ohkay Owingeh, 1982.

OVERLEAF: Comanche dancer, San Juan Feast Day, Ohkay Owingeh, 1982.

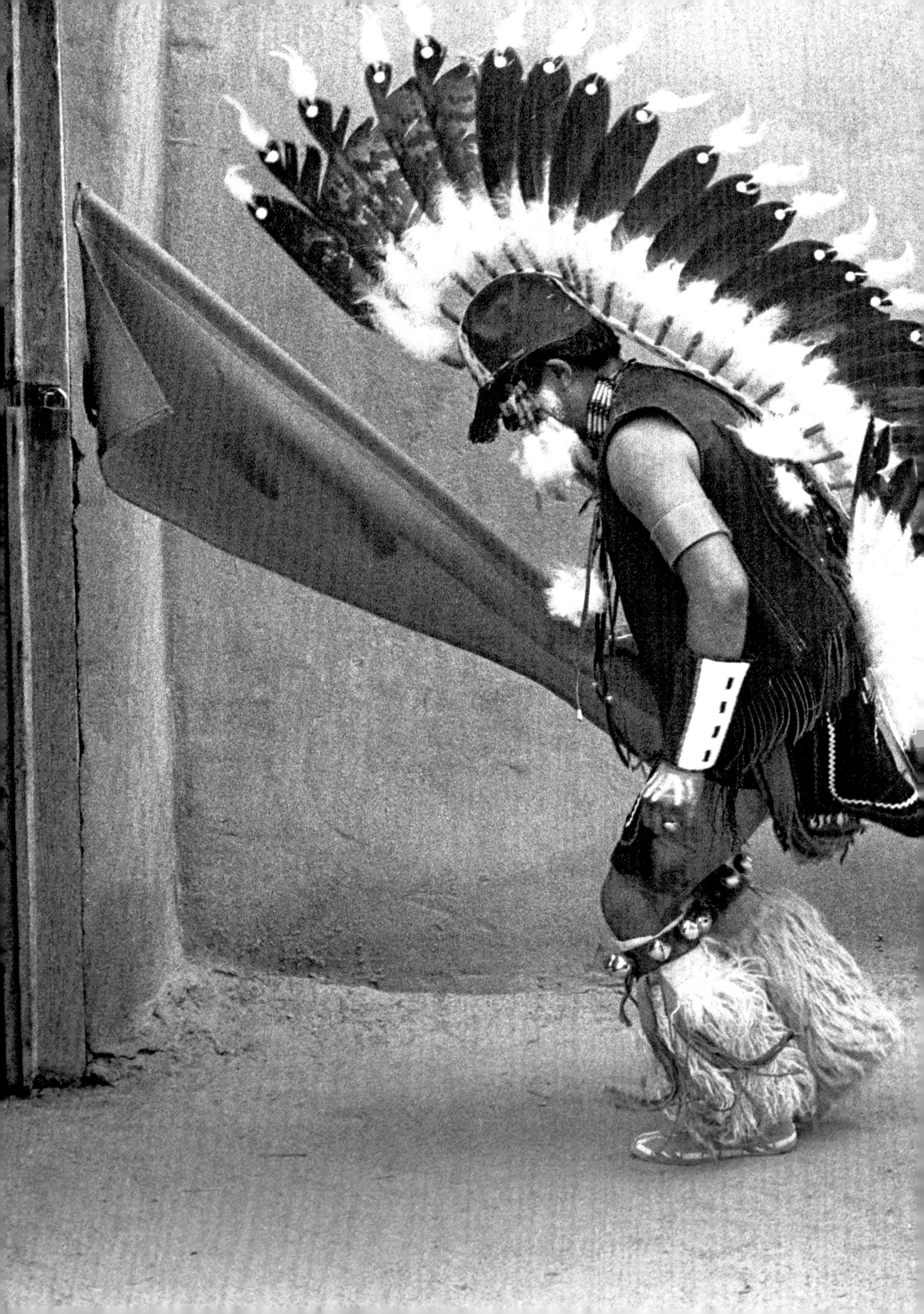

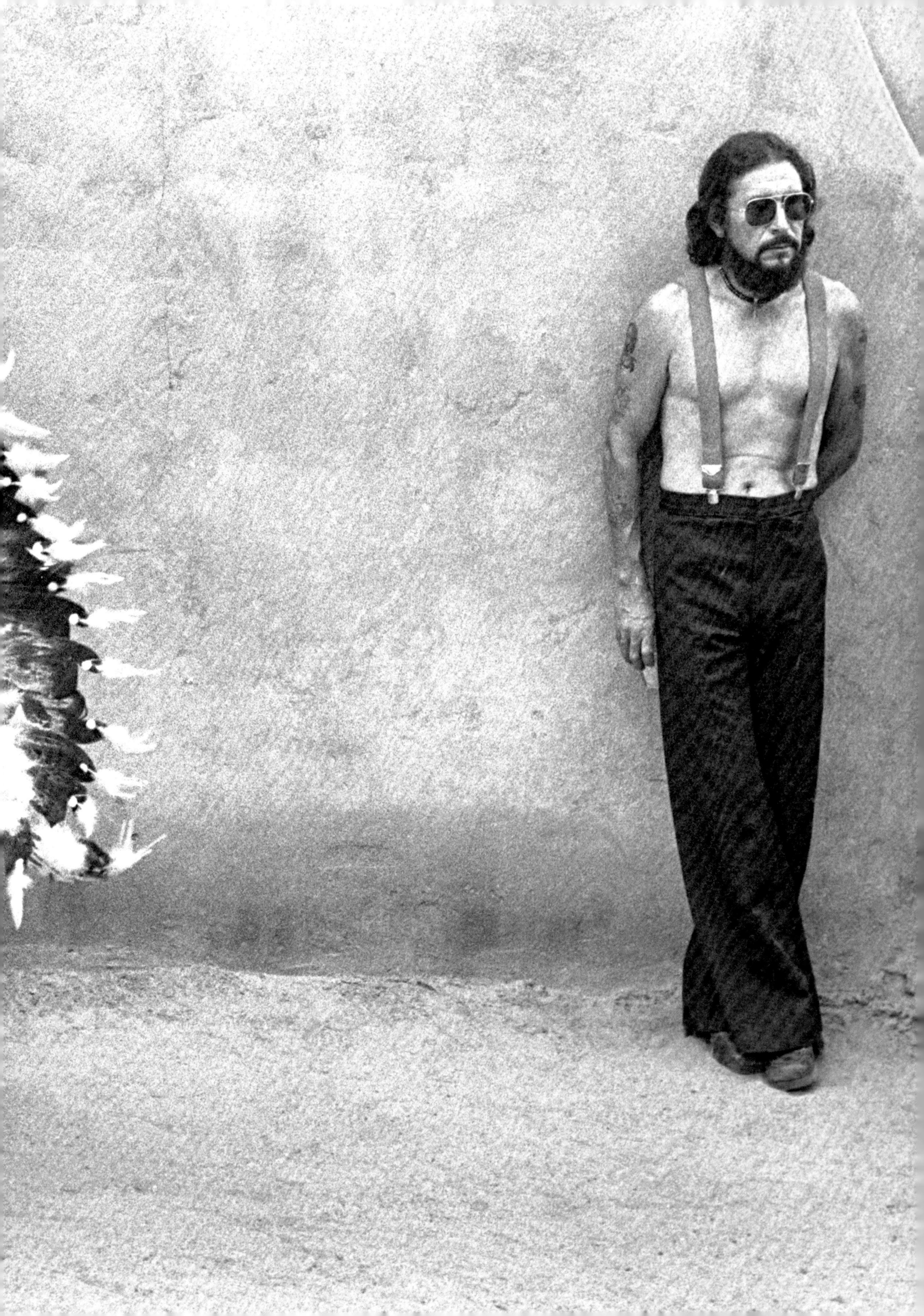

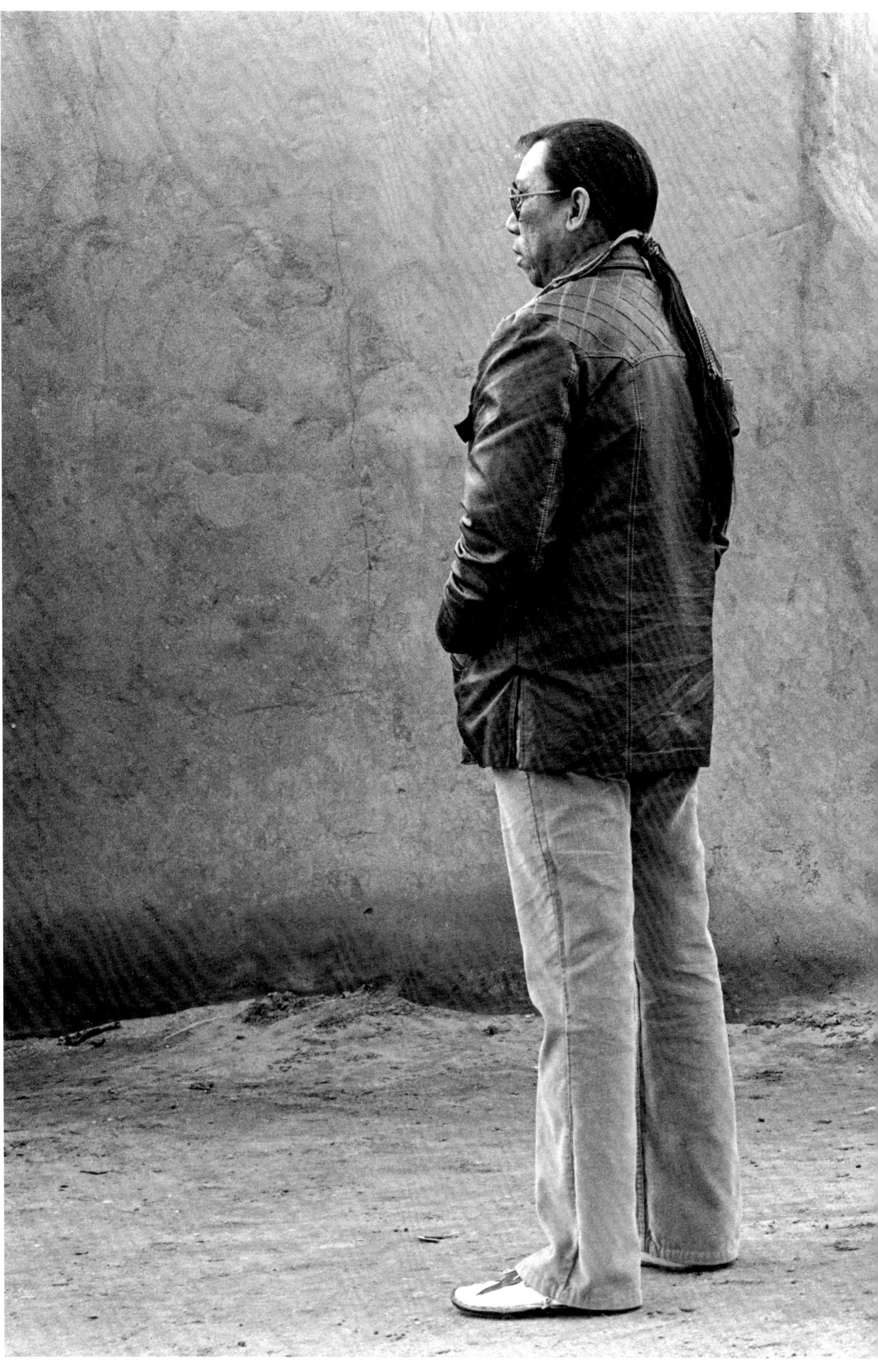

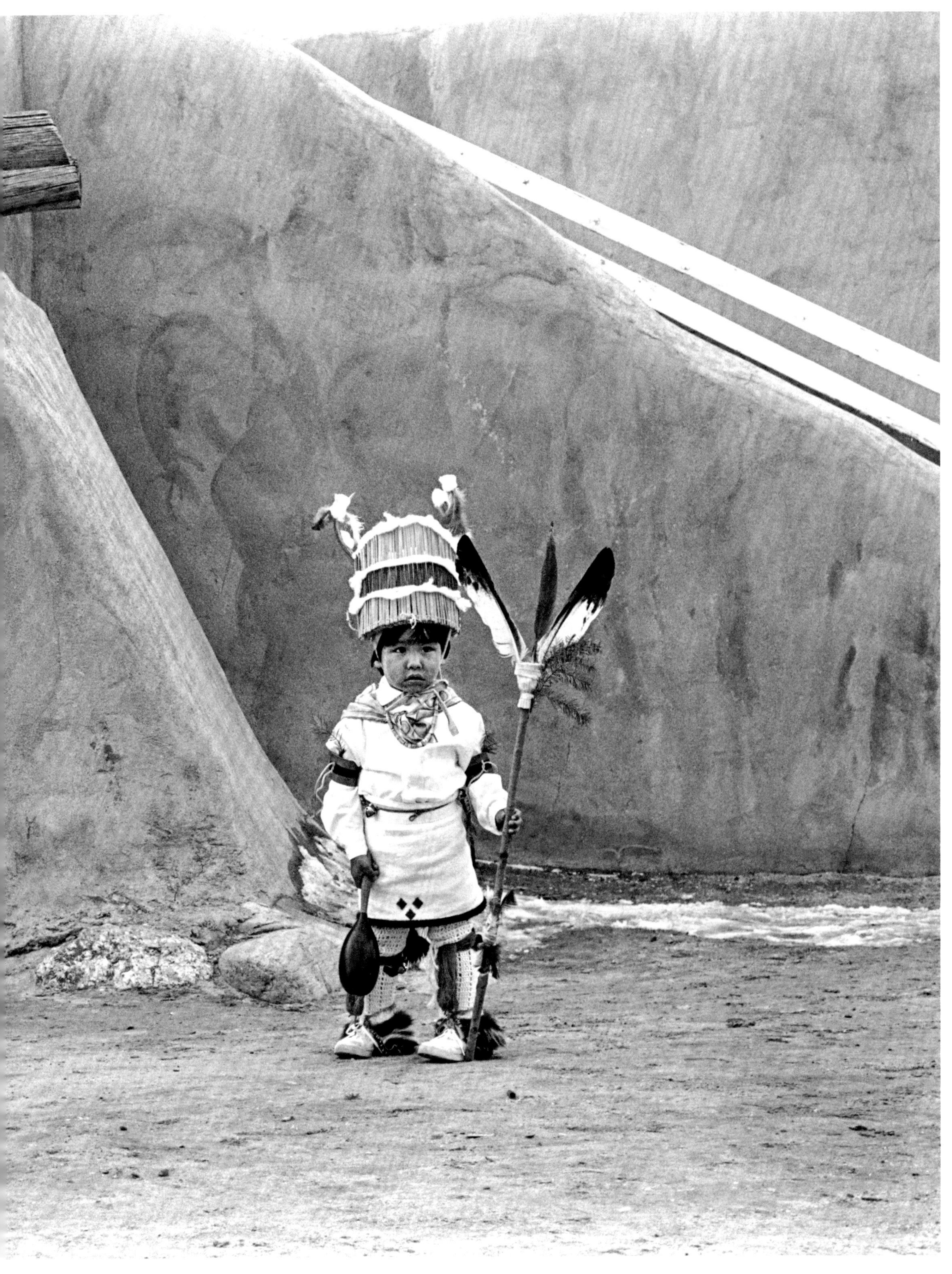

Wilfred Garcia and child dancer, Deer Dance, Ohkay Owingeh, 1982.

OVERLEAF: Joe Garcia, his wife Oneva, and daughter Star, Comanche Dance, Ohkay Owingeh, 1982.

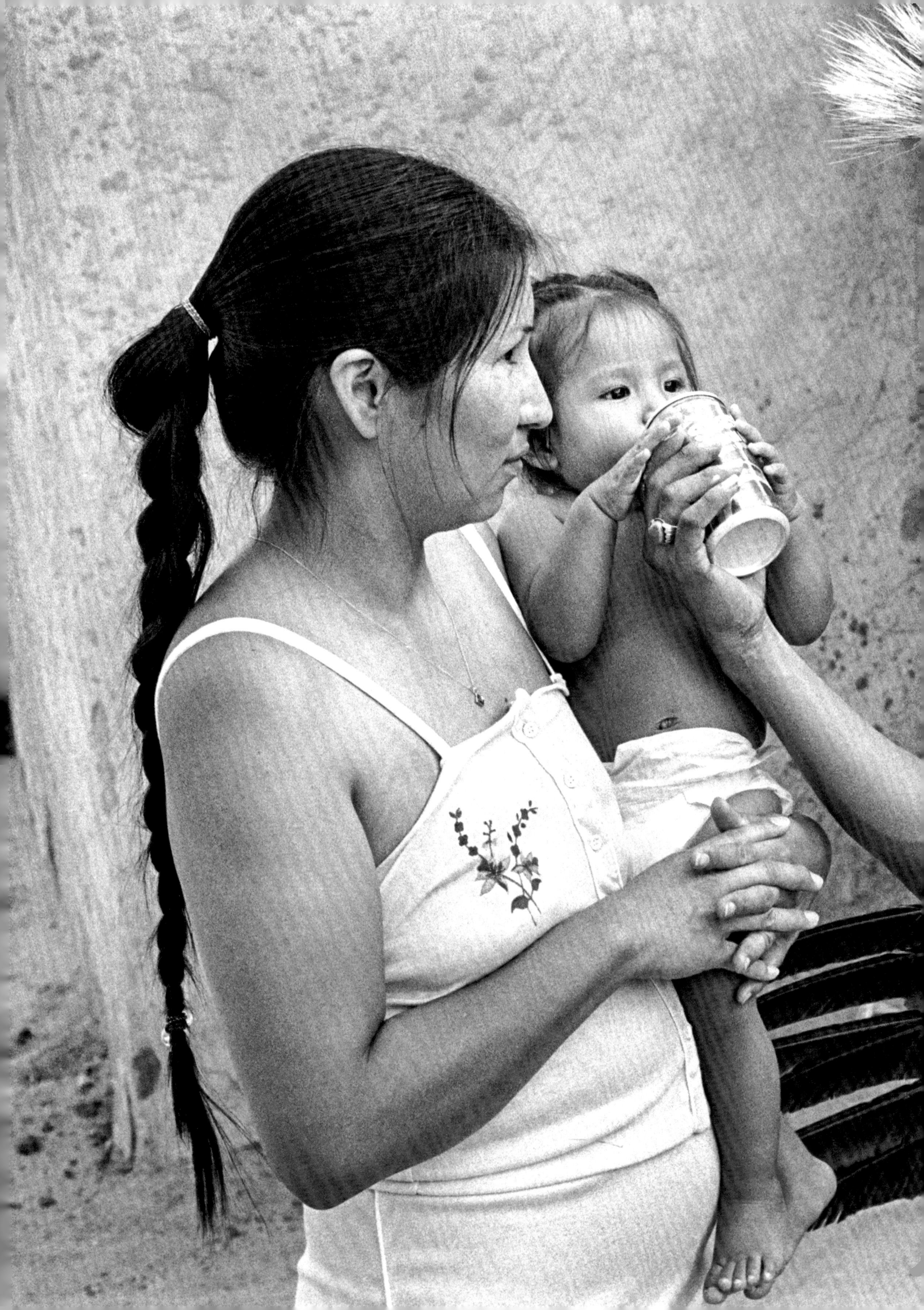

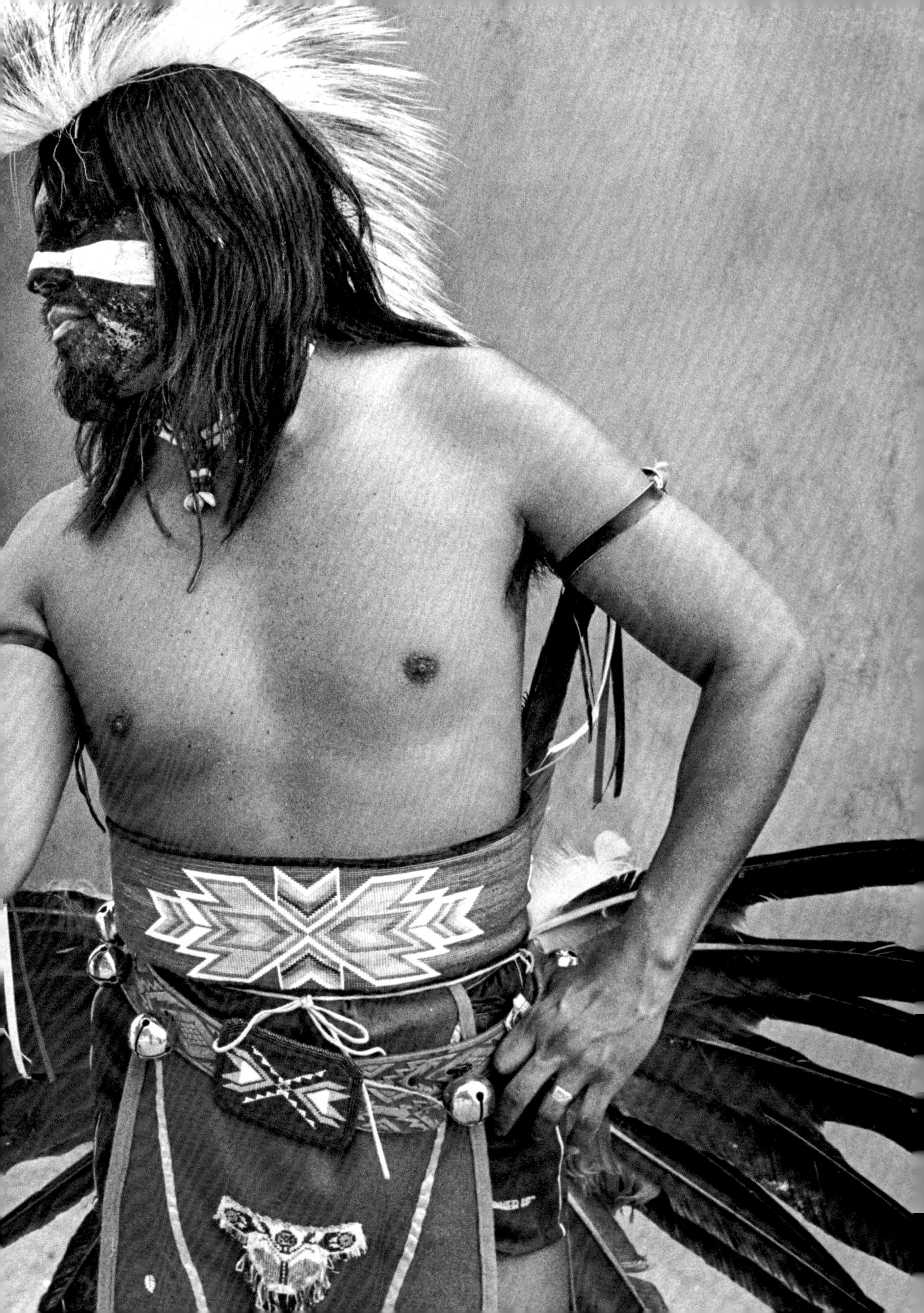

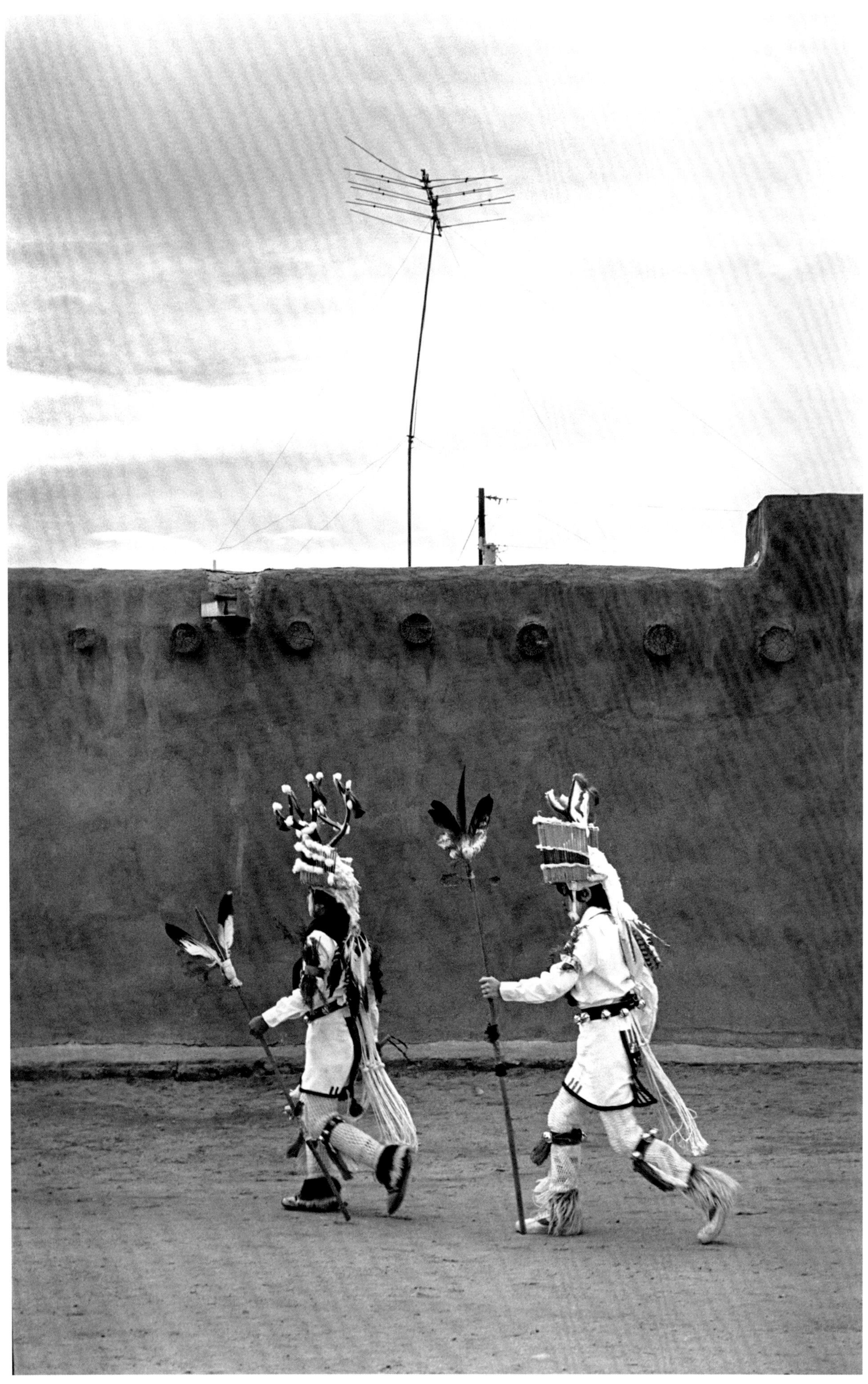

Deer dancers, Ohkay Owingeh, 1982.

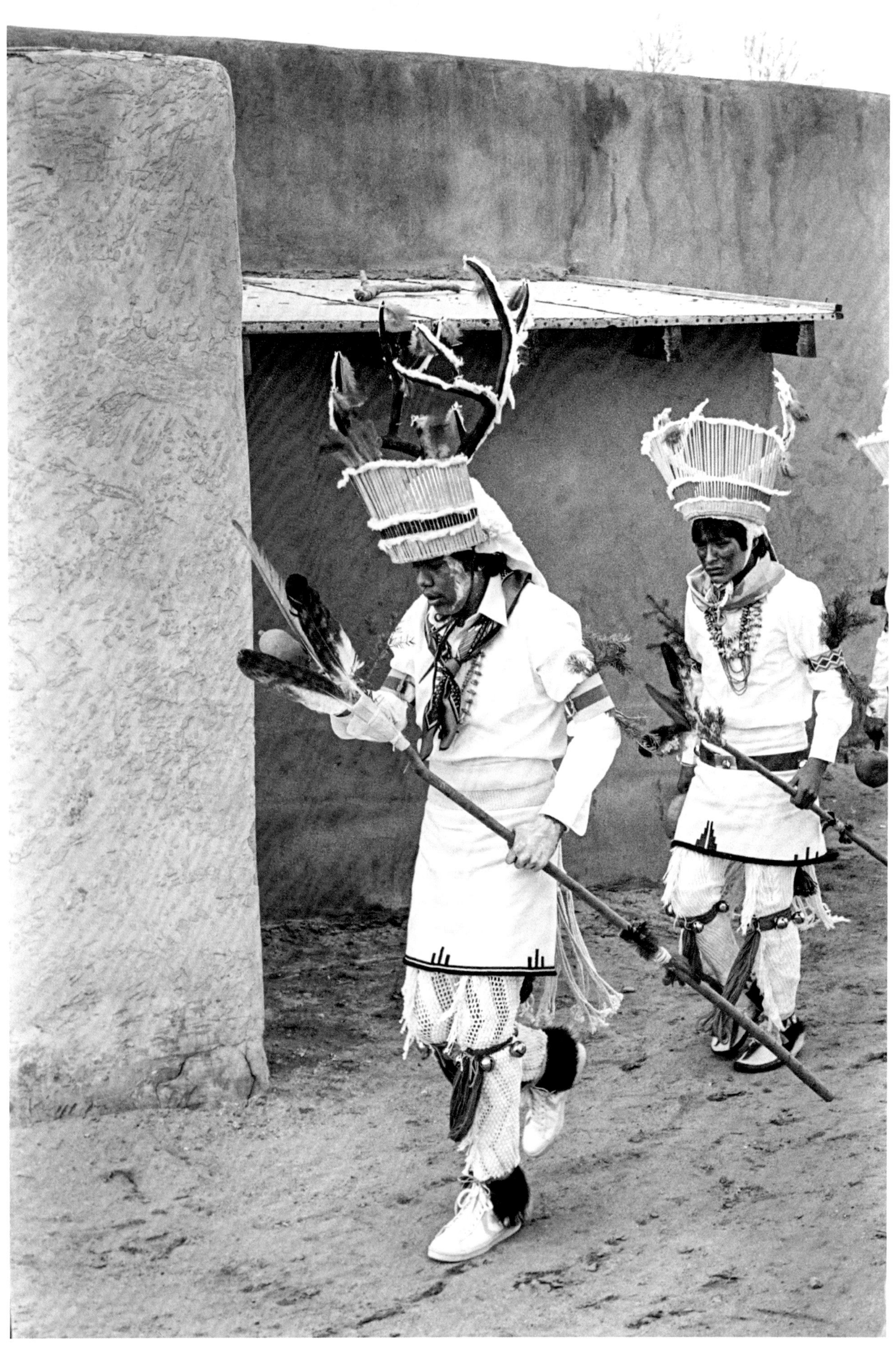

Deer dancers, Ohkay Owingeh, 1982.

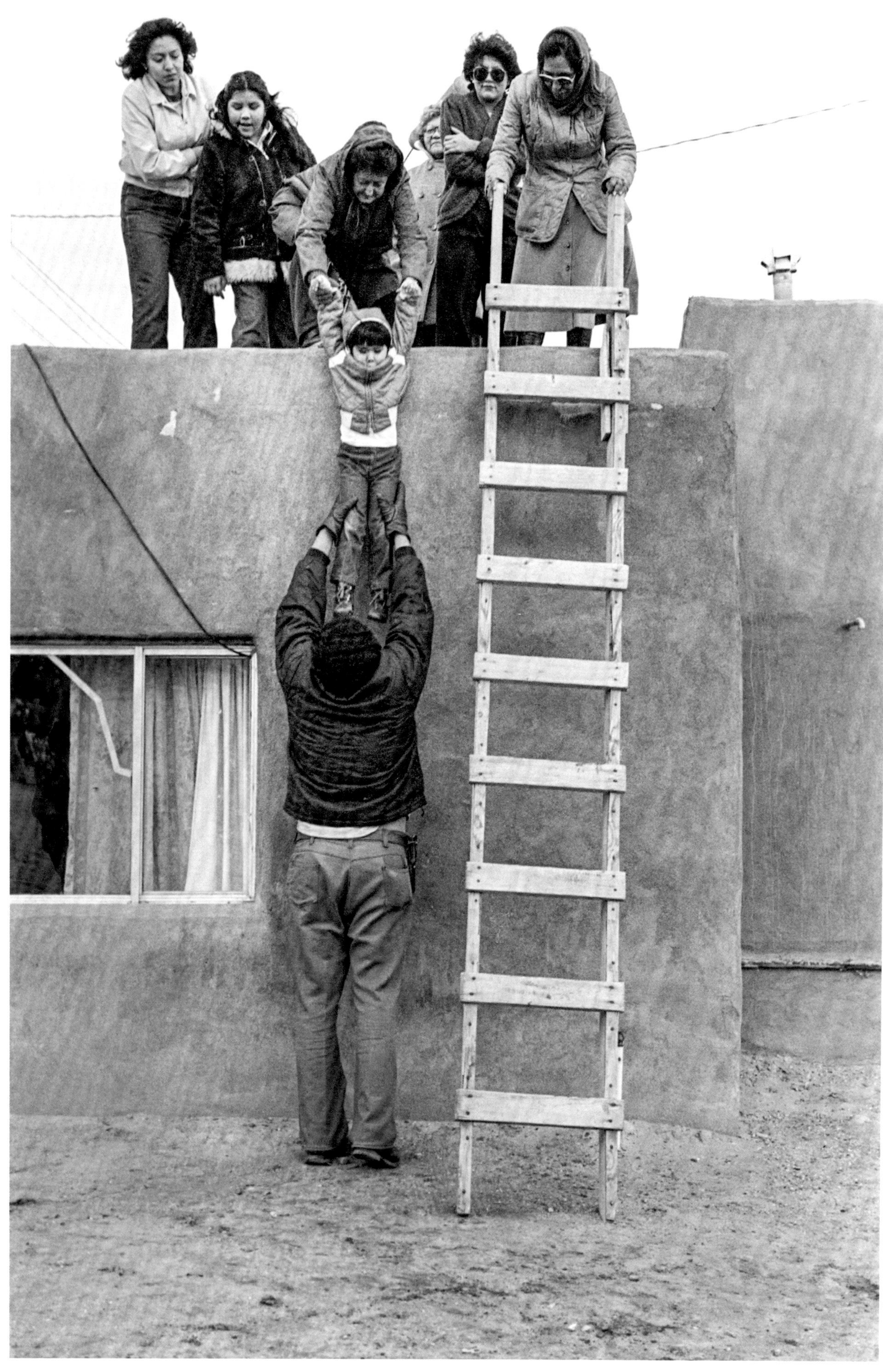

Ohkay Owingeh, 1982.

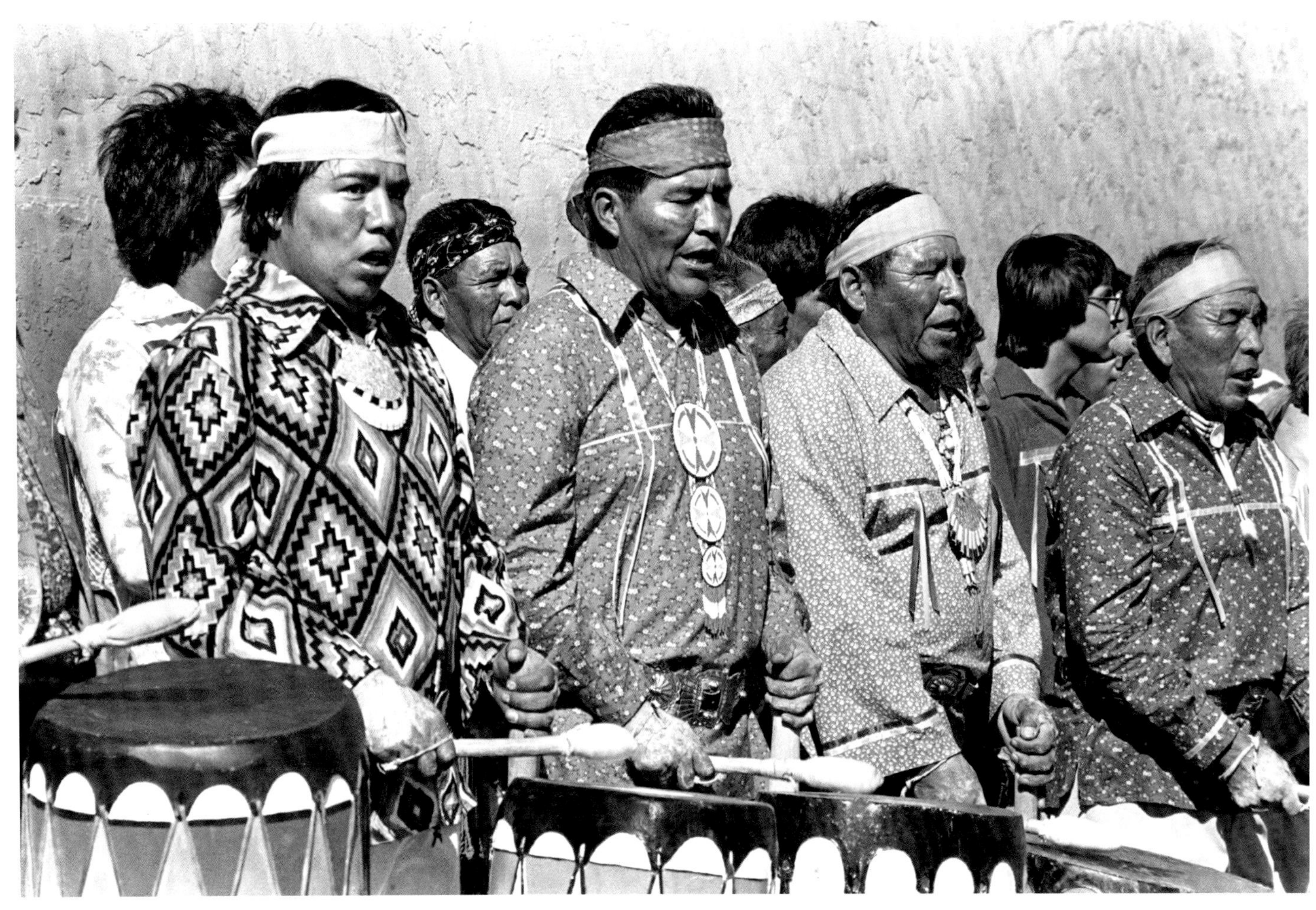

Drummers, Santa Clara Pueblo, 1981.

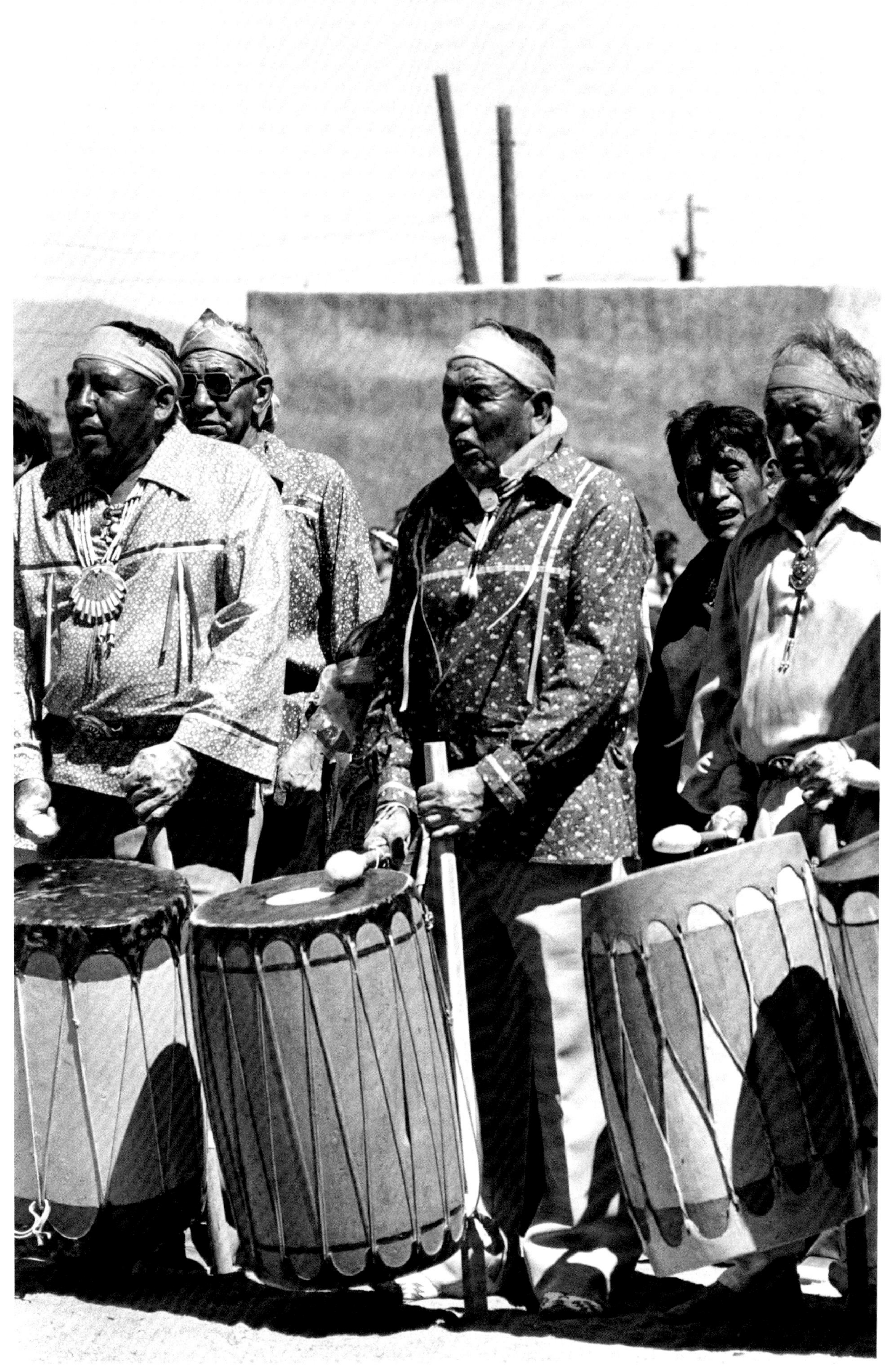

Drummers, Santa Clara Pueblo, 1981.

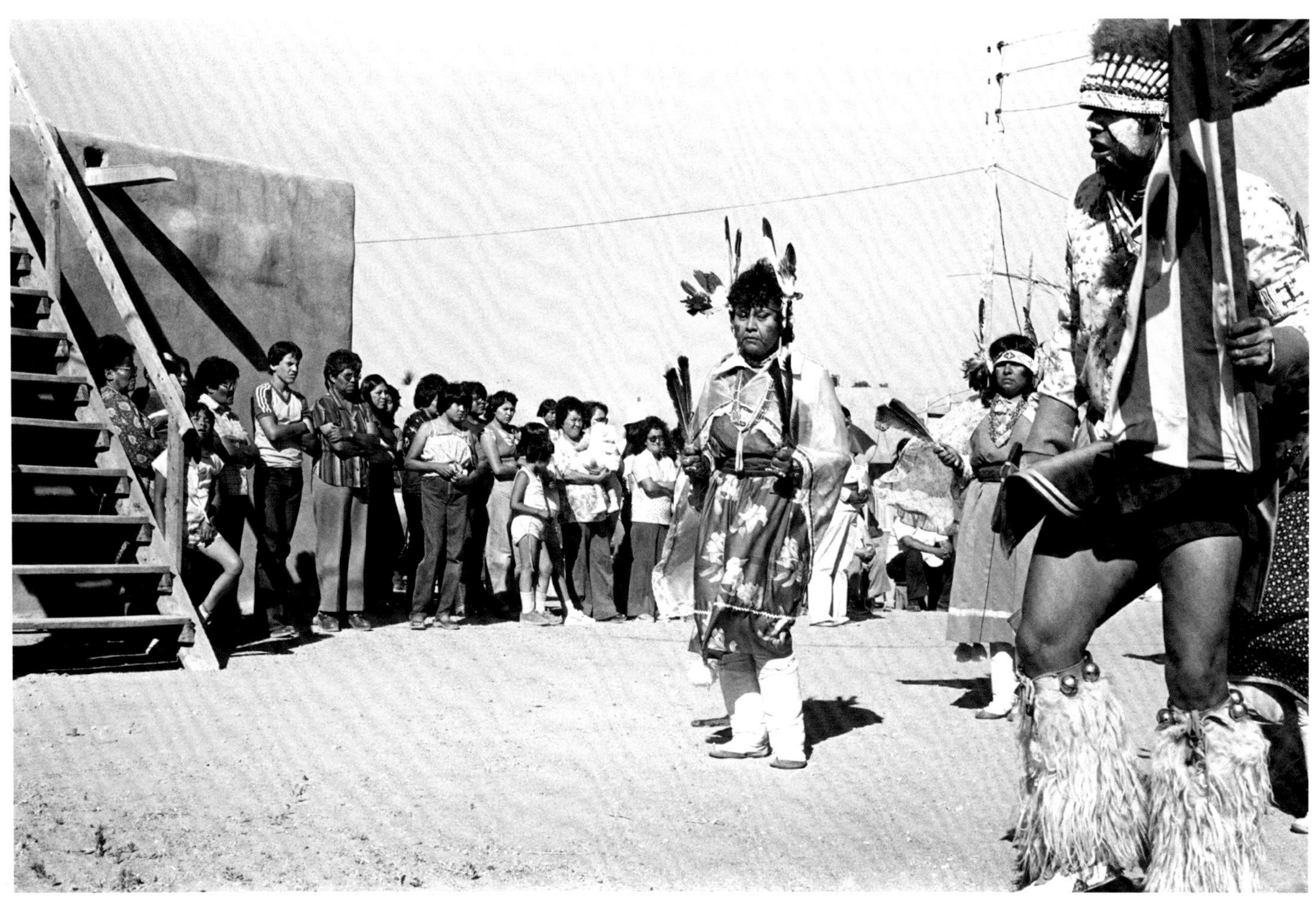

Comanche Dance, Santa Clara Pueblo, 1981.

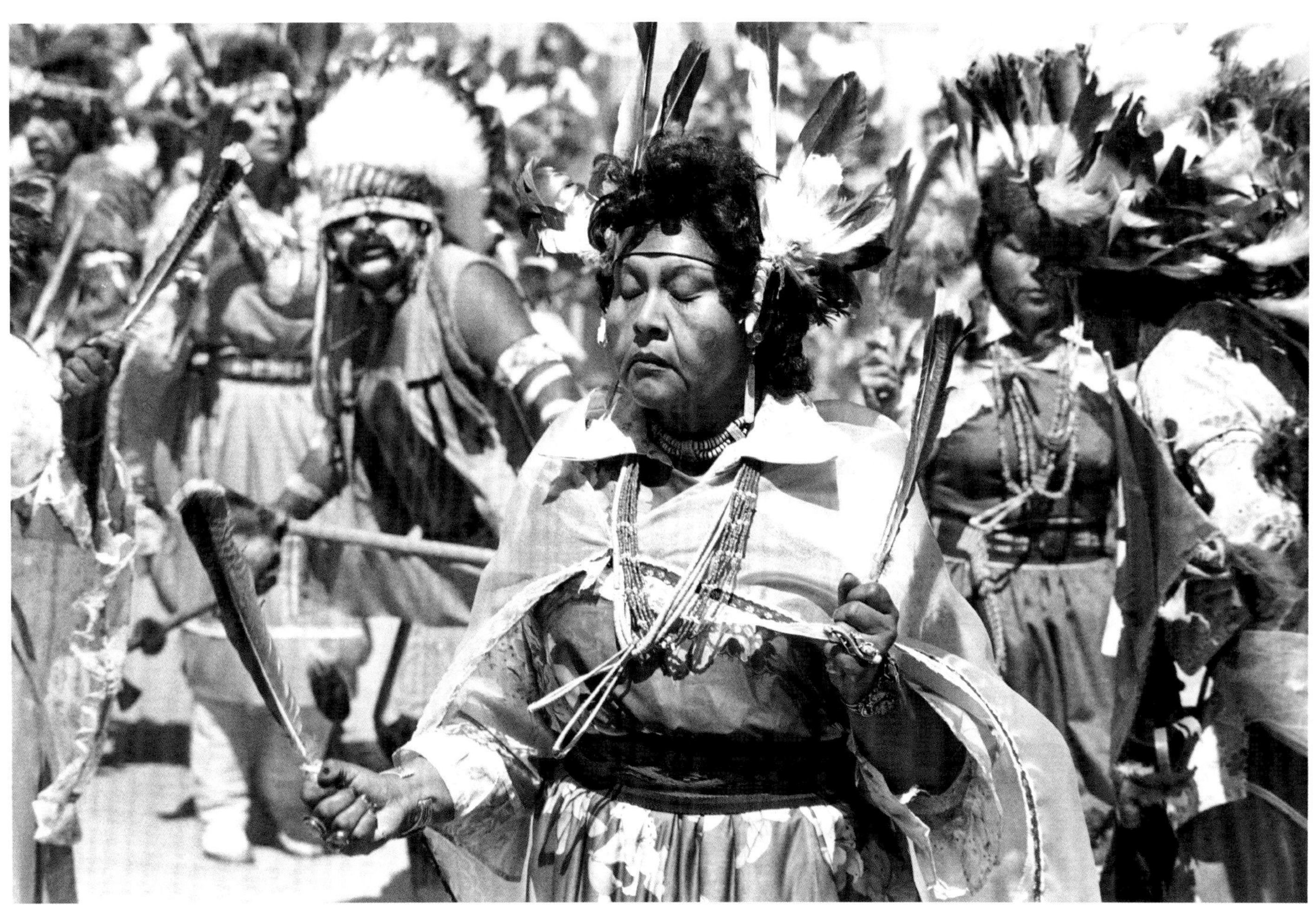

ABOVE AND OVERLEAF: Comanche Dance, Santa Clara Pueblo, 1981.

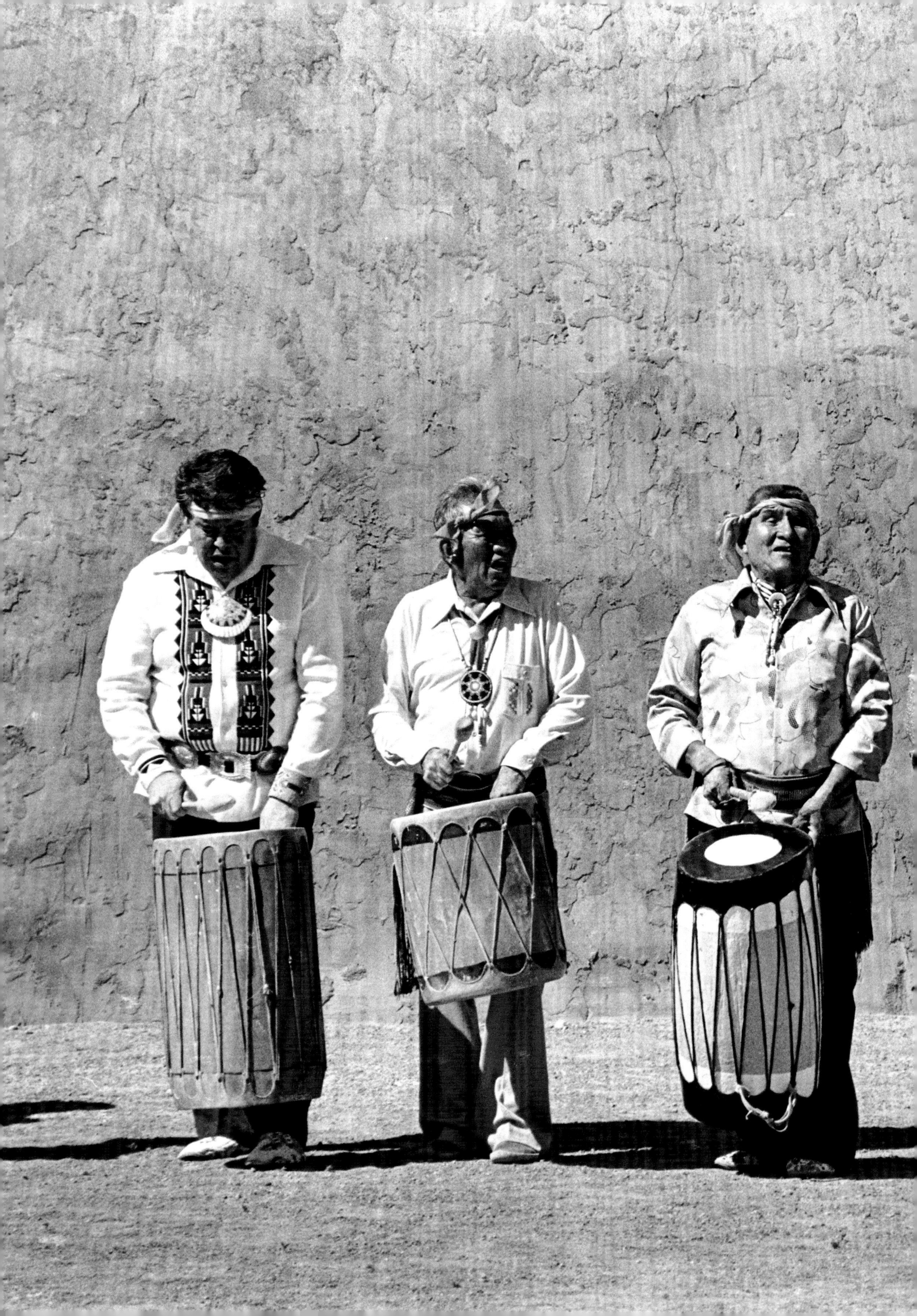

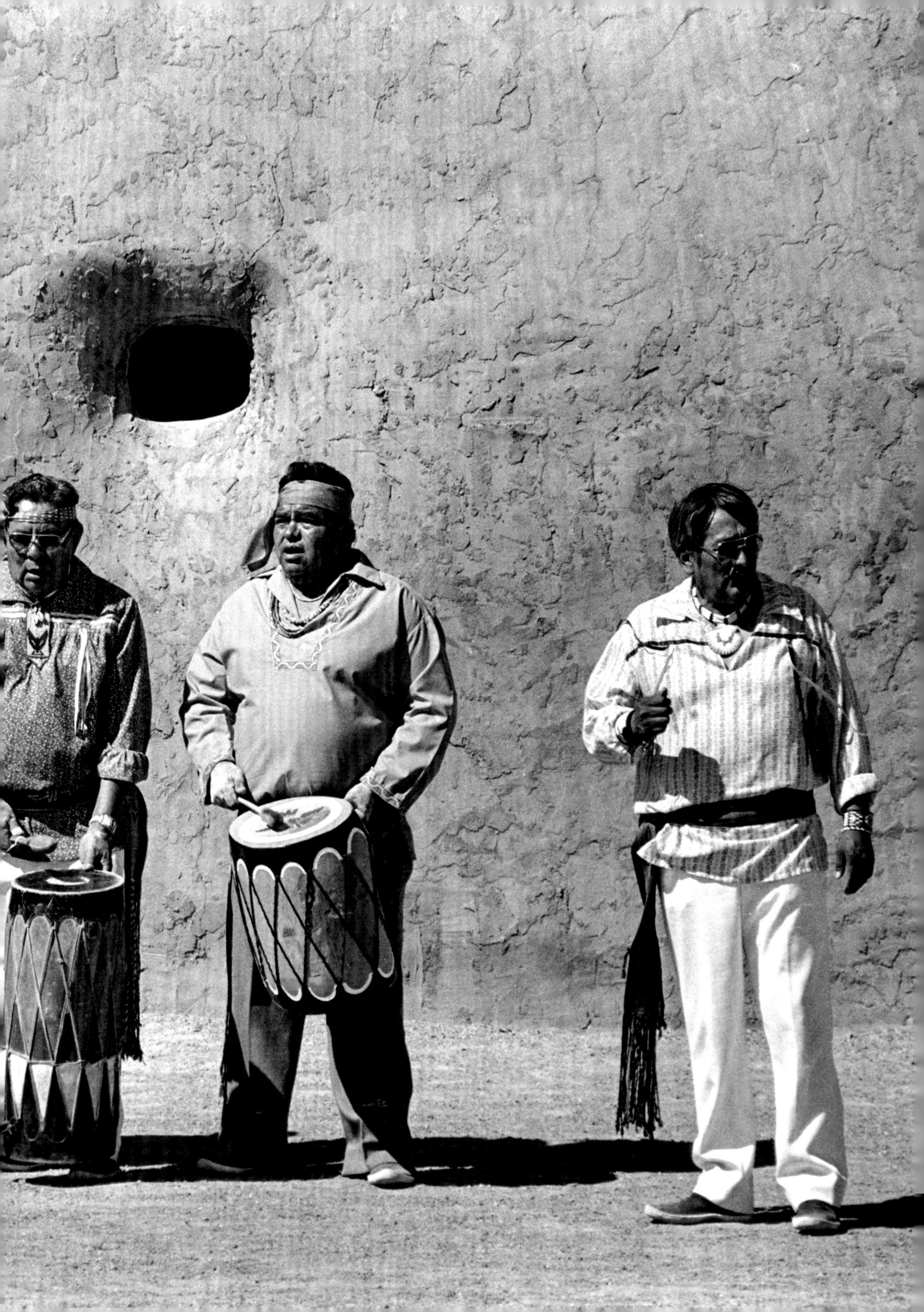

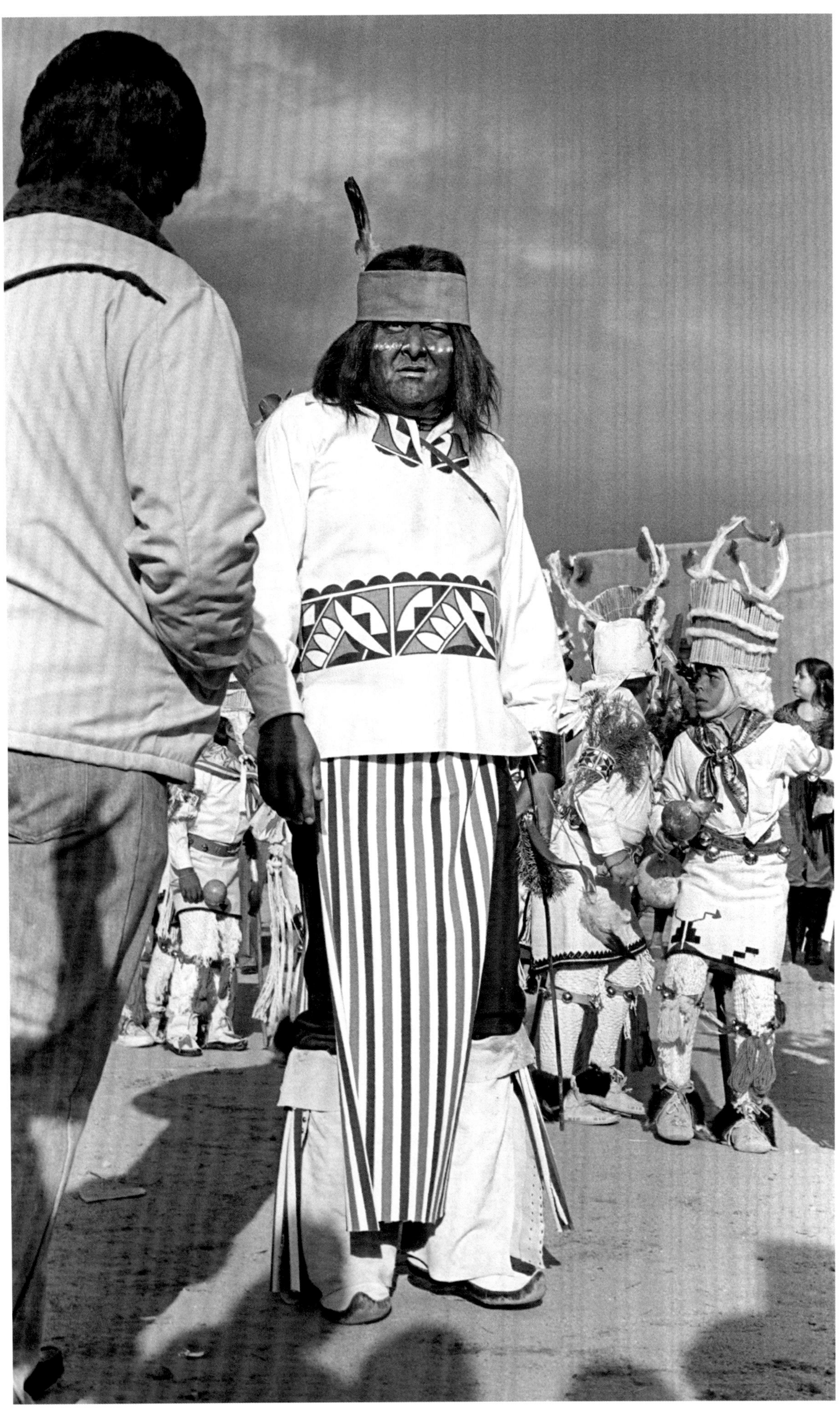

Deer Dance, Ohkay Owingeh, 1981.

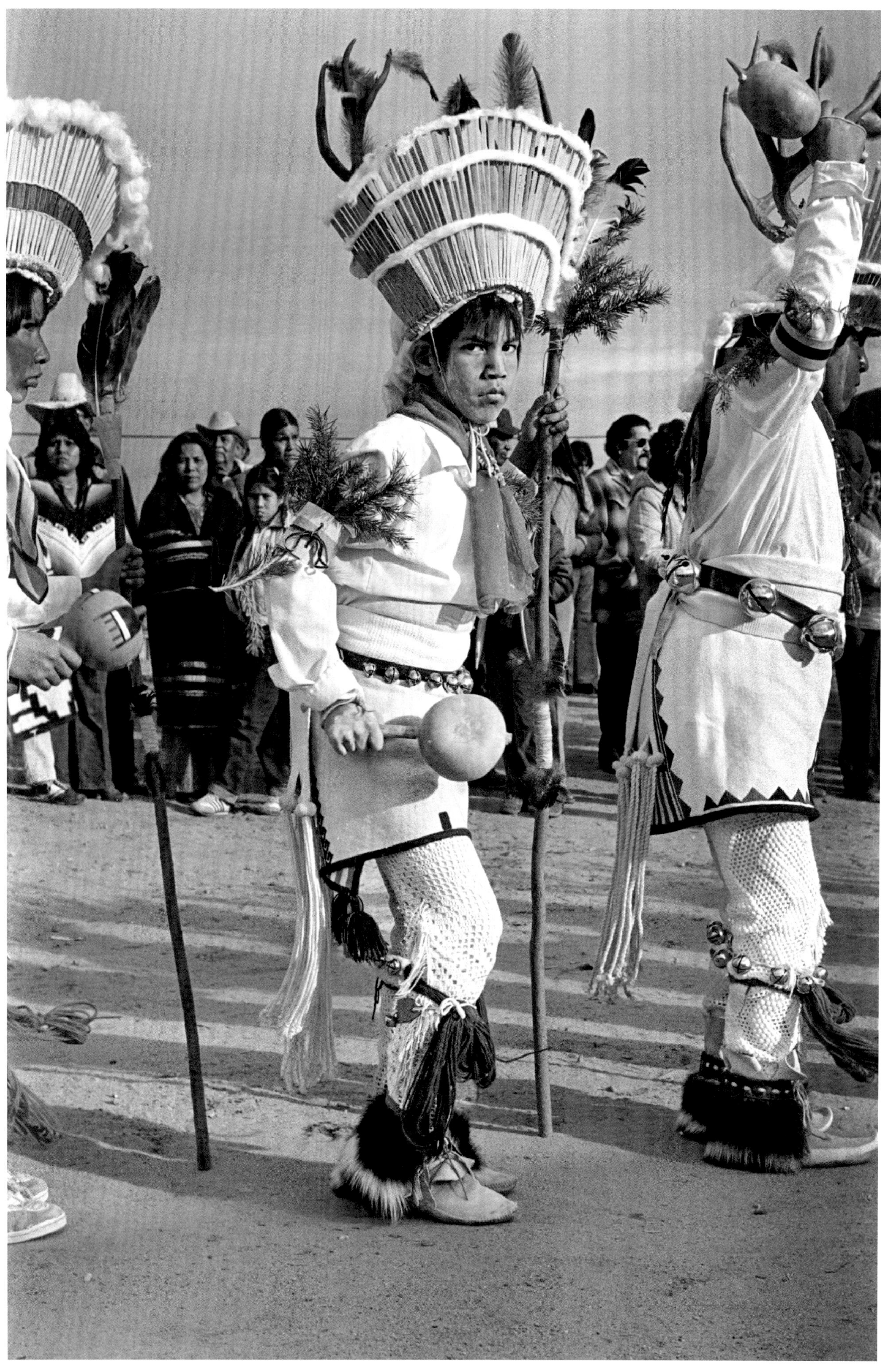

Deer Dance, Ohkay Owingeh, 1982.

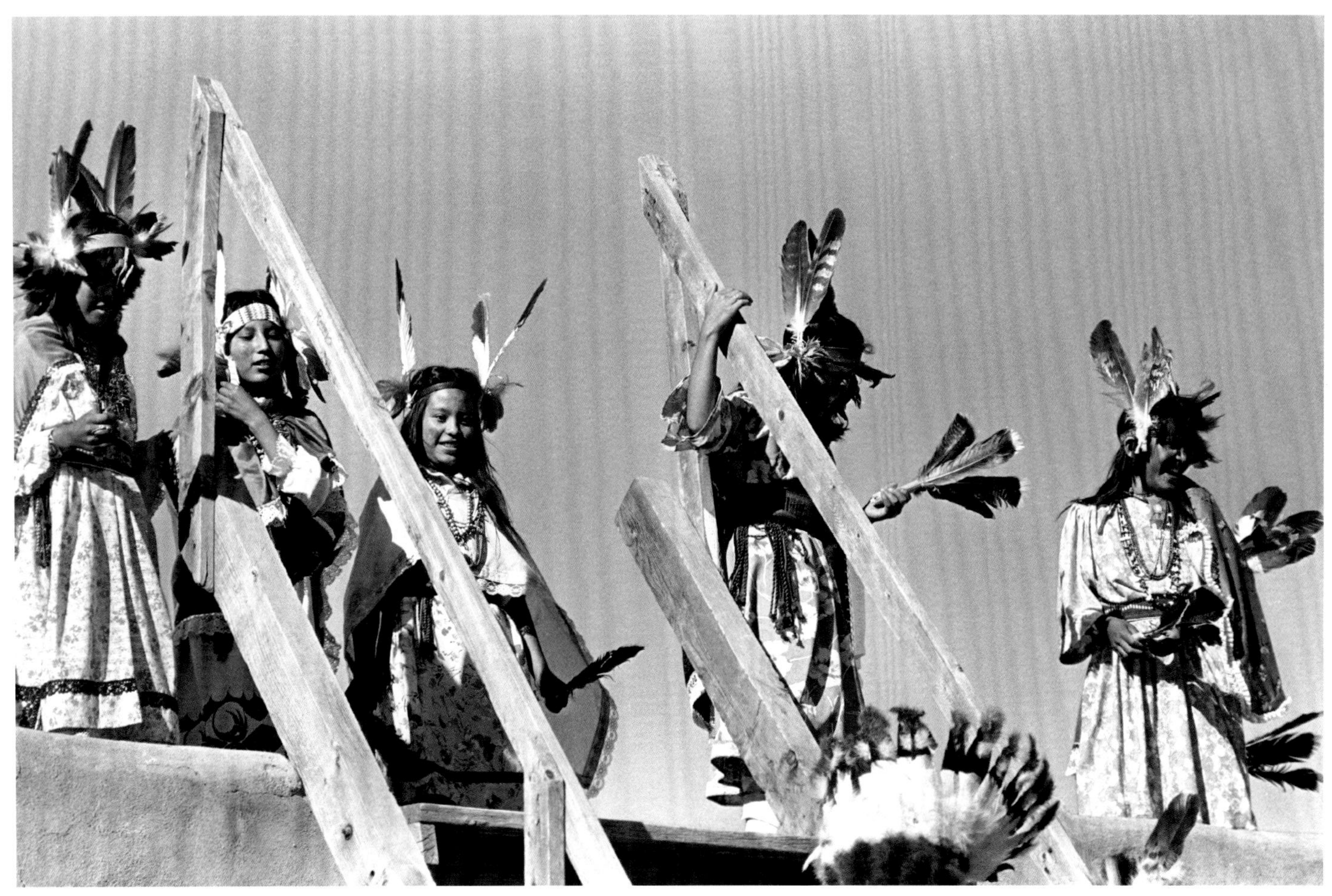

Comanche dancers, Santa Clara Pueblo, 1981.

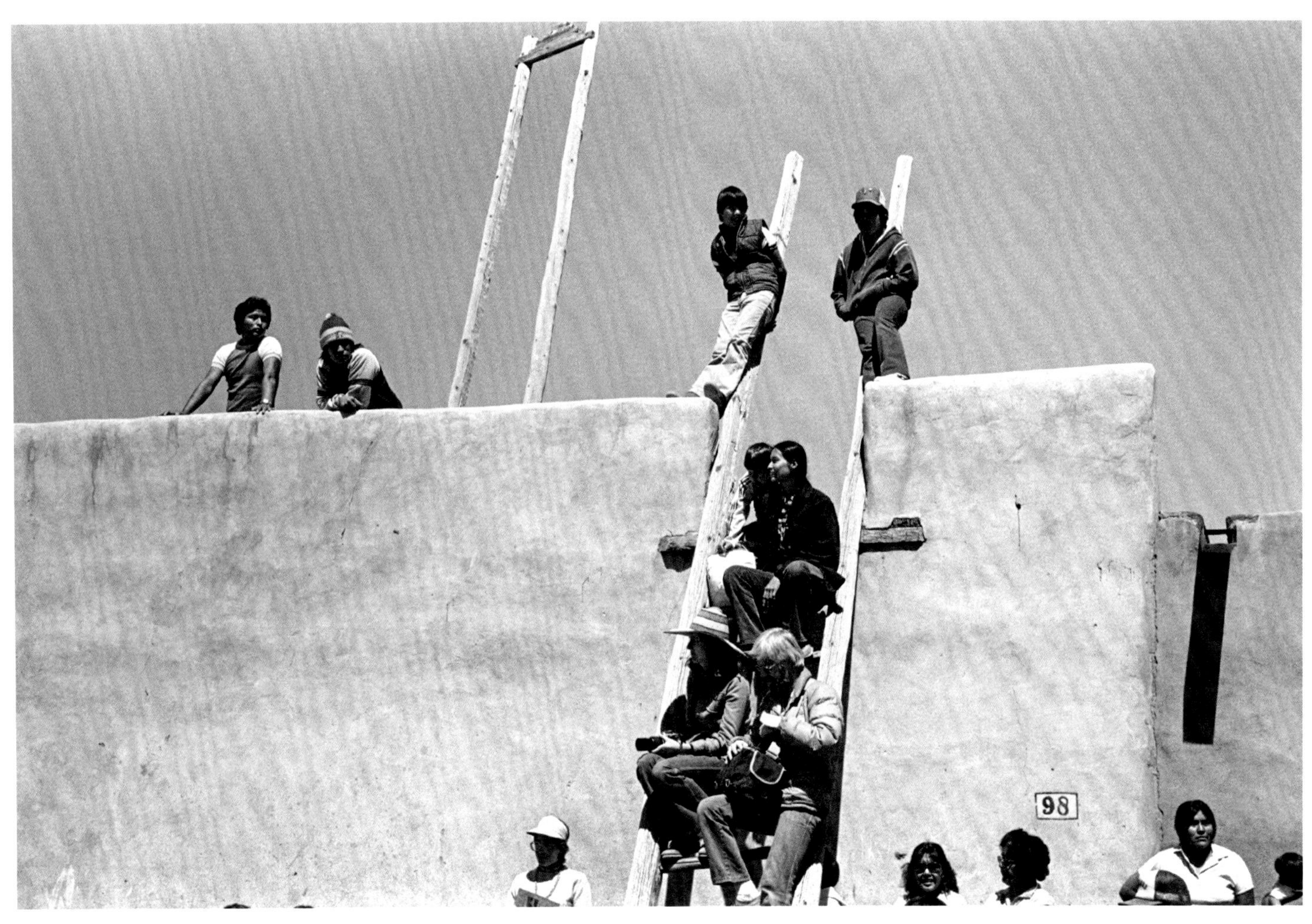

Observers at Comanche and Buffalo Dances, Santa Clara Pueblo, 1981.

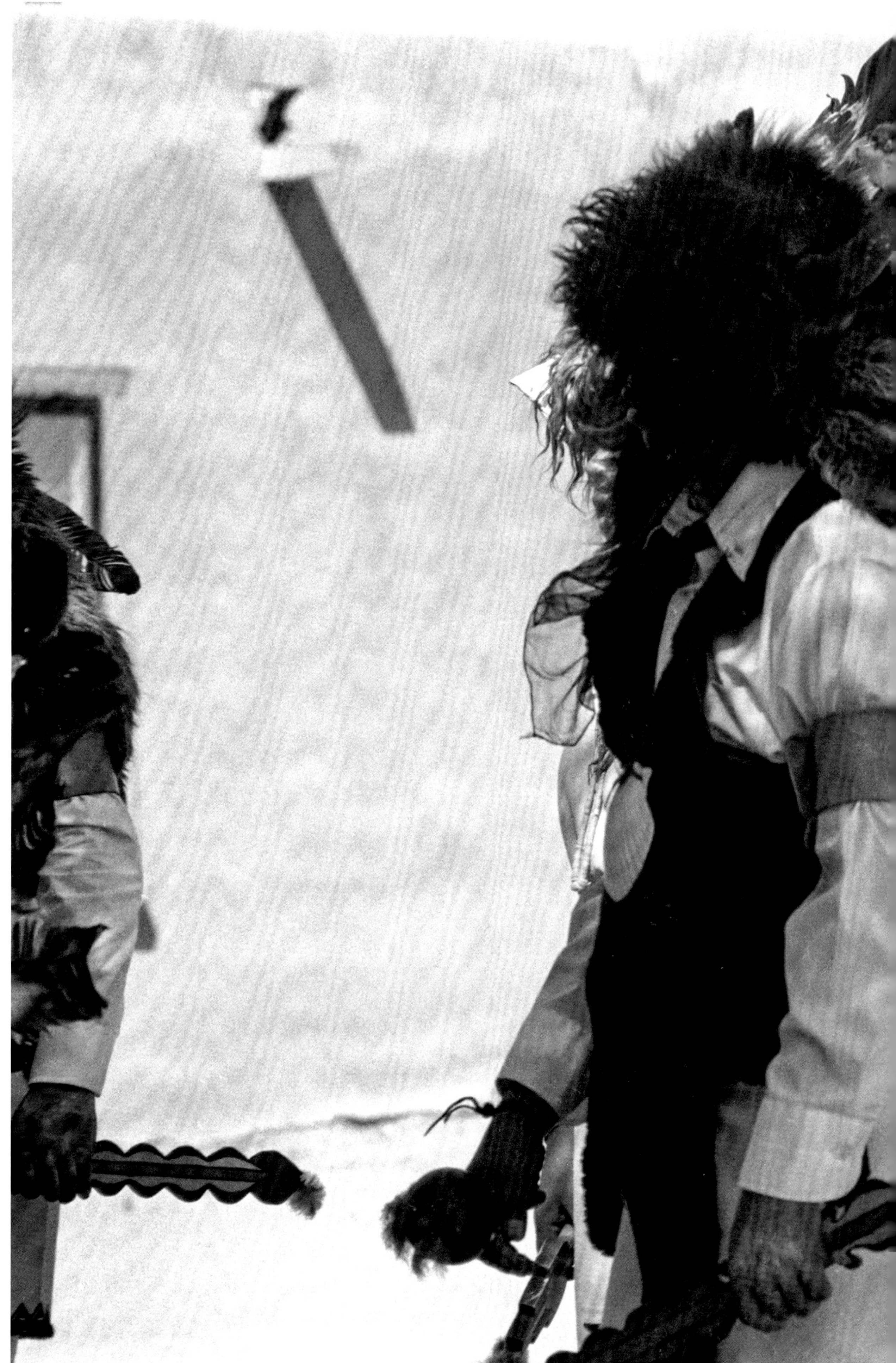

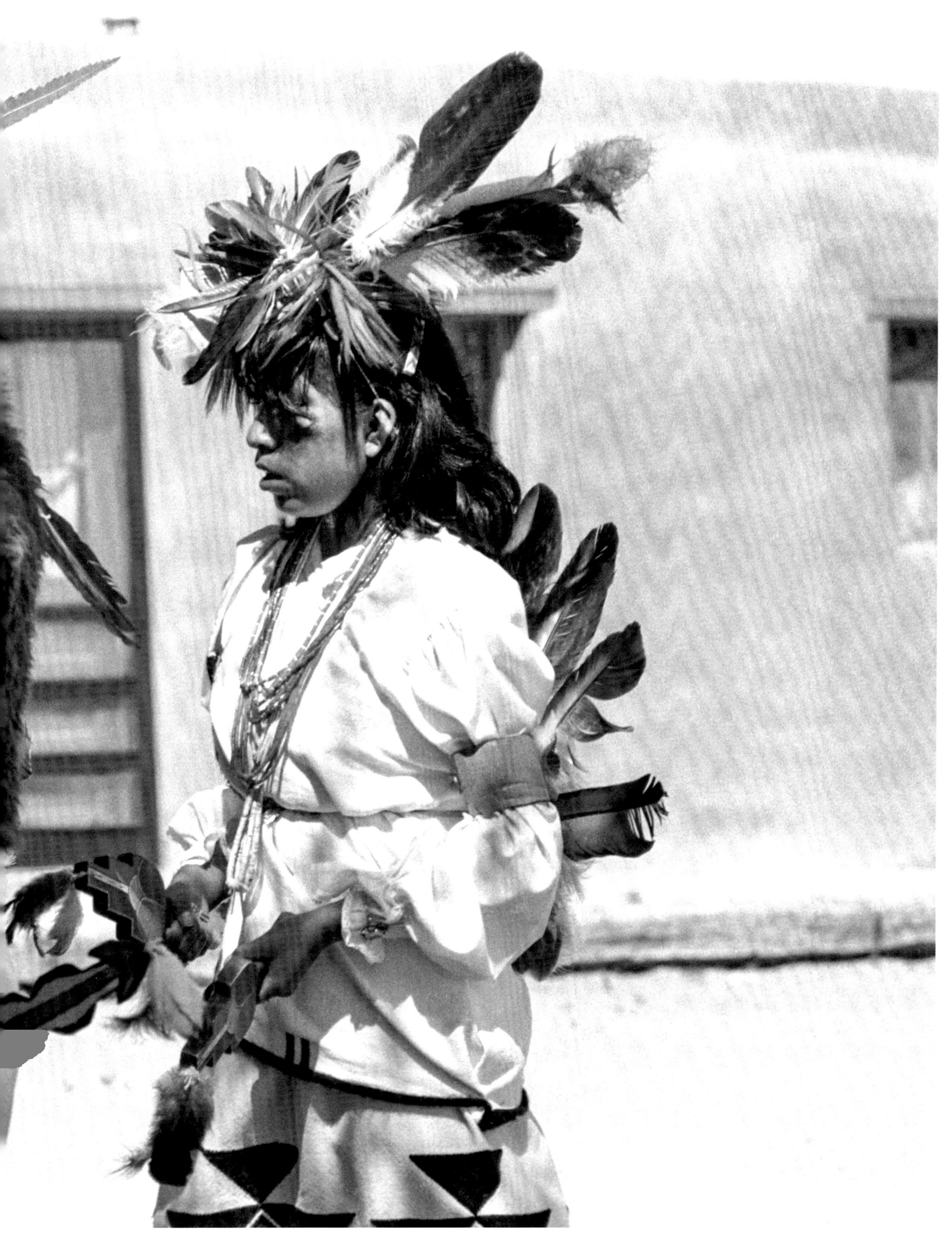

Buffalo dancers, Santa Clara Pueblo, 1981.

OVERLEAF: Anita Lujan and Juan Lujan, Deer Dance, Ohkay Owingeh, 1982.

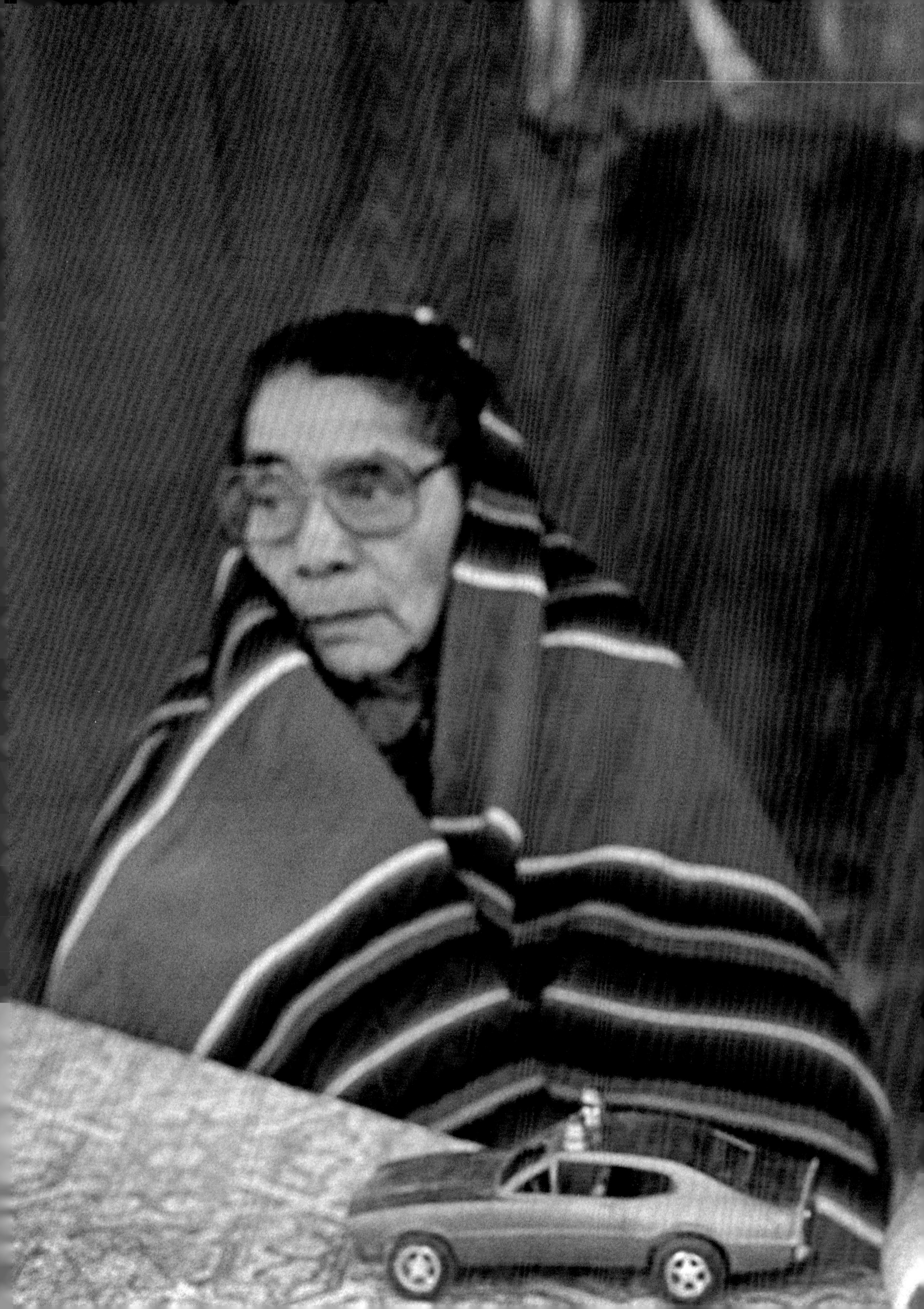

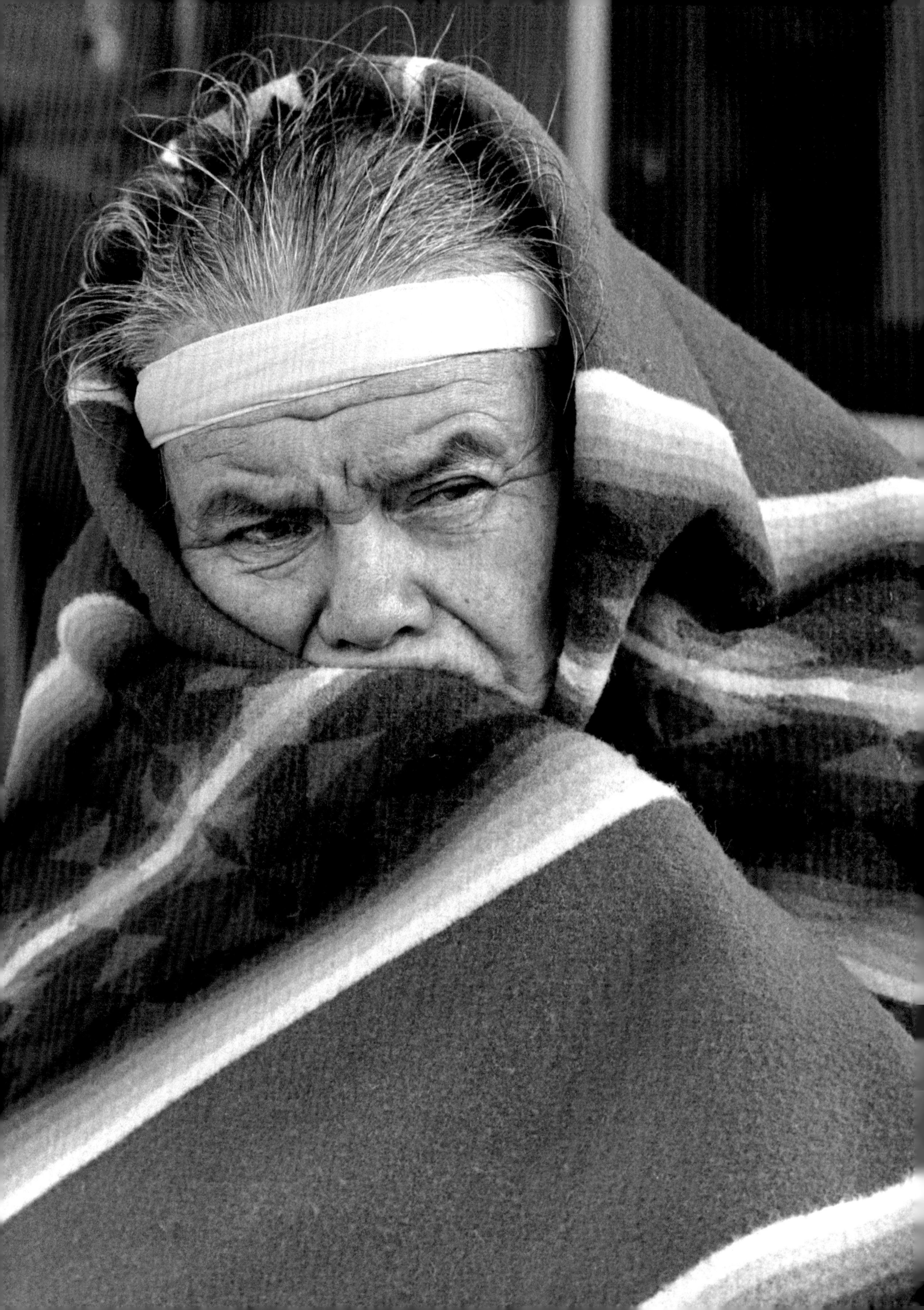

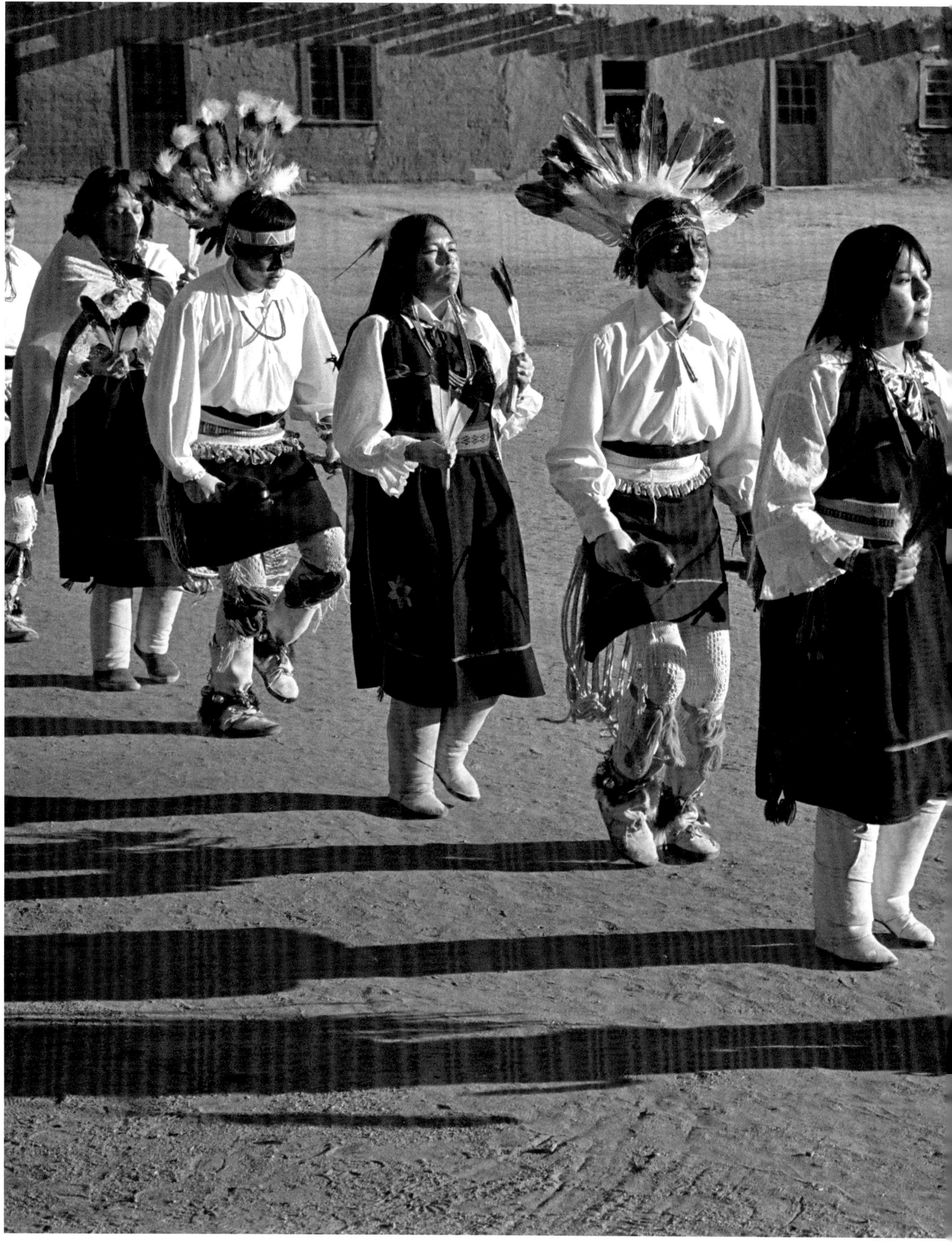

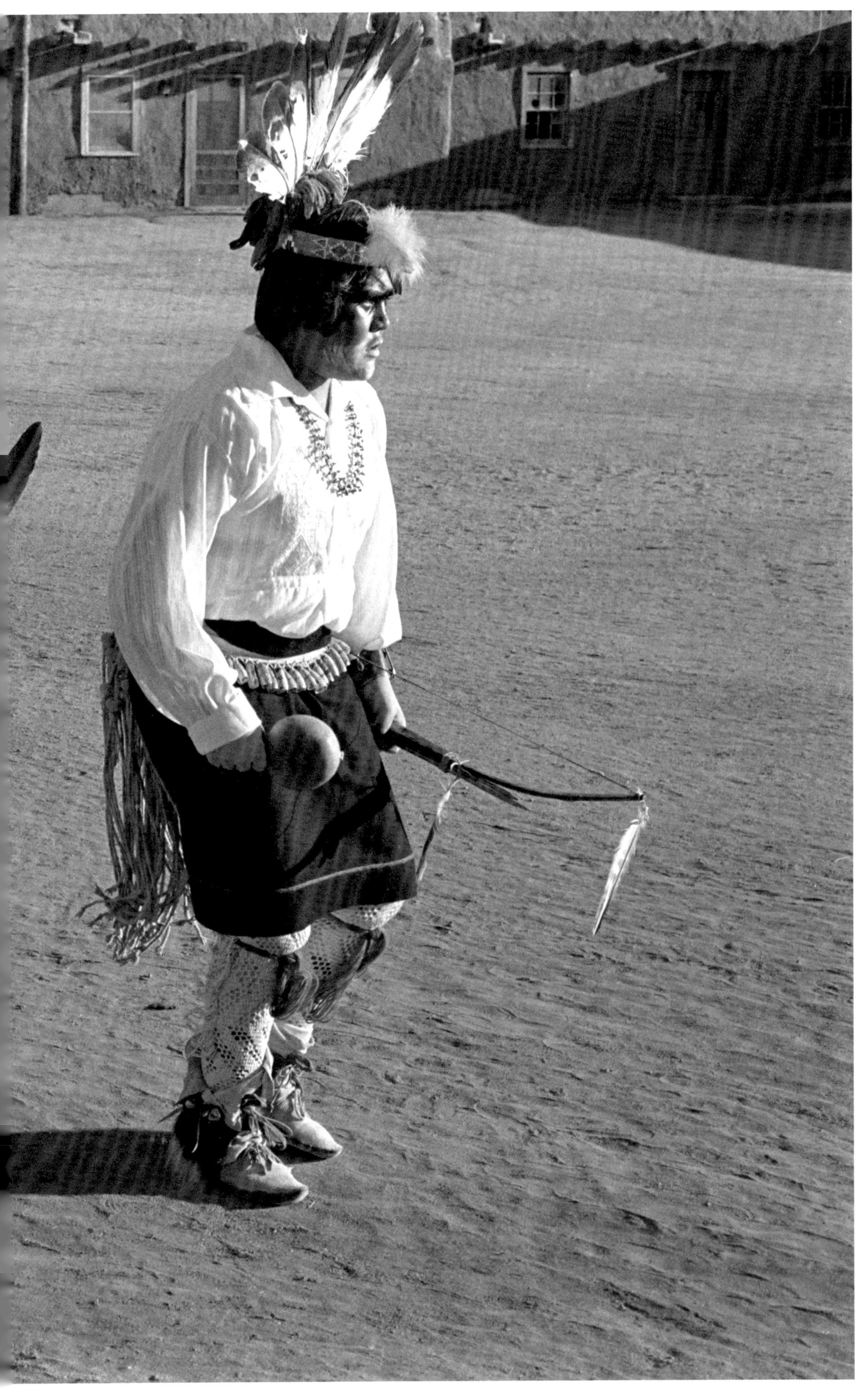

Snowbird Dance, Tesuque Pueblo, 1981.

OVERLEAF: Truchas, 1982.

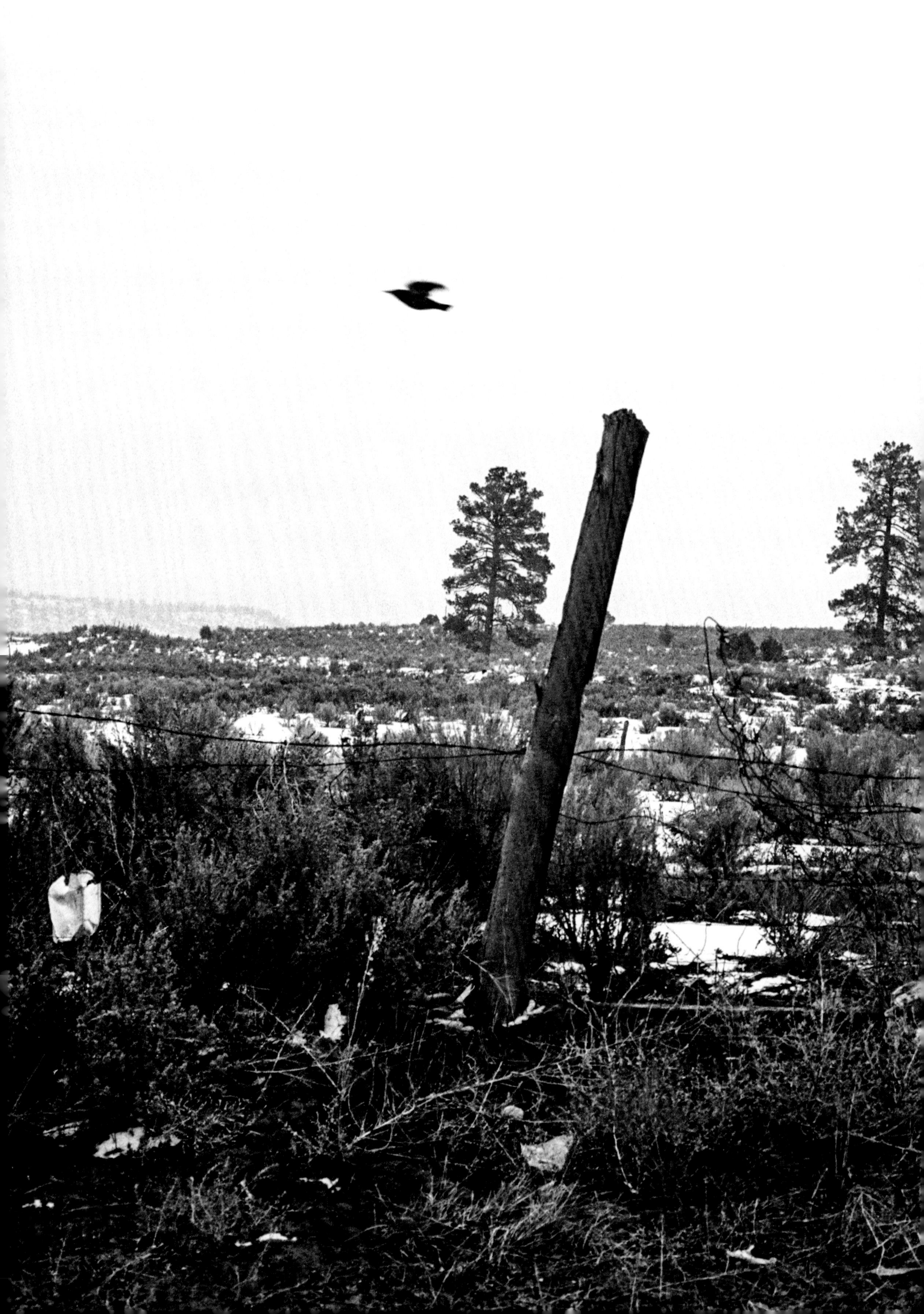

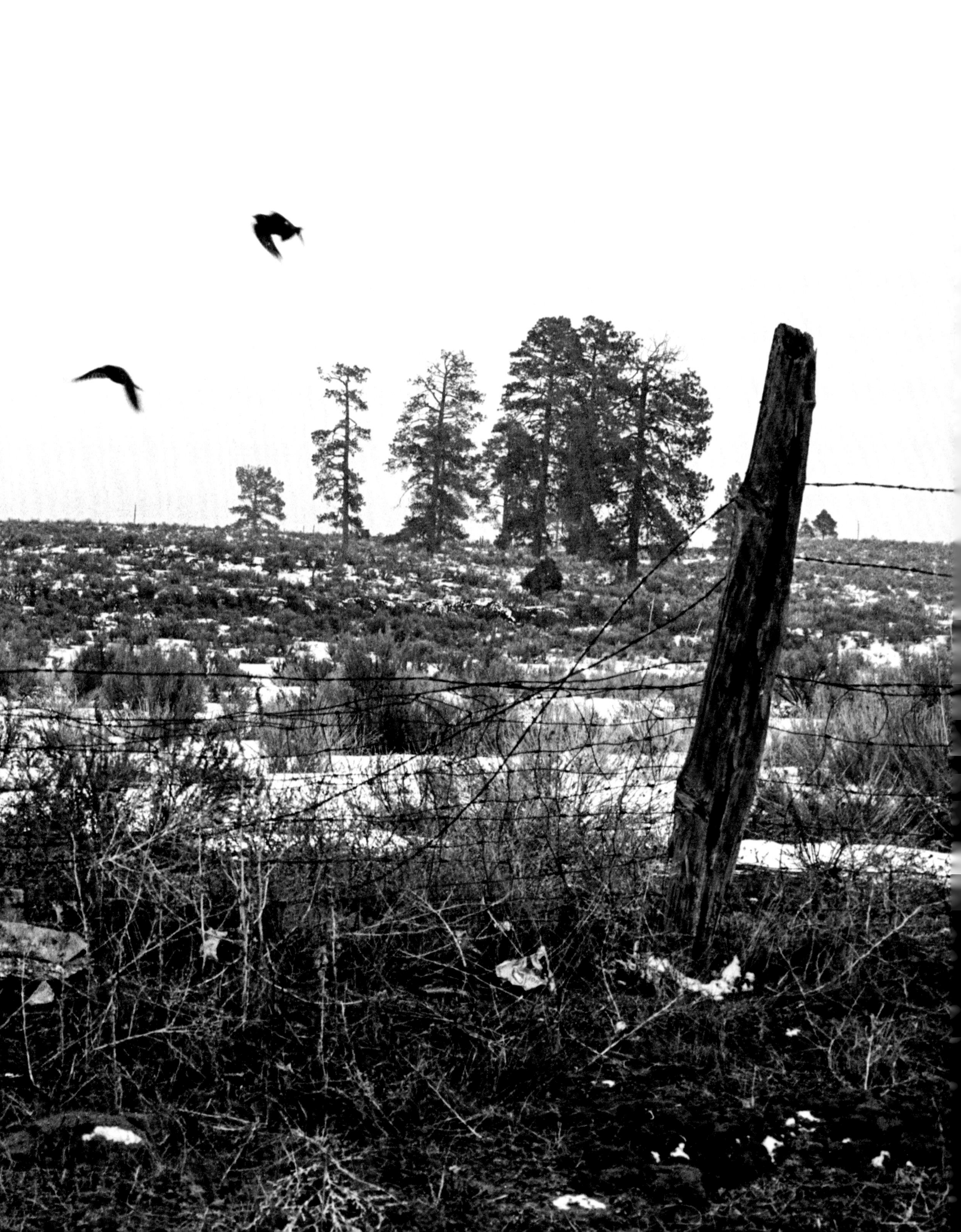

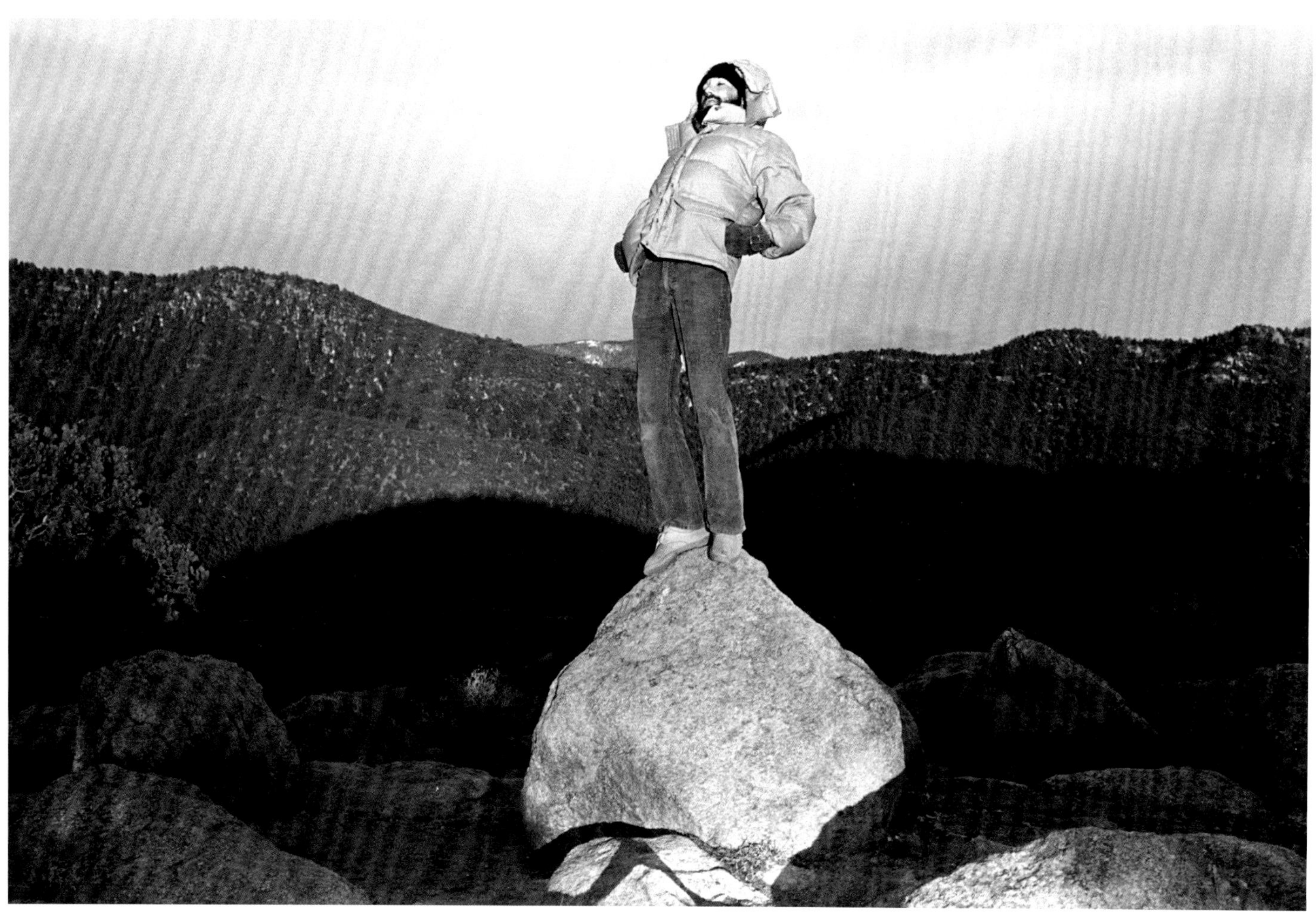

Santa Fe, 1981.

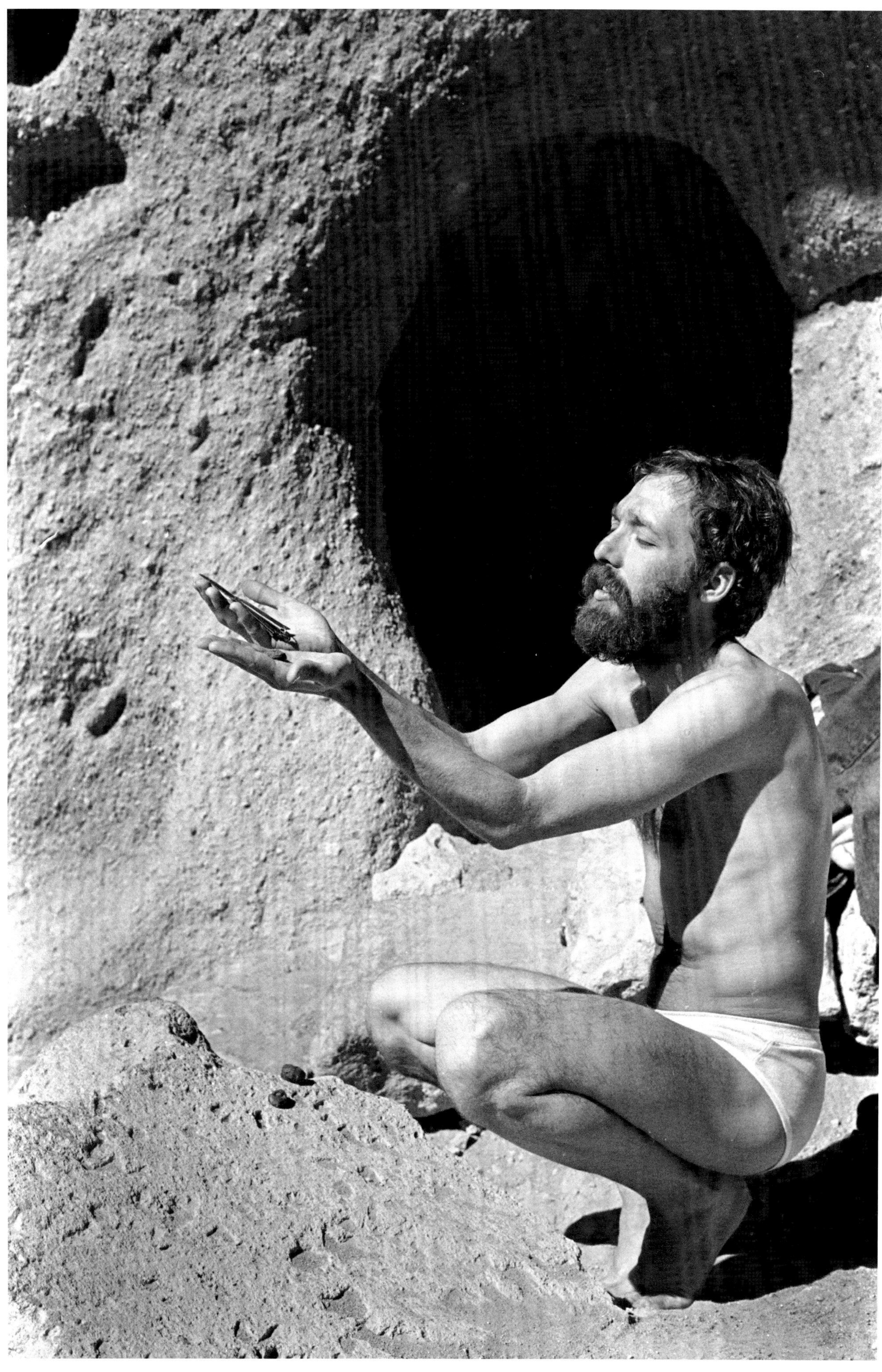

Bandelier National Monument, 1981.

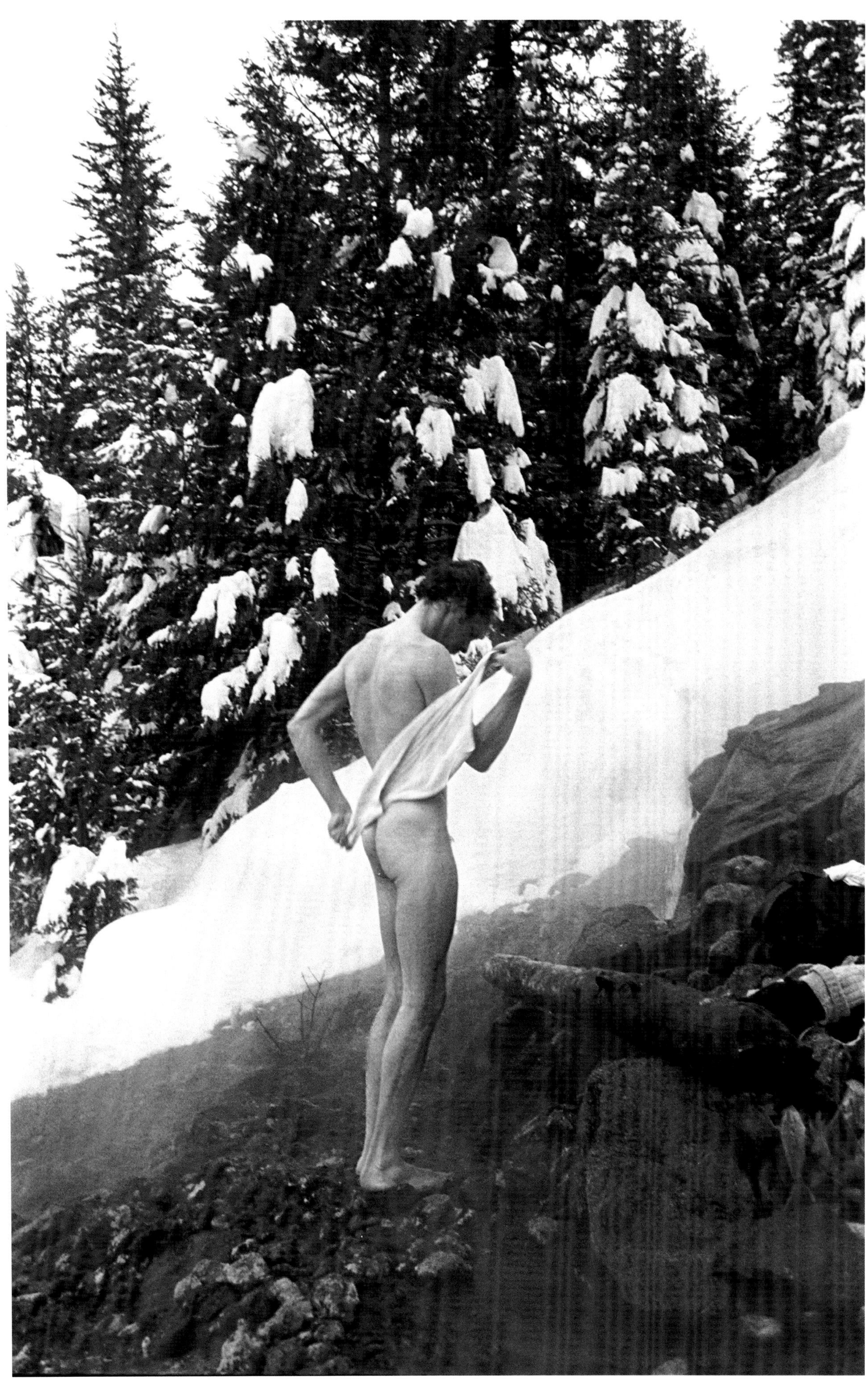

Cross-country skiers, Jemez Hot Springs, 1983.

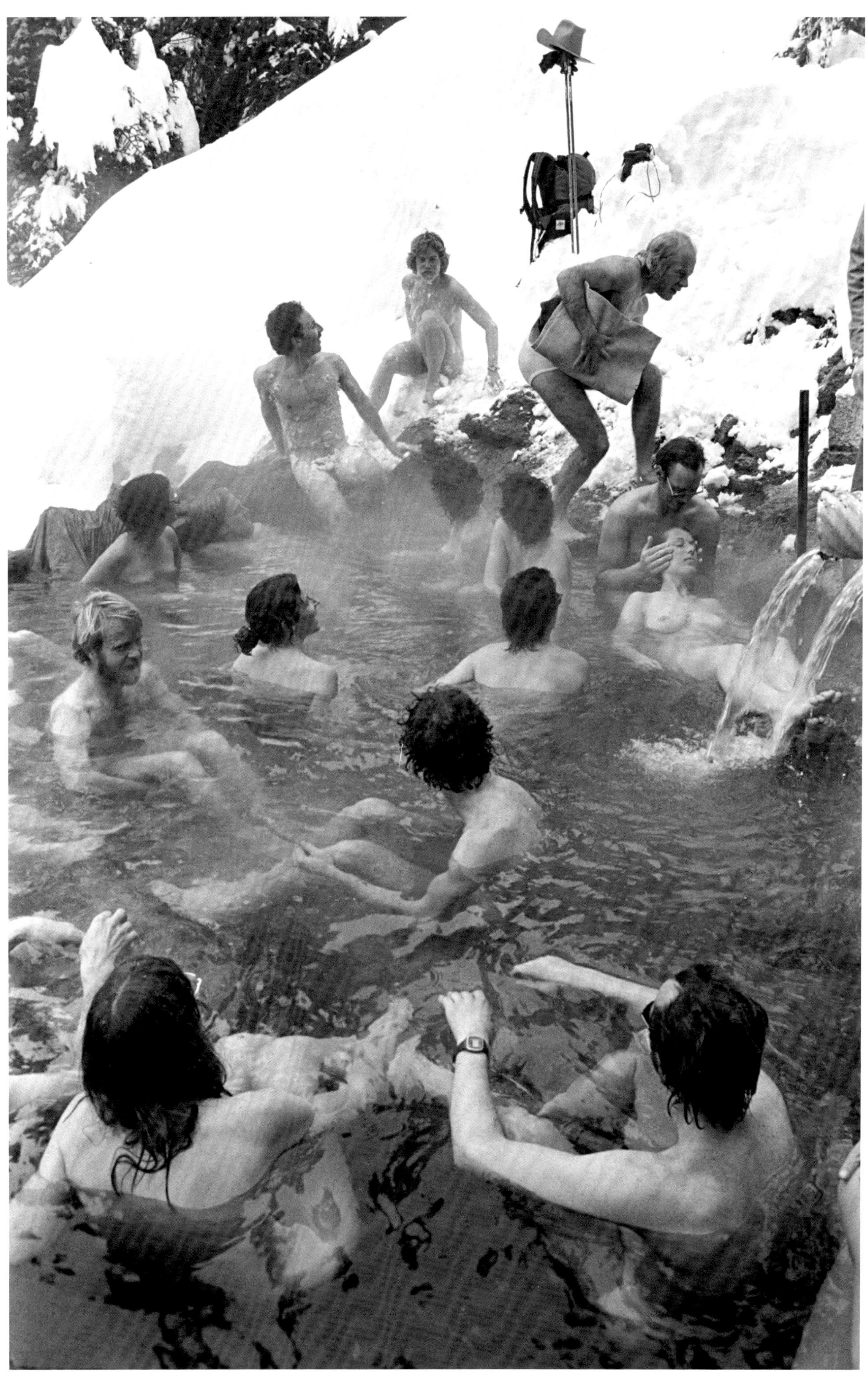

Cross-country skiers, Jemez Hot Springs, 1983.

OVERLEAF: Truchas, 1982.

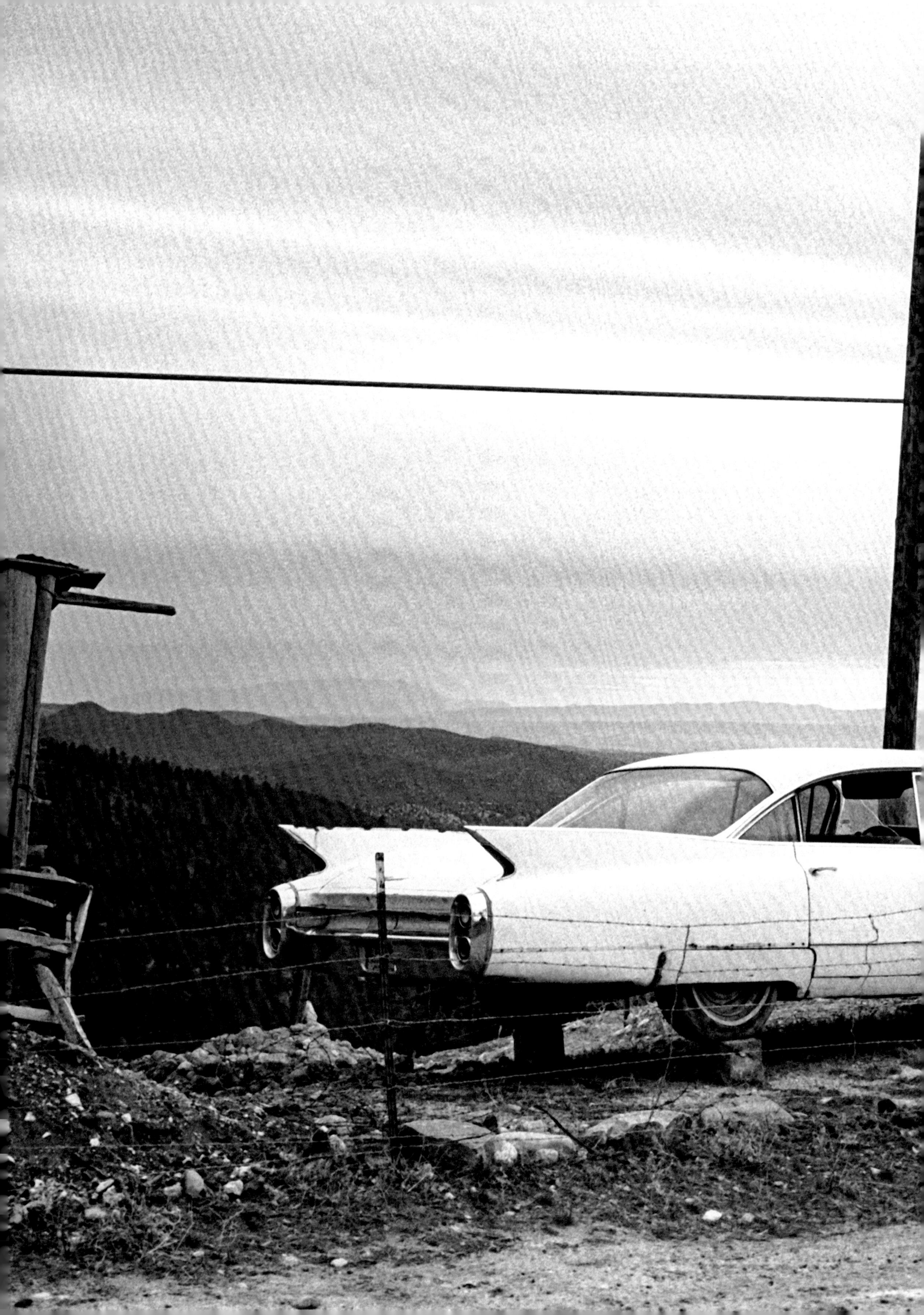

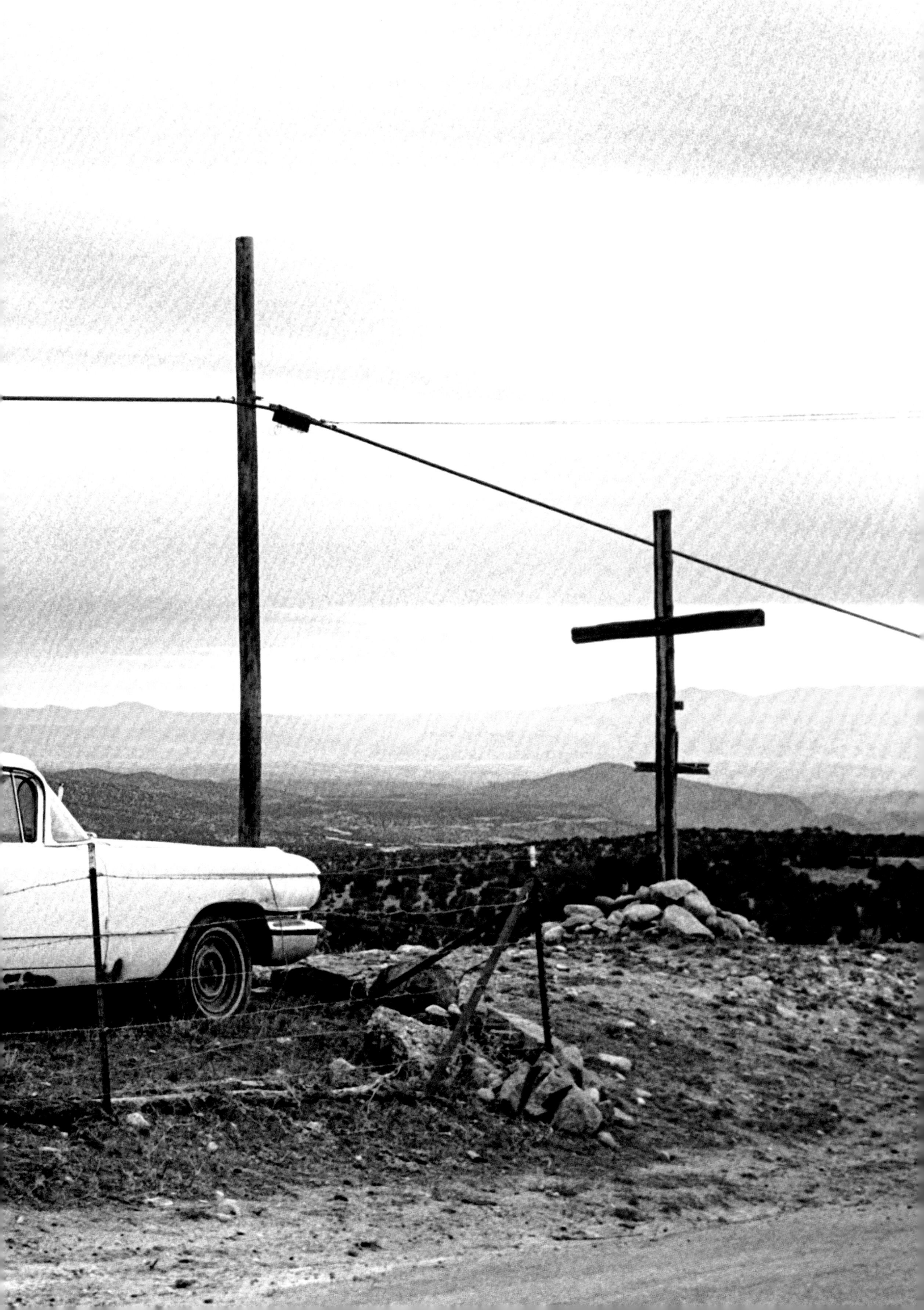

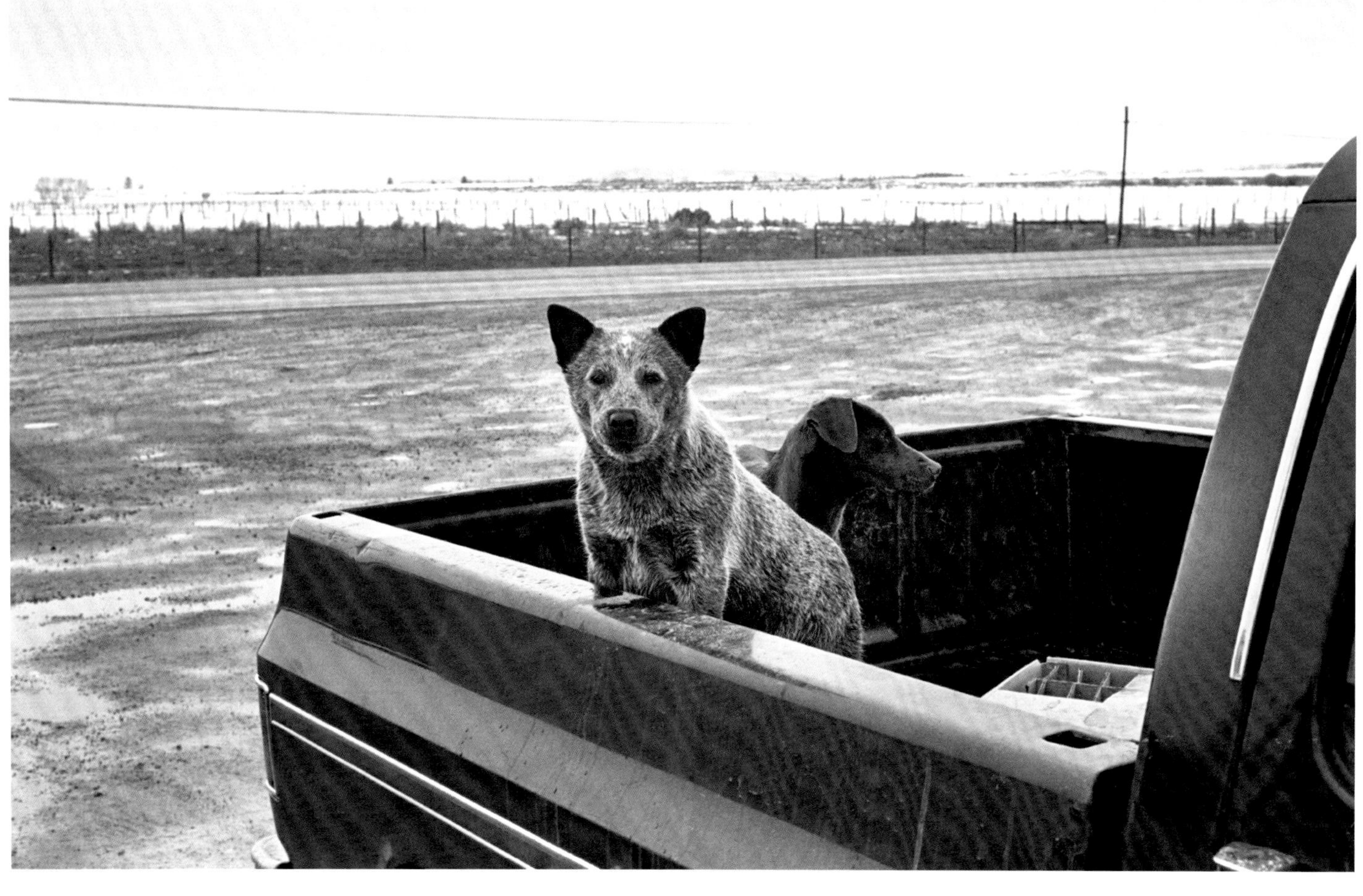

Española, 1982.

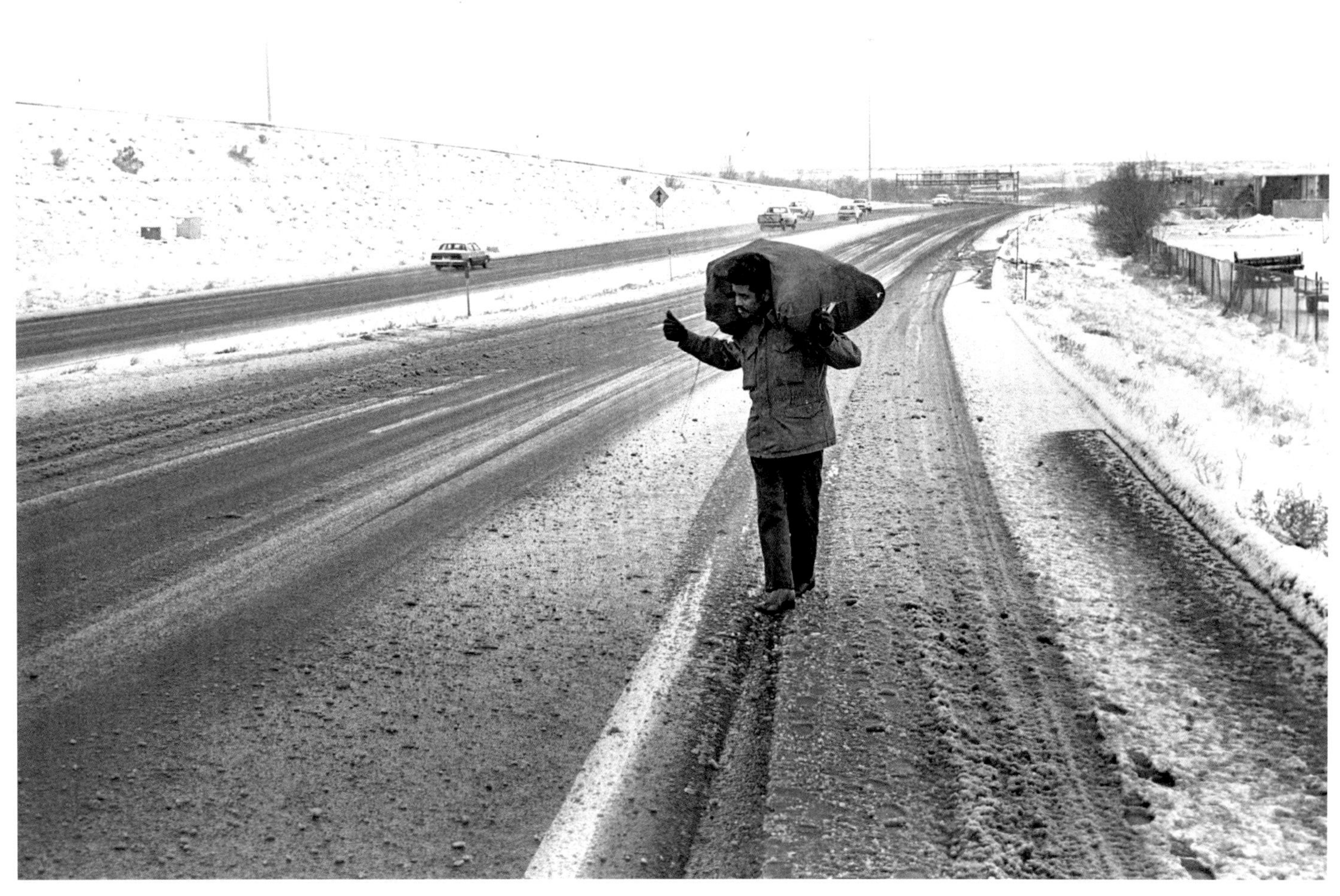

Hitchhiker, Española, 1983.

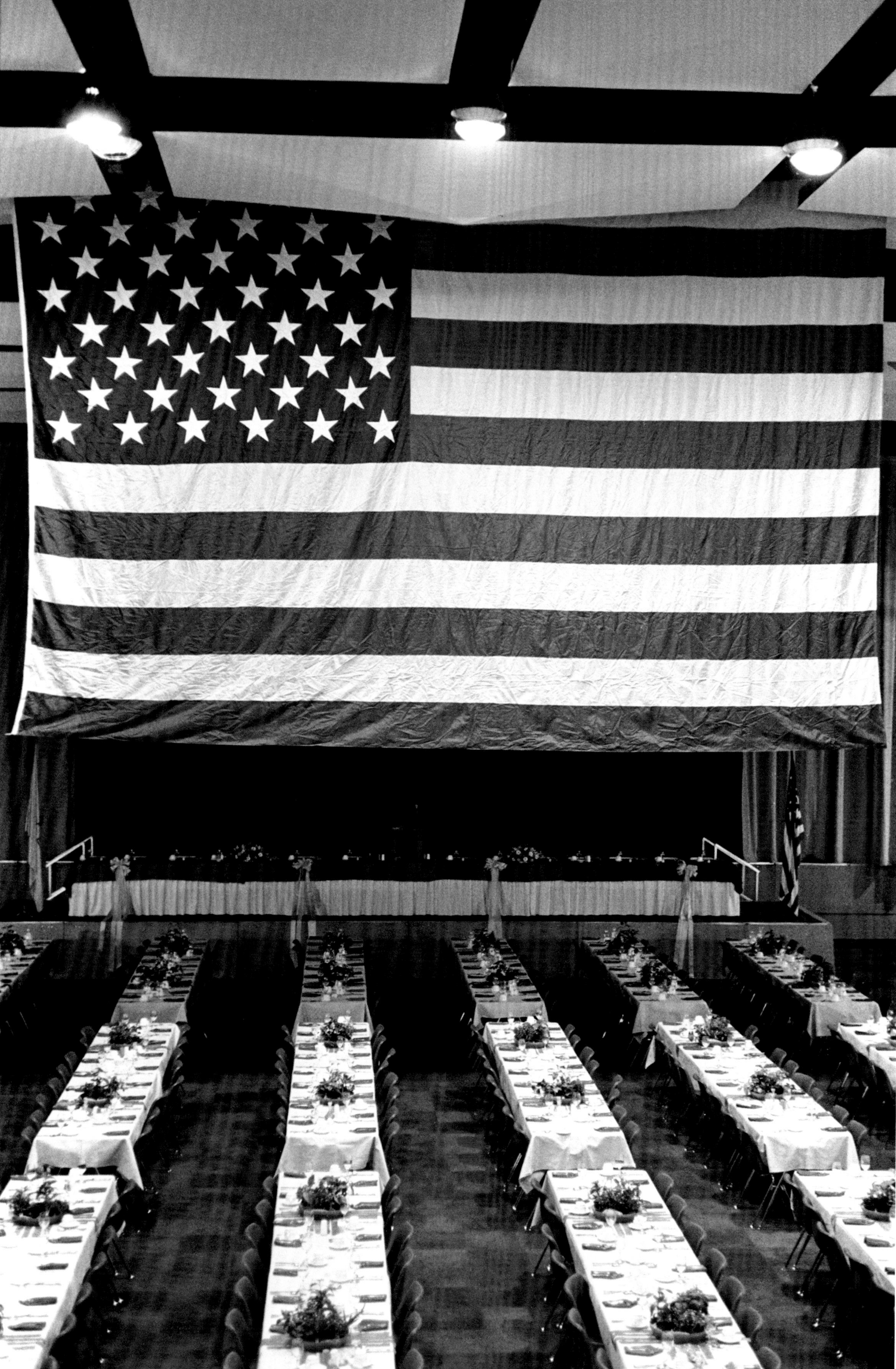

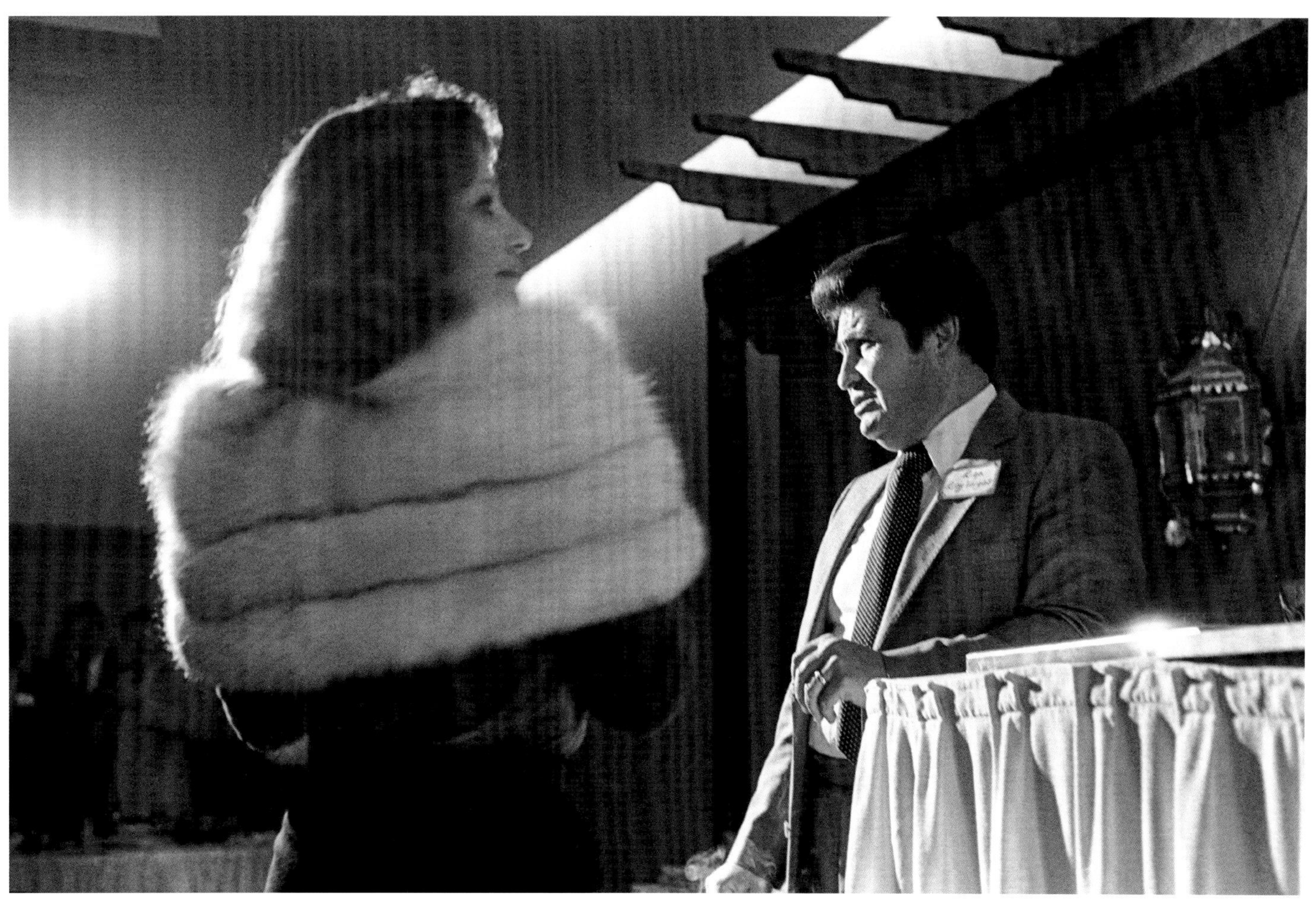

OPPOSITE AND ABOVE Political fundraising dinner, Sweeney Center, Santa Fe, 1982.

OVERLEAF: Bill Richardson campaigning for U.S. Congress, Santa Fe, 1982. Jeff Bingaman in background.

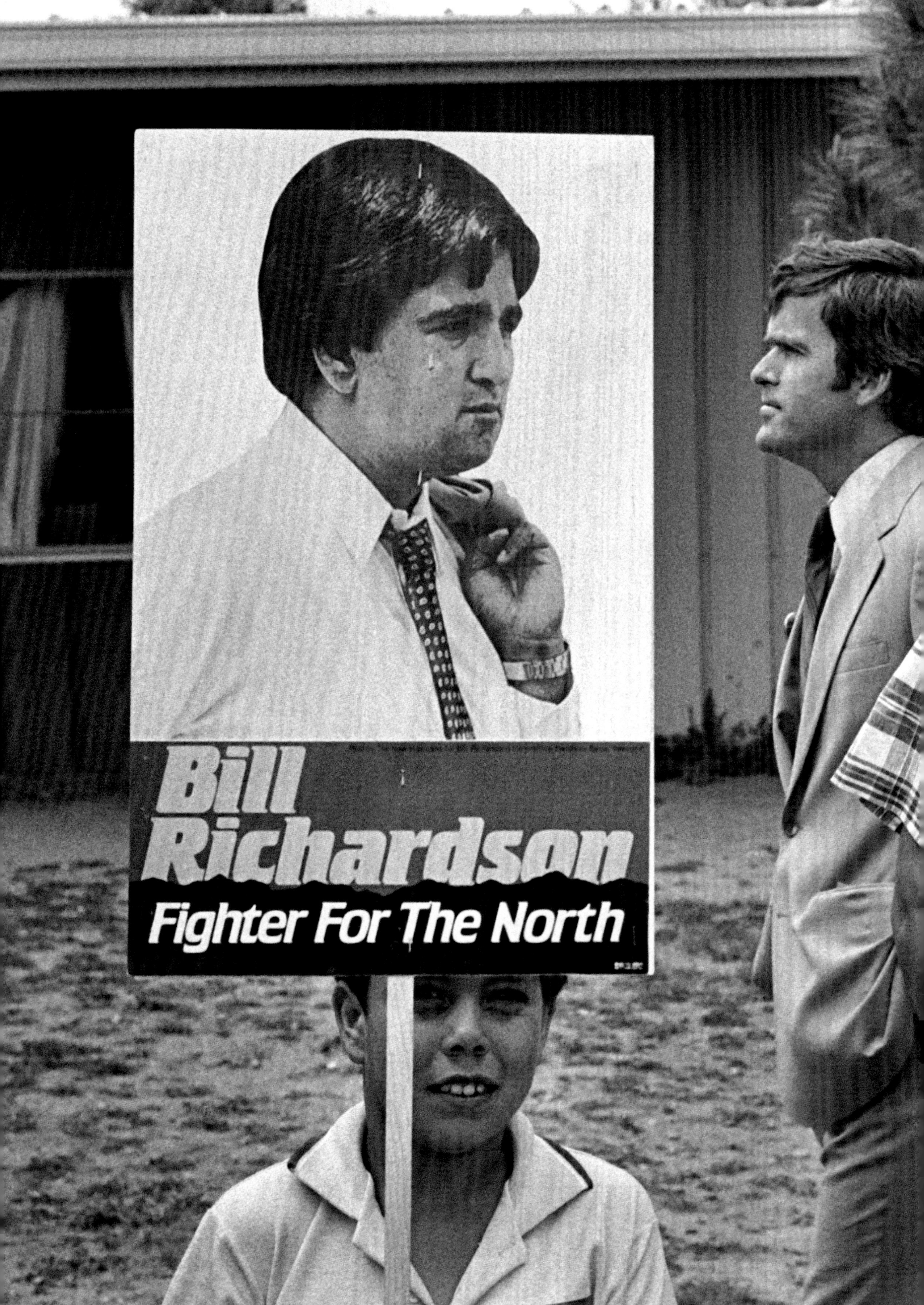
Bill
Richardson
Fighter For The North

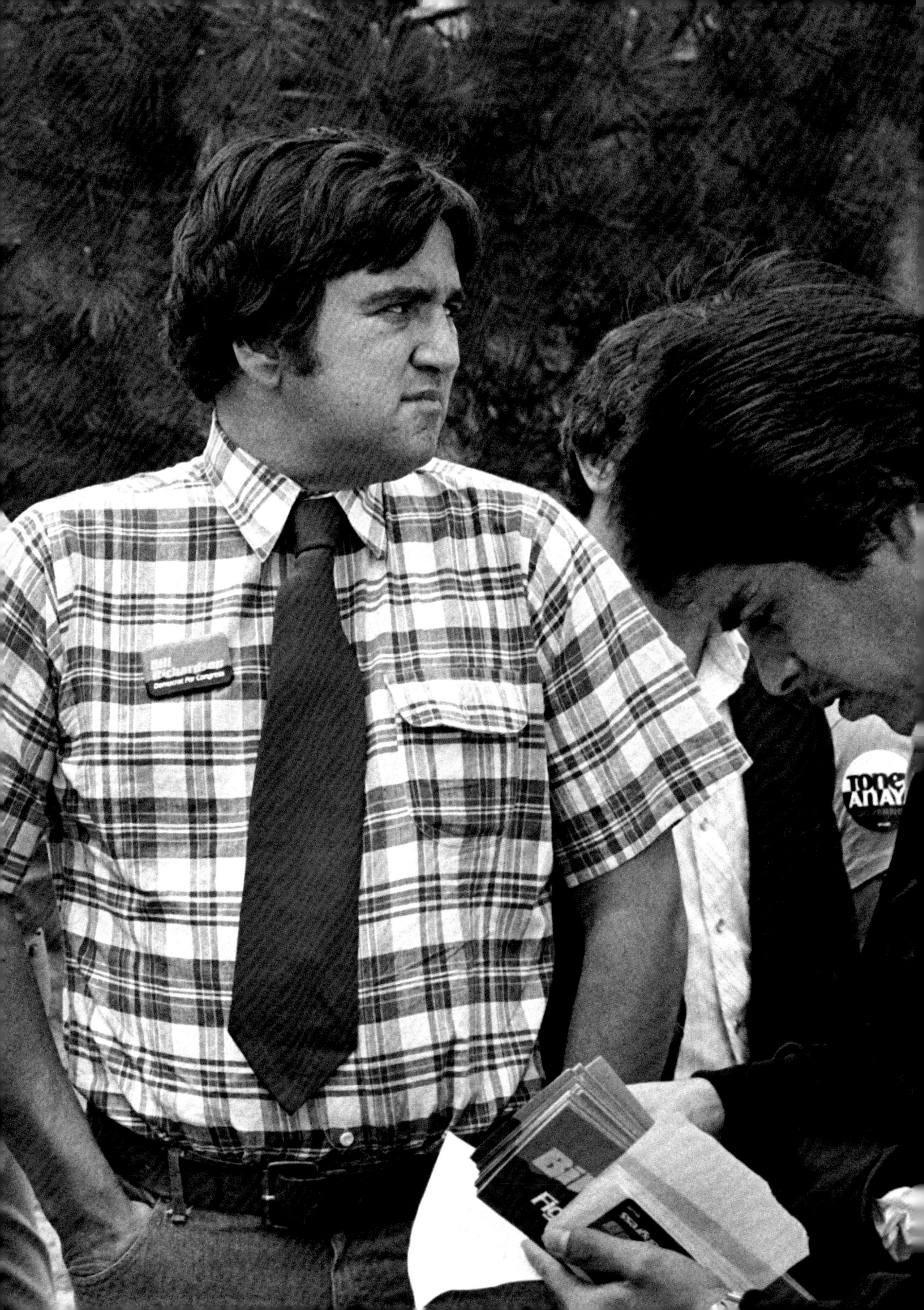
Bill Richardson
Democrat For Congress

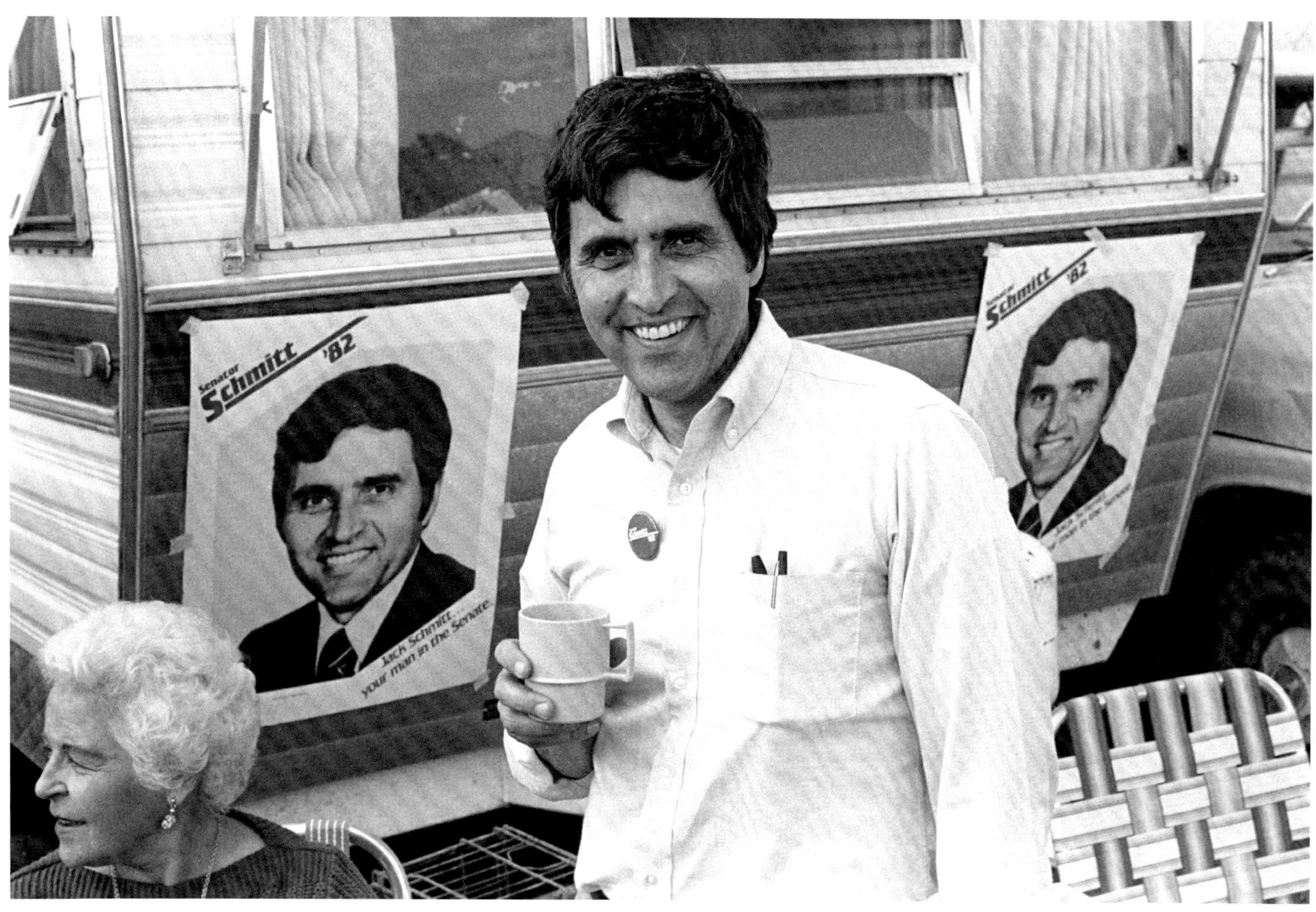

Harrison "Jack" Schmitt, former NASA moon astronaut, on the campaign trail, Albuquerque, 1982.

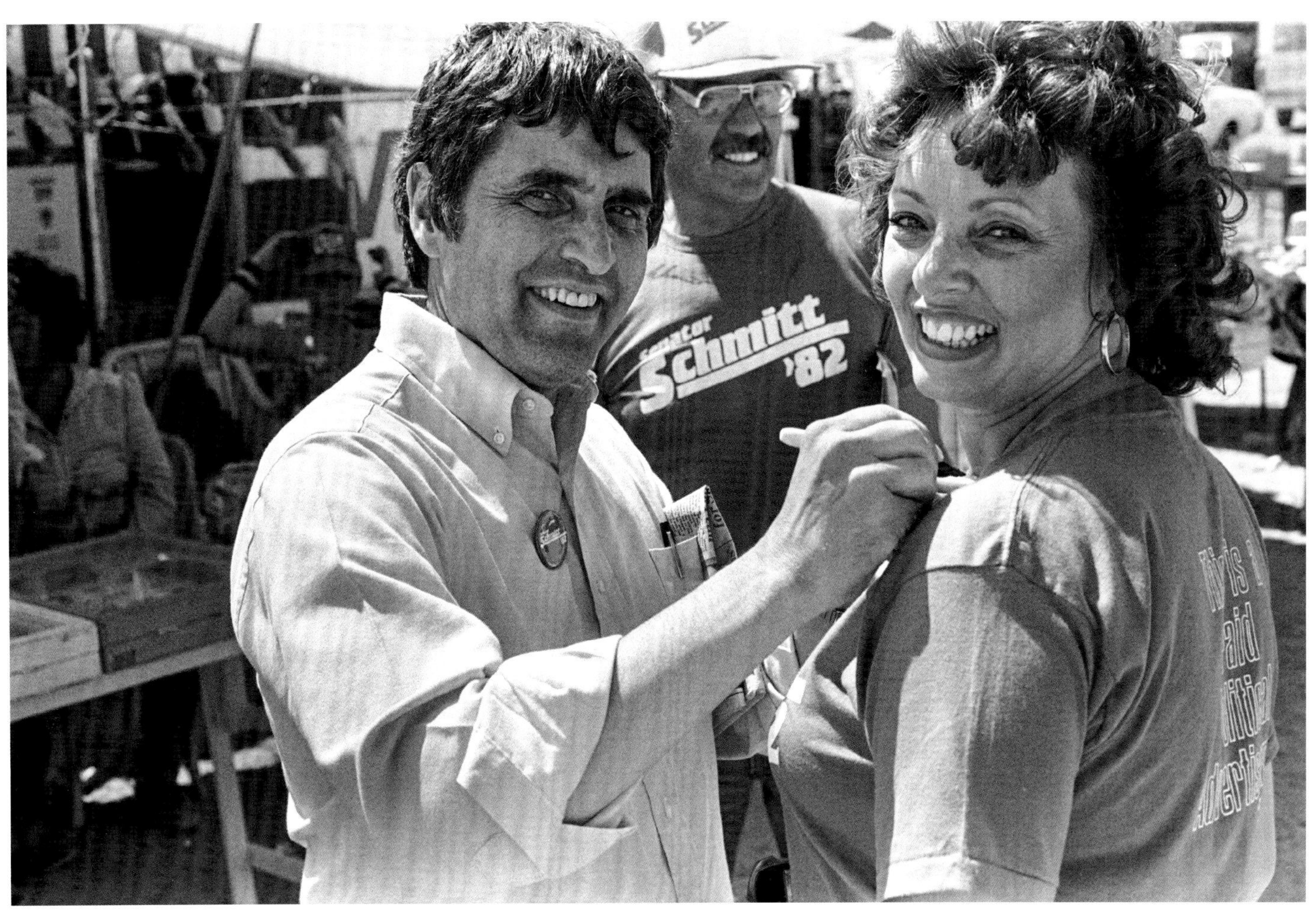

Jack Schmitt, Albuquerque, 1982.

OVERLEAF: Governor John Connolly of Texas (left) and Forrest Fenn, Santa Fe, 1982.

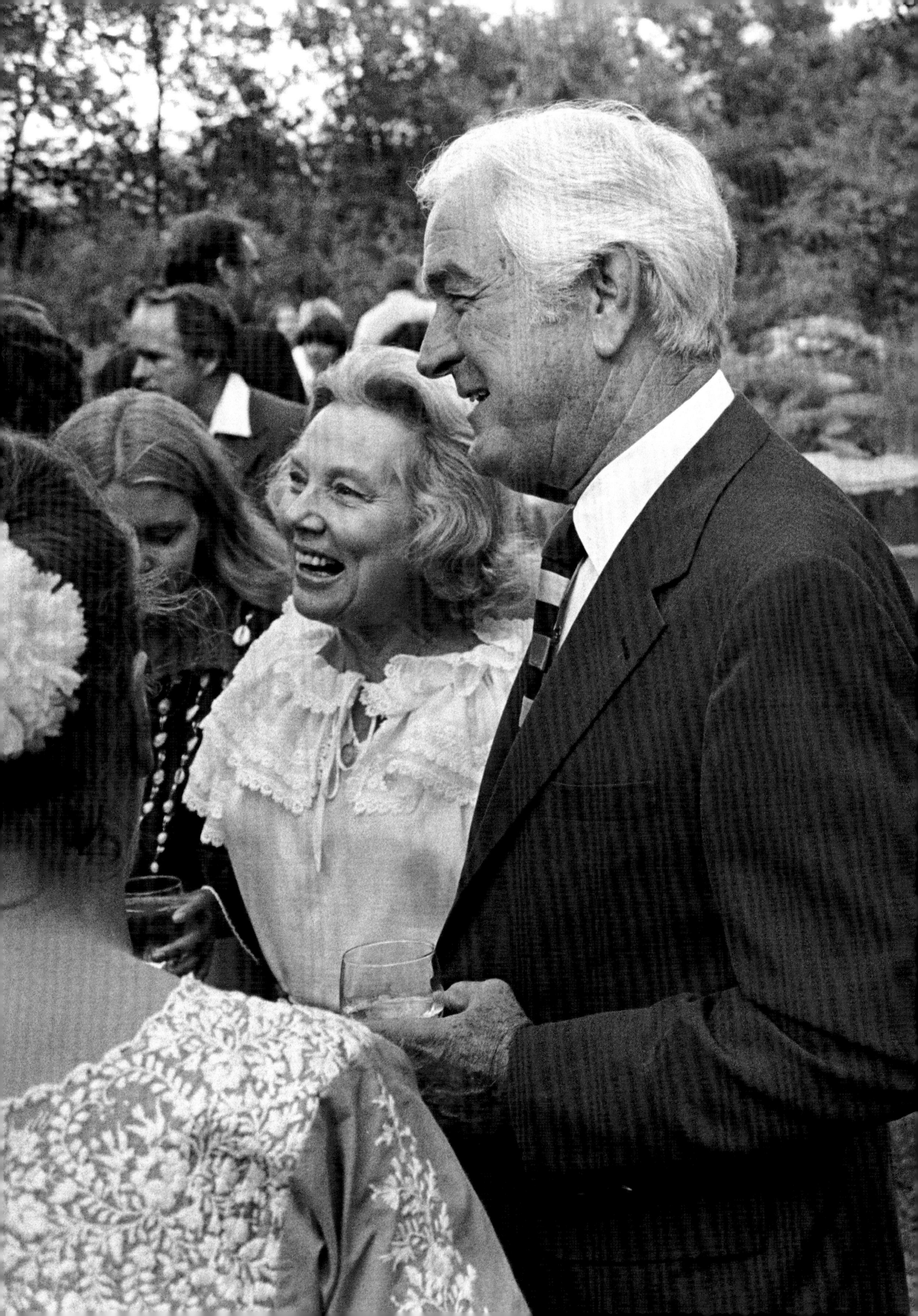

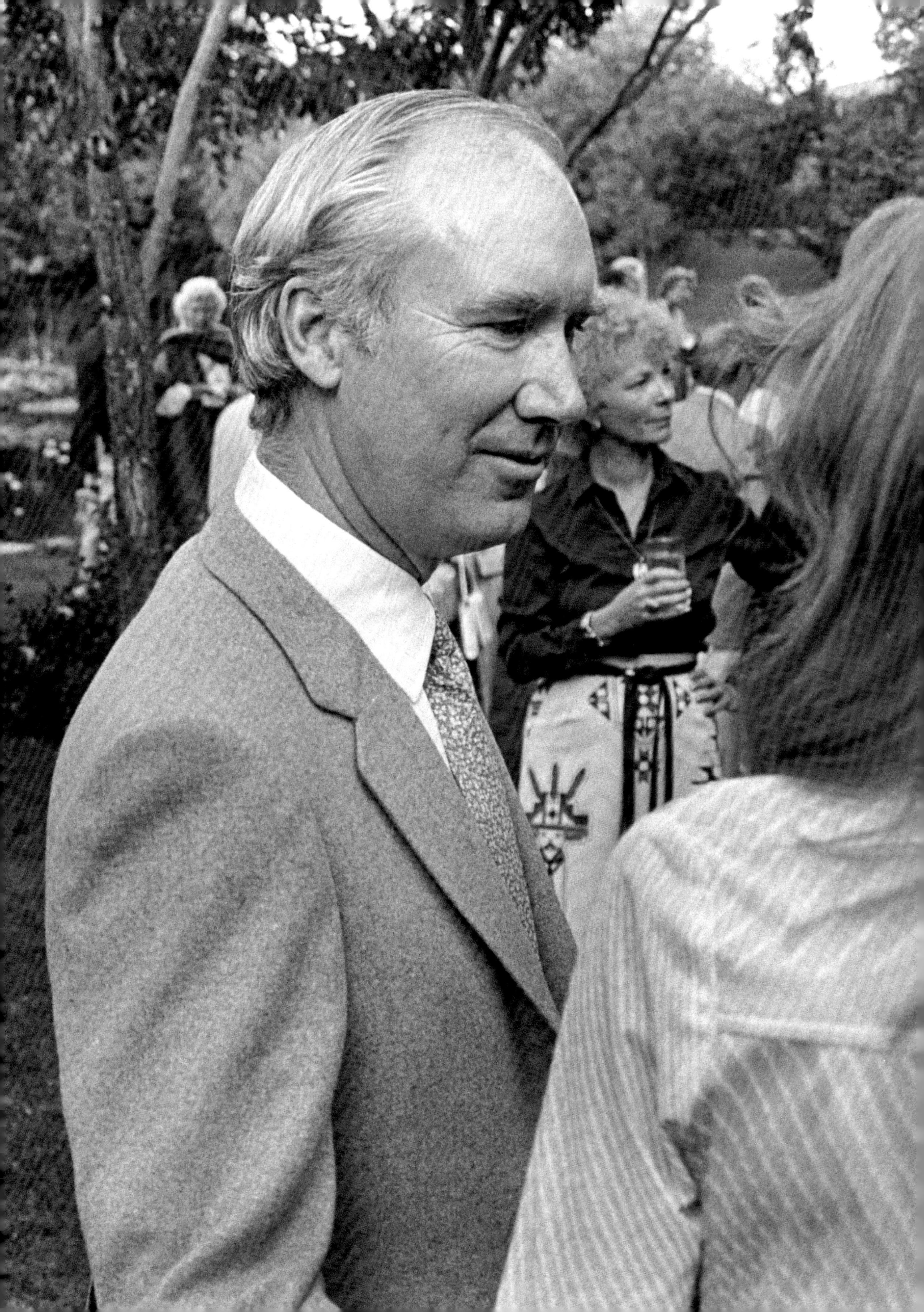

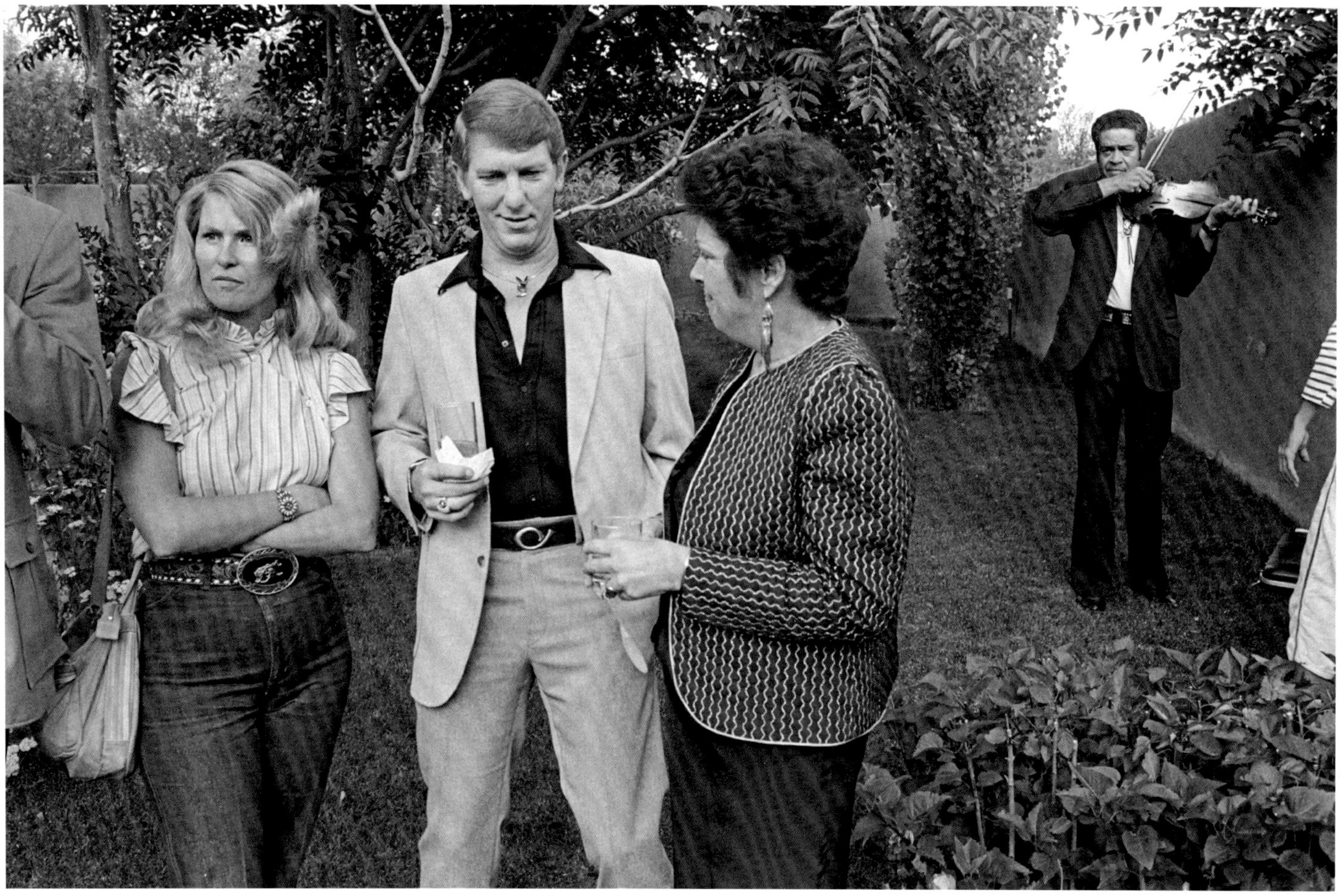

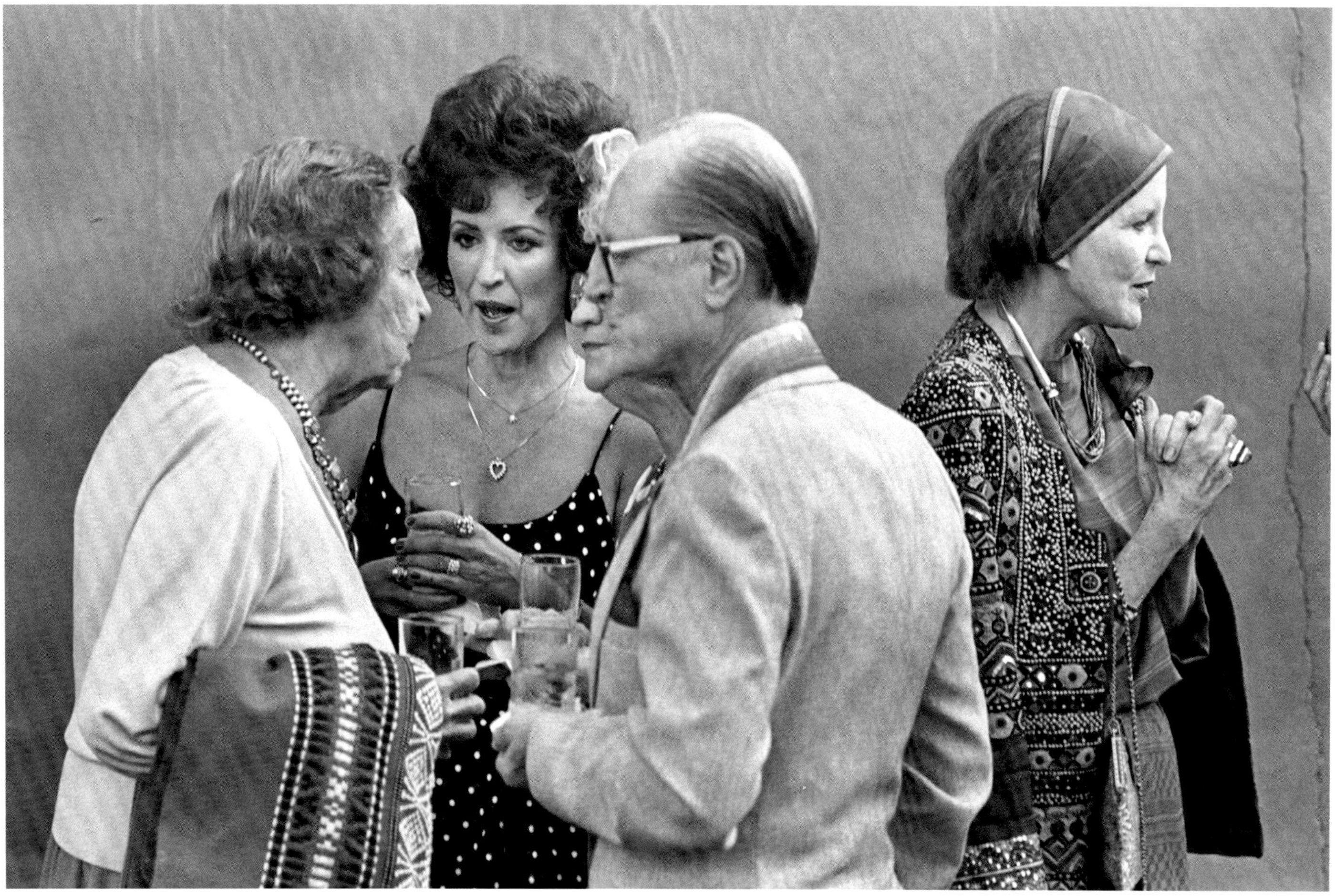

Garden party at Forrest Fenn's gallery, Santa Fe, 1982.

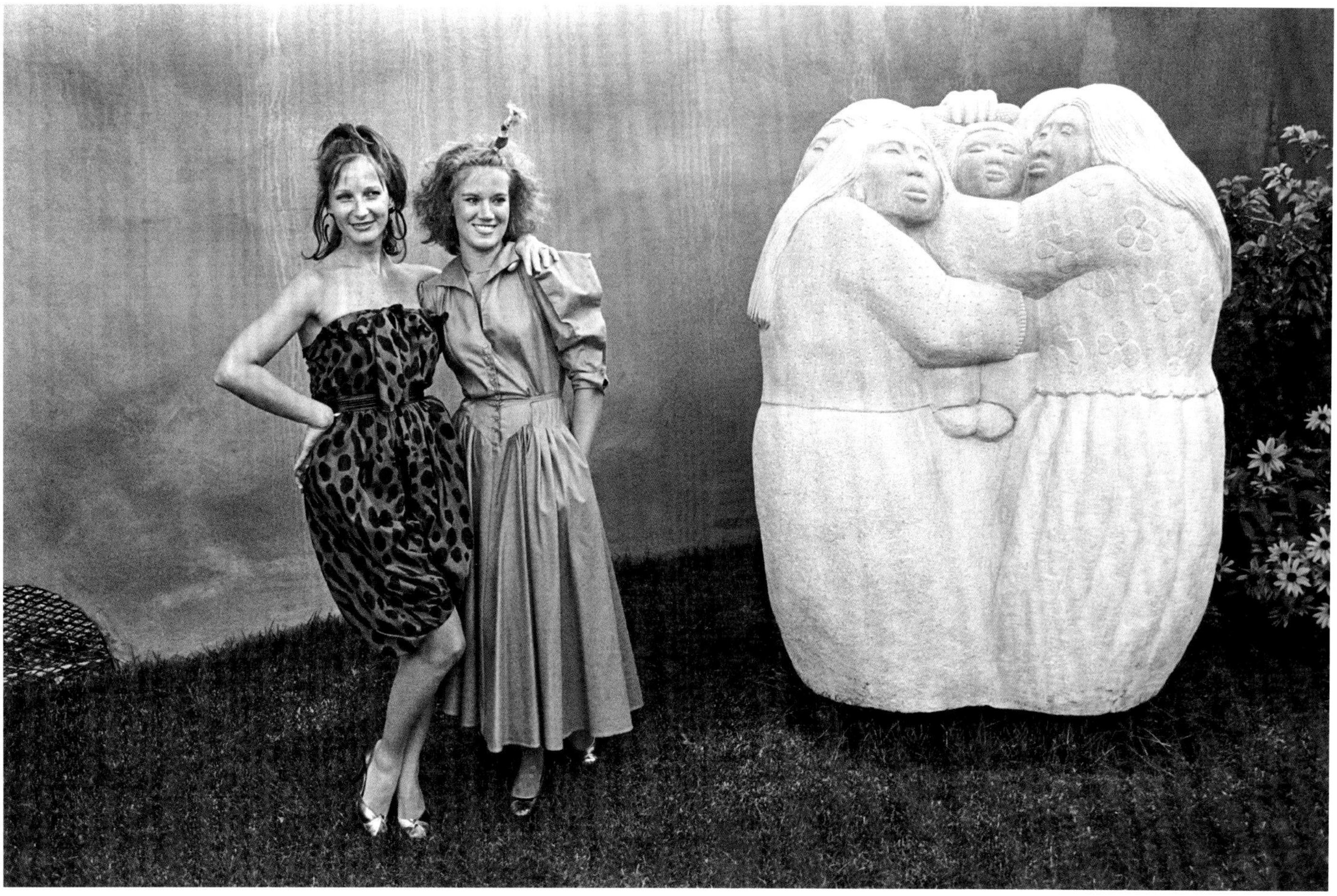

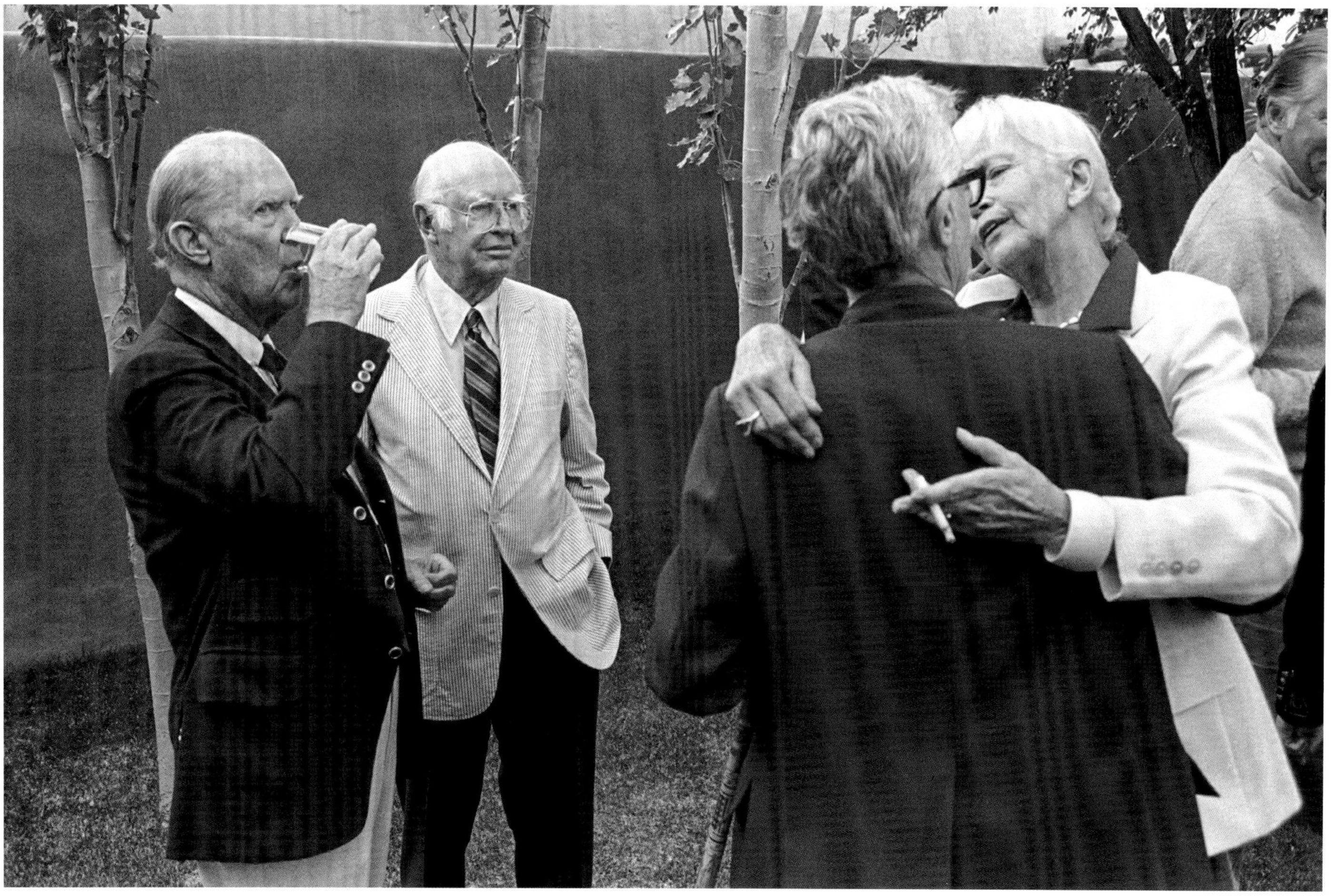

Garden party at Forrest Fenn's gallery, Santa Fe, 1982.

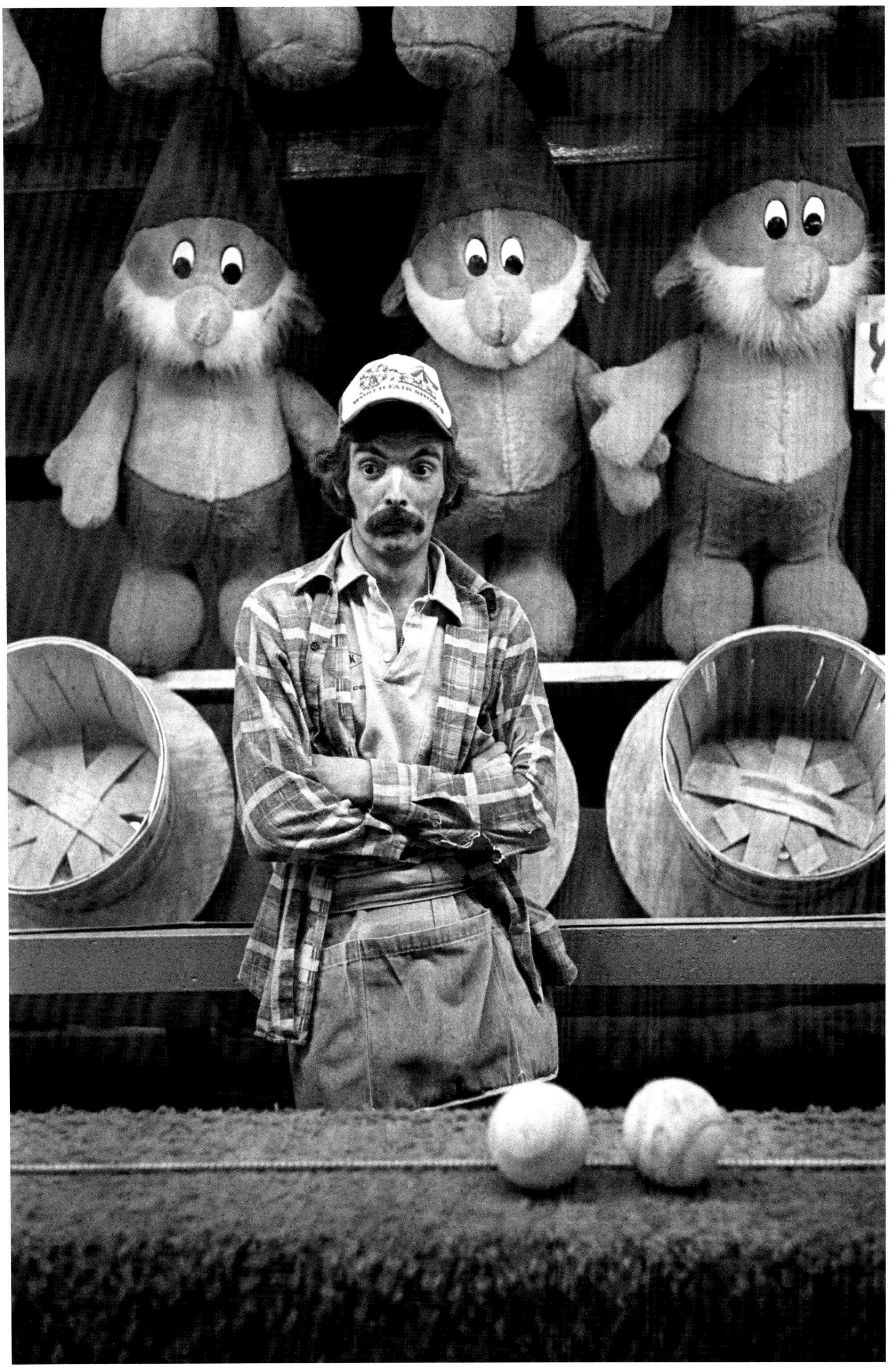

Carnival midway worker, Santa Fe, 1982.

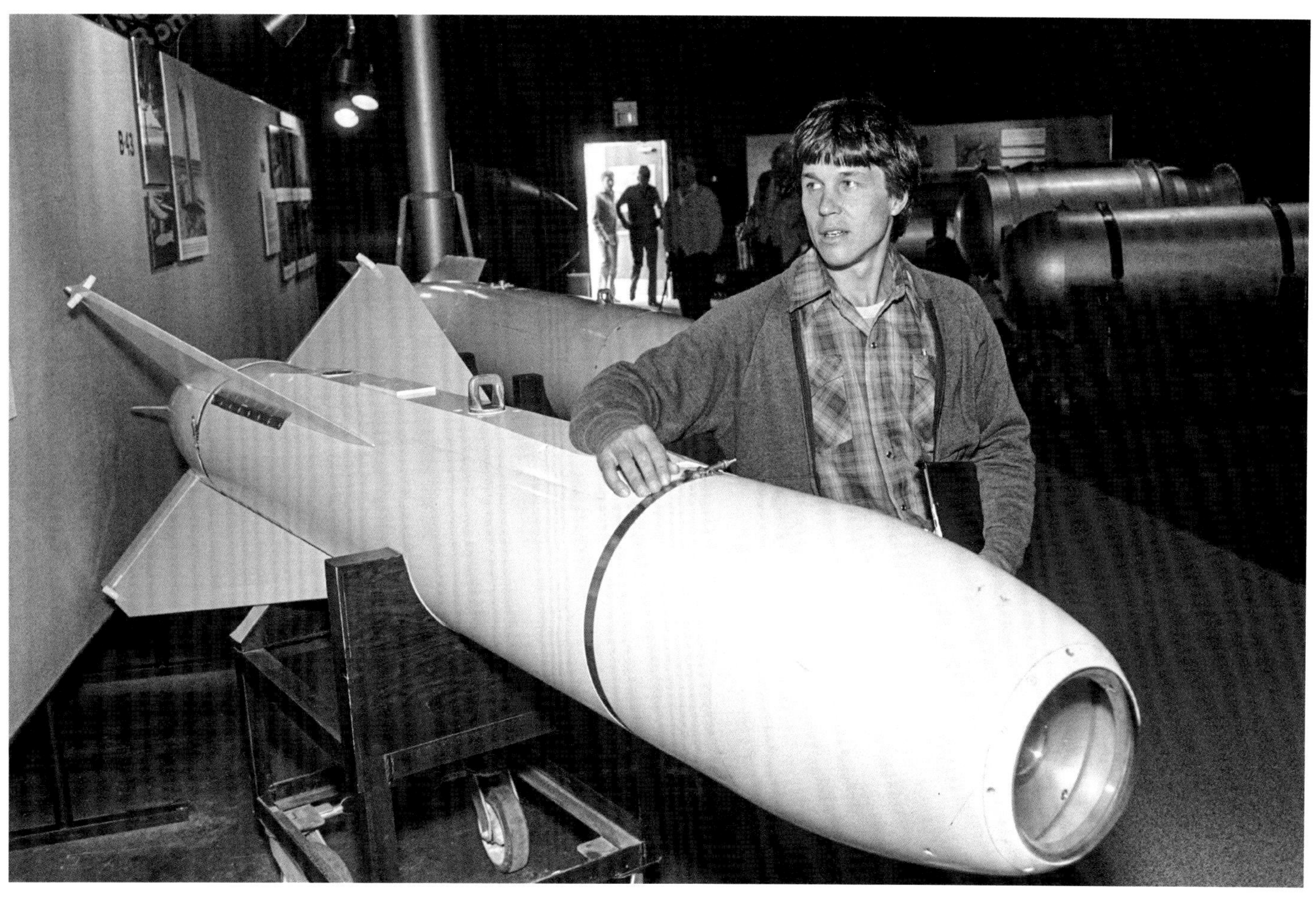

Los Alamos History Museum, 1981.

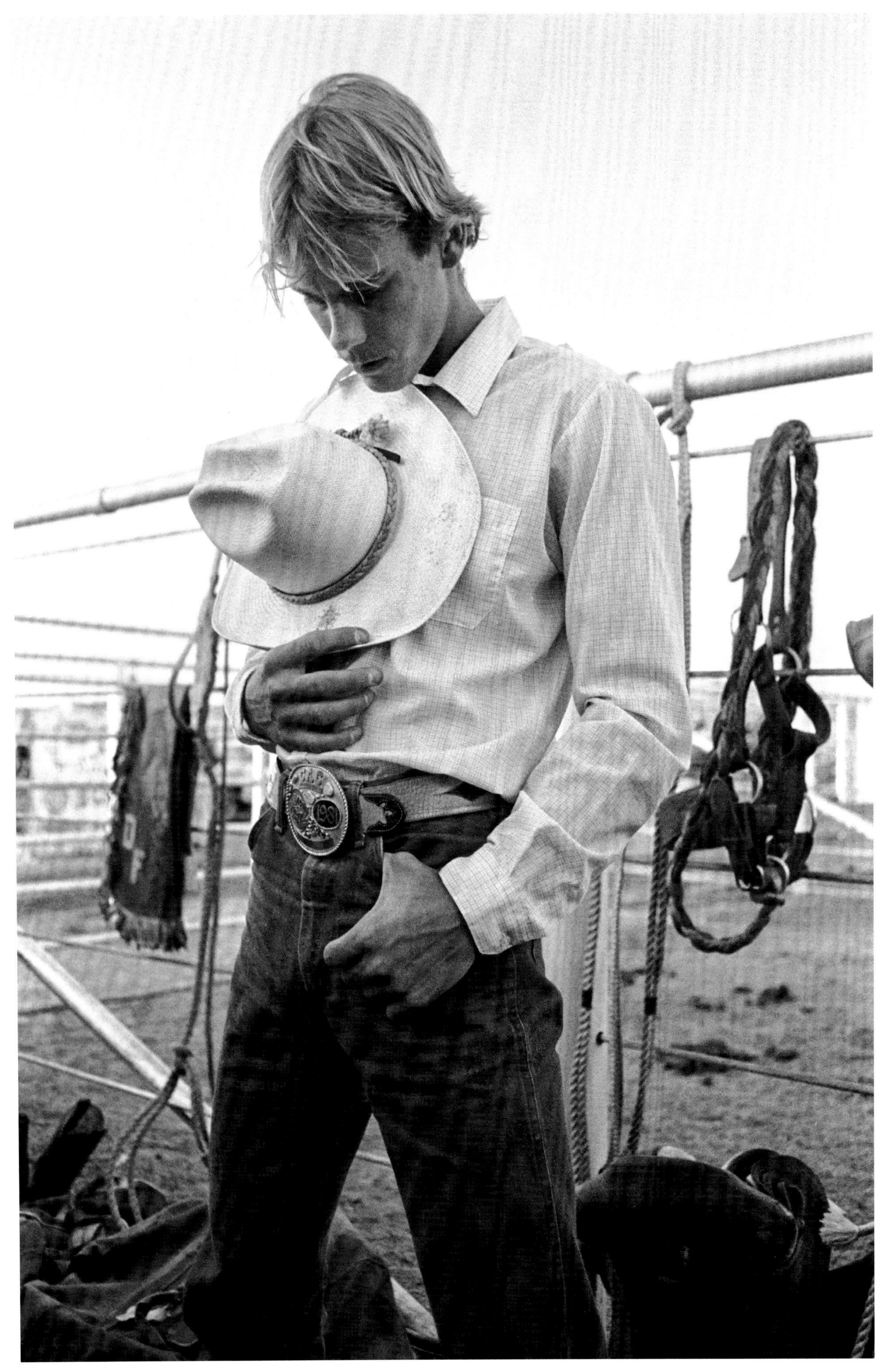

Rodeo de Santa Fe, 1982.

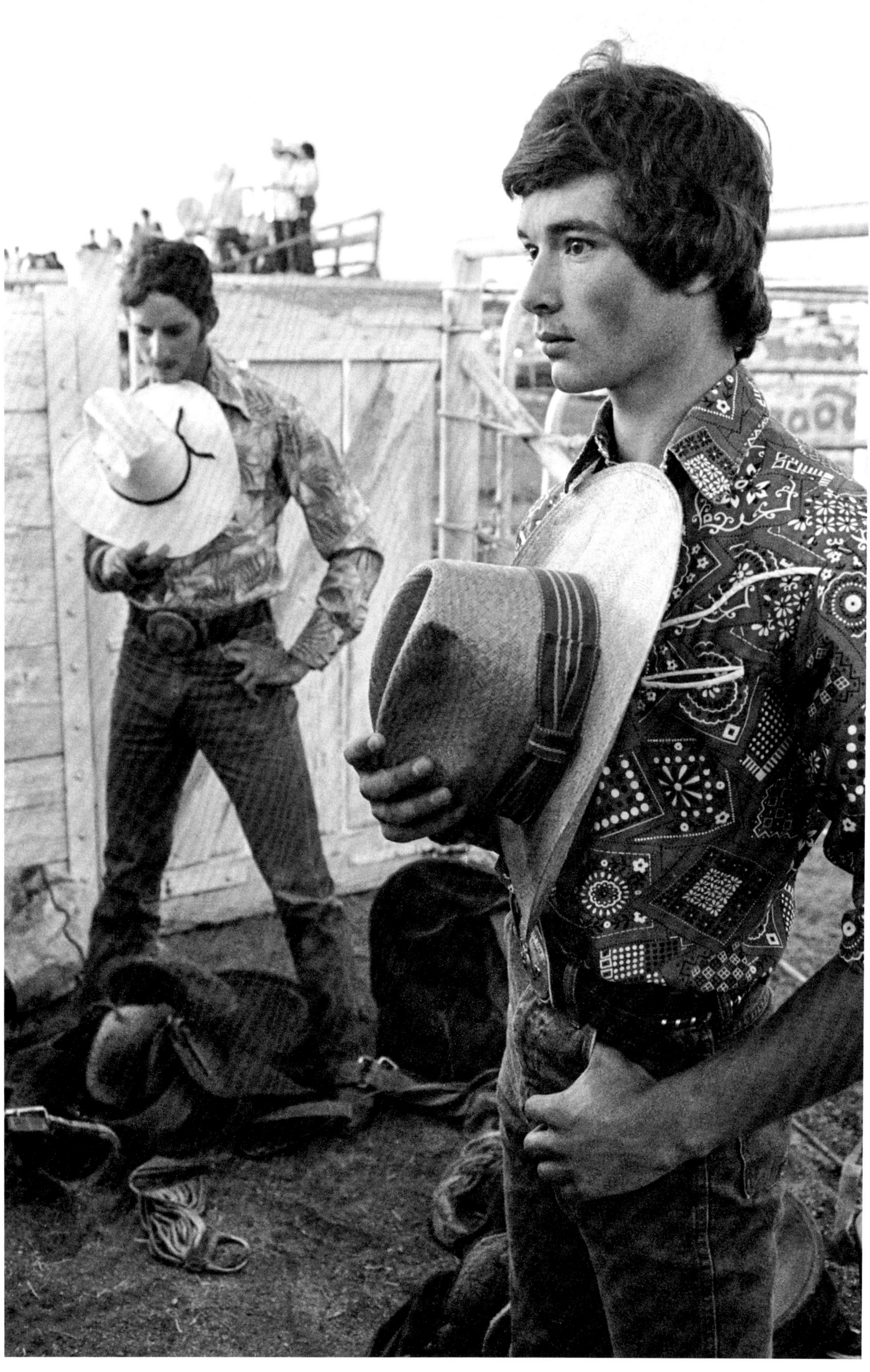

Rodeo de Santa Fe, 1982.

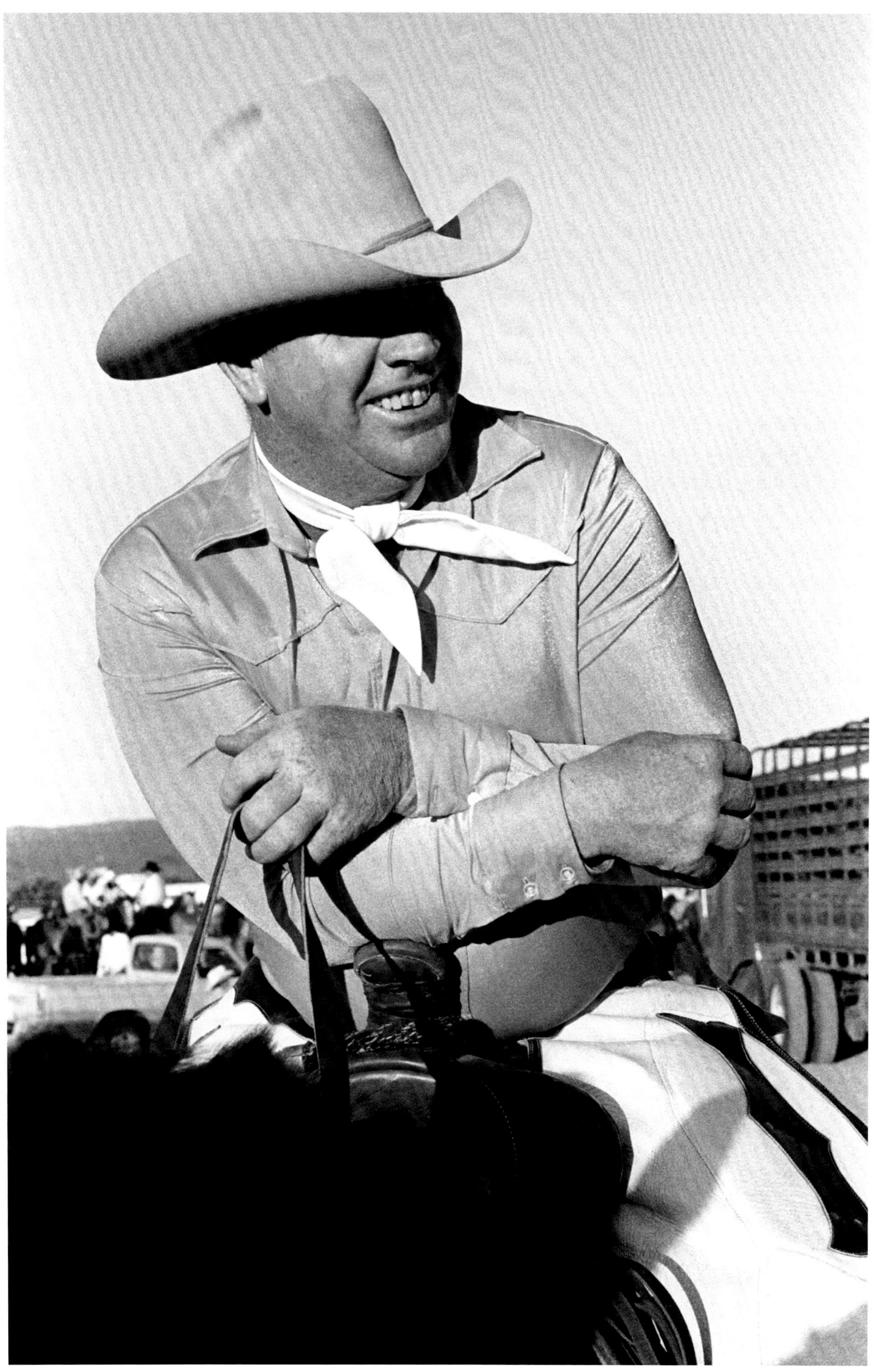

Rodeo de Santa Fe, 1982.

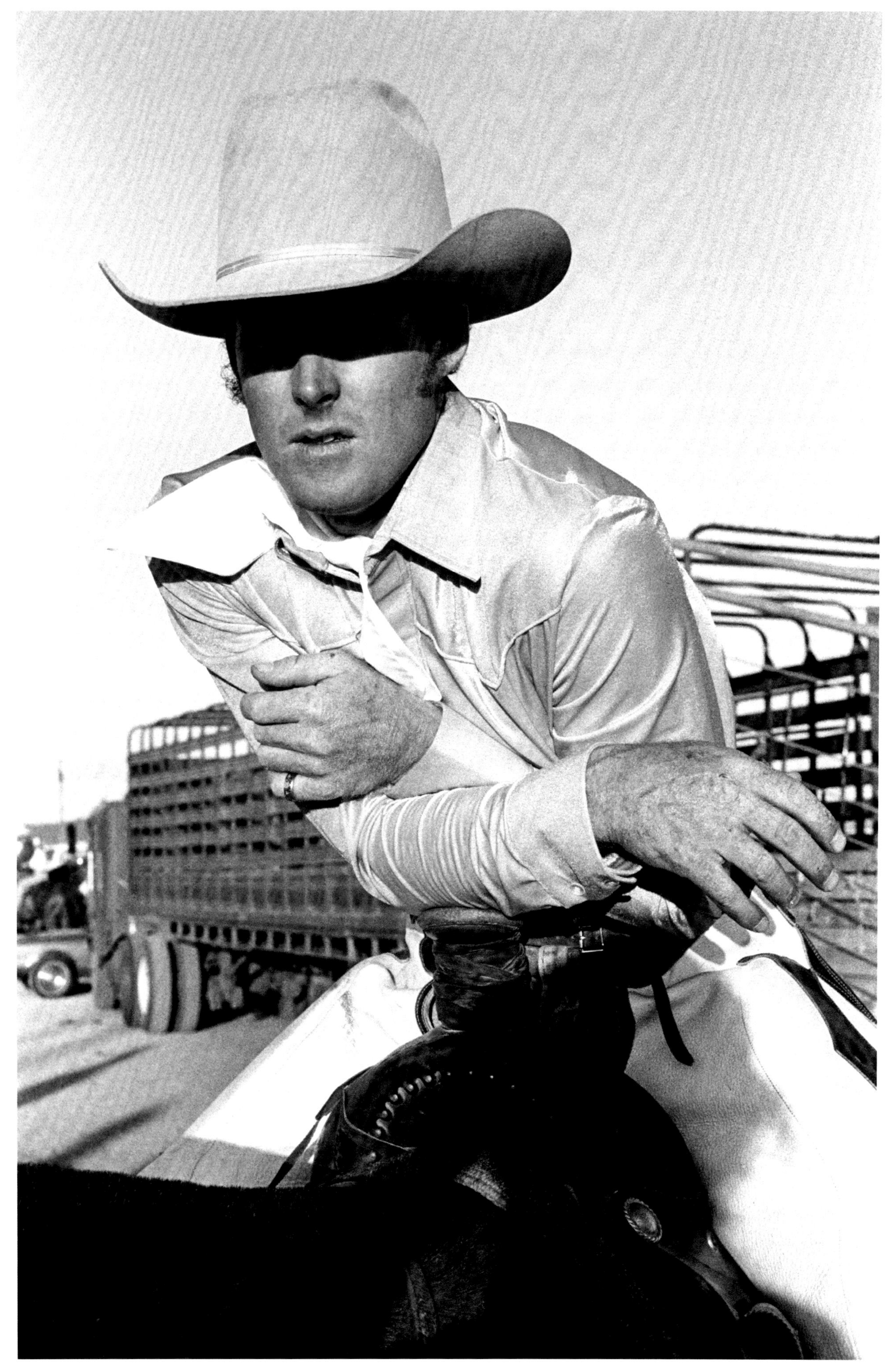

Rodeo de Santa Fe, 1982.

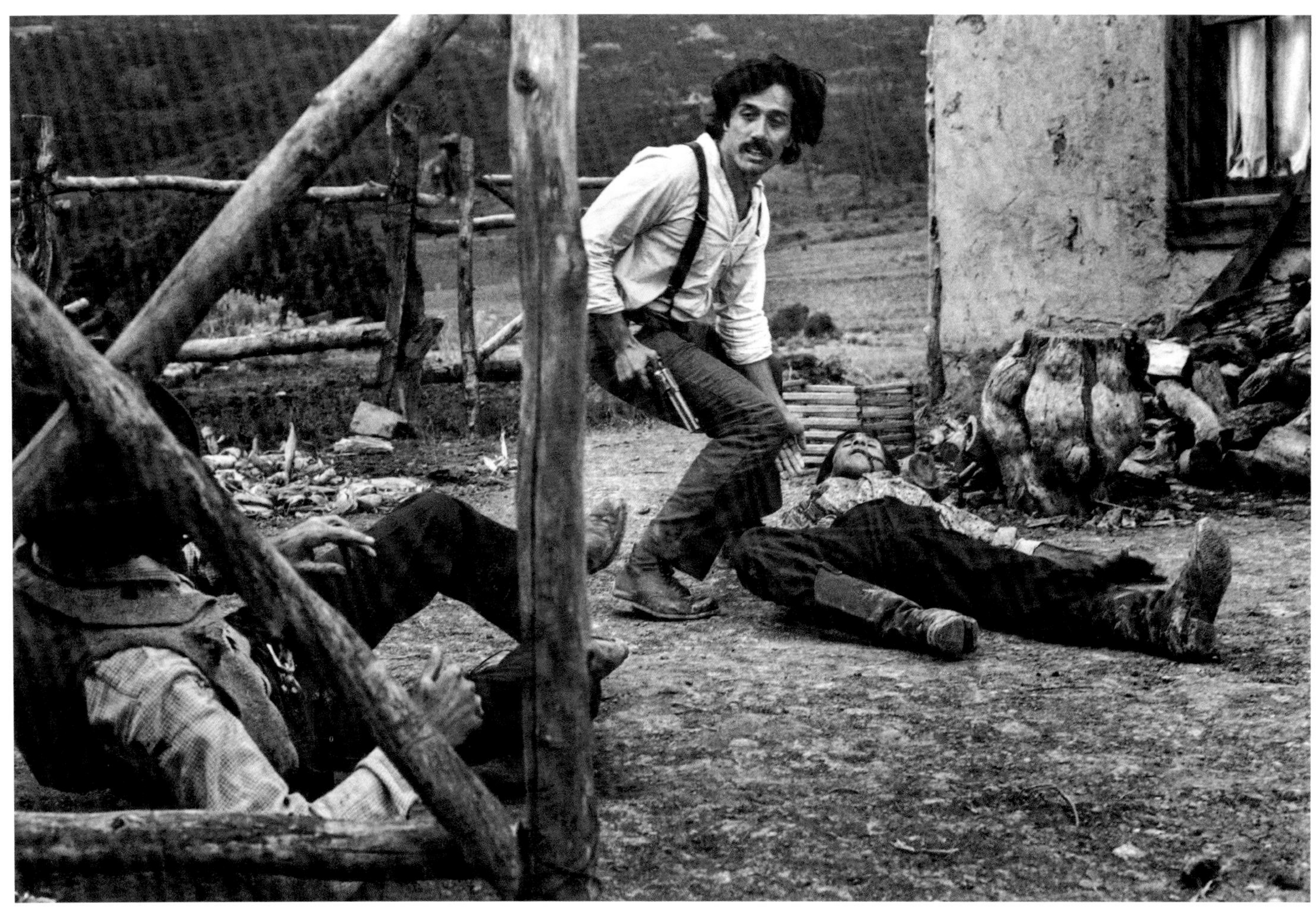

Edward James Olmos filming *The Ballad of Gregorio Cortez*, Cerrillos, 1981.

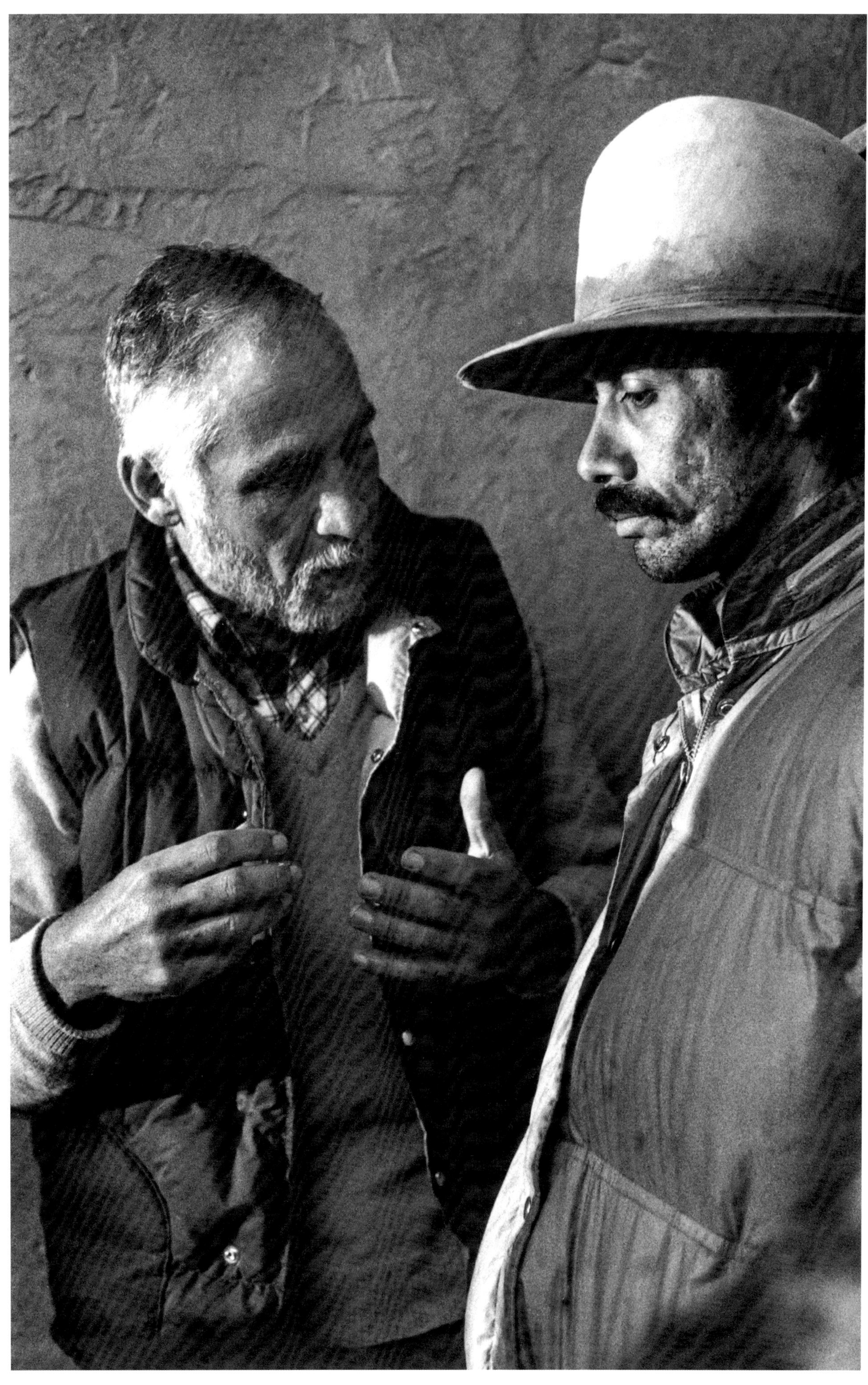

Robert Young, director of *The Ballad of Gregorio Cortez*, and Edward James Olmos, Cerrillos, 1981.

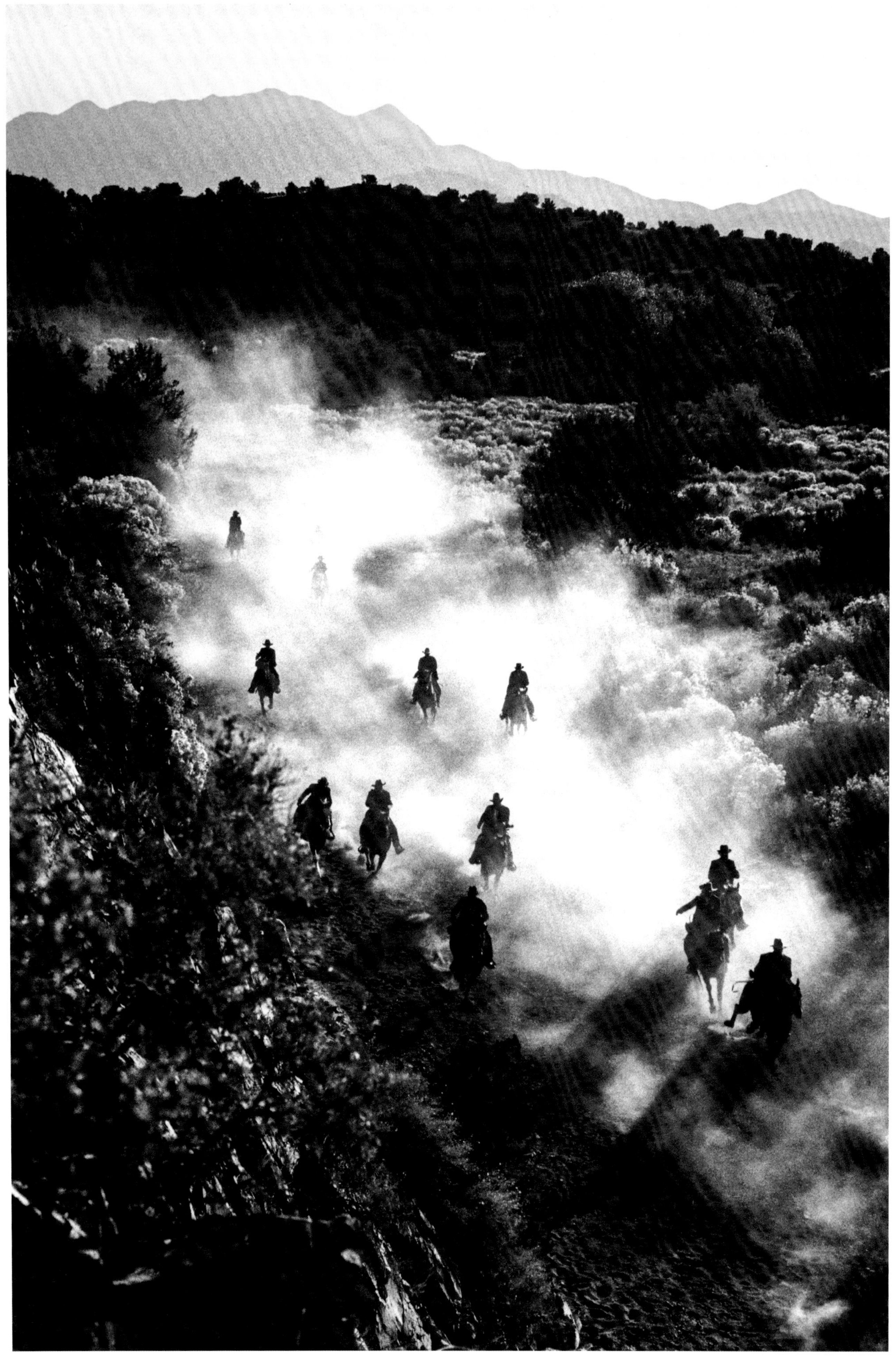

Filming *The Ballad of Gregorio Cortez*, Chama, 1981. Texas Rangers in pursuit of Gregorio Cortez.

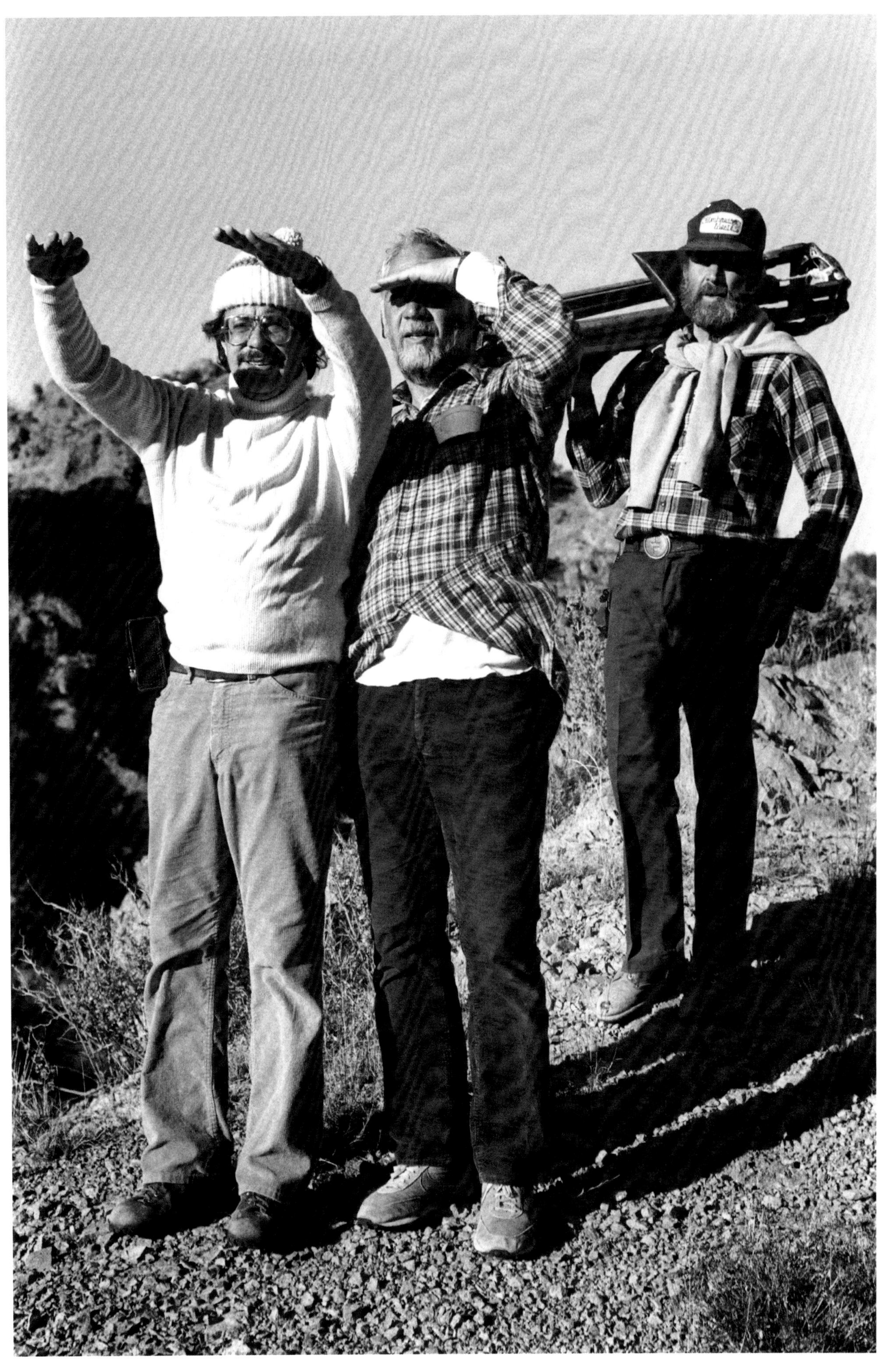

Cameraman Ray Villalobos, director Robert Young, and producer Michael Hausman filming *The Ballad of Gregorio Cortez*, Chama, 1981.

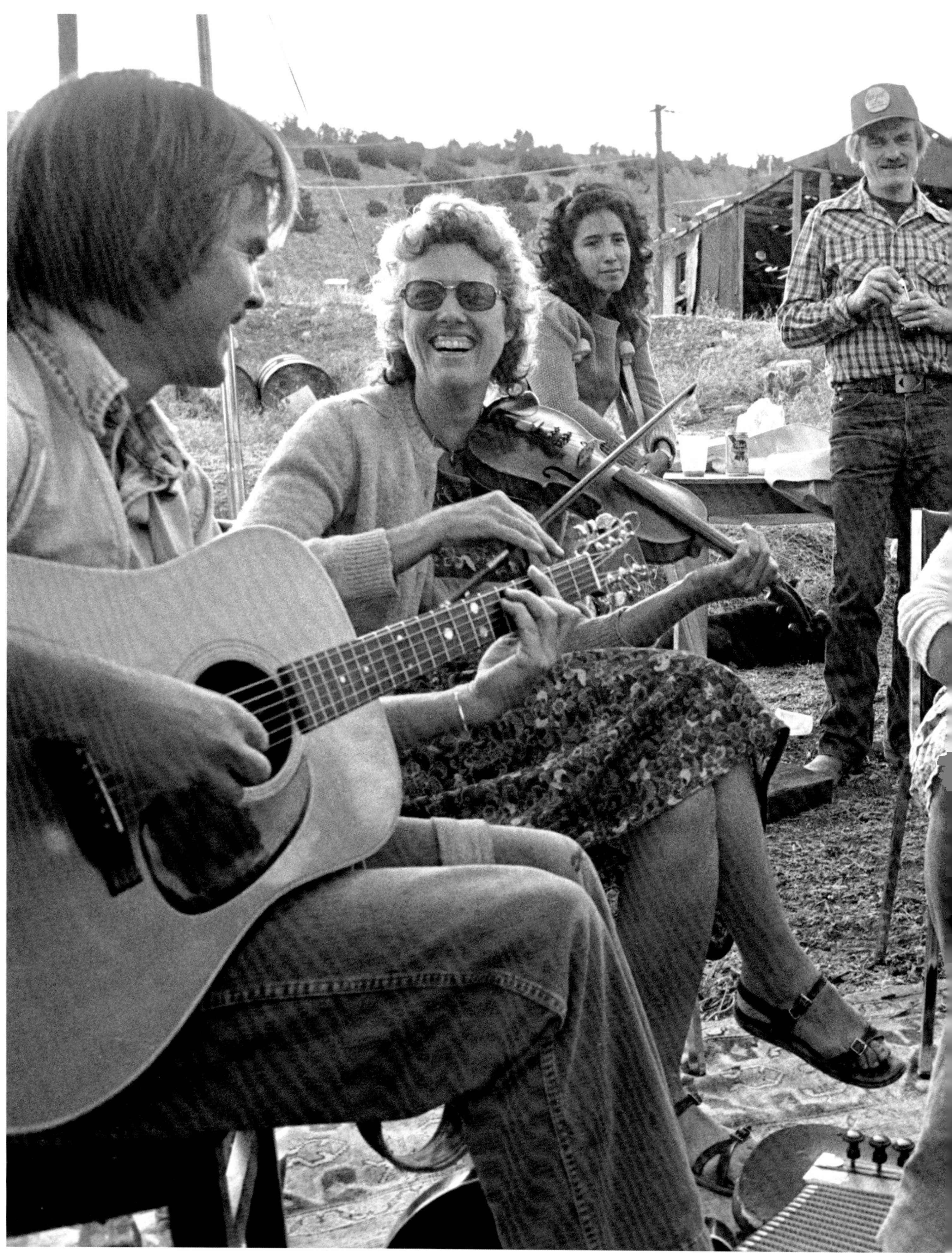

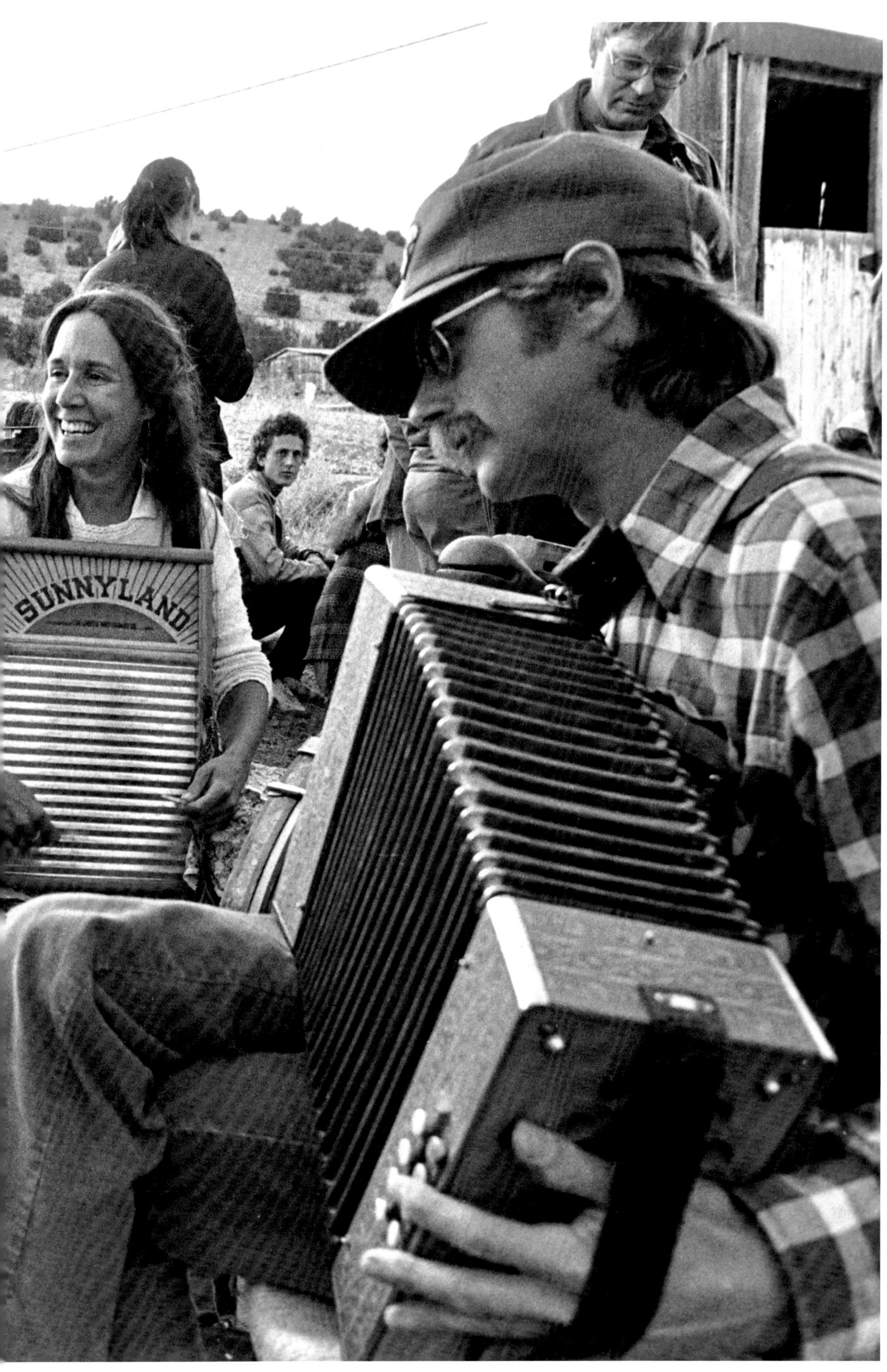

Members of Bayou Seco play at the annual *Garlic Is as Good as Ten Mothers* party, Pacho Lane's house, Madrid, 1983.

OVERLEAF: Linda Montoya and Michael Diaz at Kitty Leaken's house, Santa Fe, 1982.

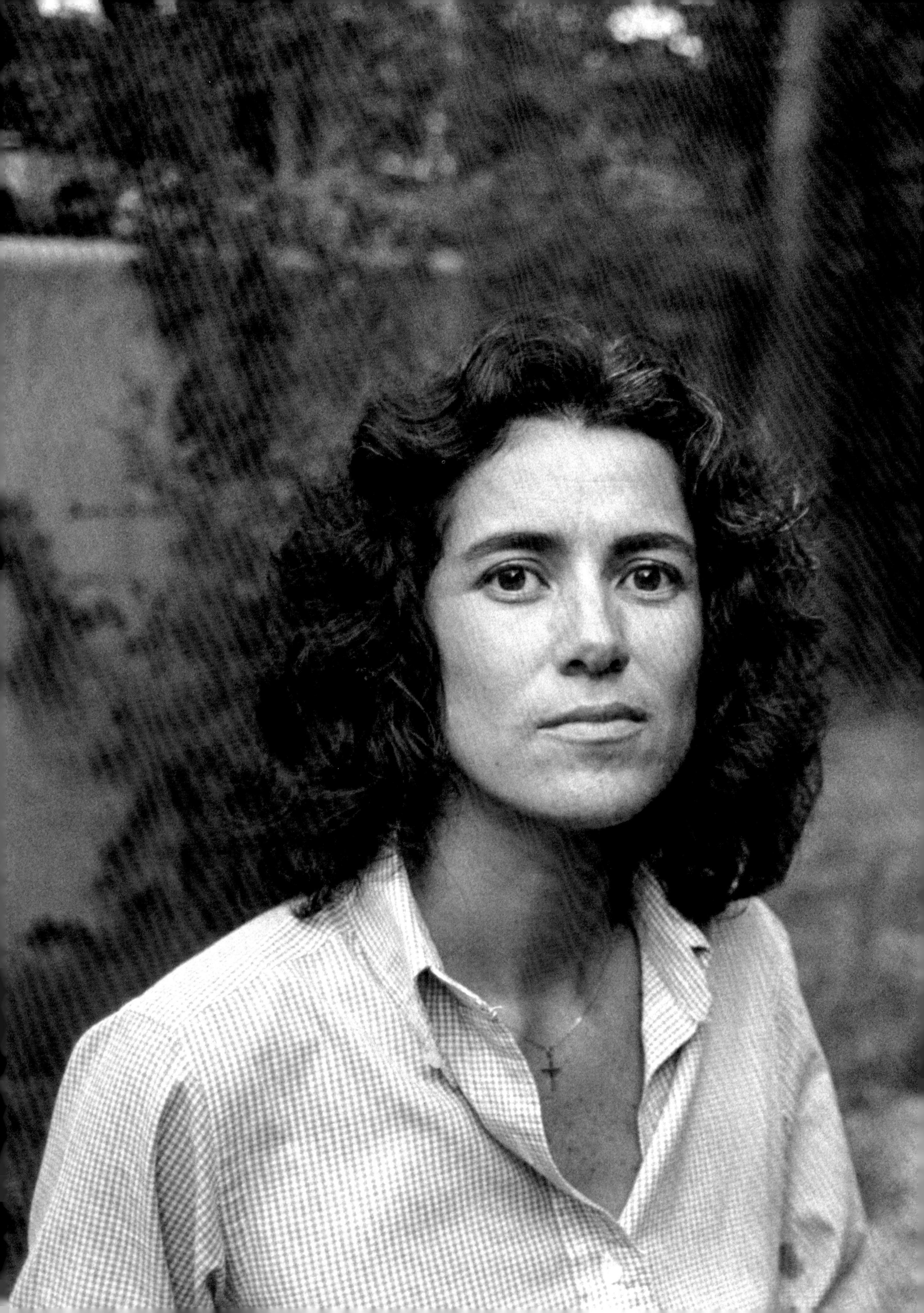

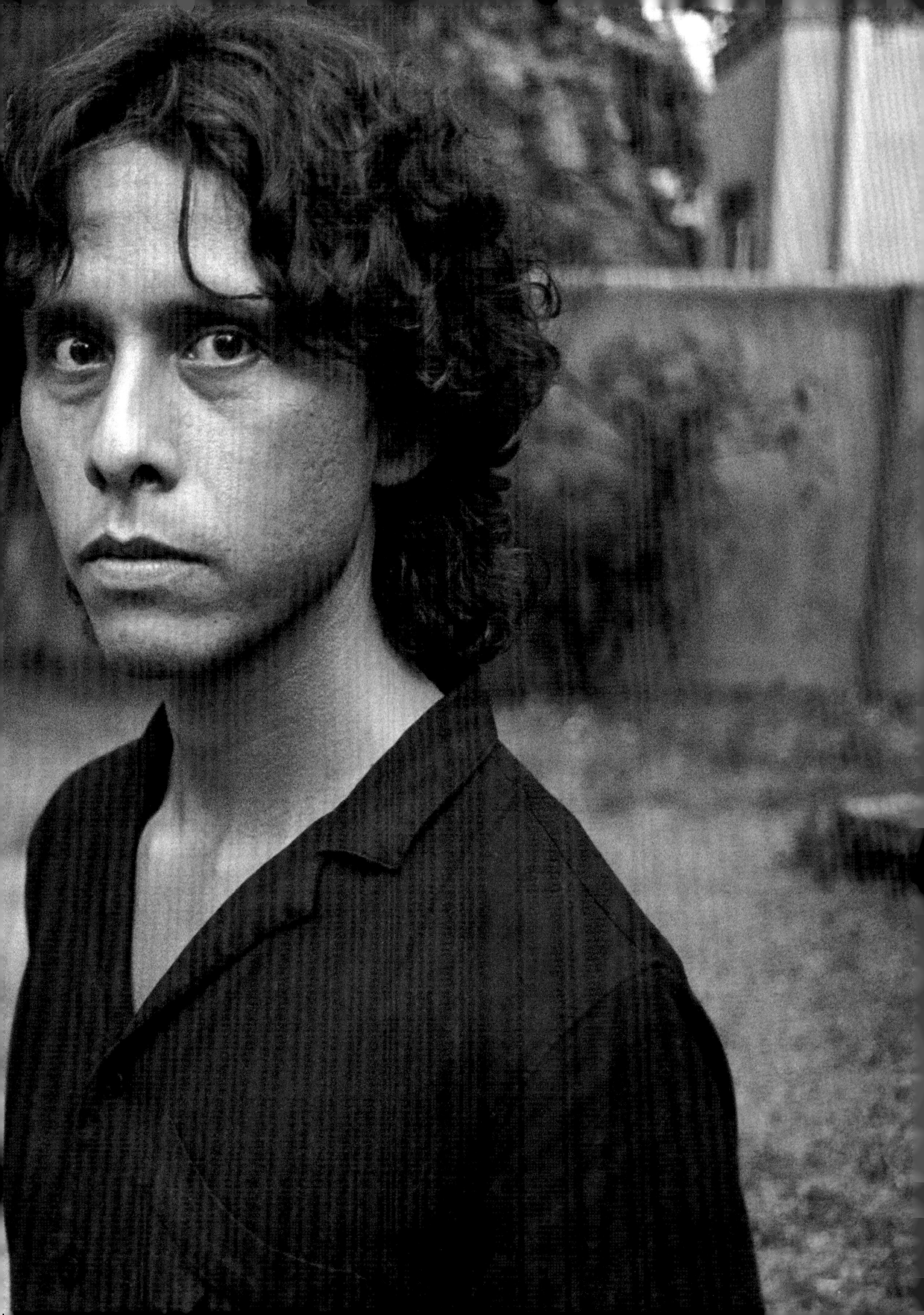

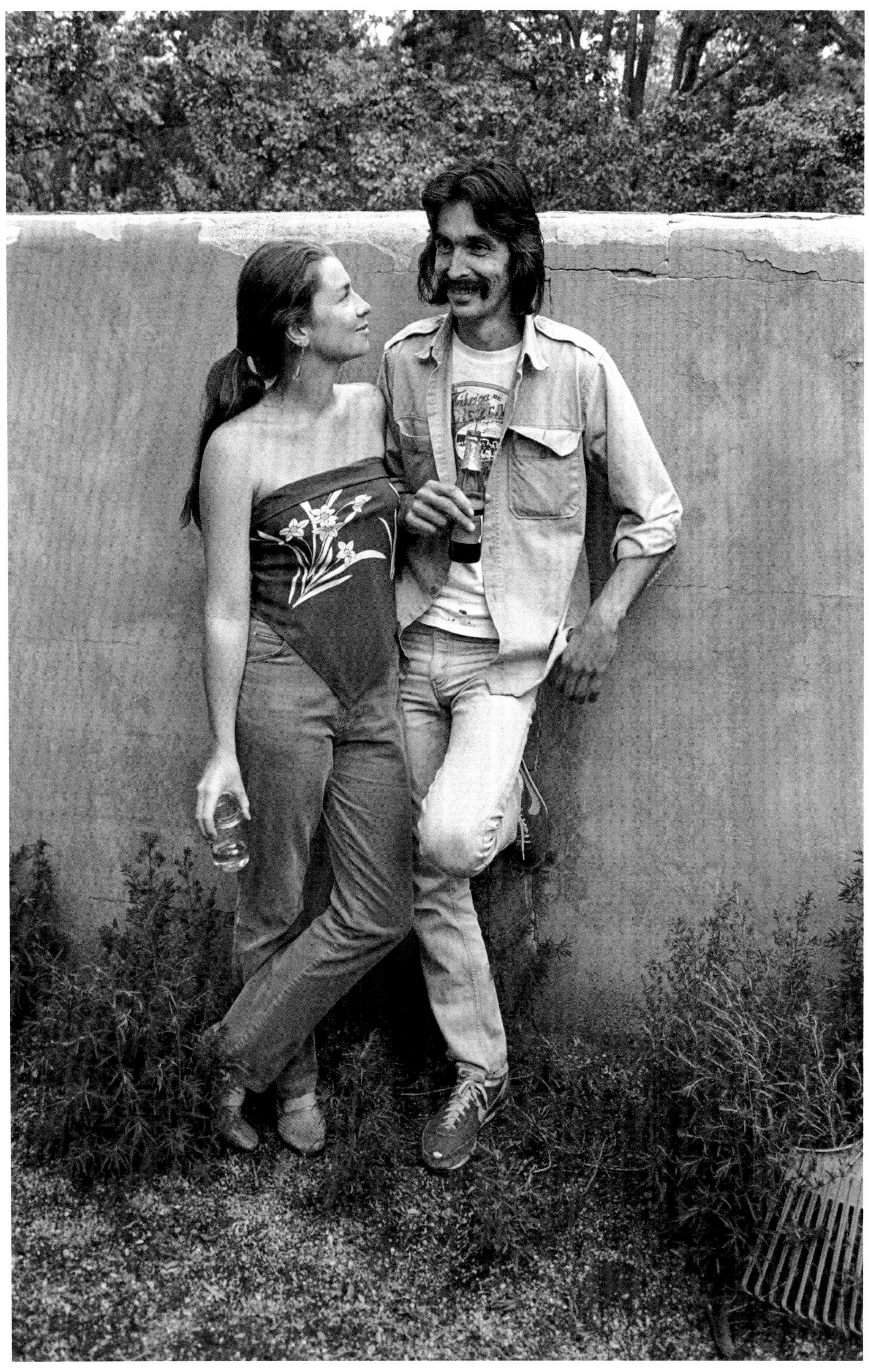

Raquel Lopez and Bob McDermot at Kitty Leaken's house, Santa Fe, 1982.

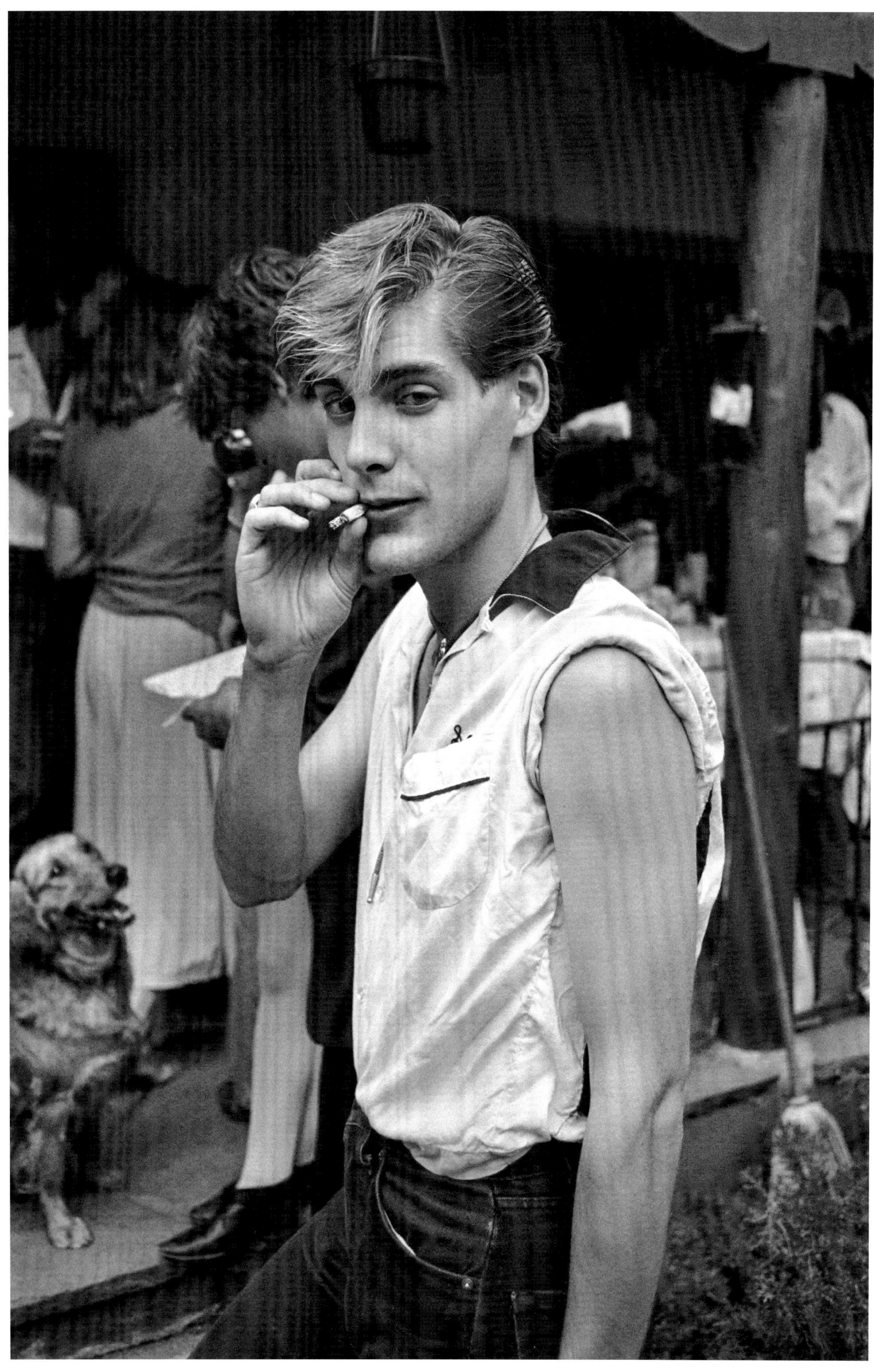

Miles Stelios Earney at Kitty Leaken's house, Santa Fe, 1982.

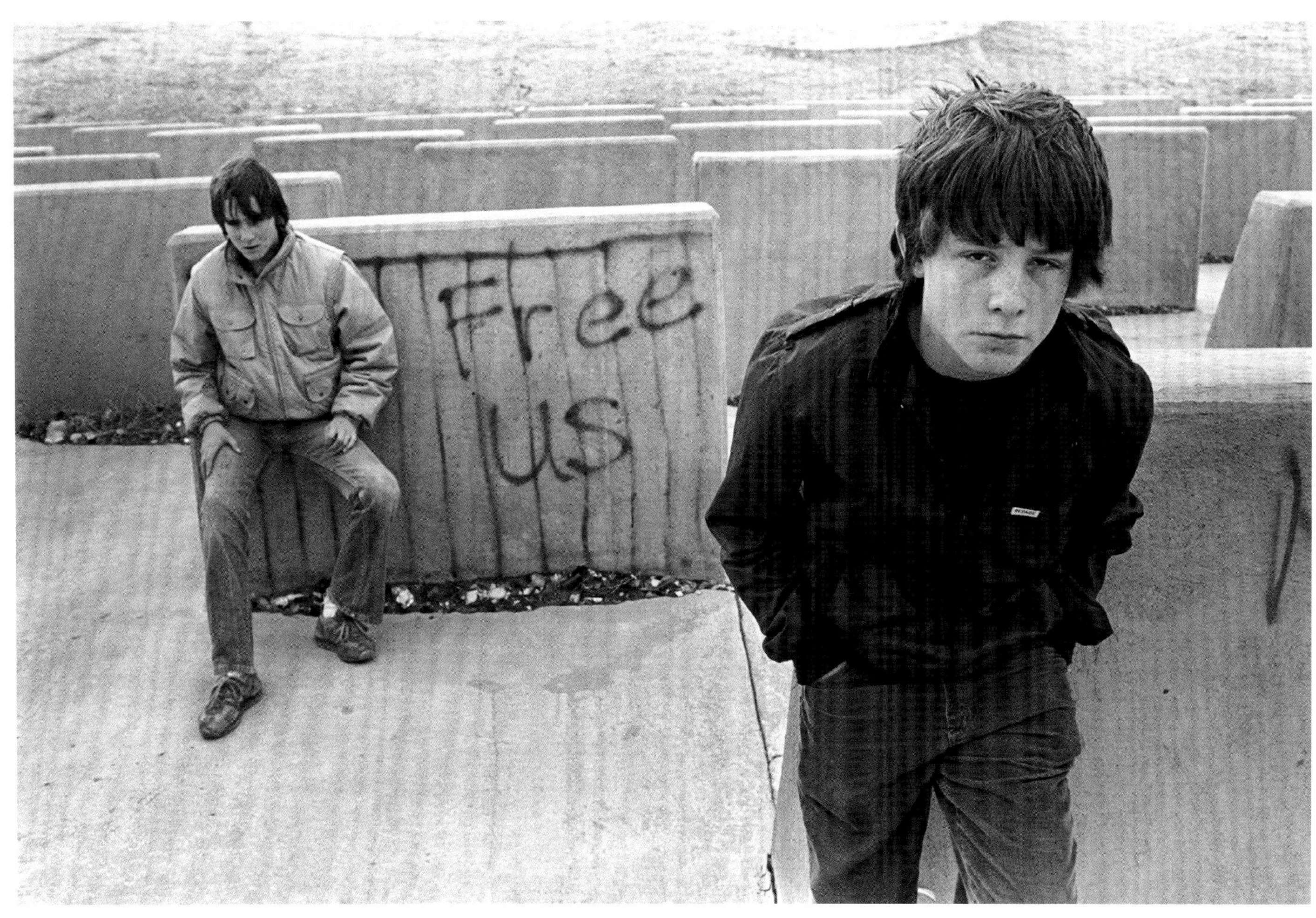

Albuquerque, 1983.

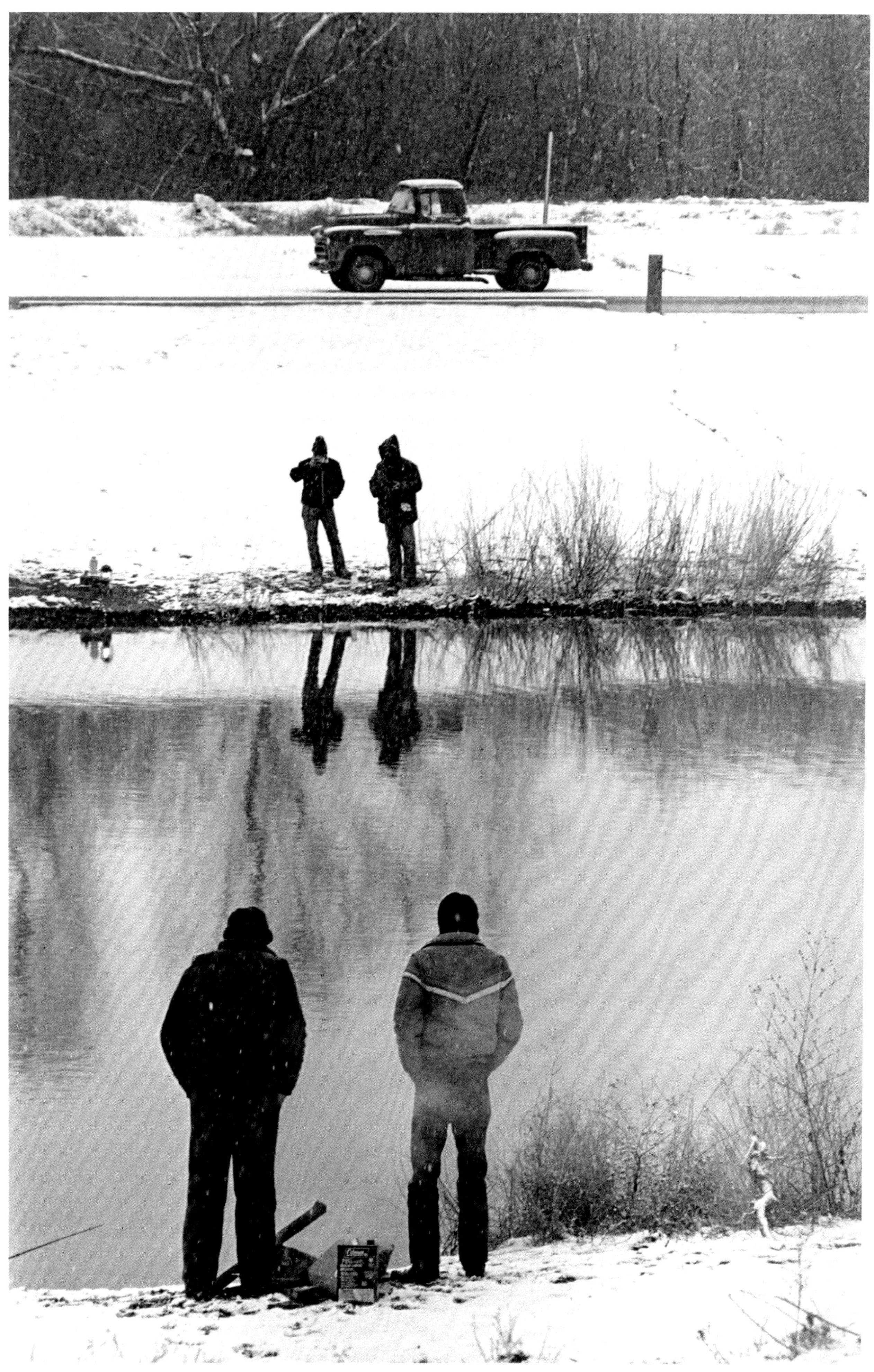

Albuquerque, 1983.

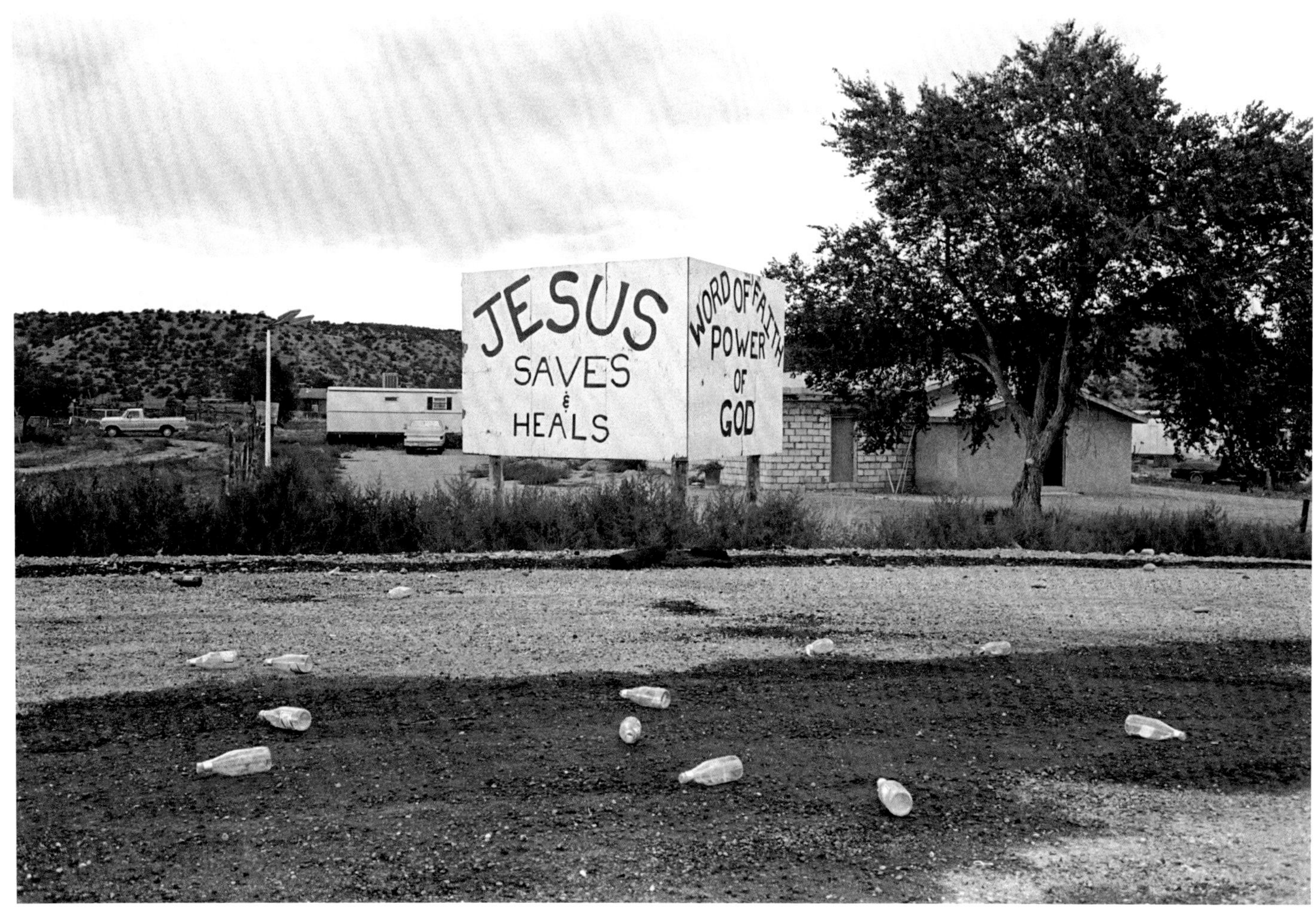

Albuquerque, 1982.

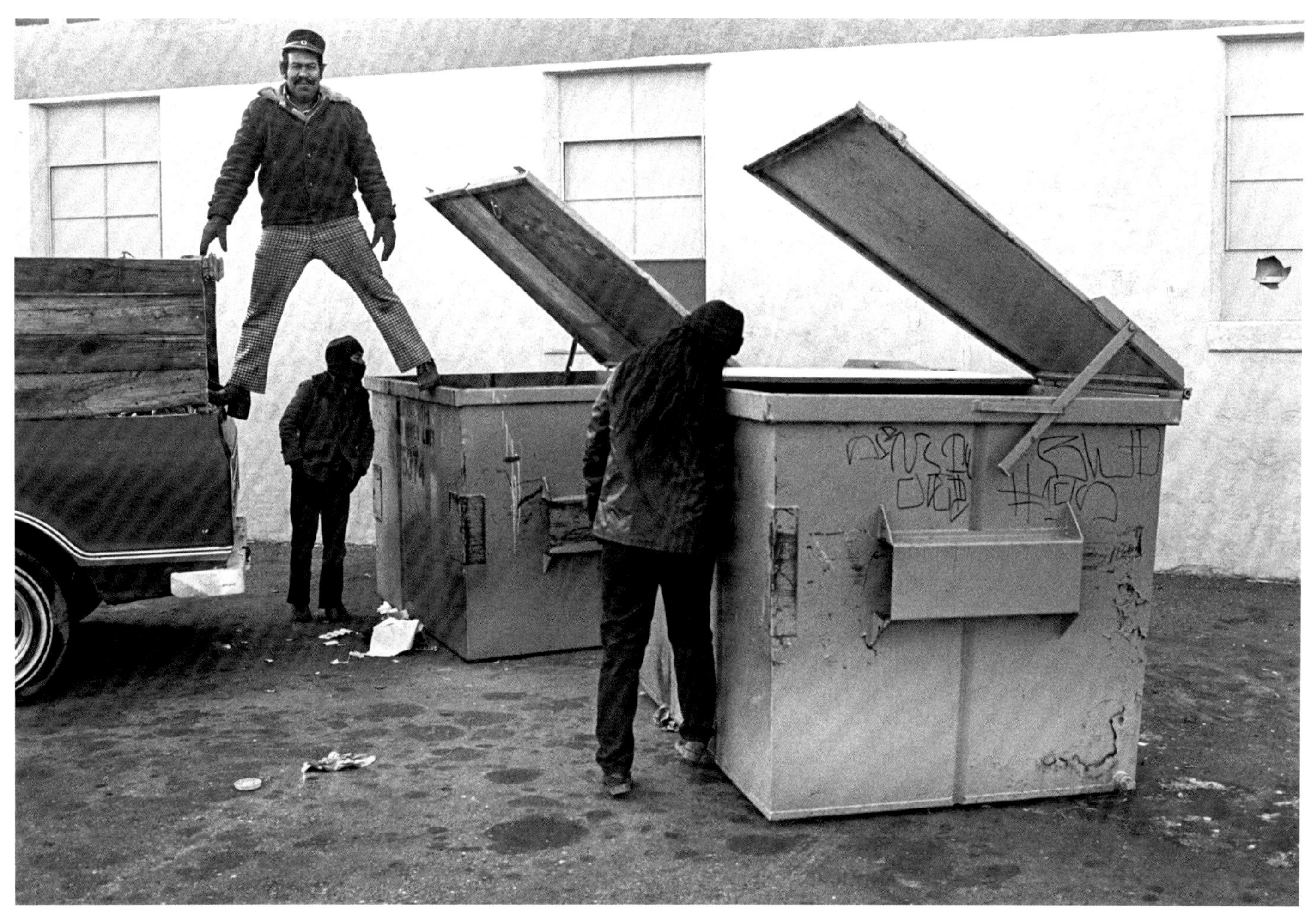

Recycling center, Albuquerque, 1983.

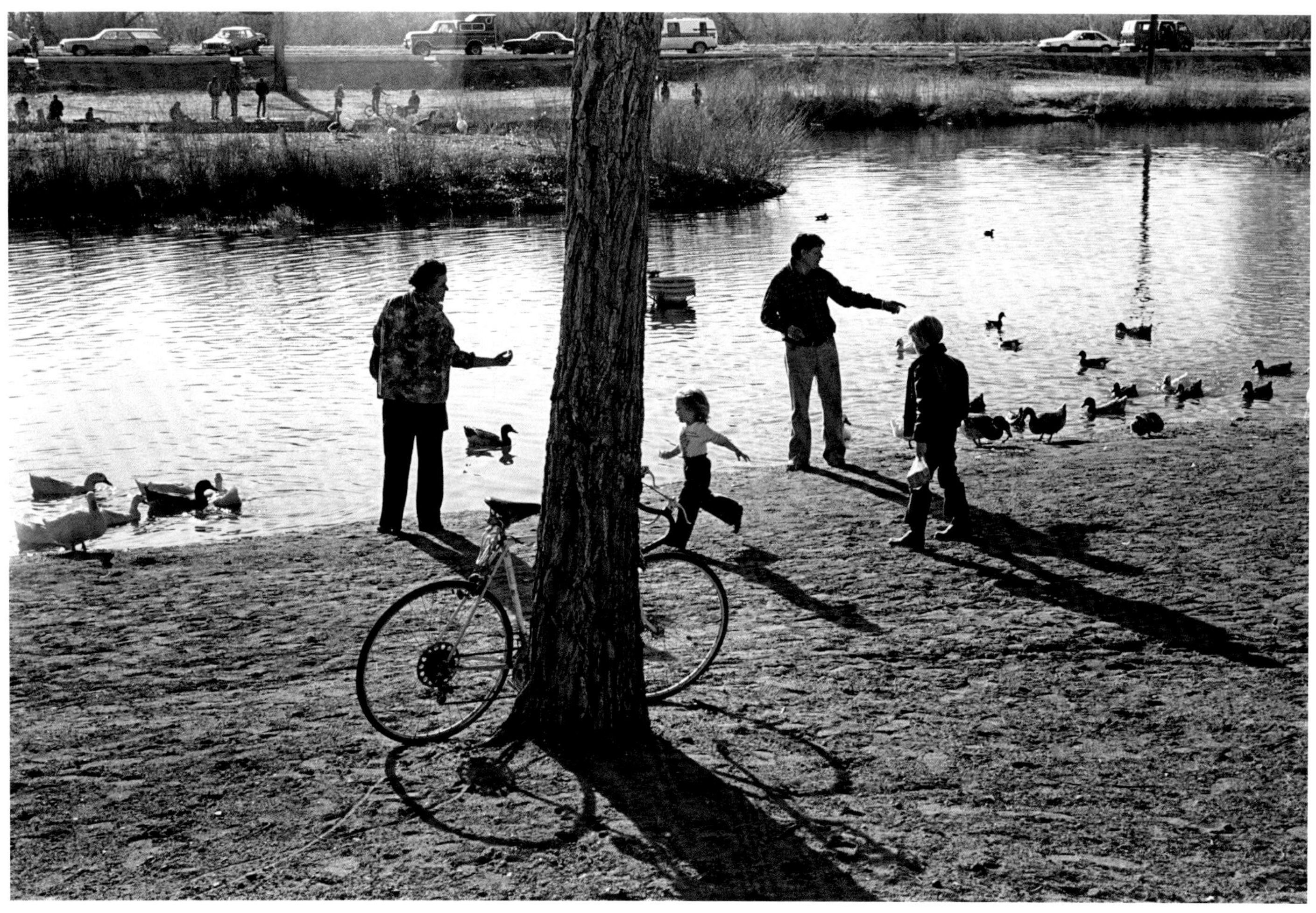

South Valley along the Rio Grande, Albuquerque, 1982.

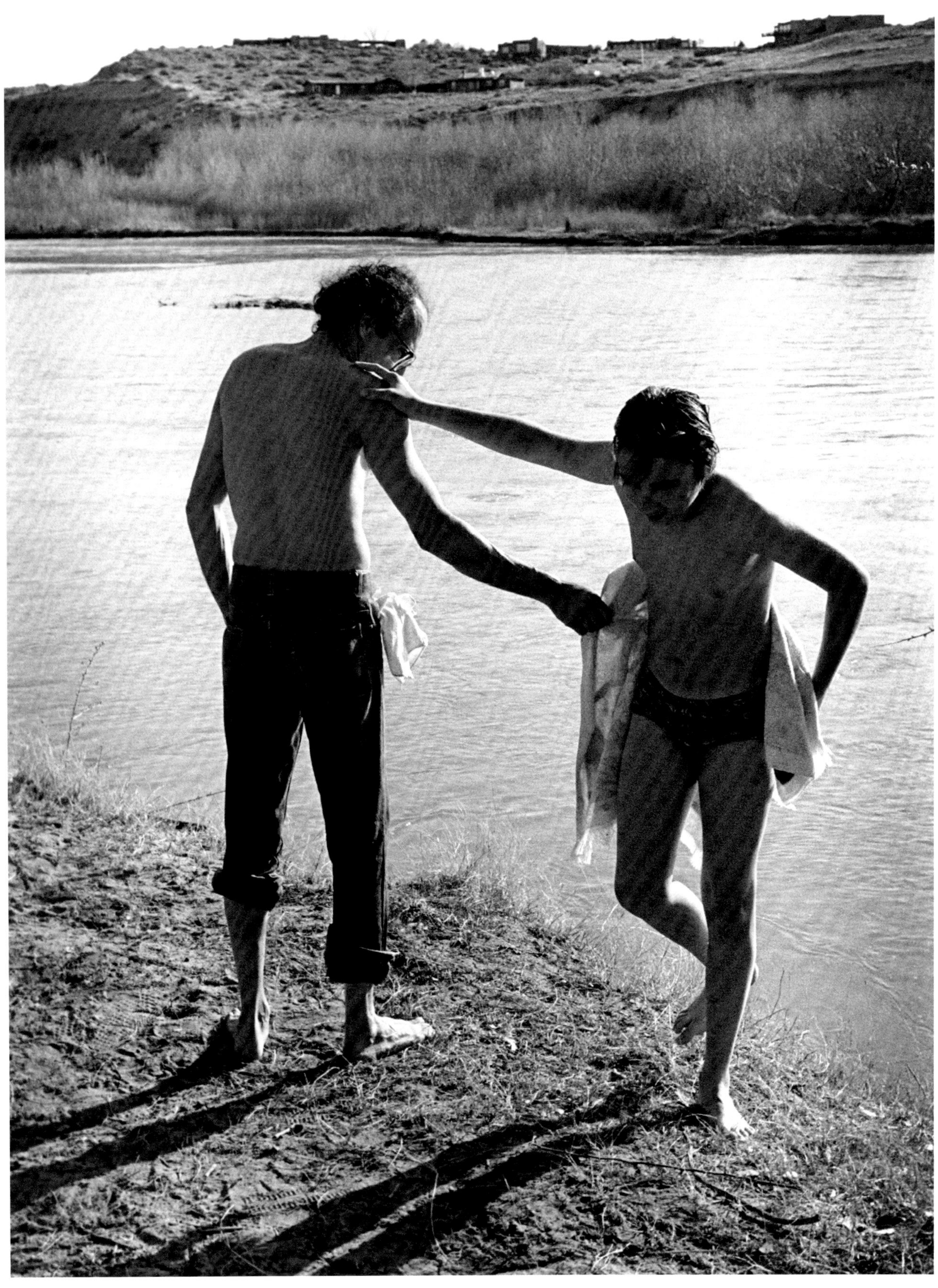

ABOVE AND OVERLEAF: South Valley along the Rio Grande, Albuquerque, 1982.

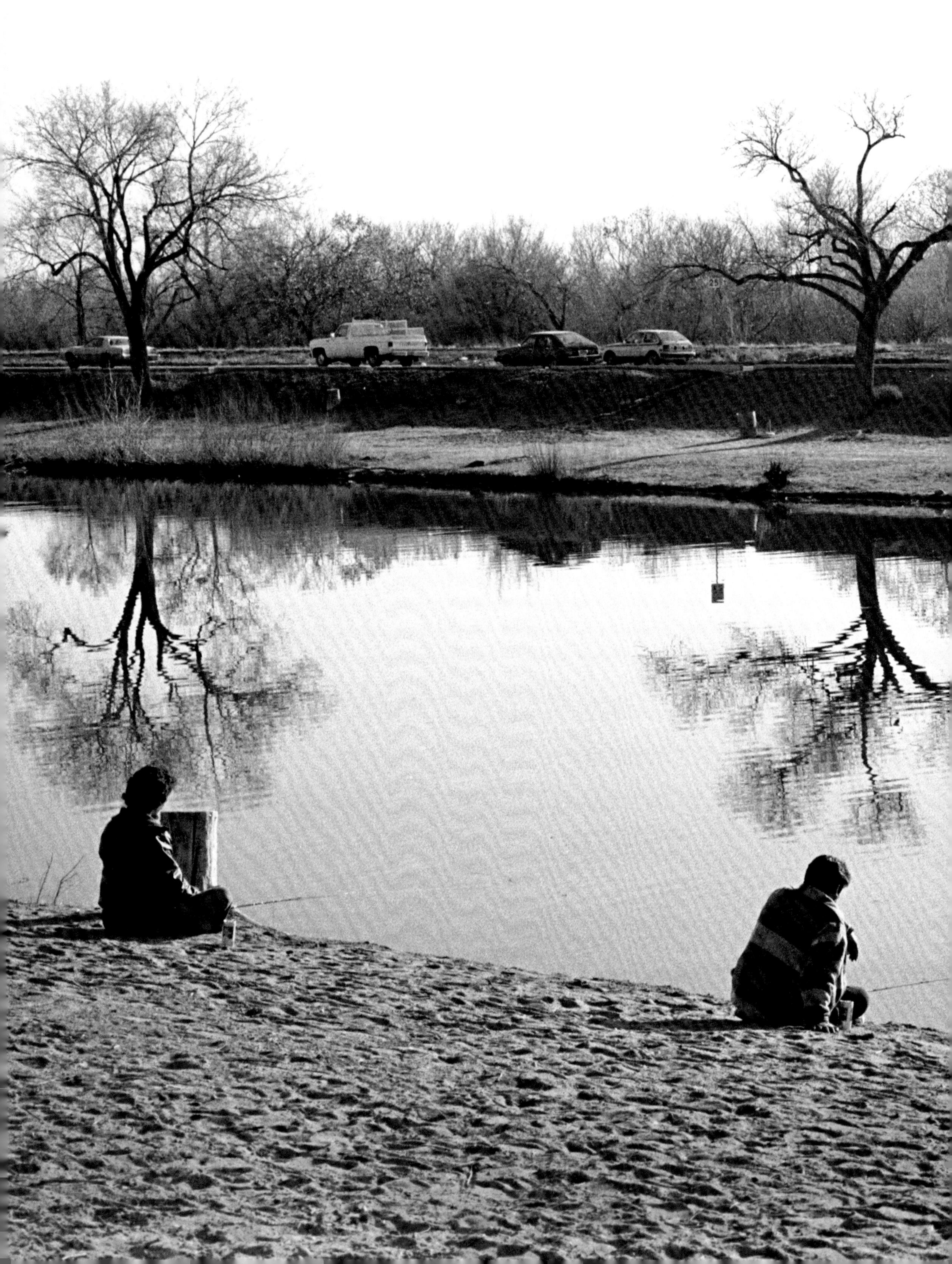

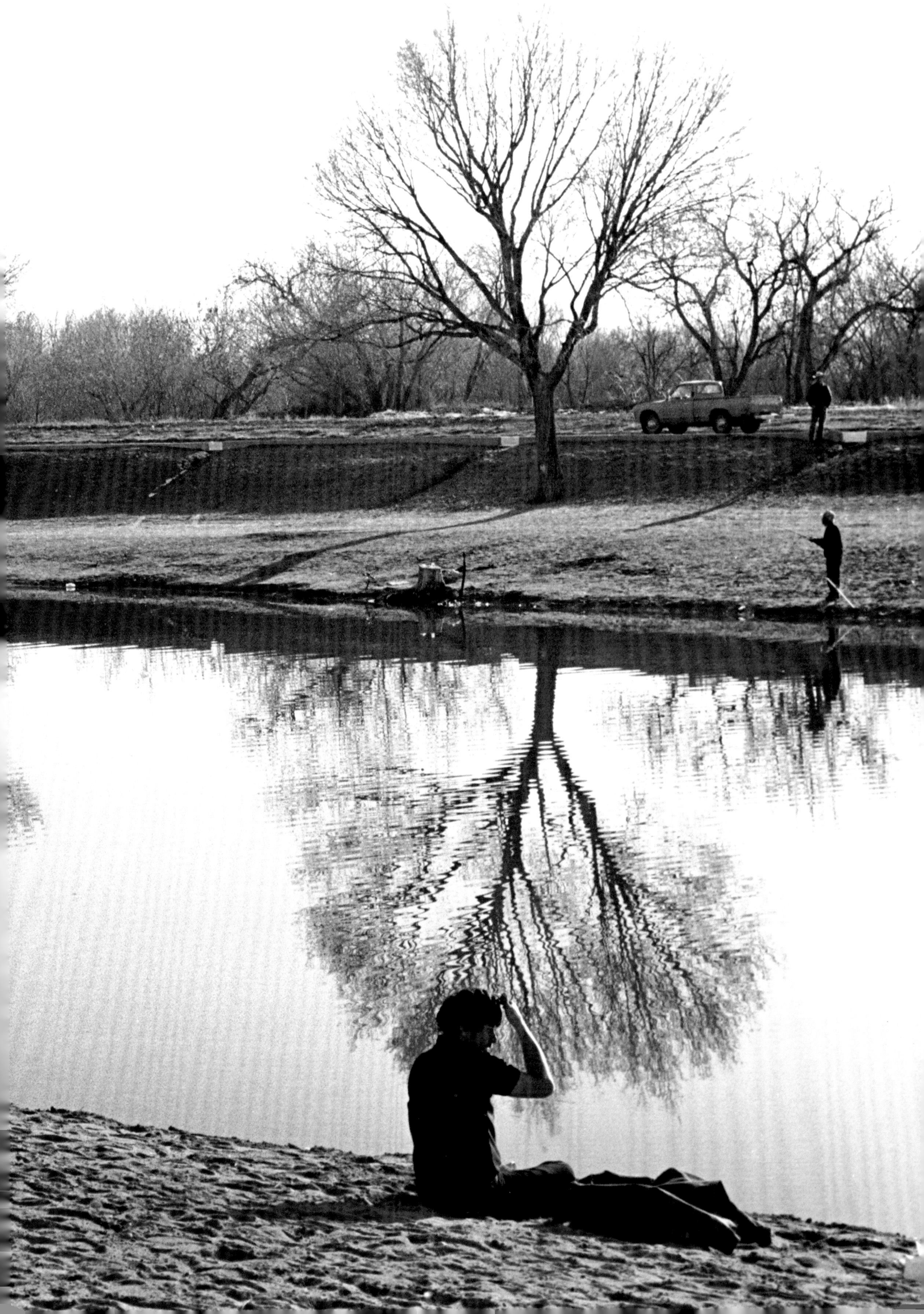

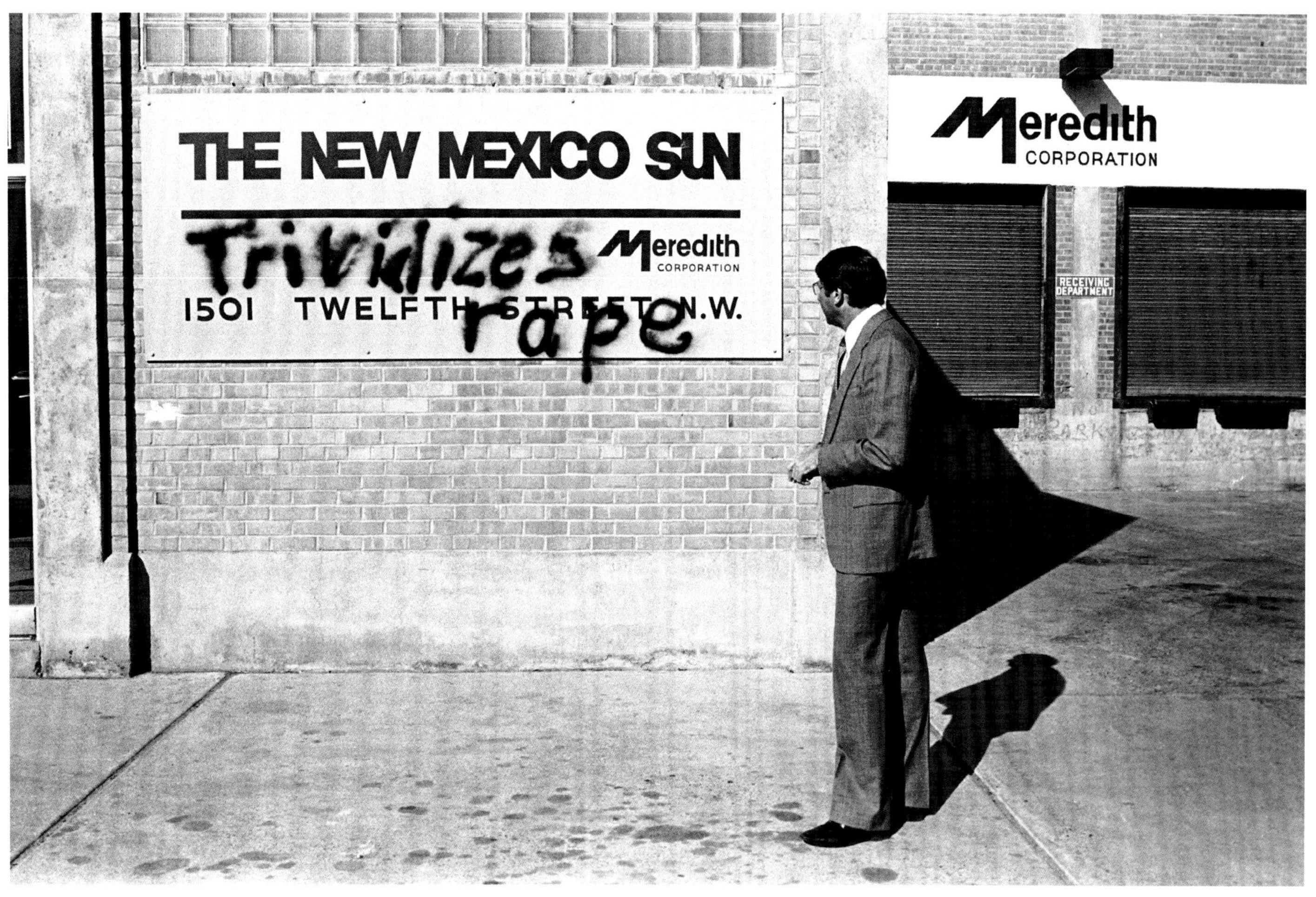

Outside *The New Mexico Sun* offices at the Meredith Corporation building, Albuquerque, 1983.

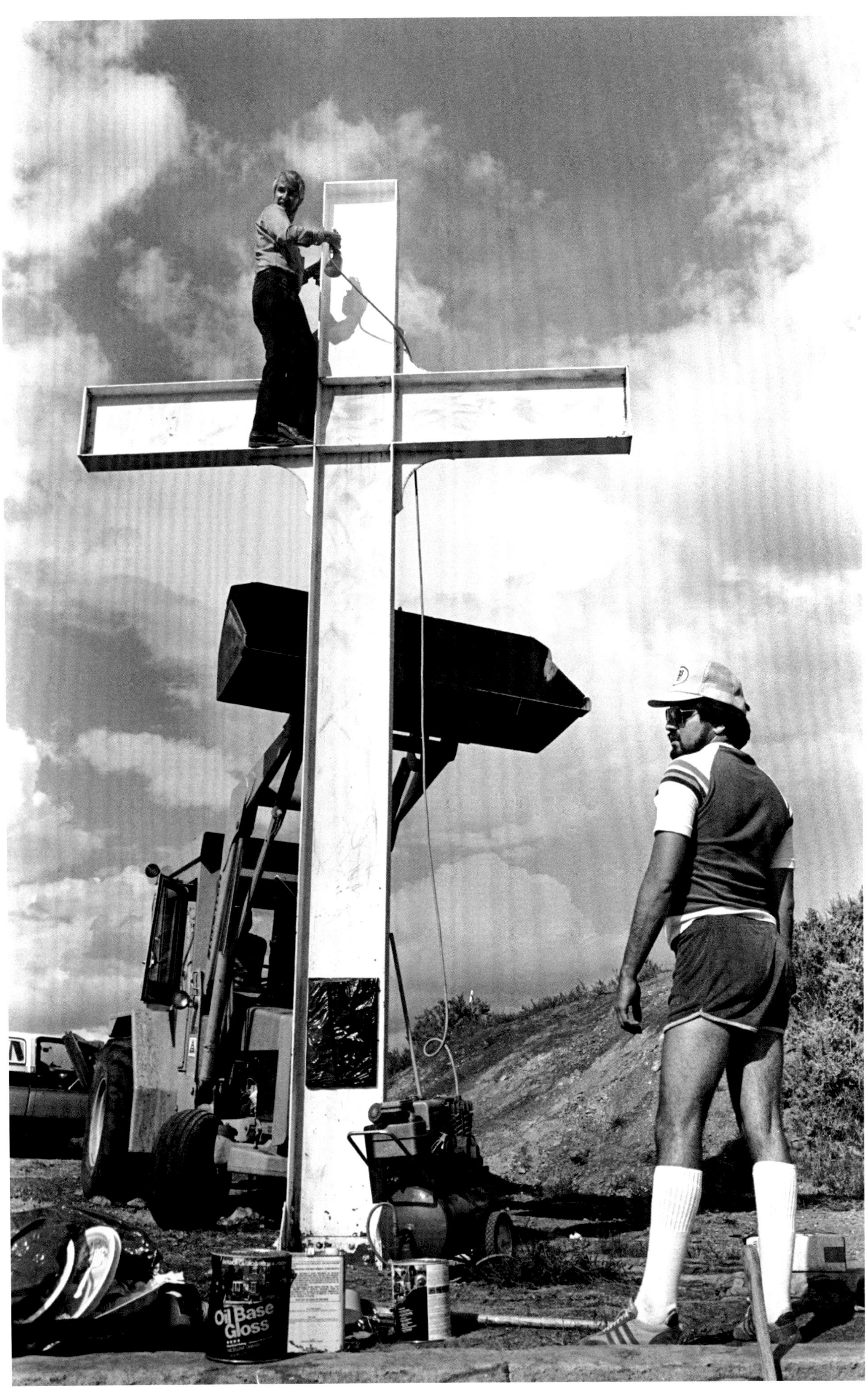

Painting crew at the Cross of the Martyrs, Santa Fe, 1981.

OVERLEAF: Chimayó, 1982.

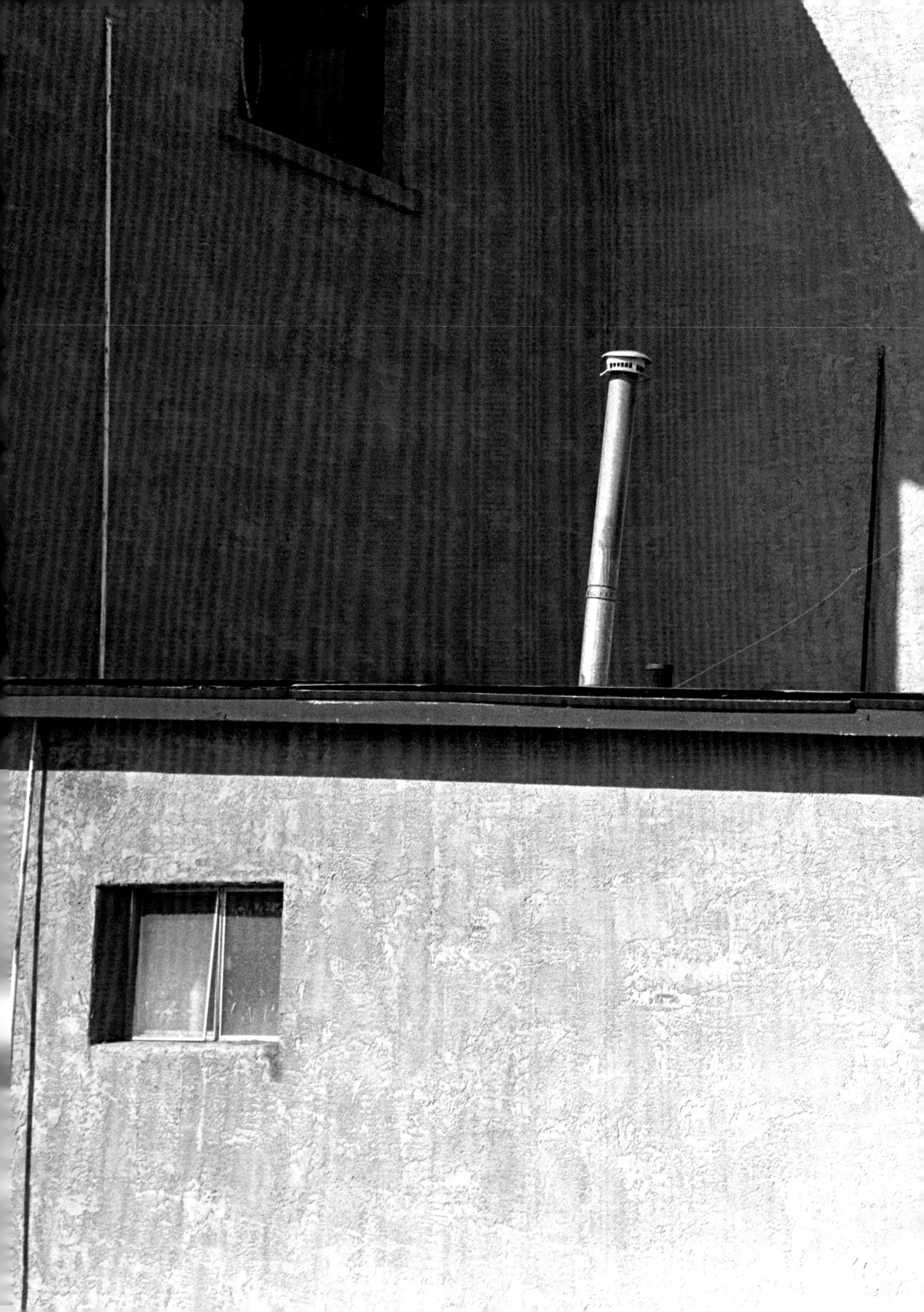

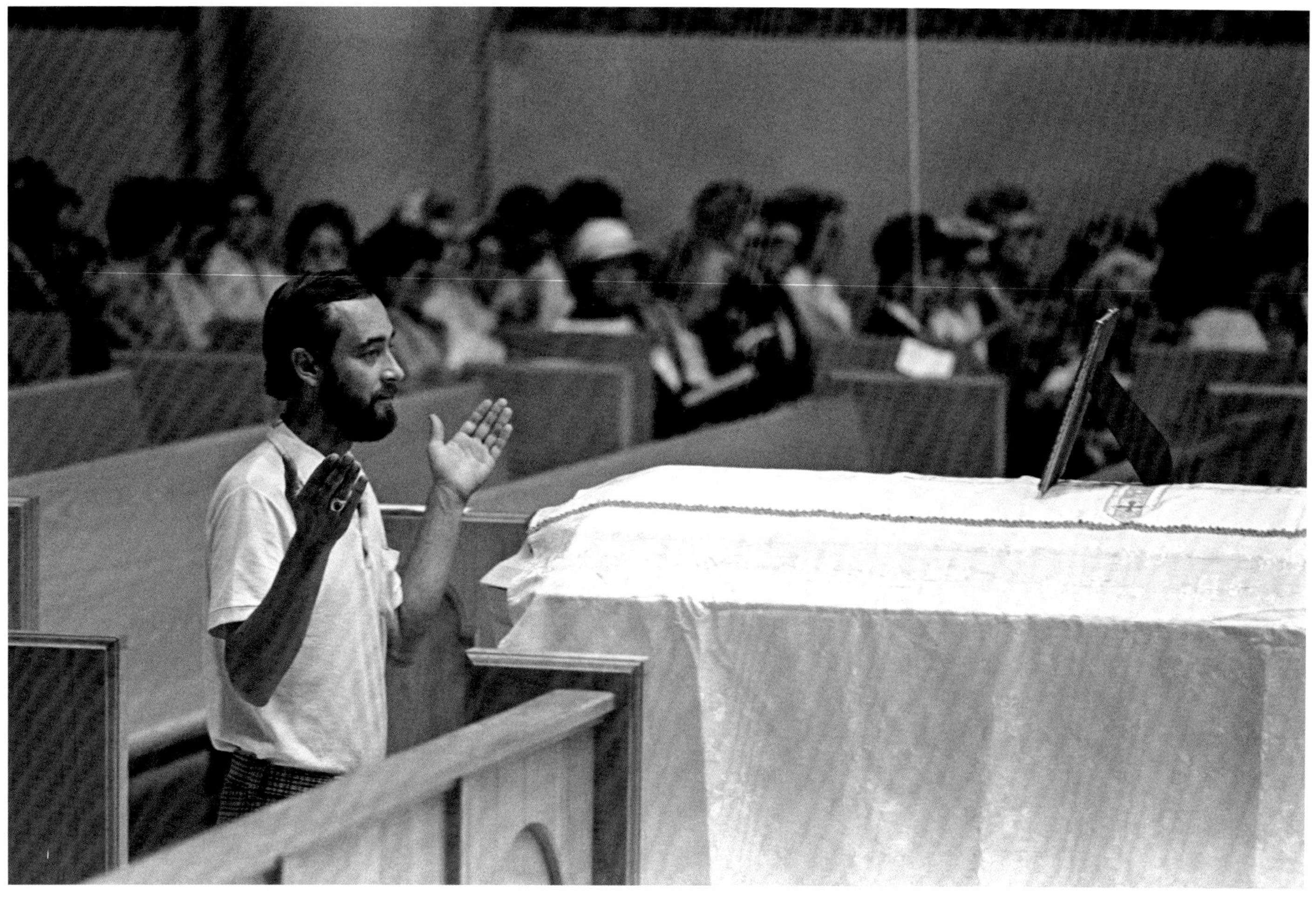

ABOVE AND OPPOSITE: Funeral of Father Reynaldo Rivera, Cathedral Basilica of Saint Francis of Assisi, Santa Fe, 1982.

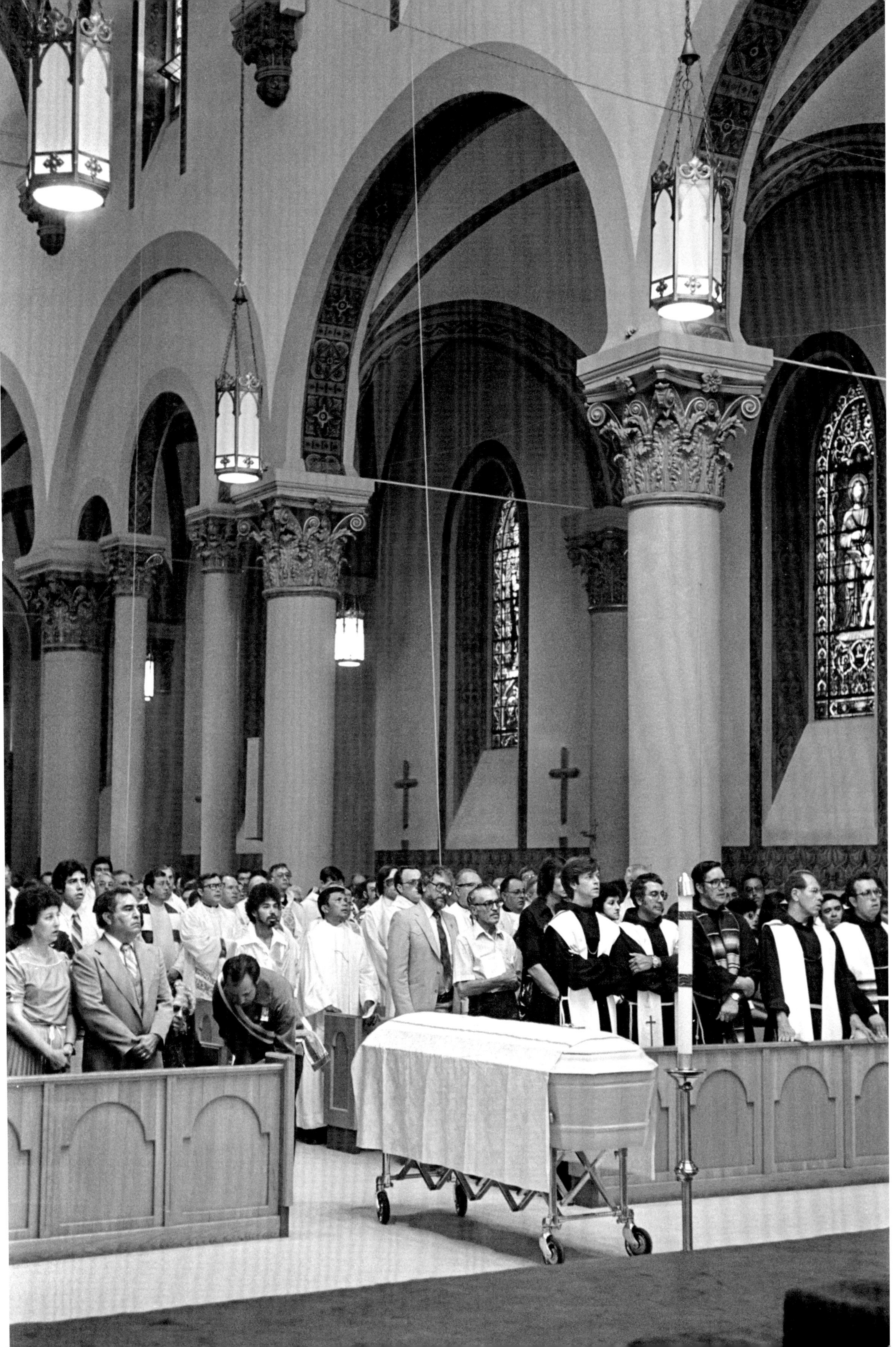

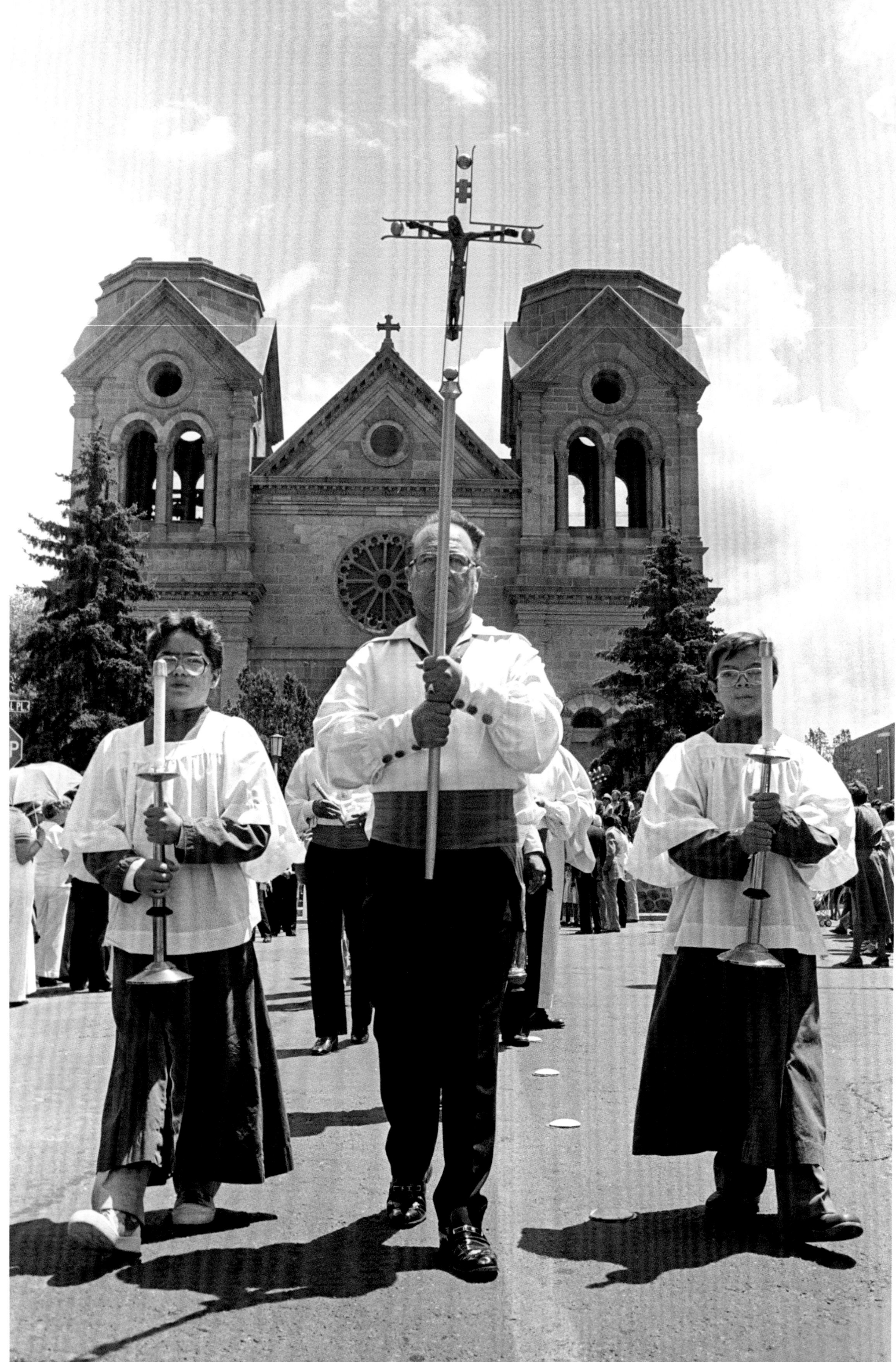

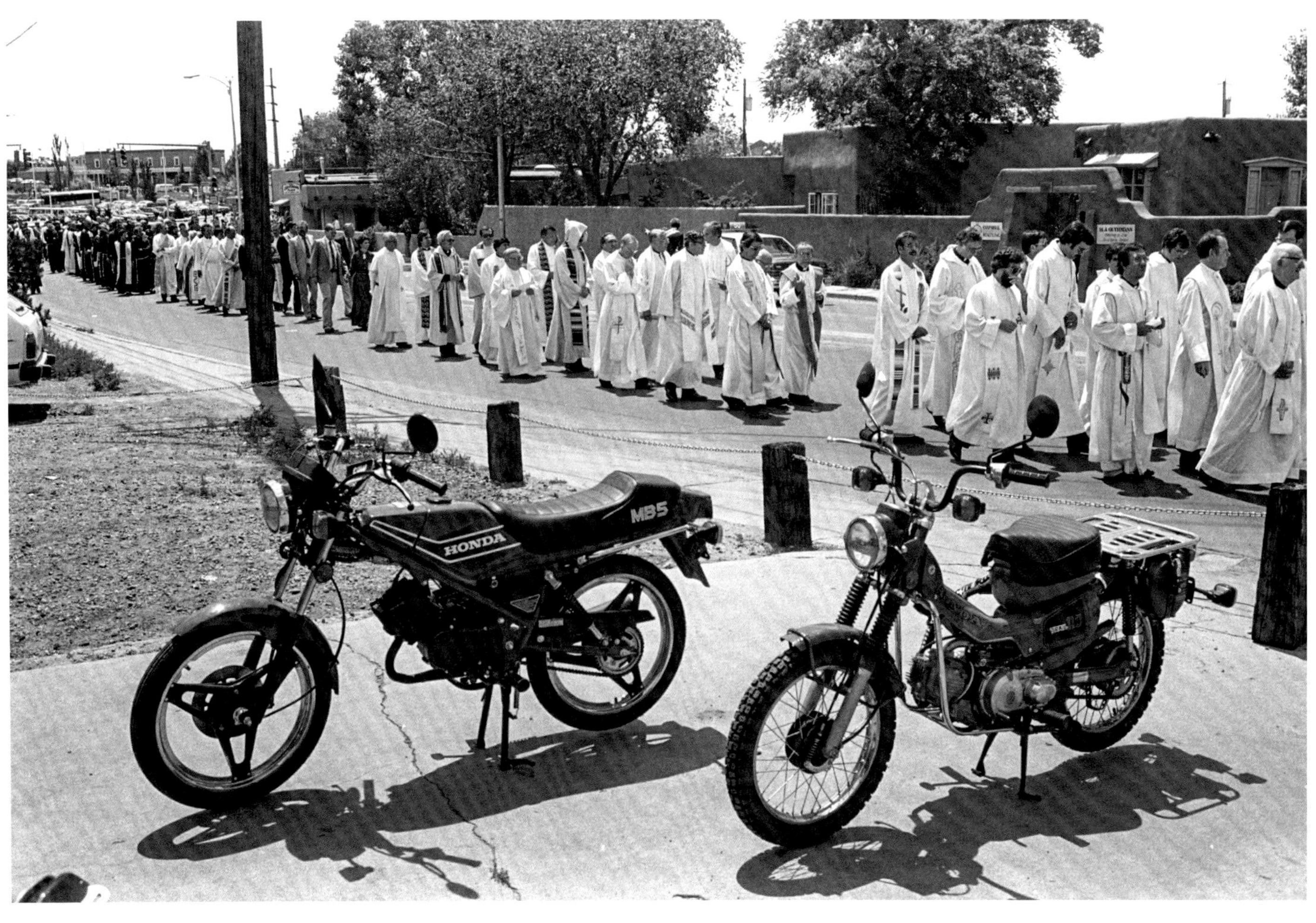

OPPOSITE AND ABOVE: Funeral procession of Fr. Reynaldo Rivera from the Cathedral to Rosario Cemetery, Santa Fe, 1982.

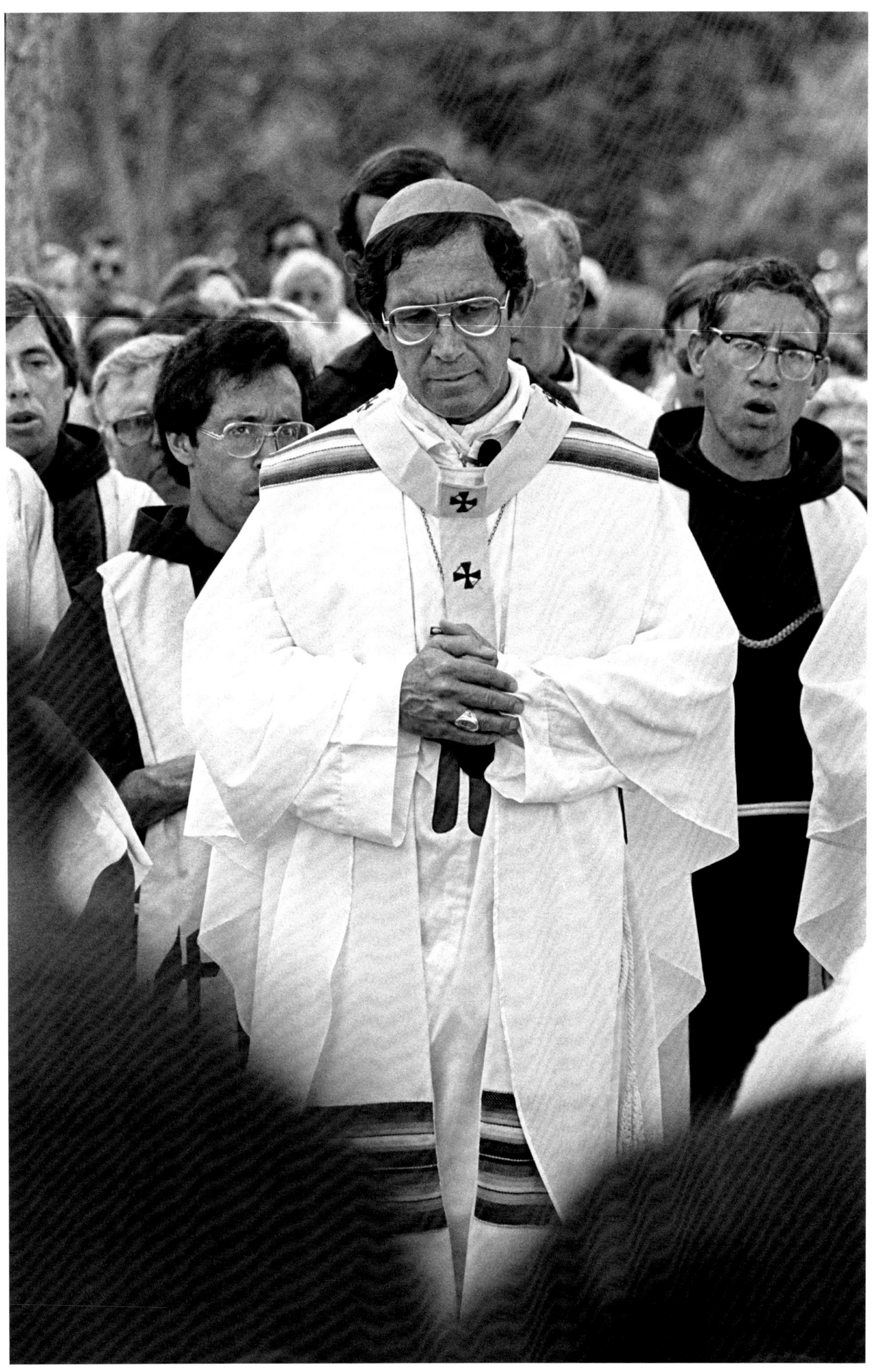

Archbishop Robert Sanchez at the graveside of Fr. Reynaldo Rivera, Rosario Cemetery, Santa Fe, 1982.

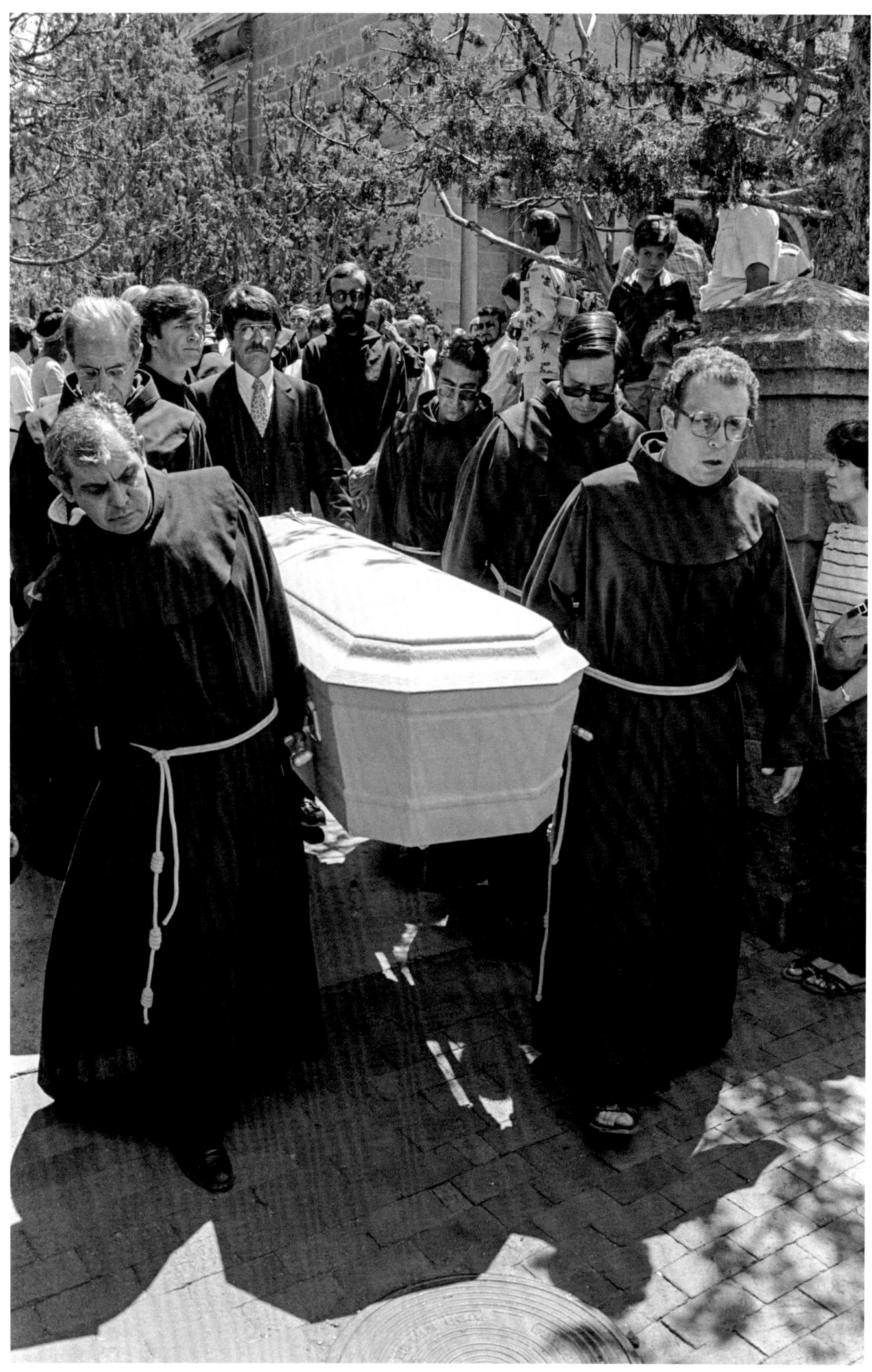

Franciscan priests carry the coffin of Fr. Reynaldo Rivera, Rosario Cemetery, Santa Fe, 1982.

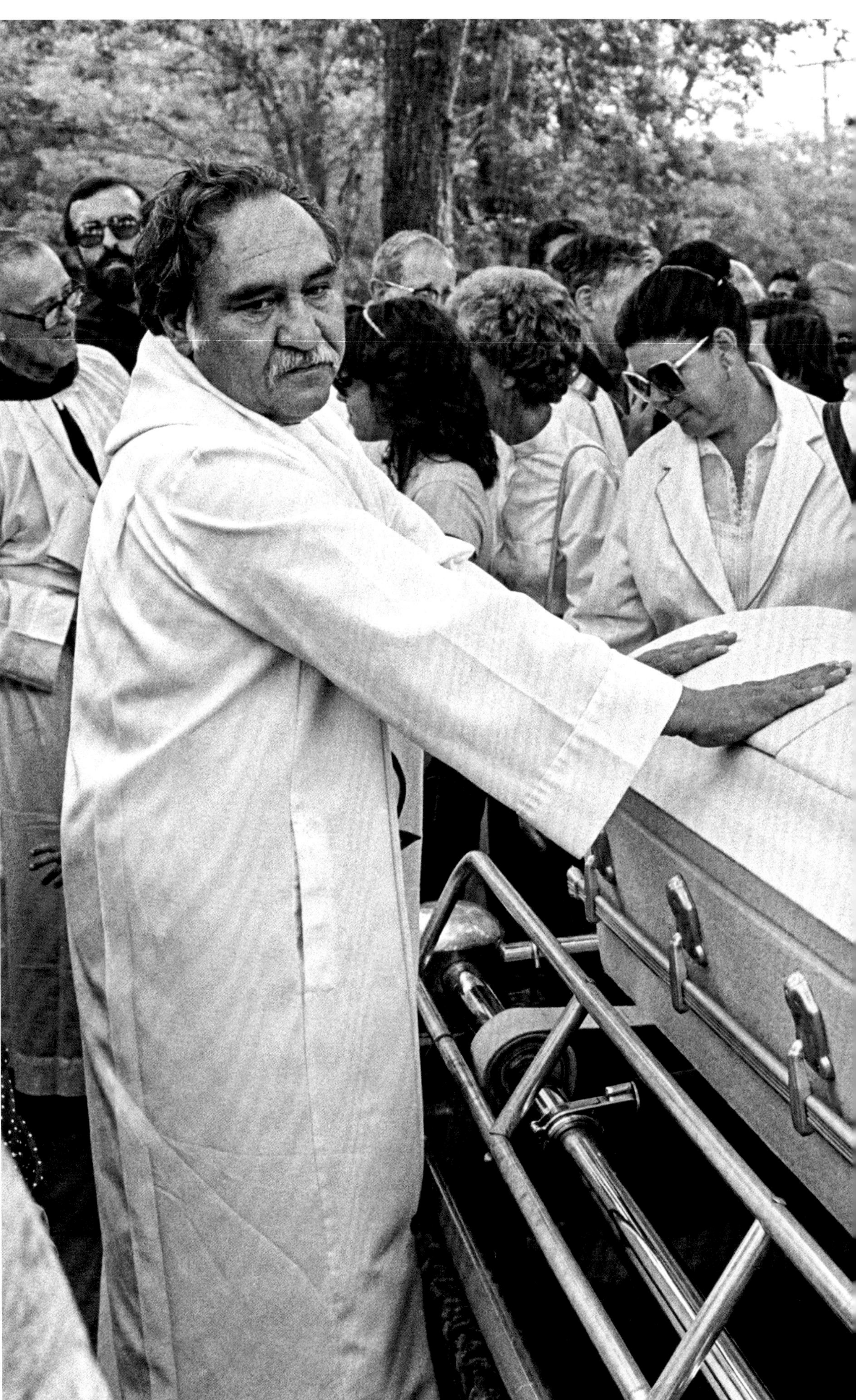

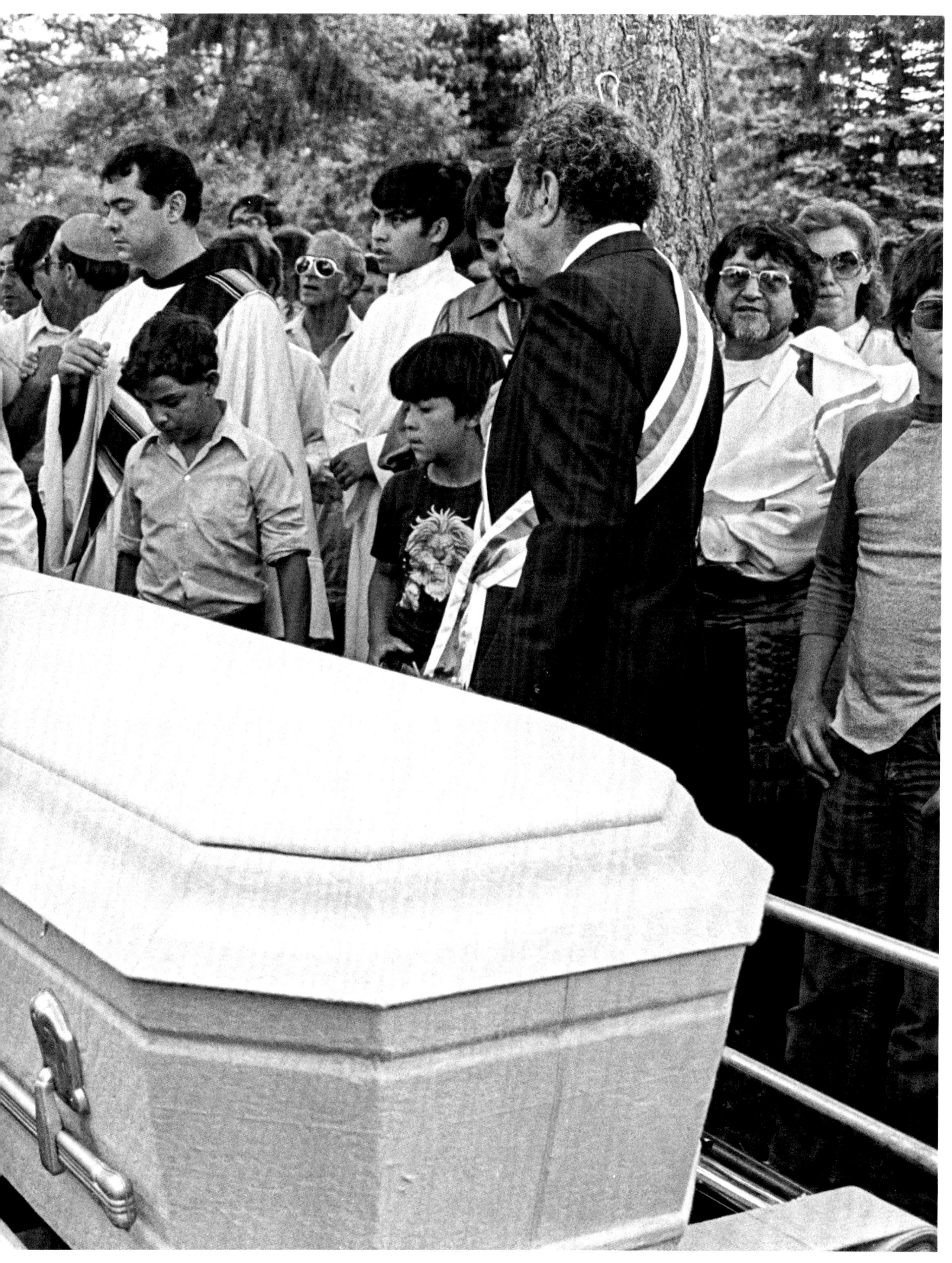

Burial of Fr. Reynaldo Rivera, Rosario Cemetery, Santa Fe, 1982.

OVERLEAF: Santo Niño de Atocha Chapel, Chimayó, 1981.

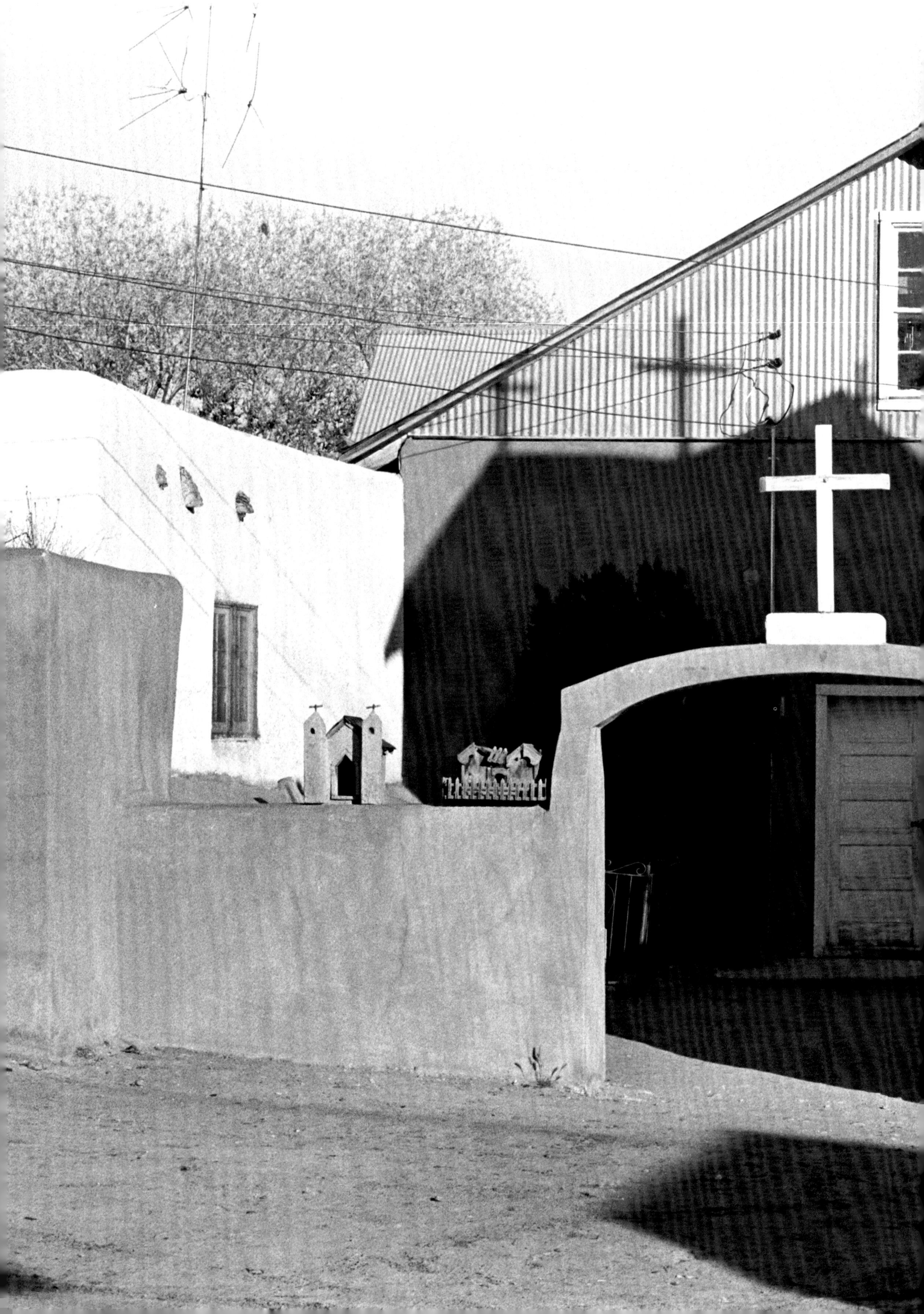

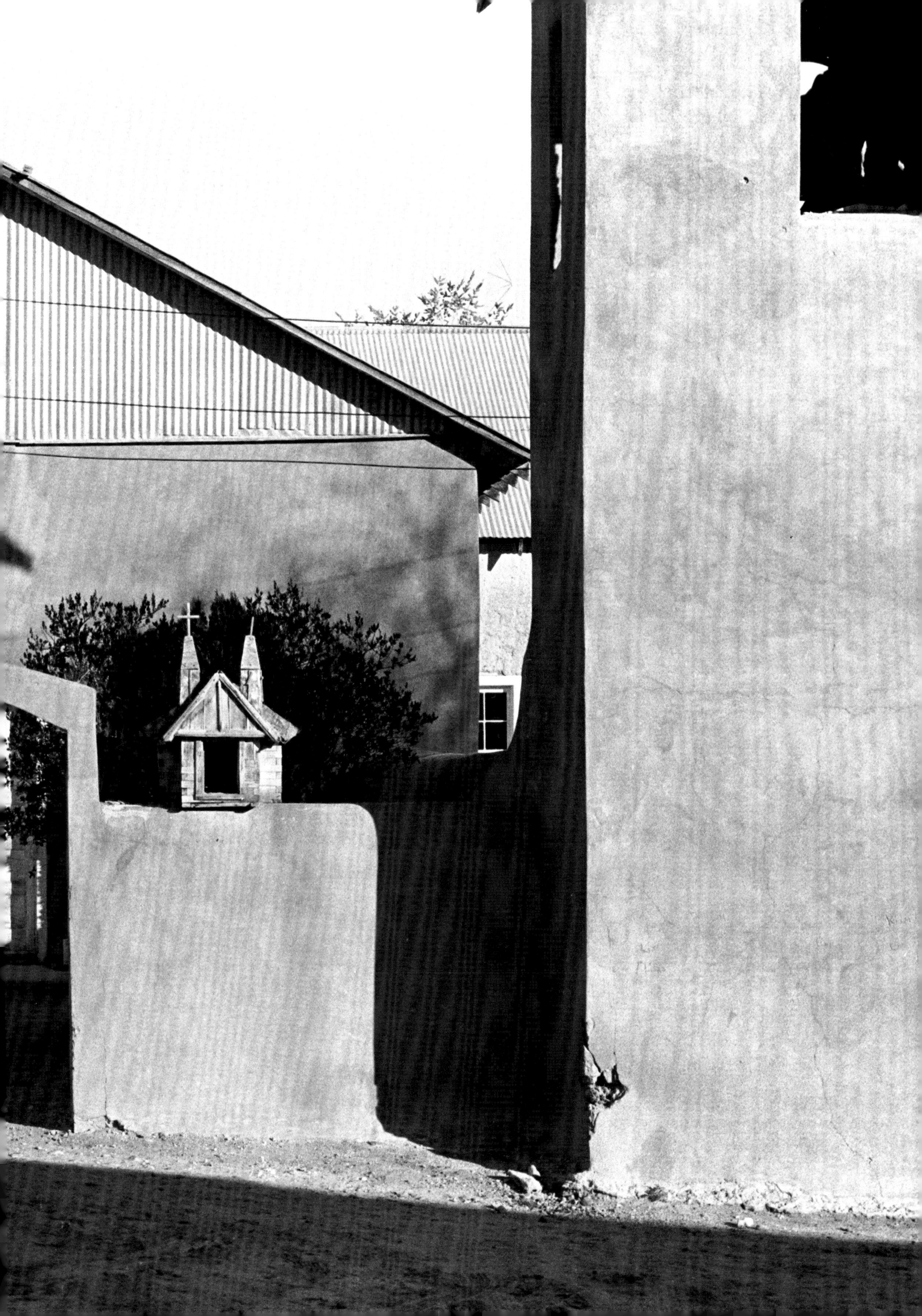

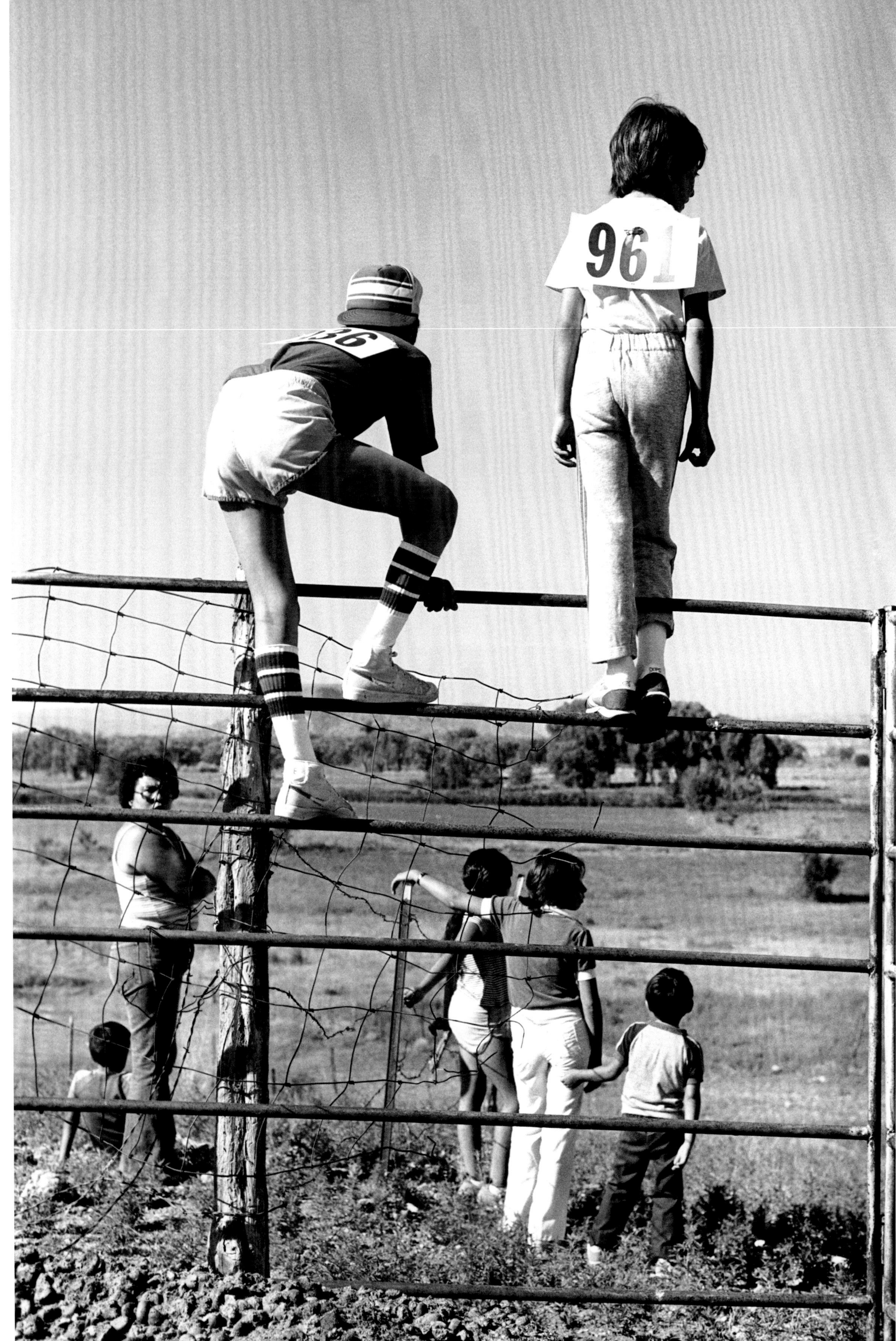
961

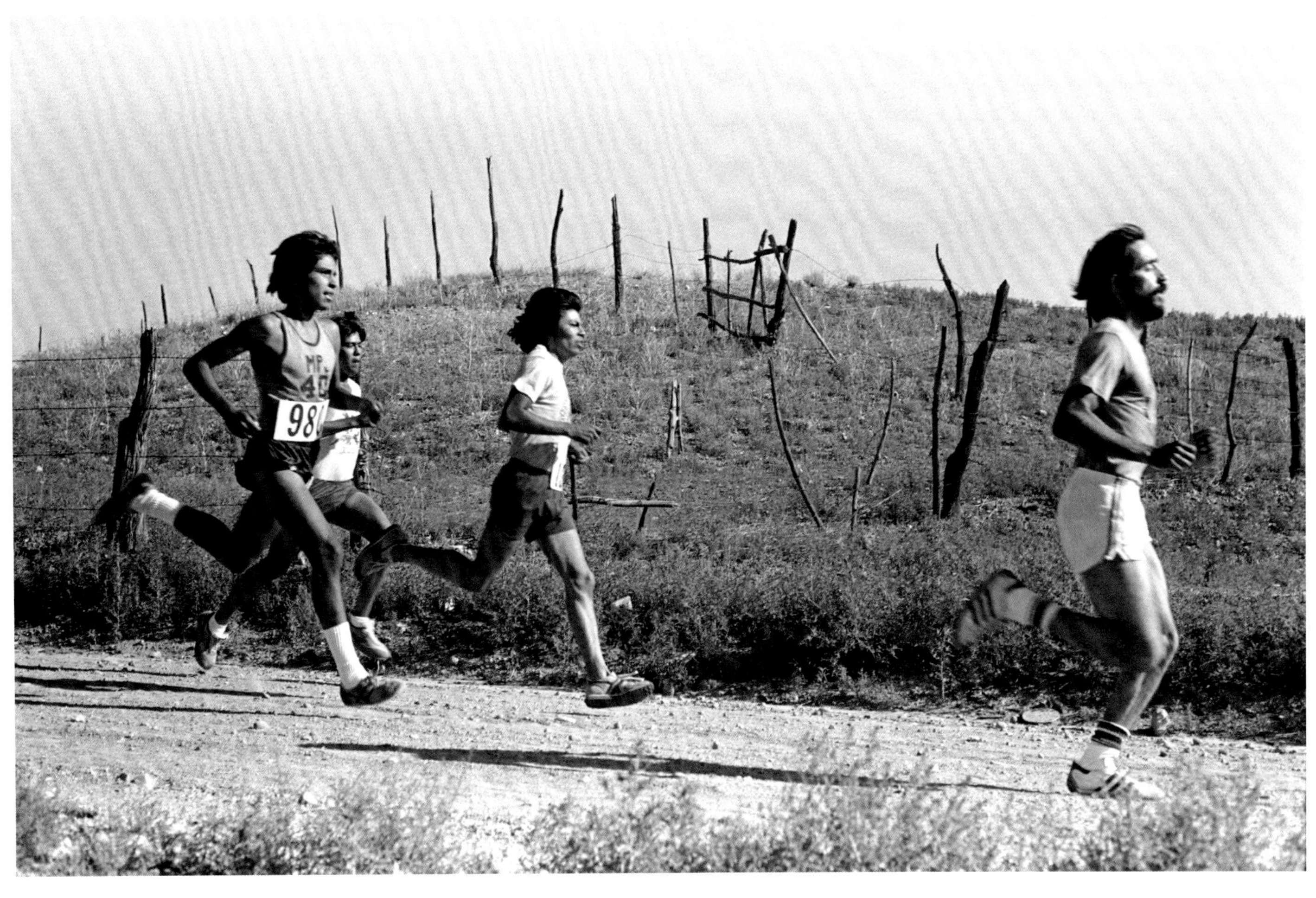

OPPOSITE, ABOVE, AND OVERLEAF: "Save the Jemez Mountains" footrace, Santa Clara Pueblo, 1981.

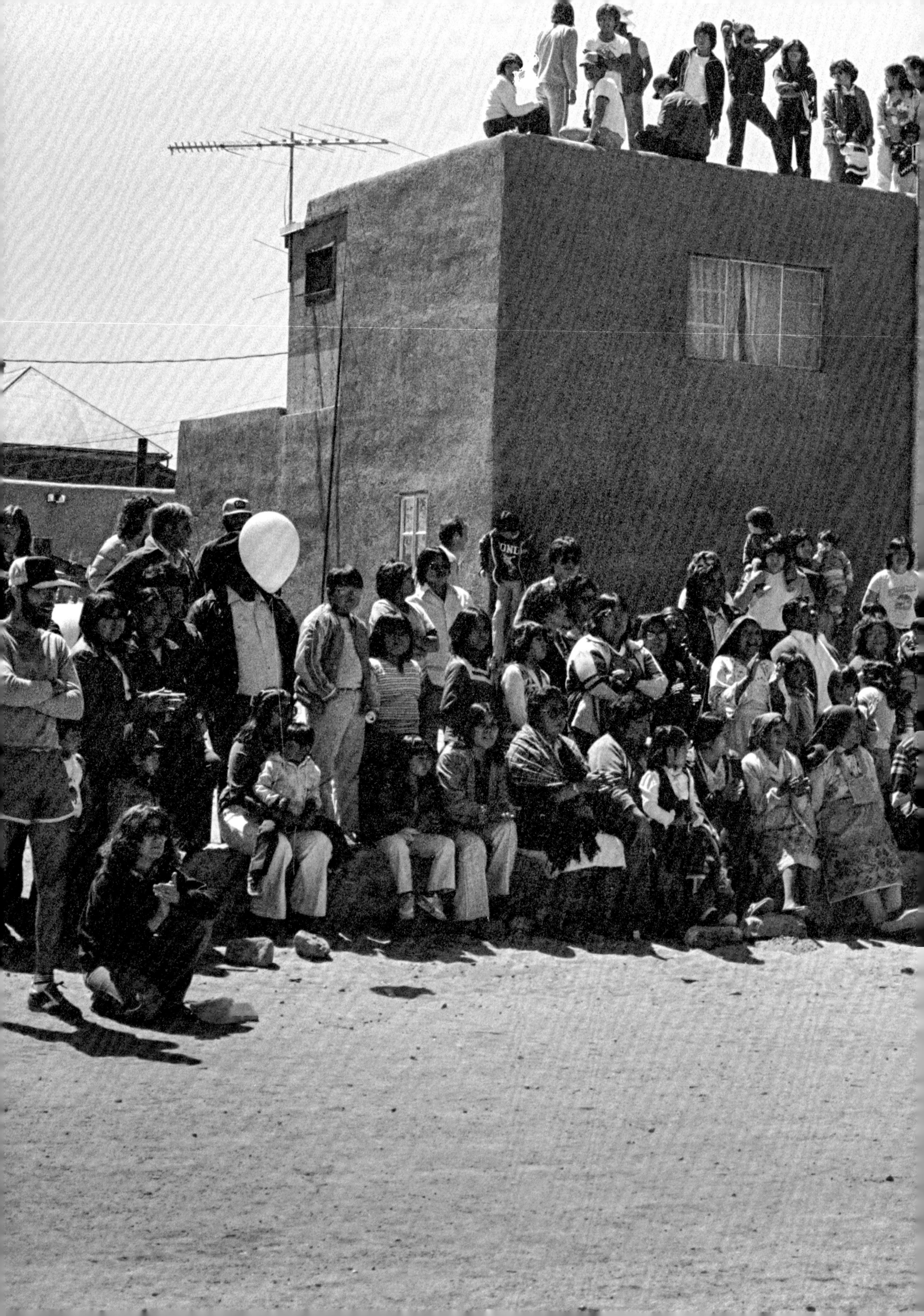

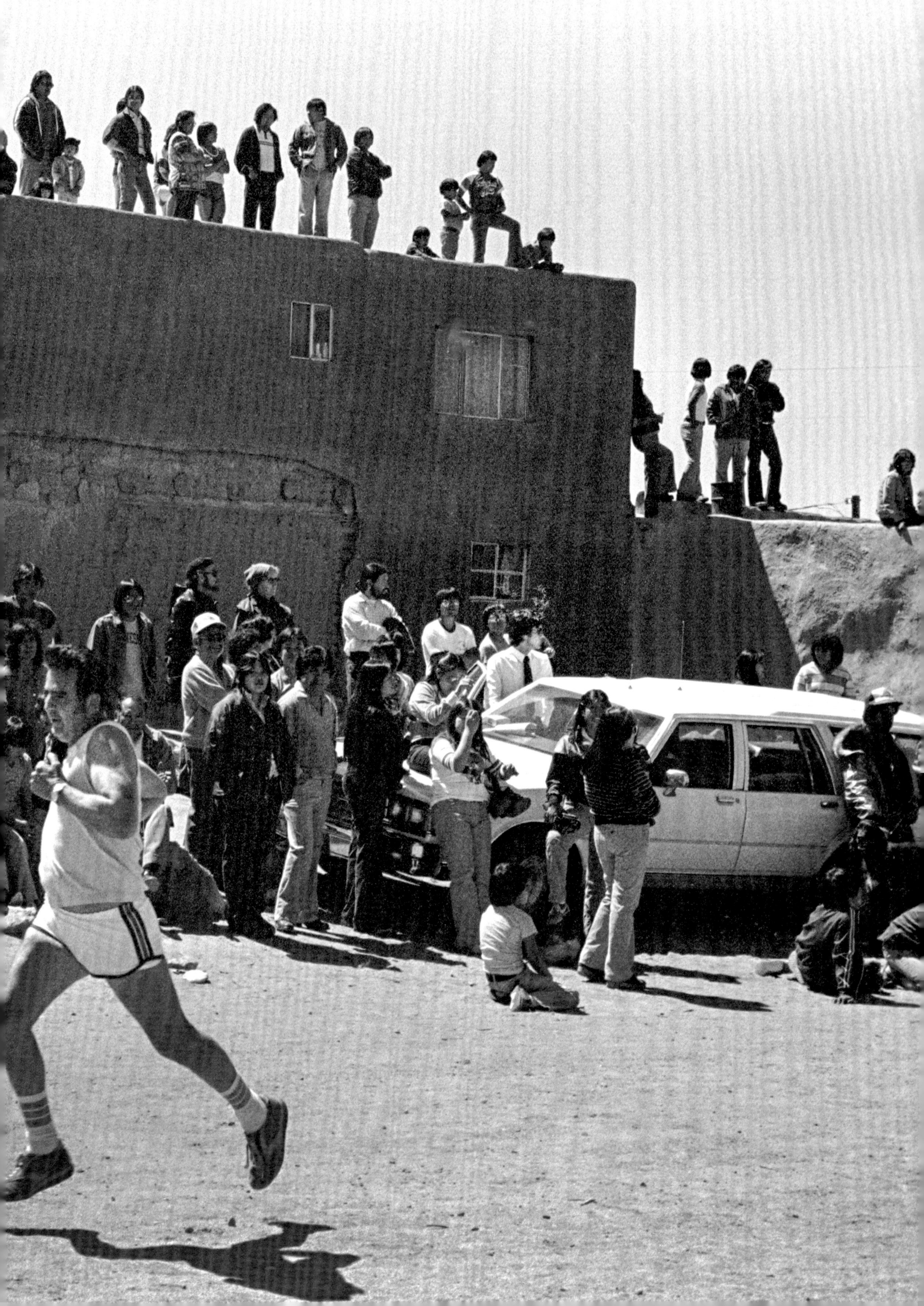

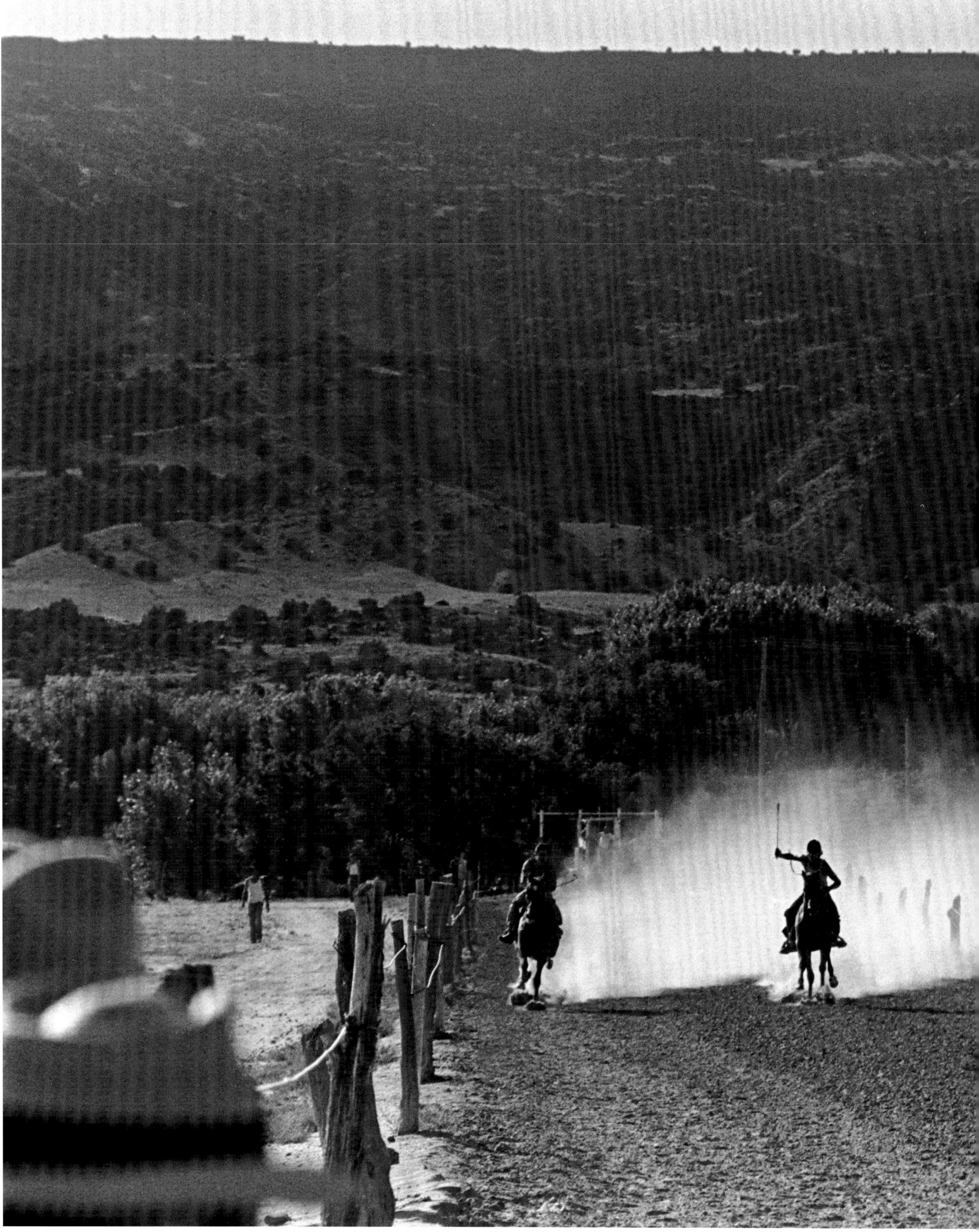

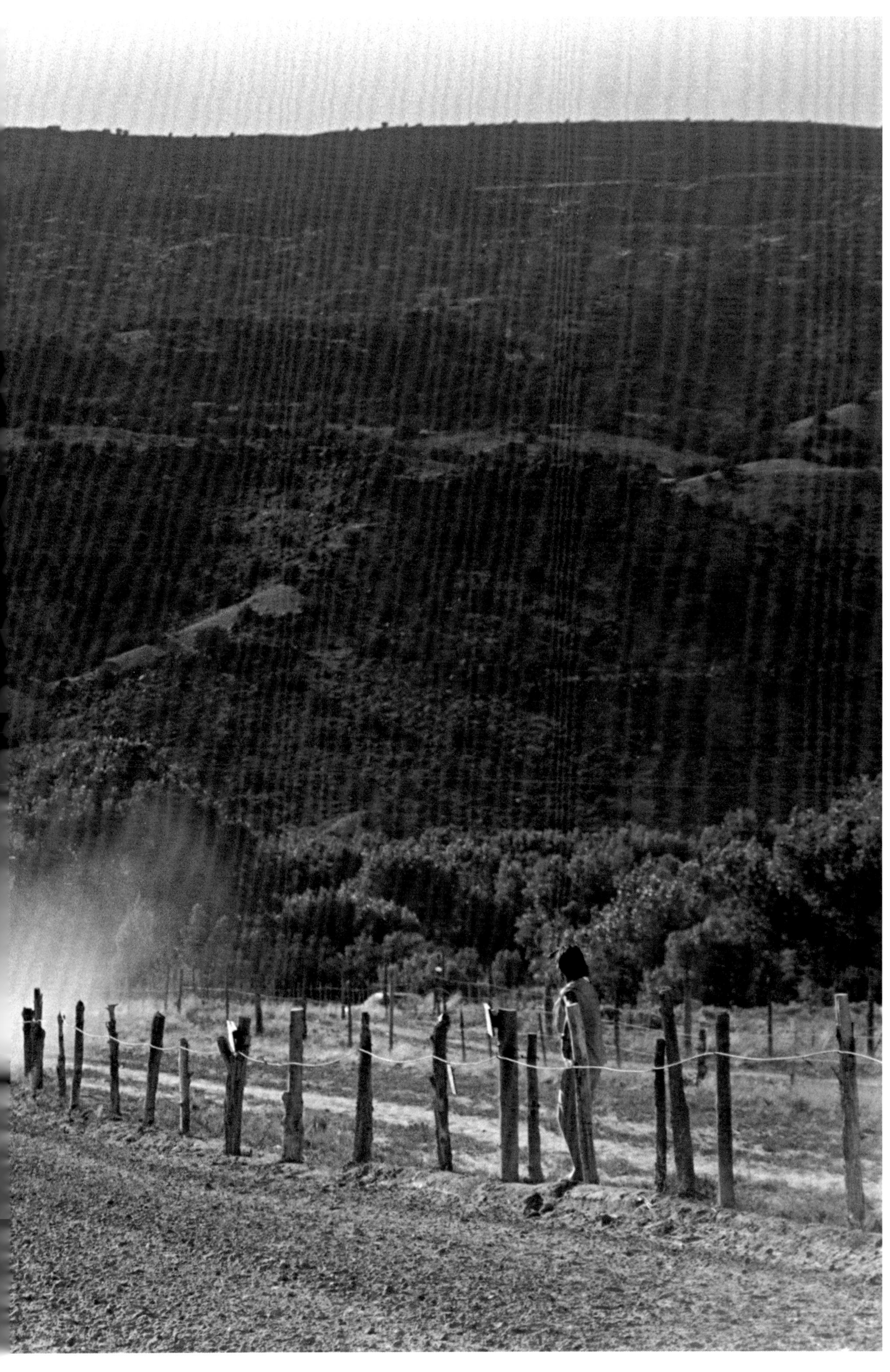

Horse races, Velarde, 1981.

OVERLEAF: Santa Fe Indian Market, Santa Fe Plaza, 1982.

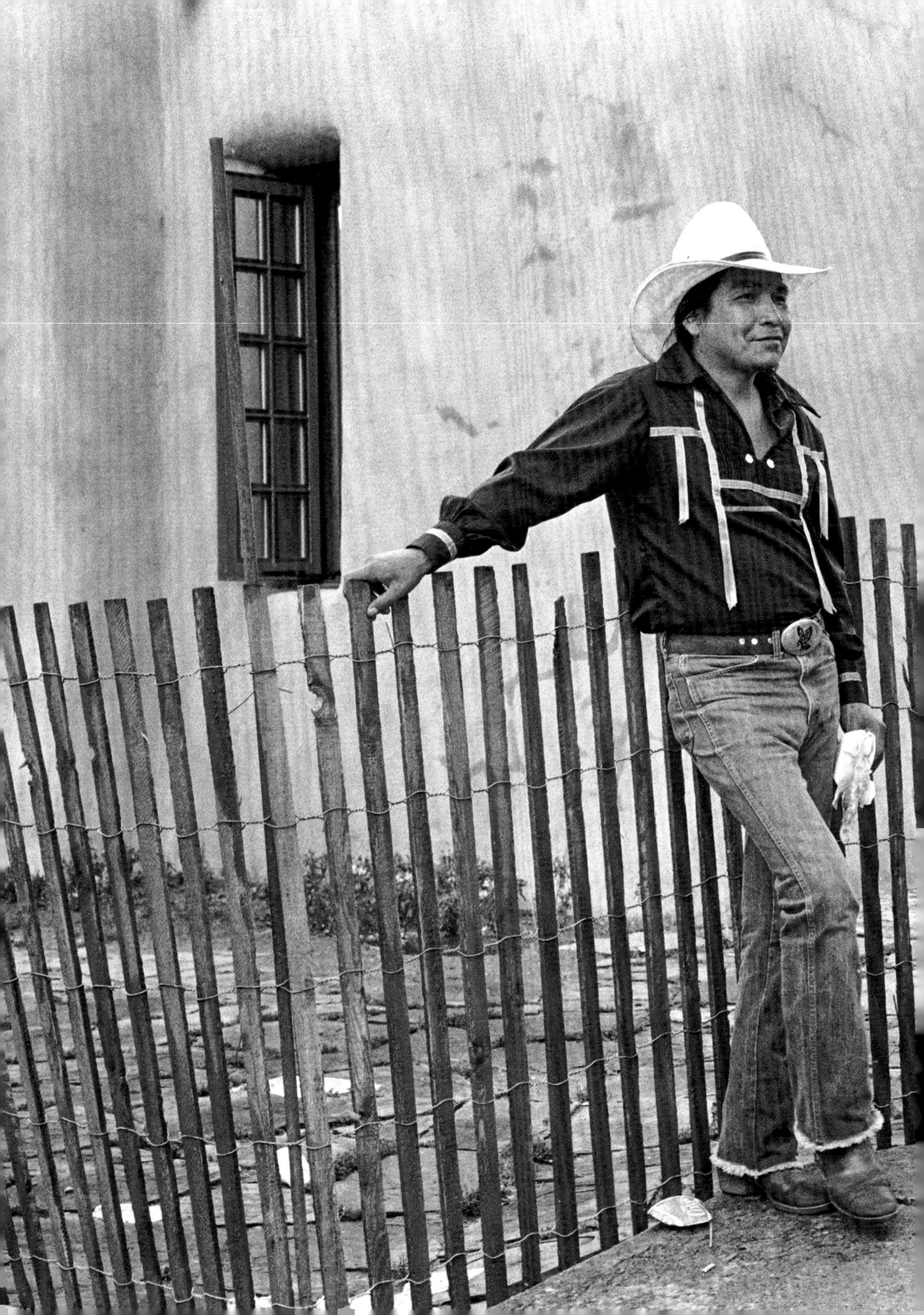

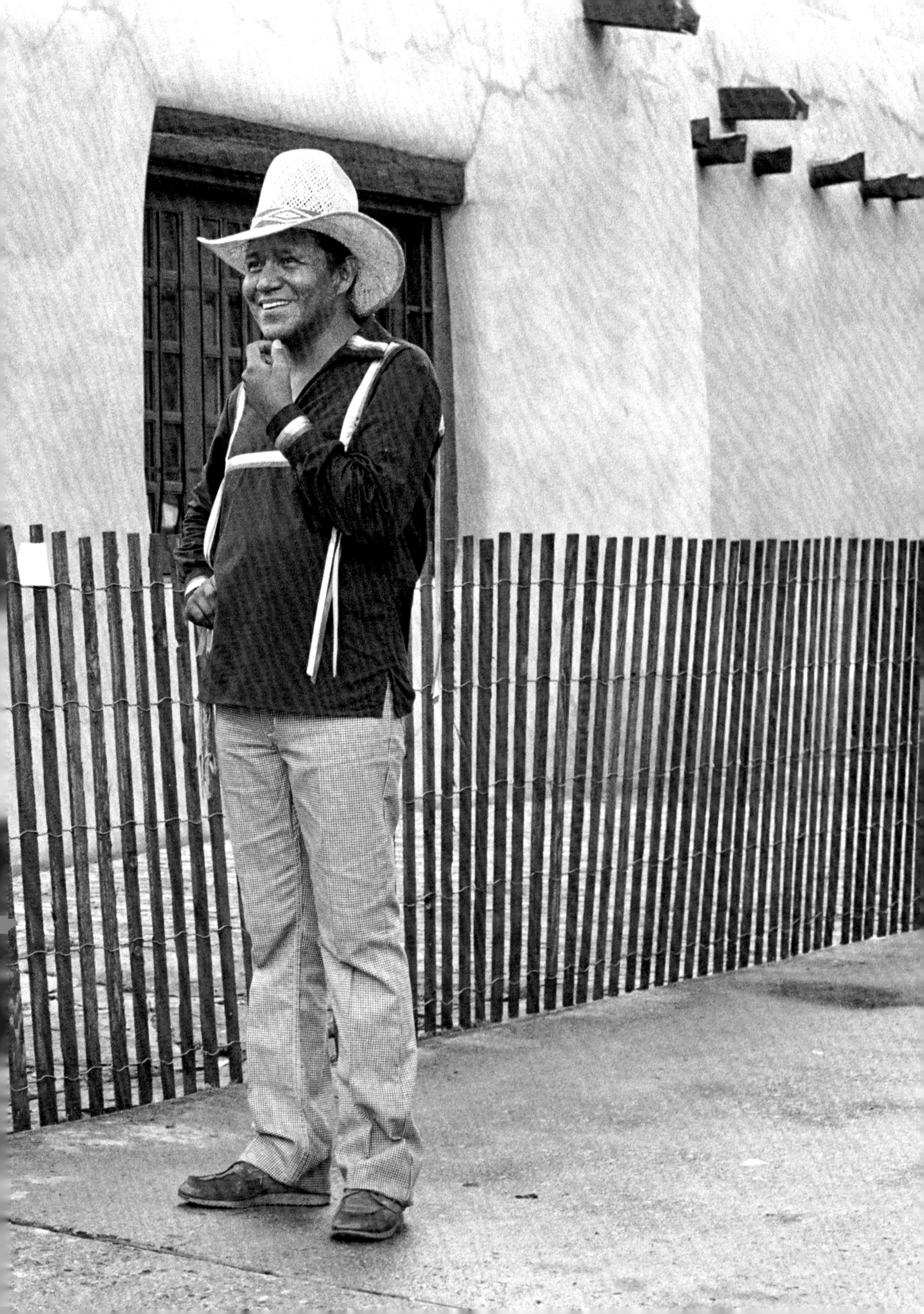

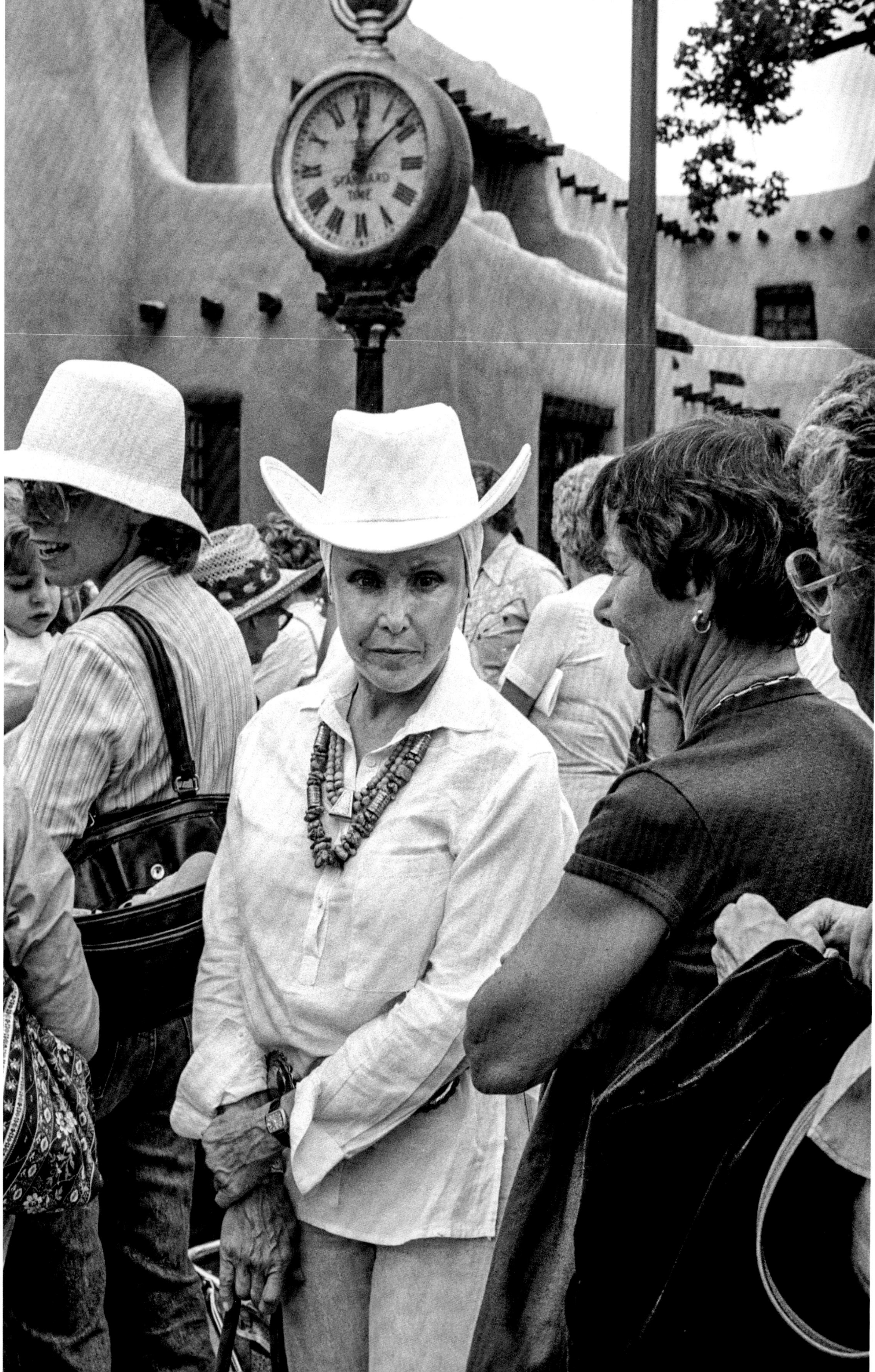

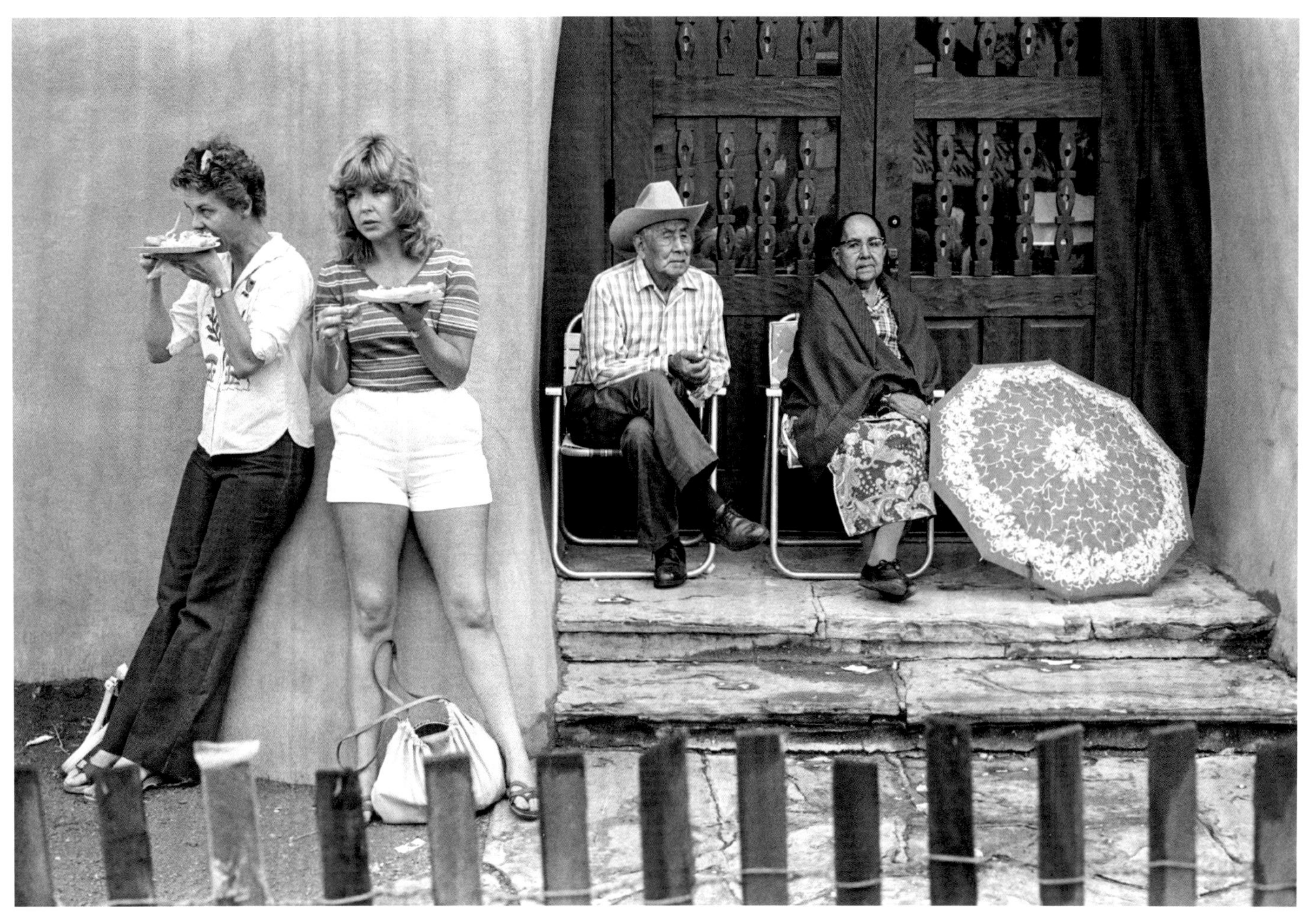

OPPOSITE AND ABOVE: Santa Fe Indian Market, Santa Fe Plaza, 1982.

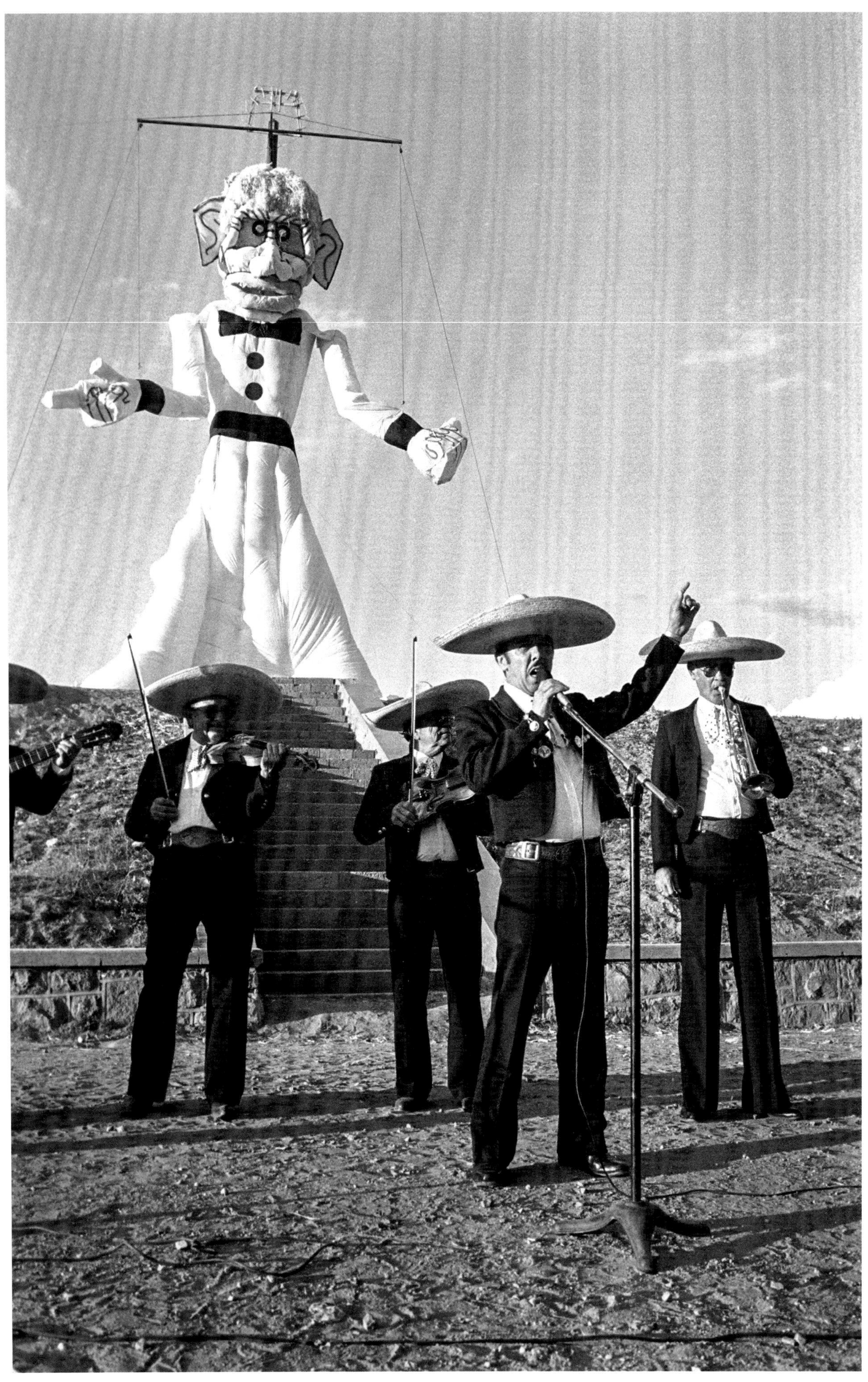

Mariachi band plays prior to the Burning of Zozobra, Fiesta de Santa Fe, 1982.

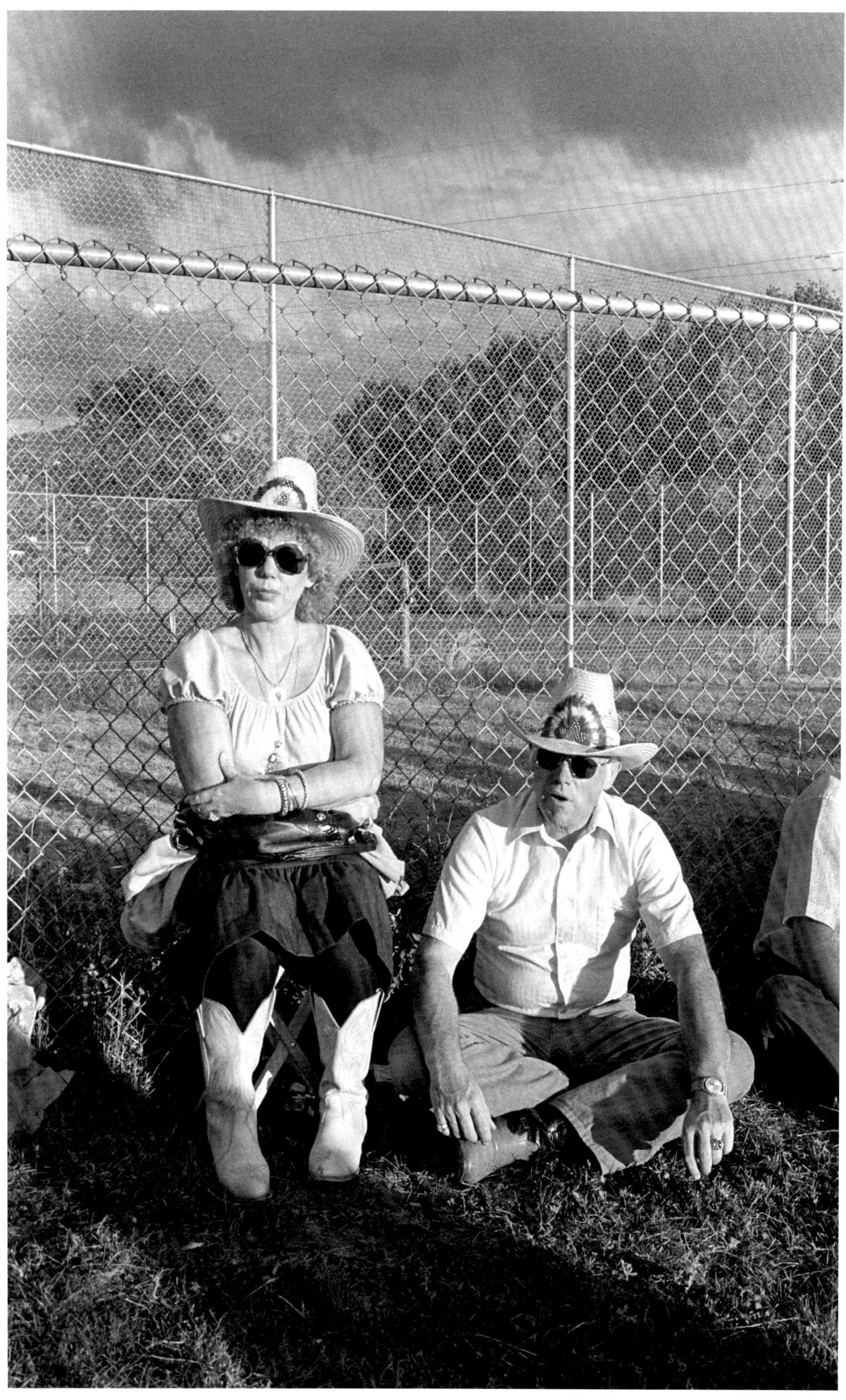

At the Burning of Zozobra, Fiesta de Santa Fe, 1982.

OVERLEAF: Gallery owner Martha Keats and photographer Douglas Keats, Santa Fe, 1982.

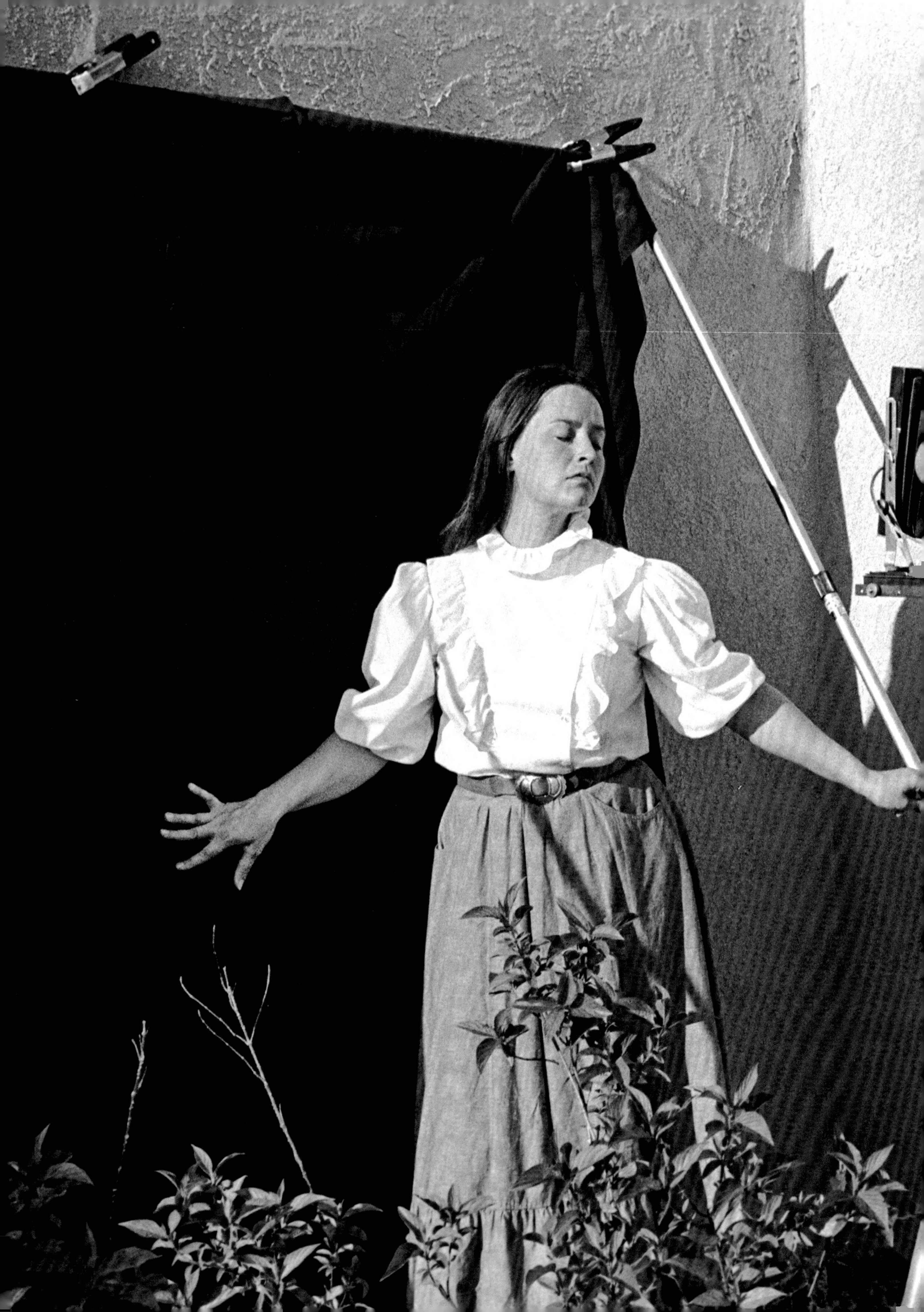

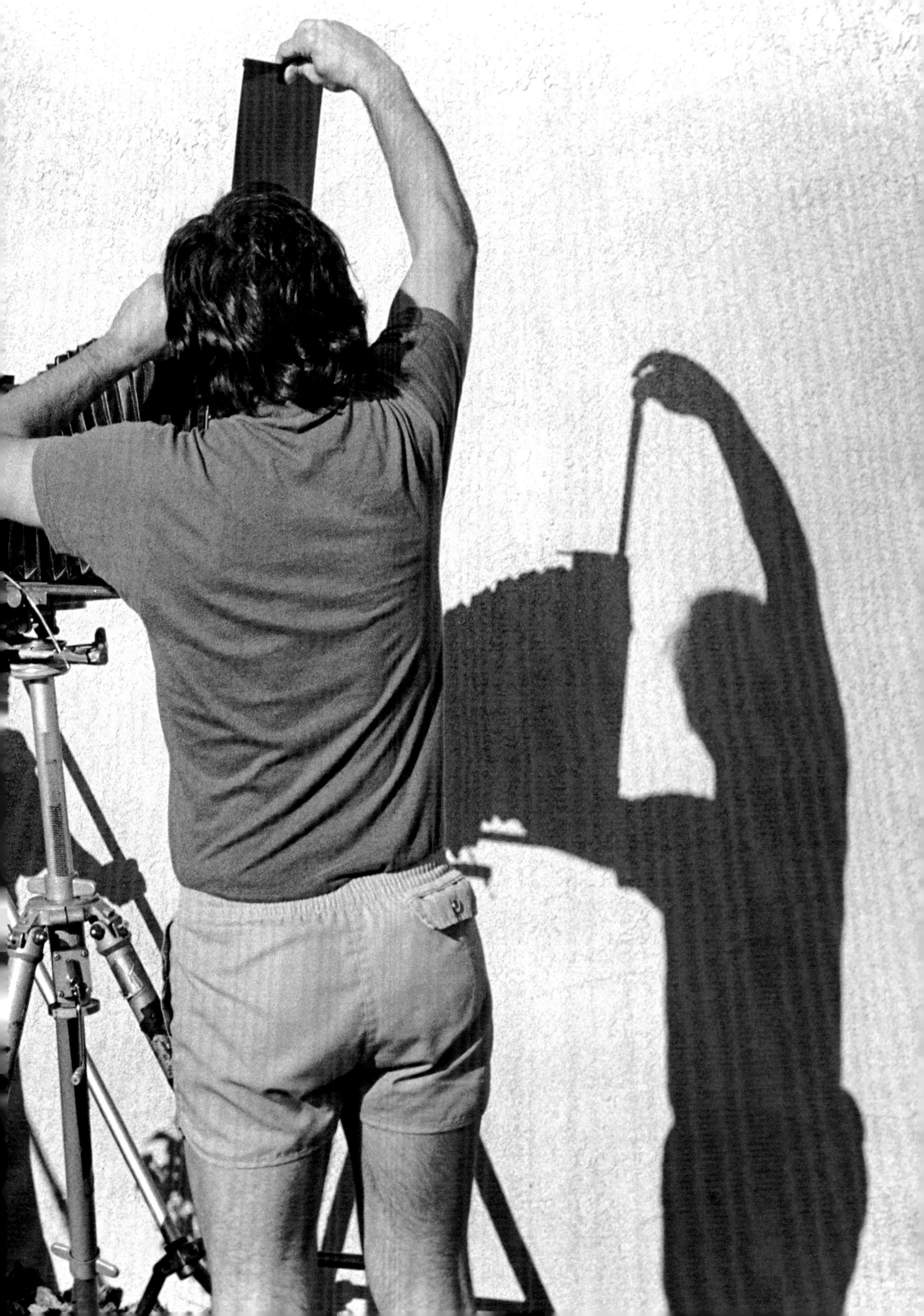

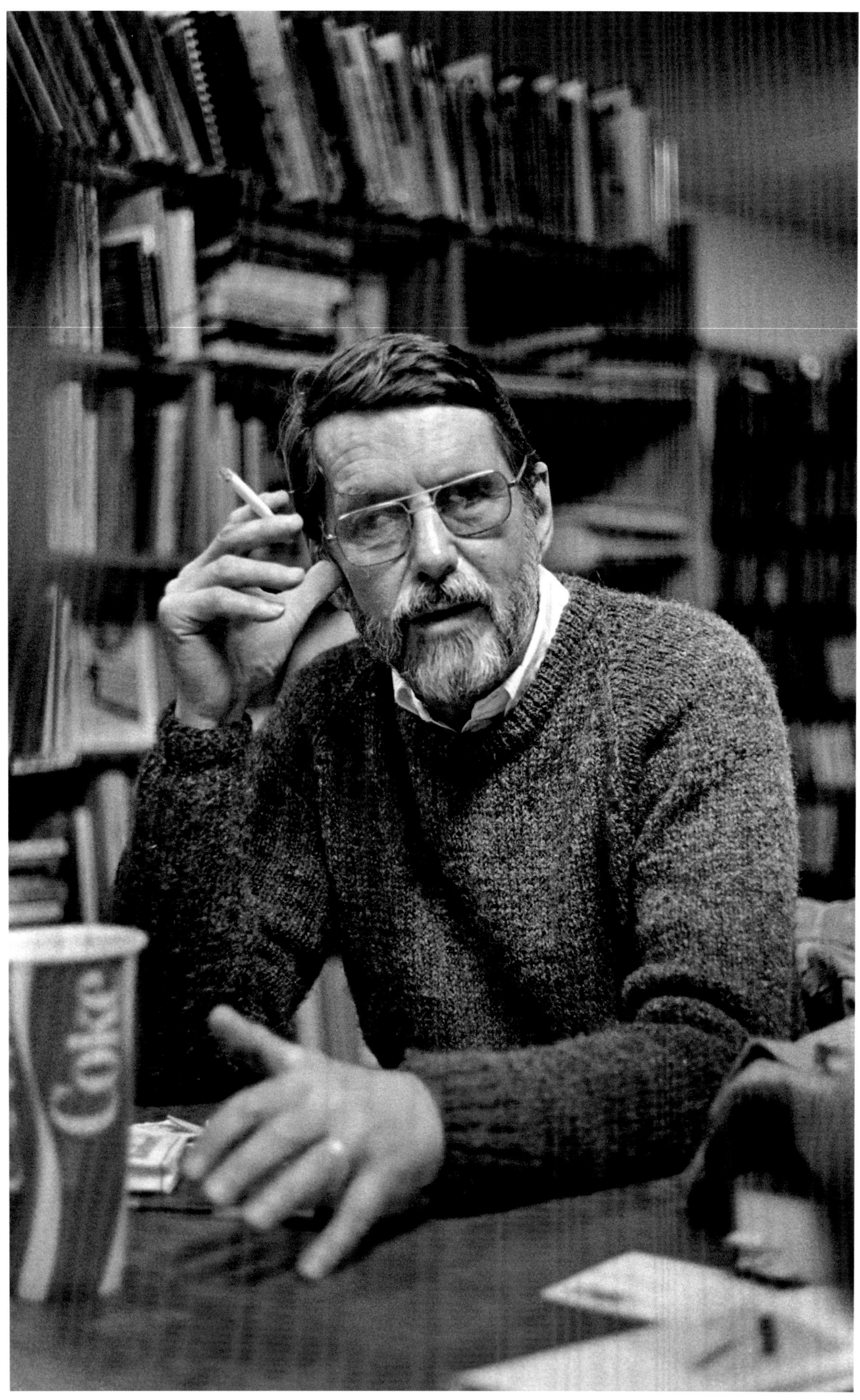

Poet Robert Creeley, University of New Mexico, Albuquerque, 1983.

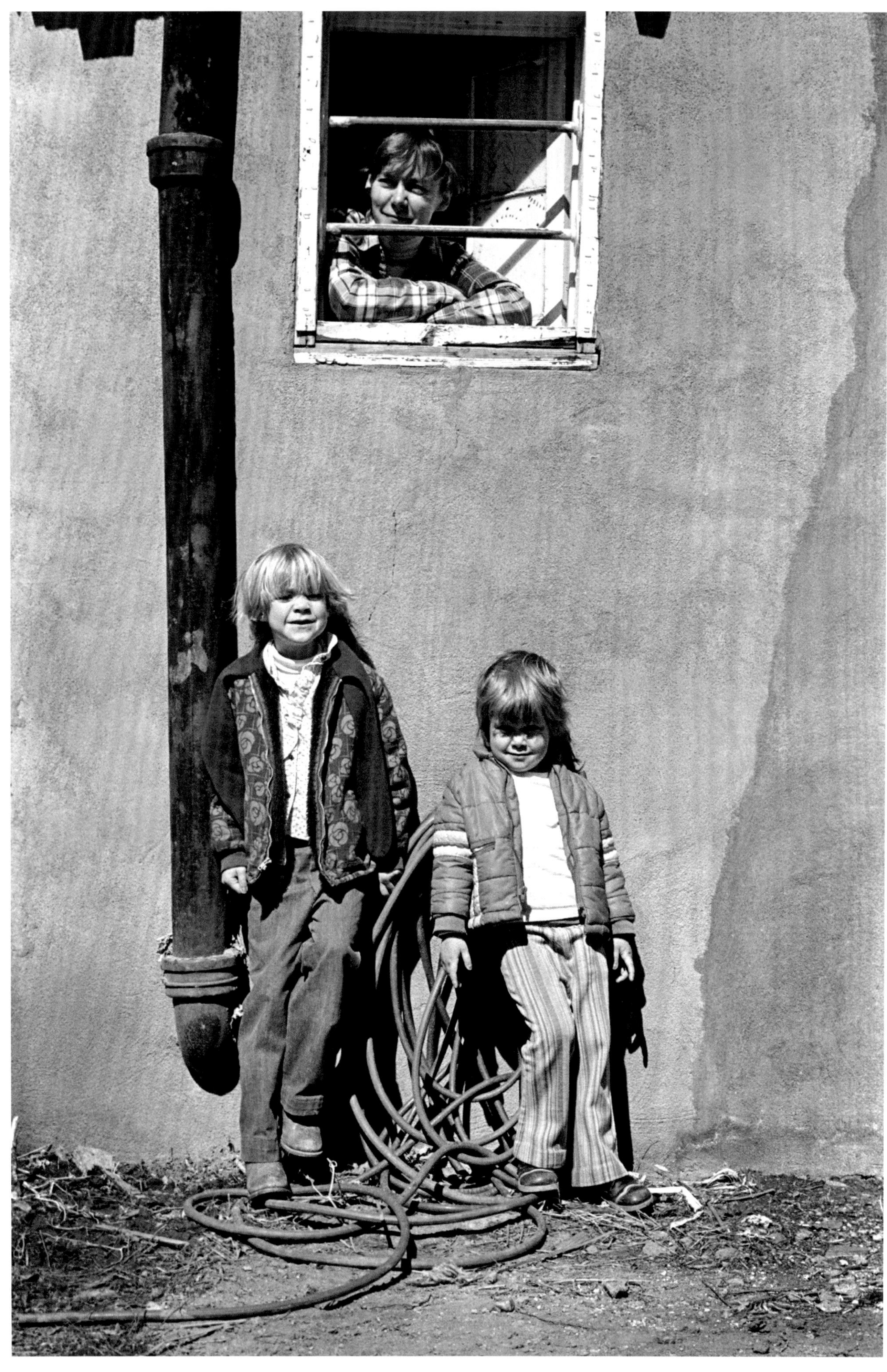

Holly Bealmear and daughters Zoe and Farrar, Santa Fe, 1982.

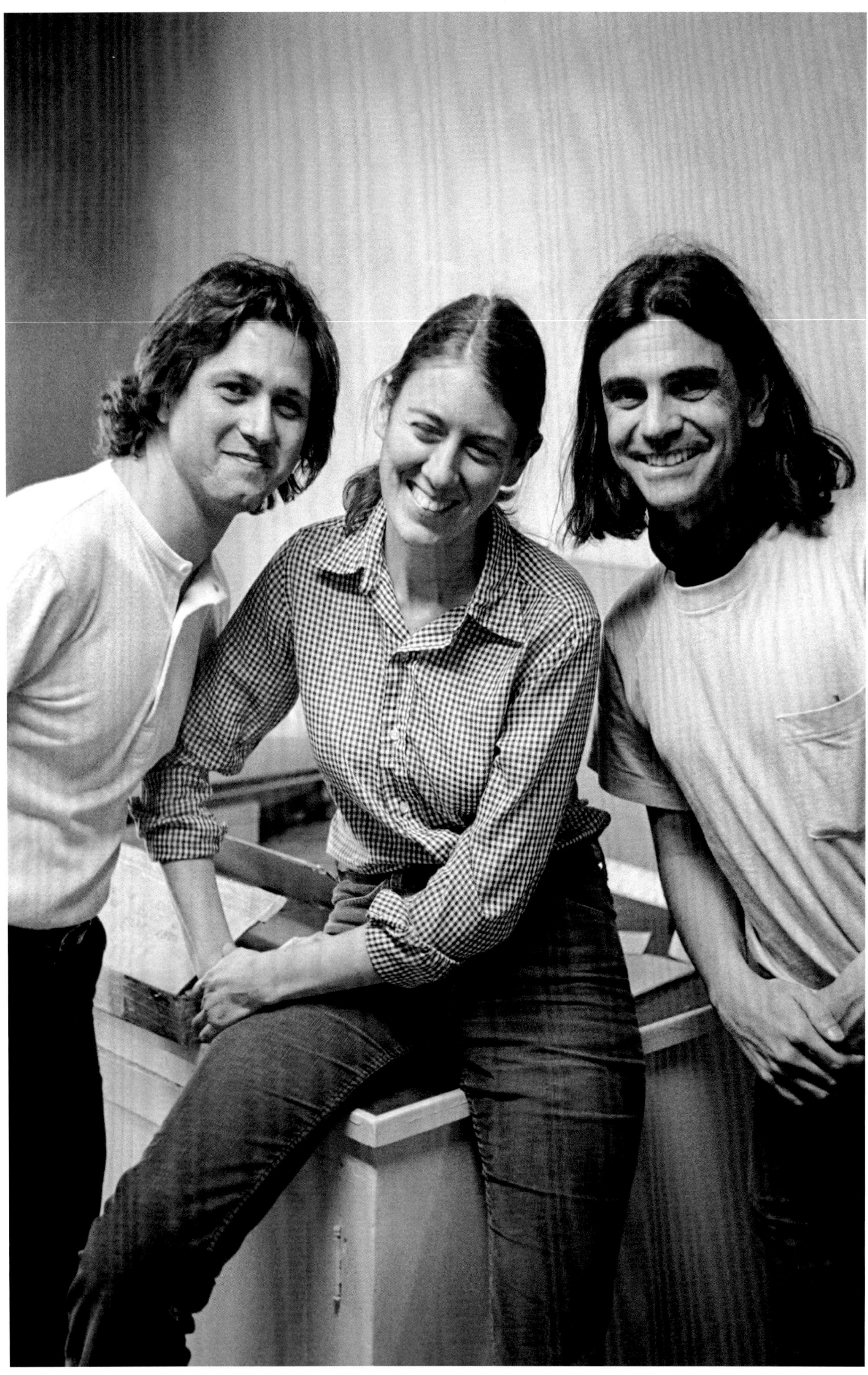

Photographers Doug Keats, Mary Peck, and Bernard Plossu at Mary Peck's studio, Santa Fe, 1982.

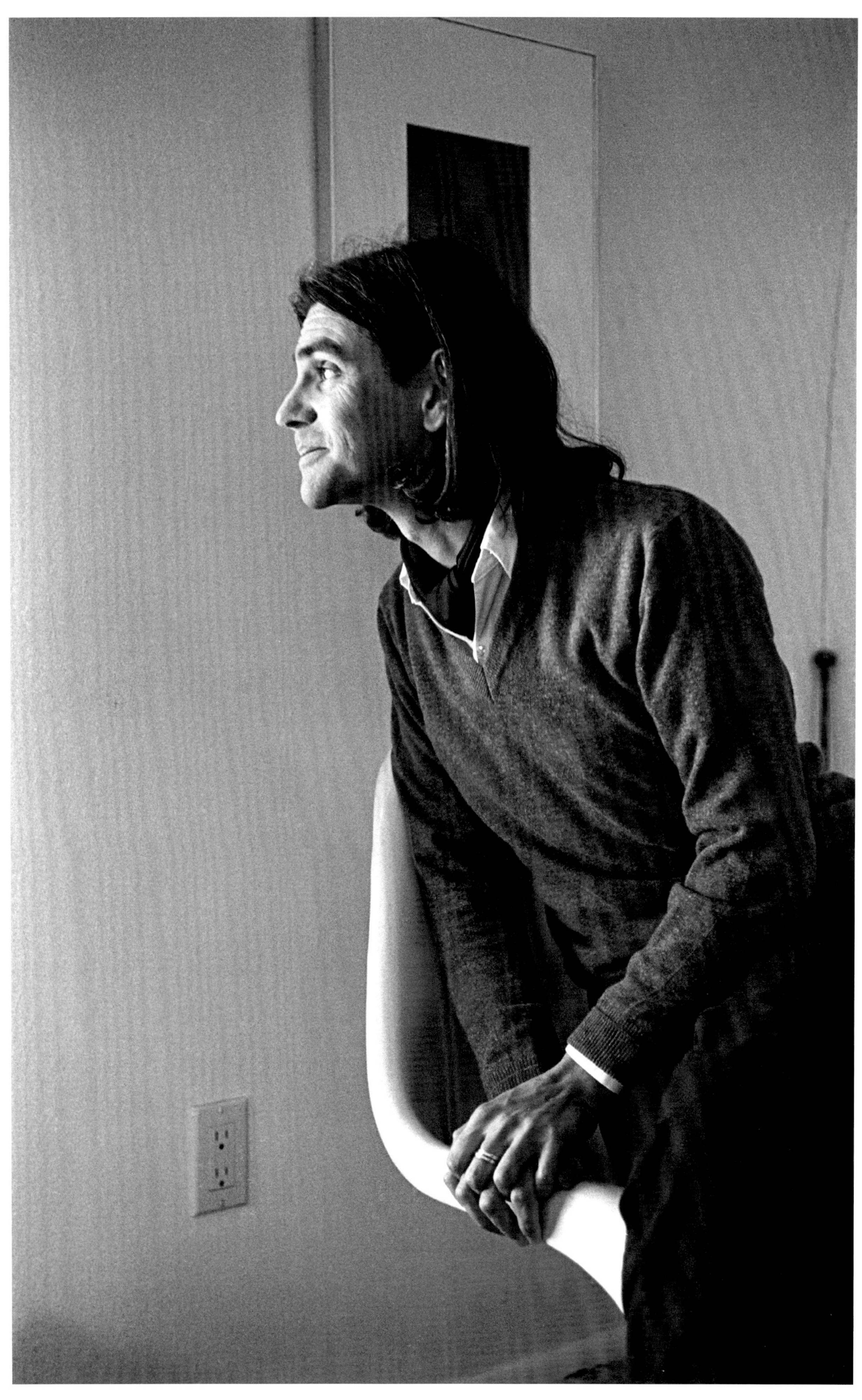

Bernard Plossu, Santa Fe, 1982.

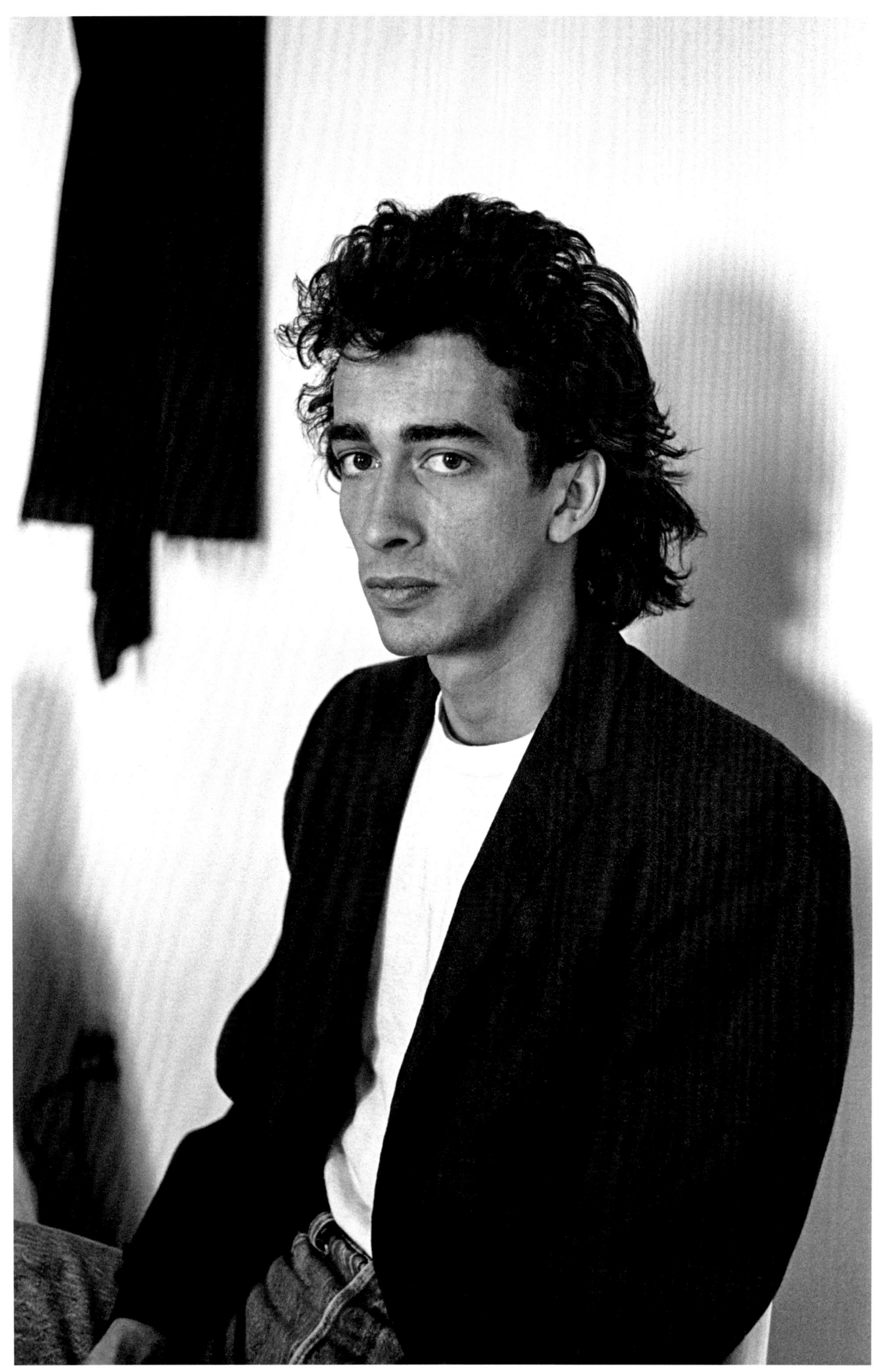

Photographer Pierre Mahaim, Santa Fe, 1982.

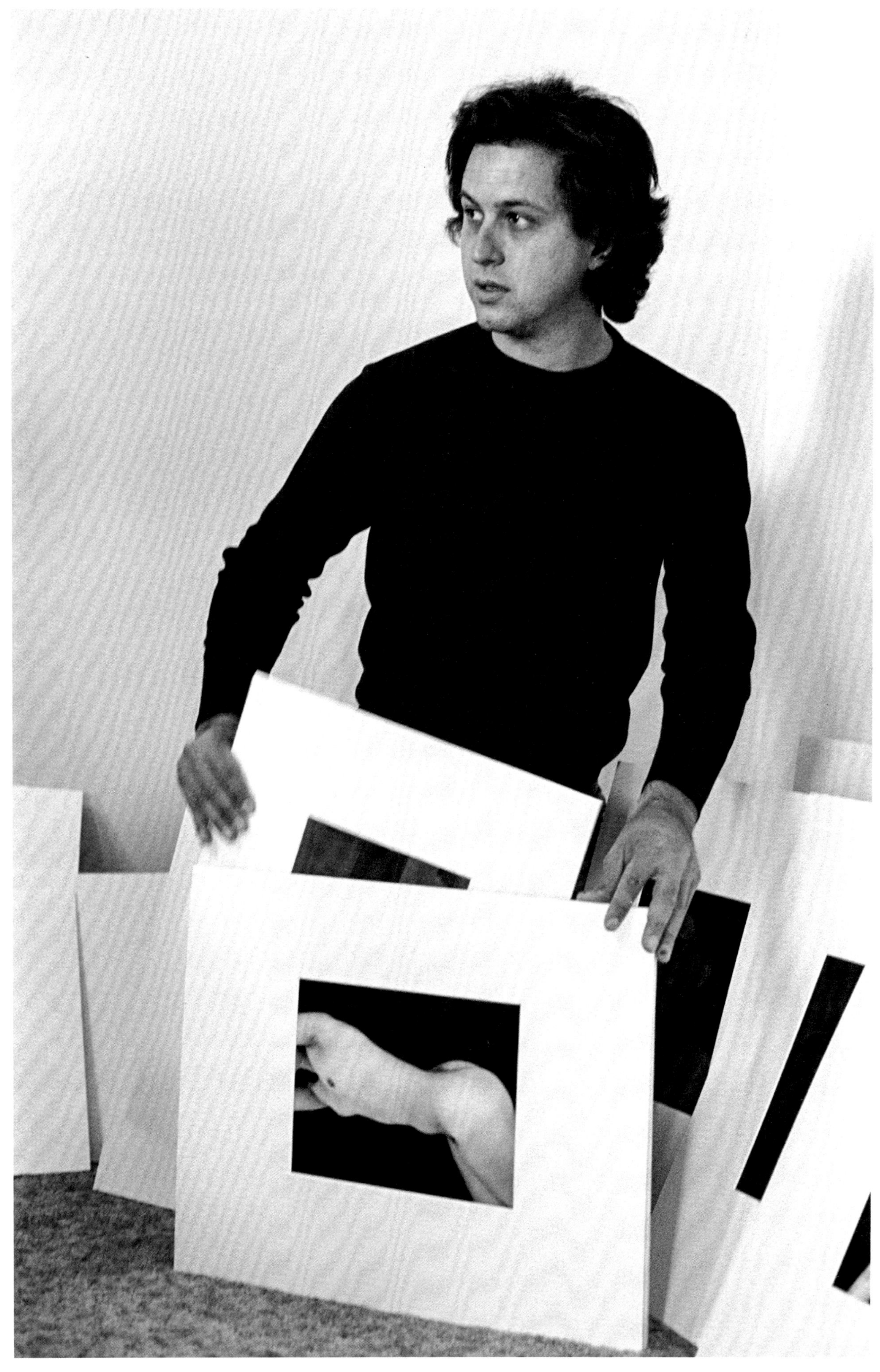

Doug Keats, Santa Fe, 1982.

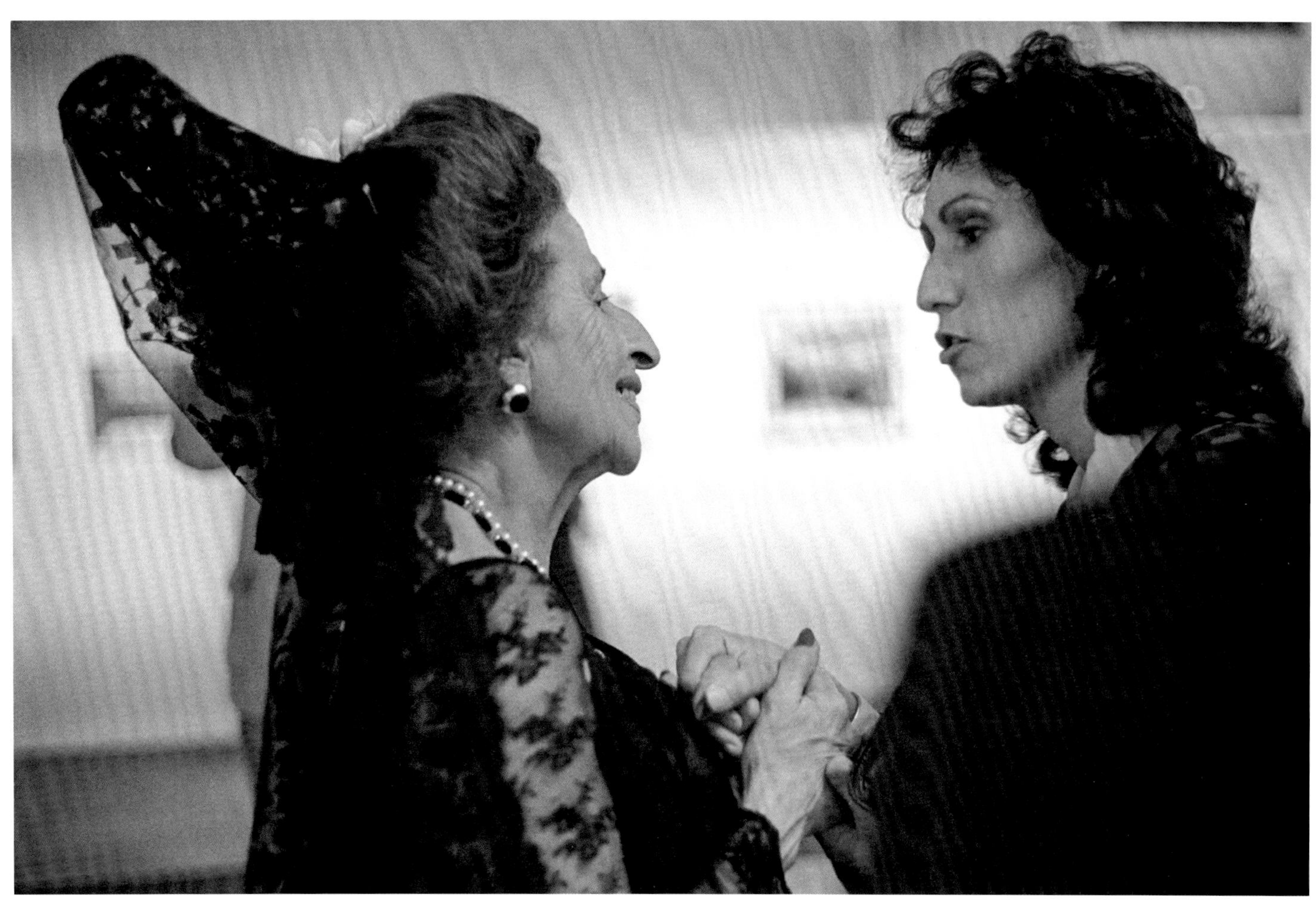

Concha Ortiz y Pino de Kleven and Teresa Archuleta-Sagel, Santa Fe, 1982.

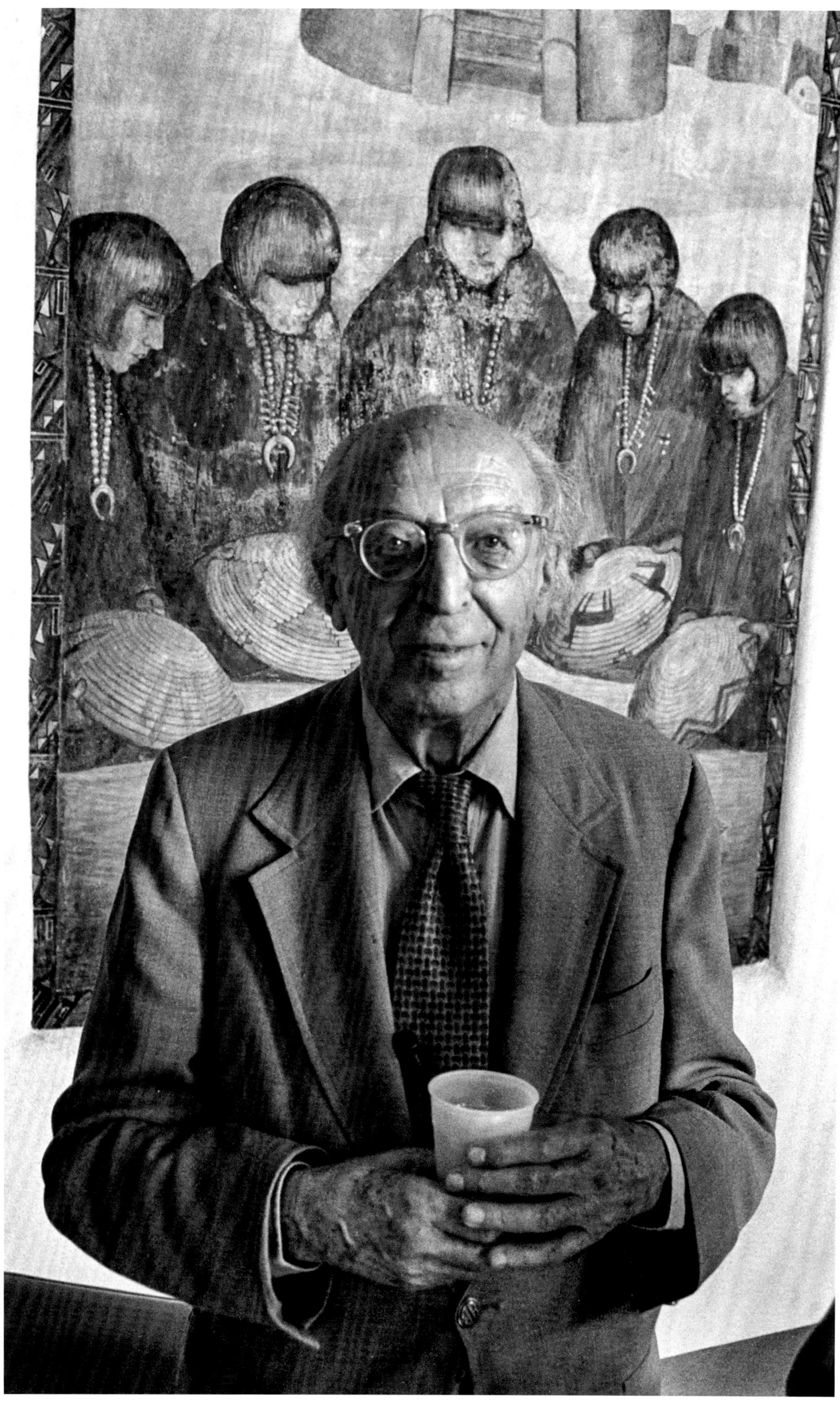

Aaron Copland visiting with the Santa Fe Chamber Music Festival, 1982.

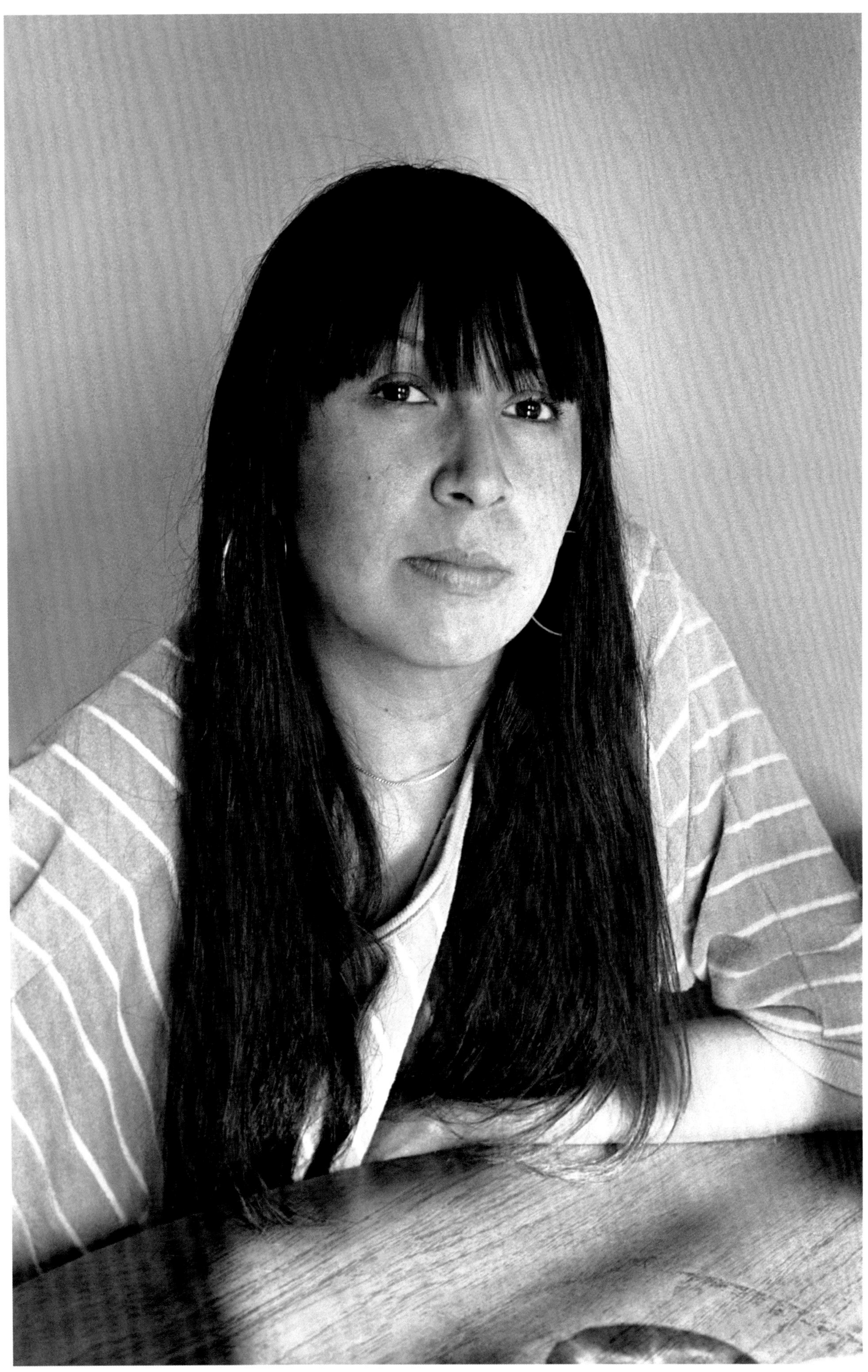

Marilyn Garcia, Albuquerque, 1983.

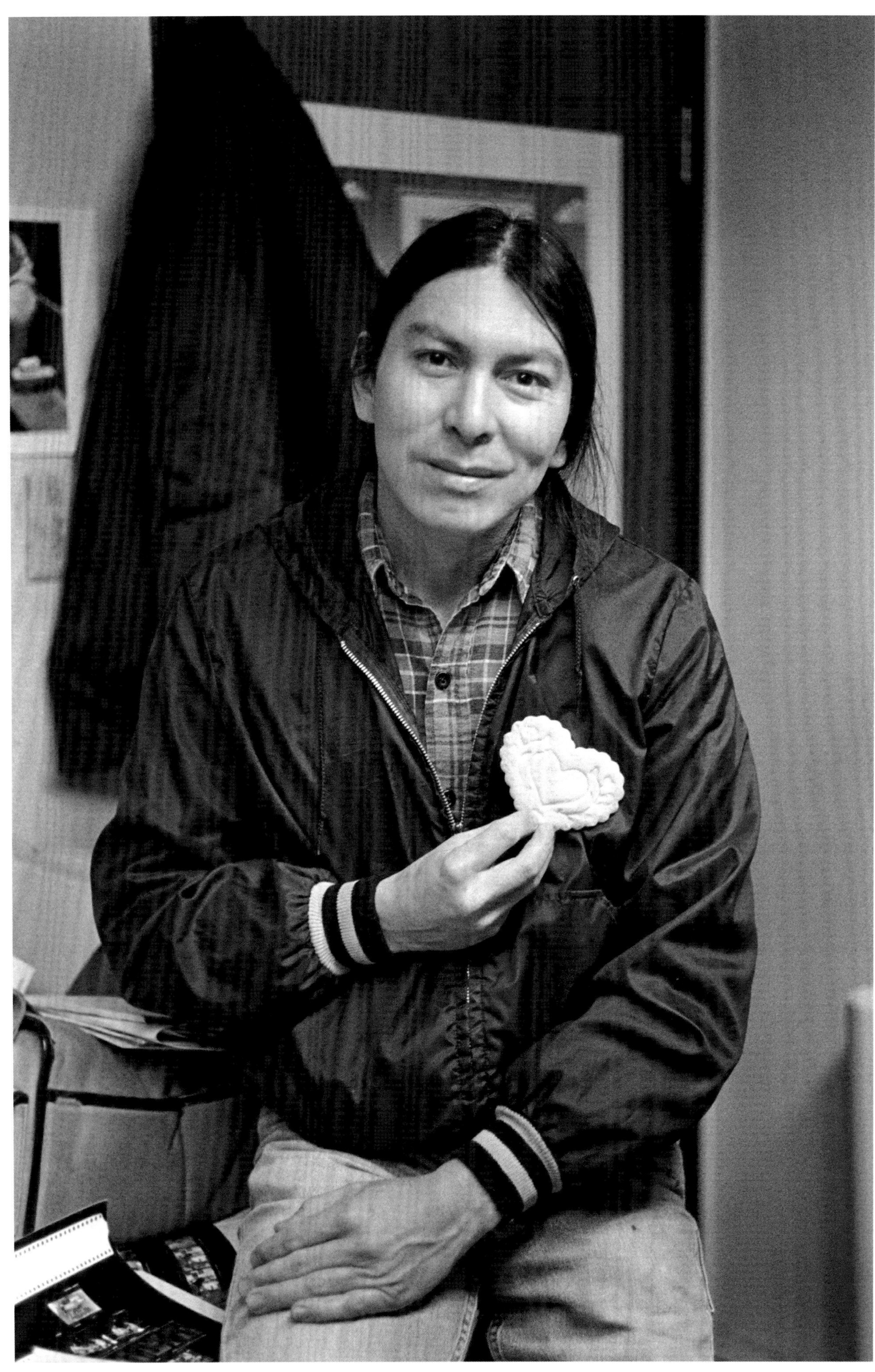

Photographer Elray Deroin in the darkroom at *The New Mexico Sun*, Albuquerque, 1983.

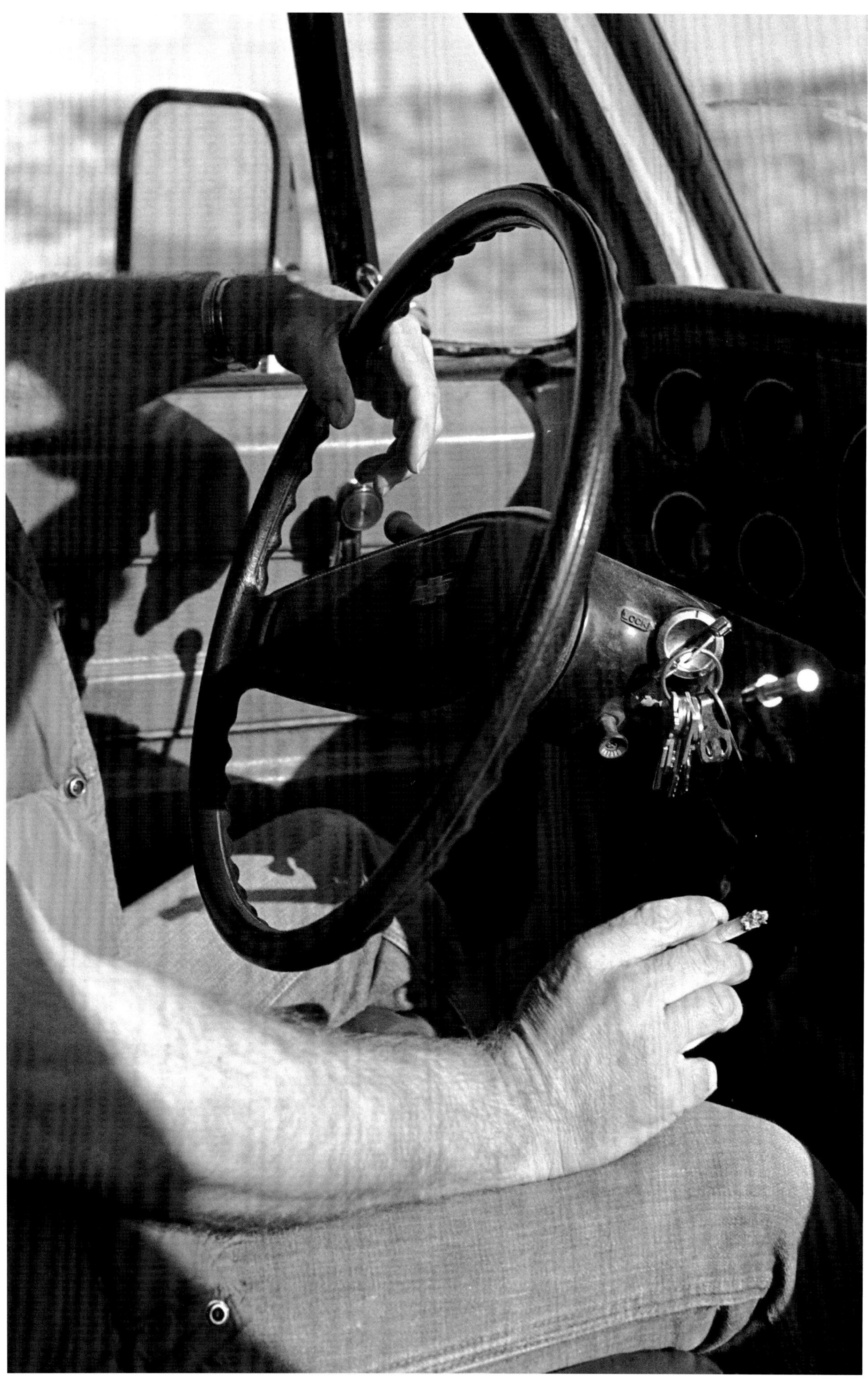

Photographer Walter Nelson, Coyote, 1982.

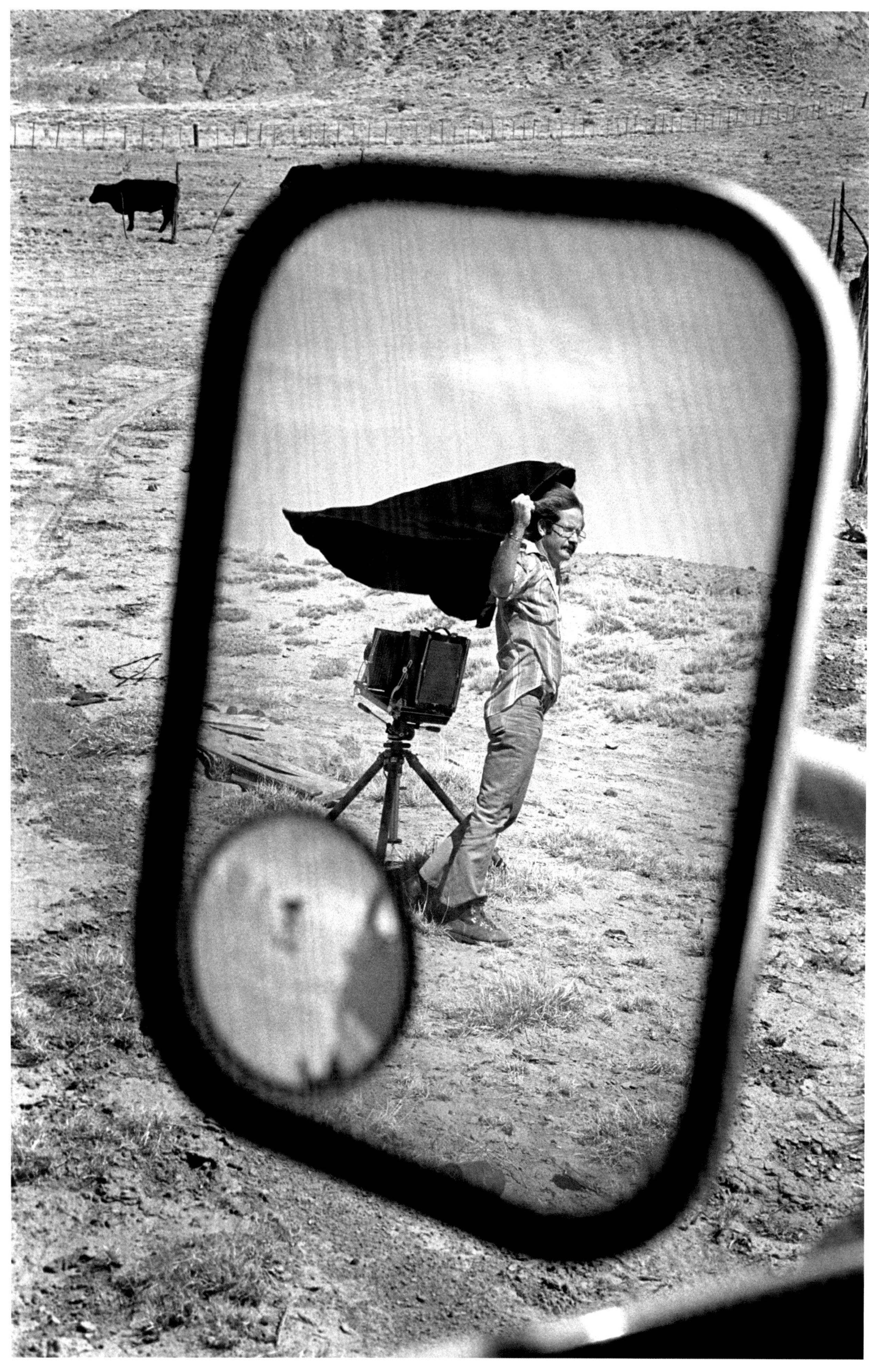

Walter Nelson, Coyote, 1982.

OVERLEAF: Photographer Ray Belcher and family, Galisteo, 1982.

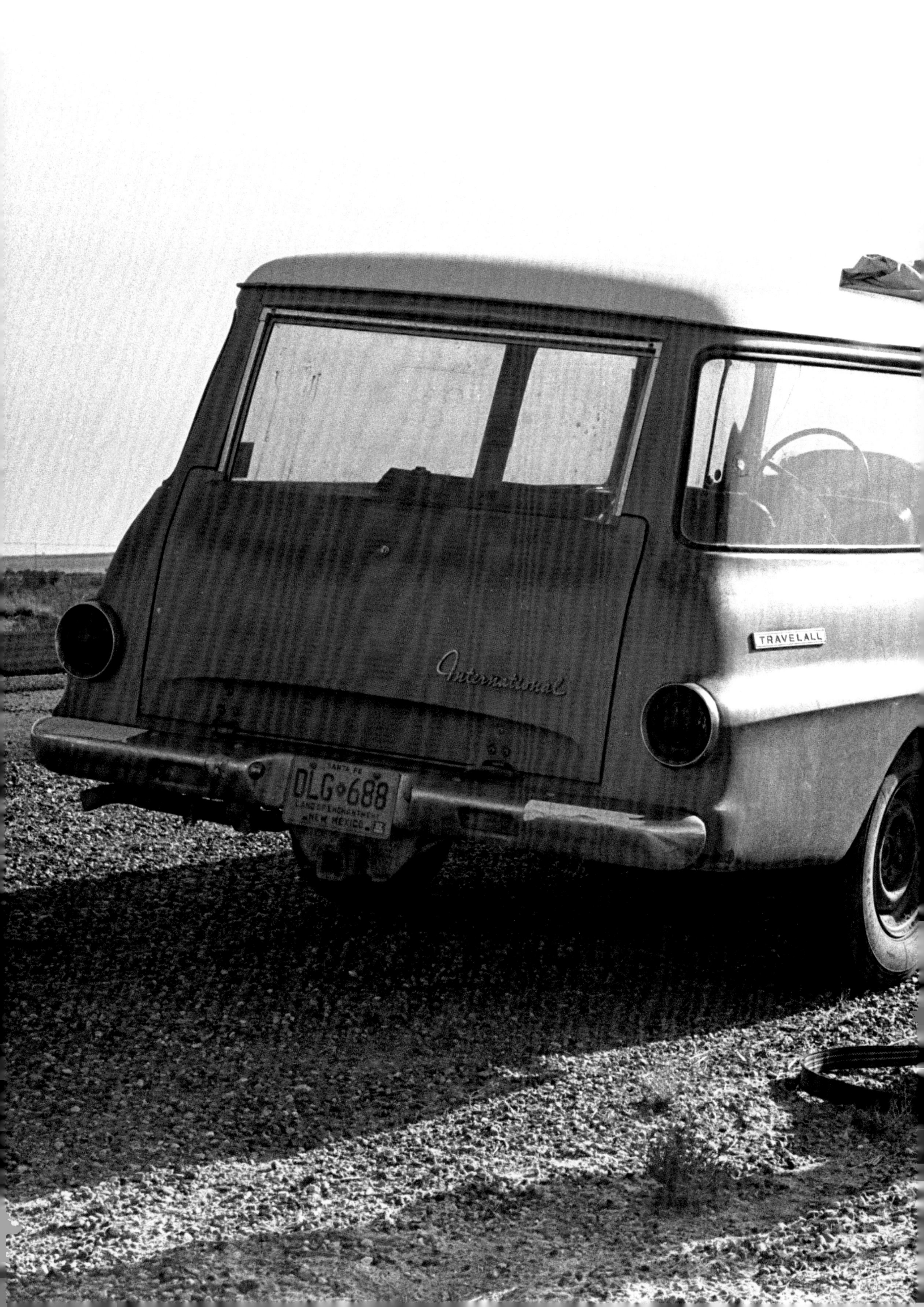
TRAVELALL
International
SANTA FE
DLG 688
LAND OF ENCHANTMENT
NEW MEXICO

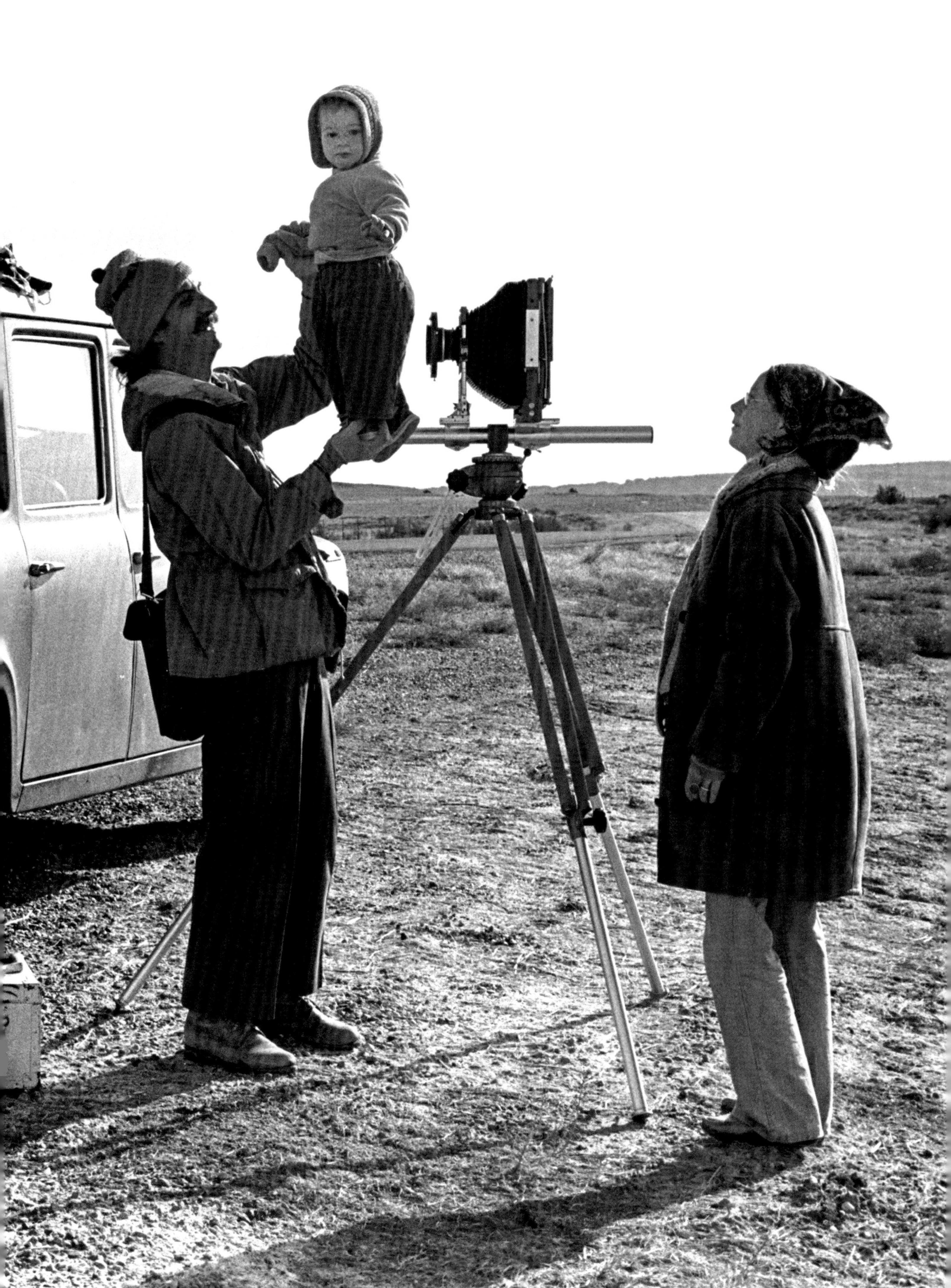

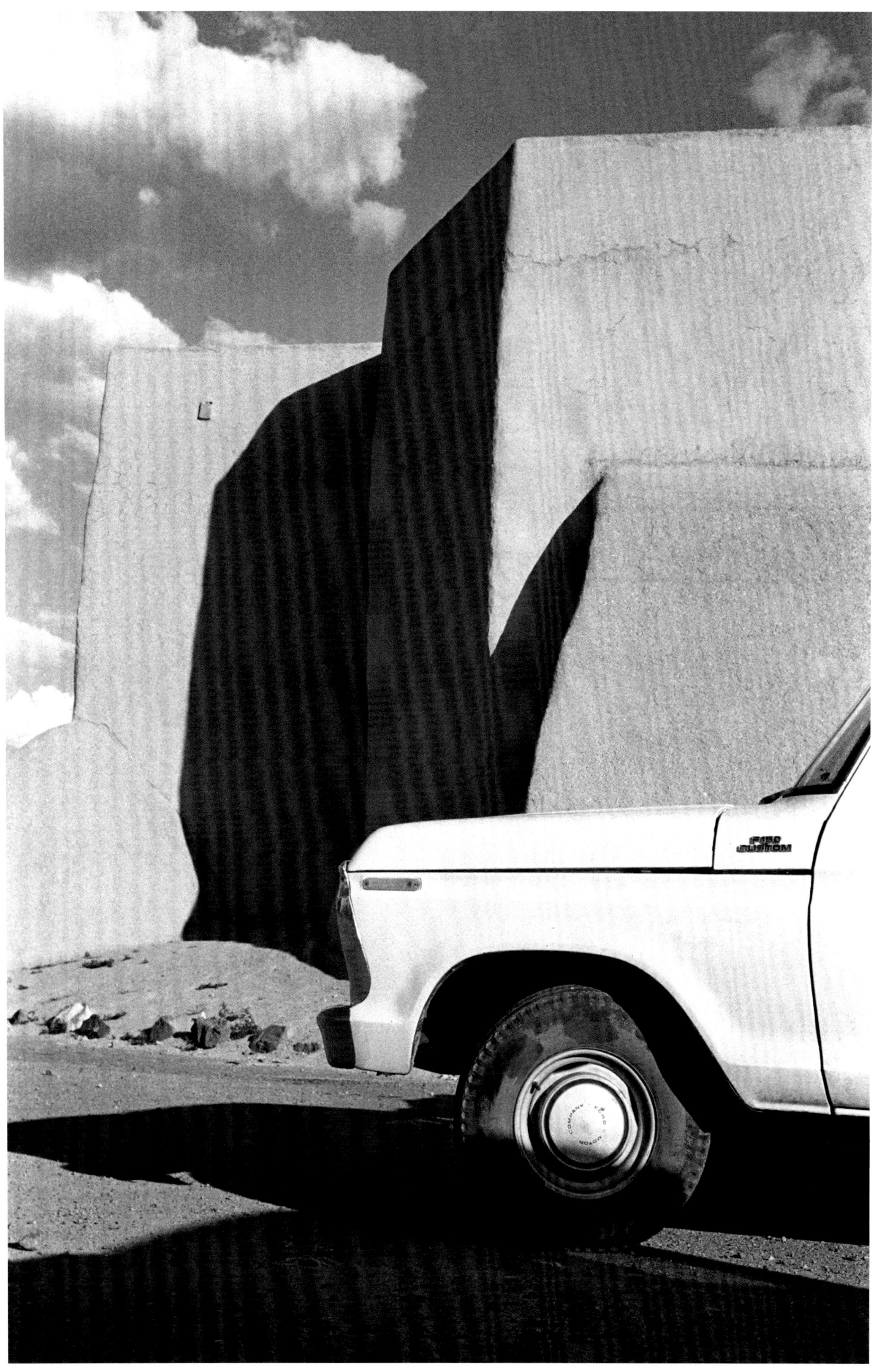

Saint Francis de Asís Mission Church, Ranchos de Taos, 1982.

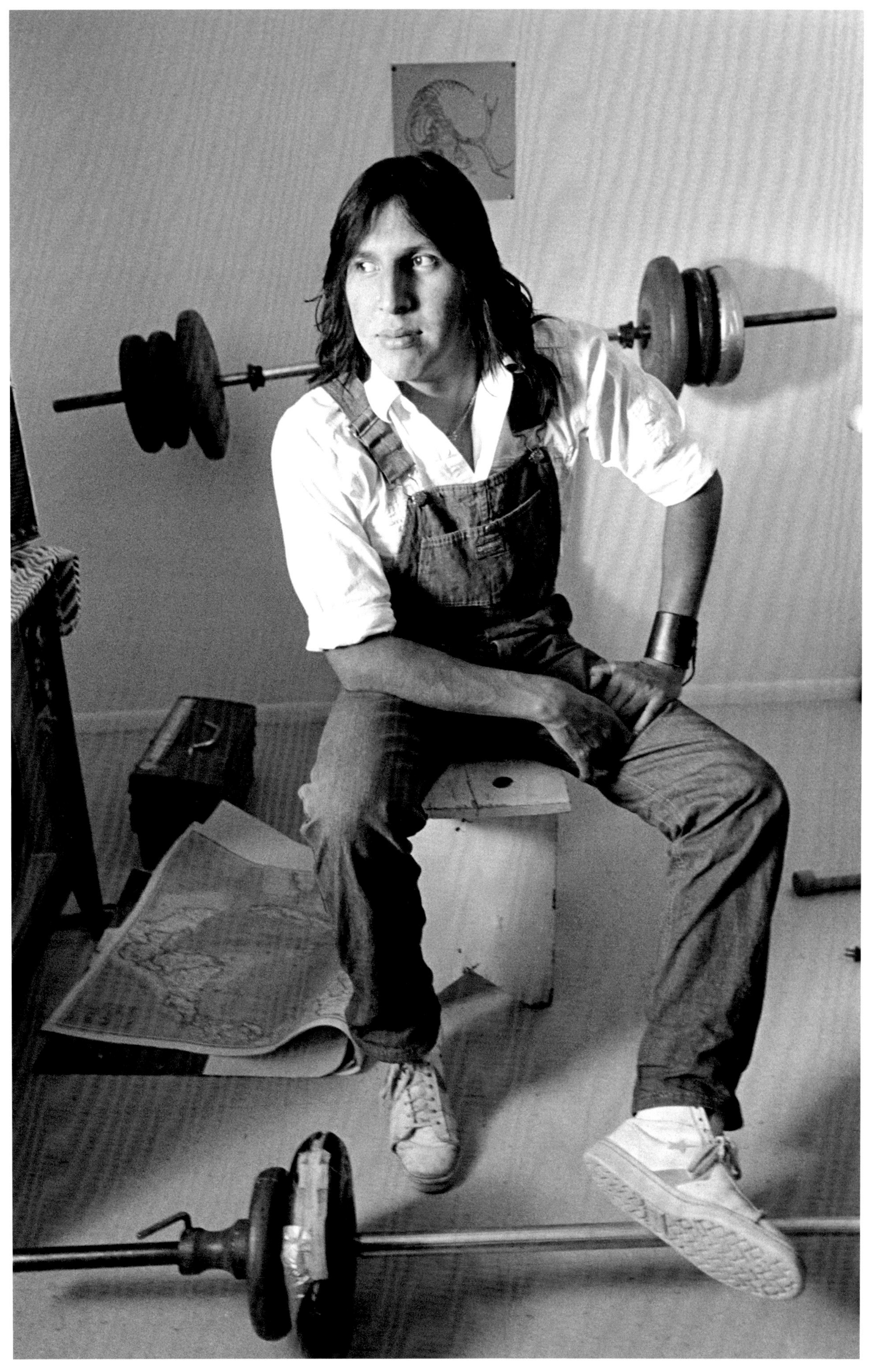

Marvin Garcia, Santa Ana Pueblo, 1983.

OVERLEAF: Marilyn Garcia and Marvin Garcia at the Mission Church of Santa Ana, Santa Ana Pueblo, 1983.

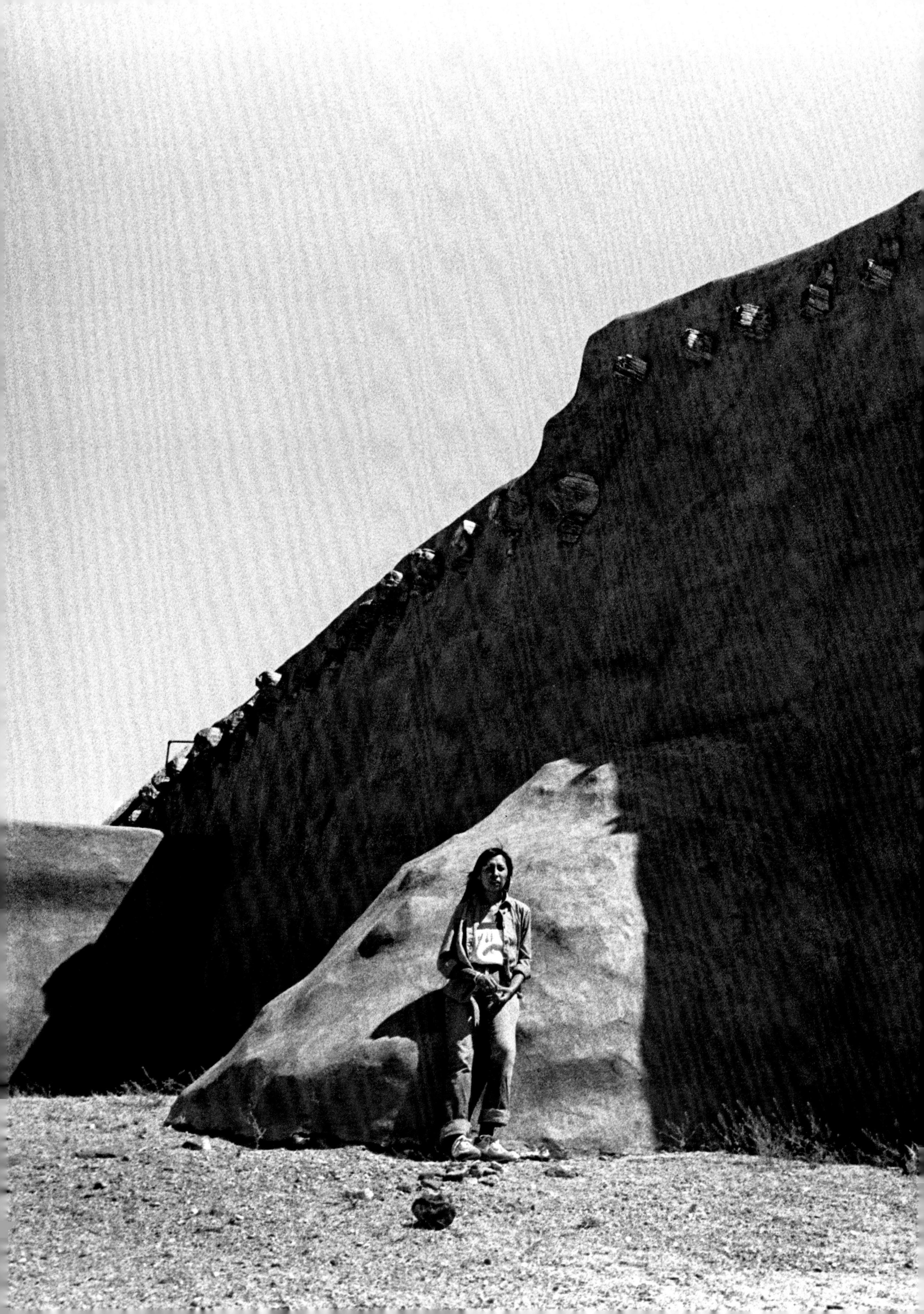

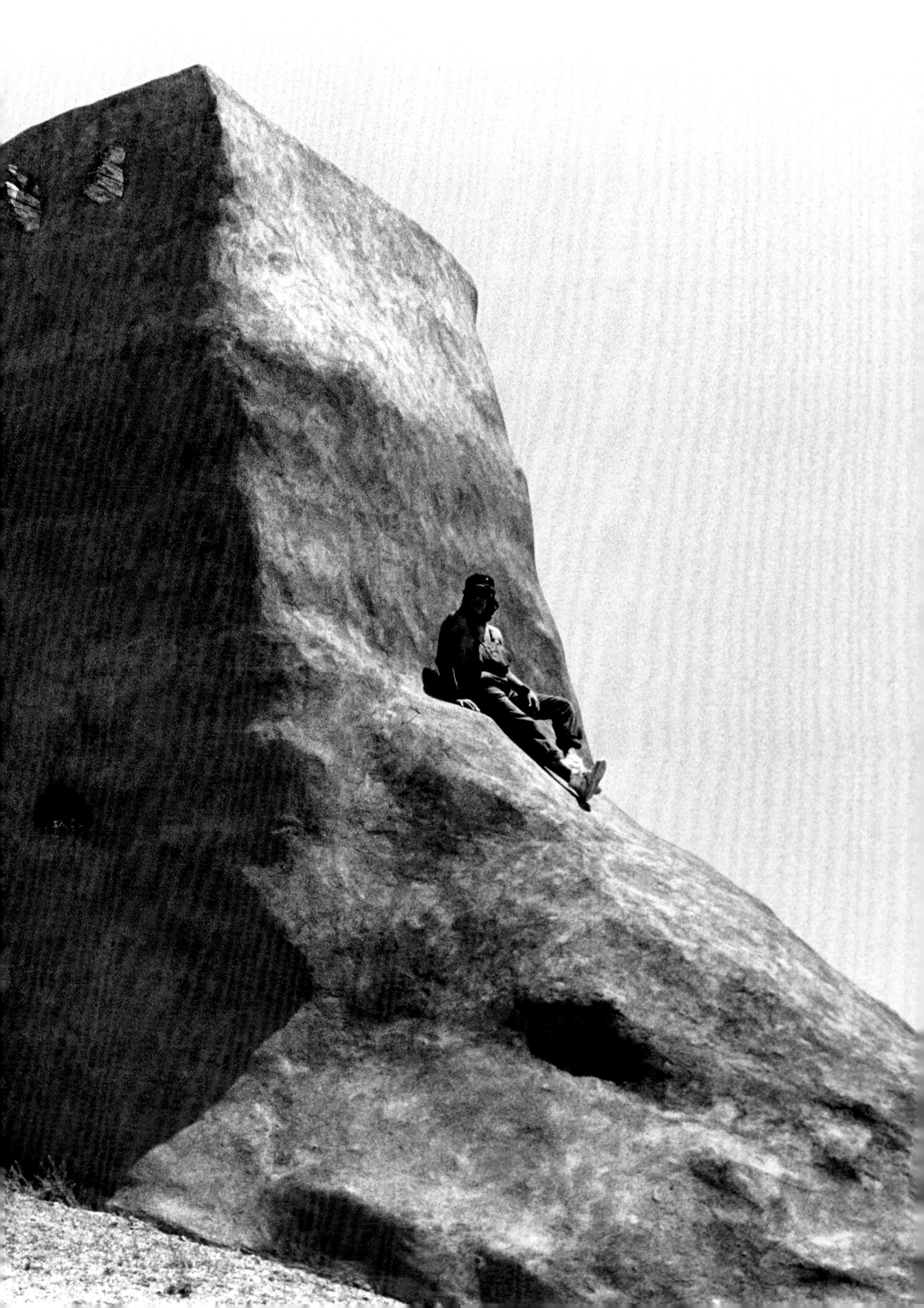

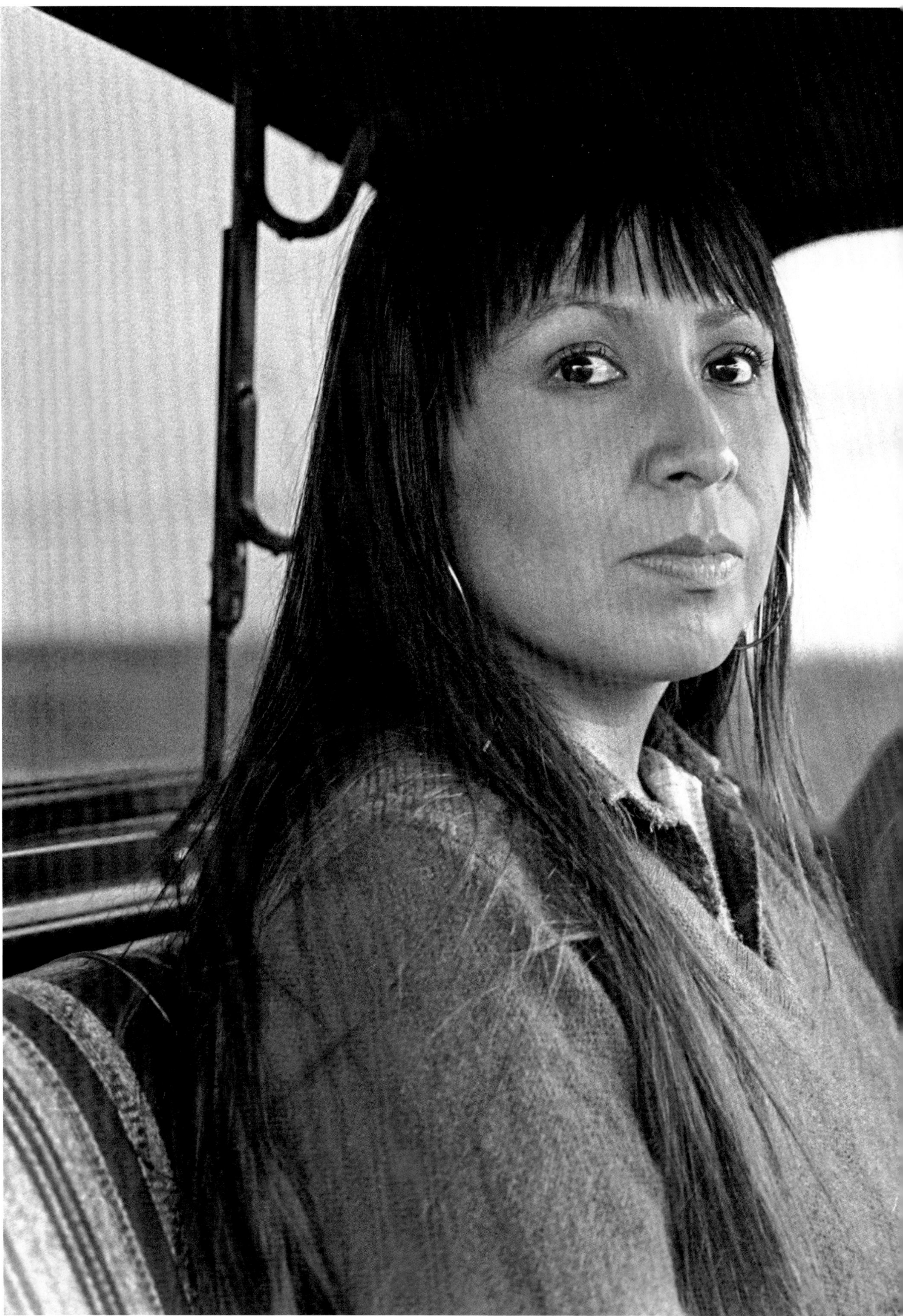

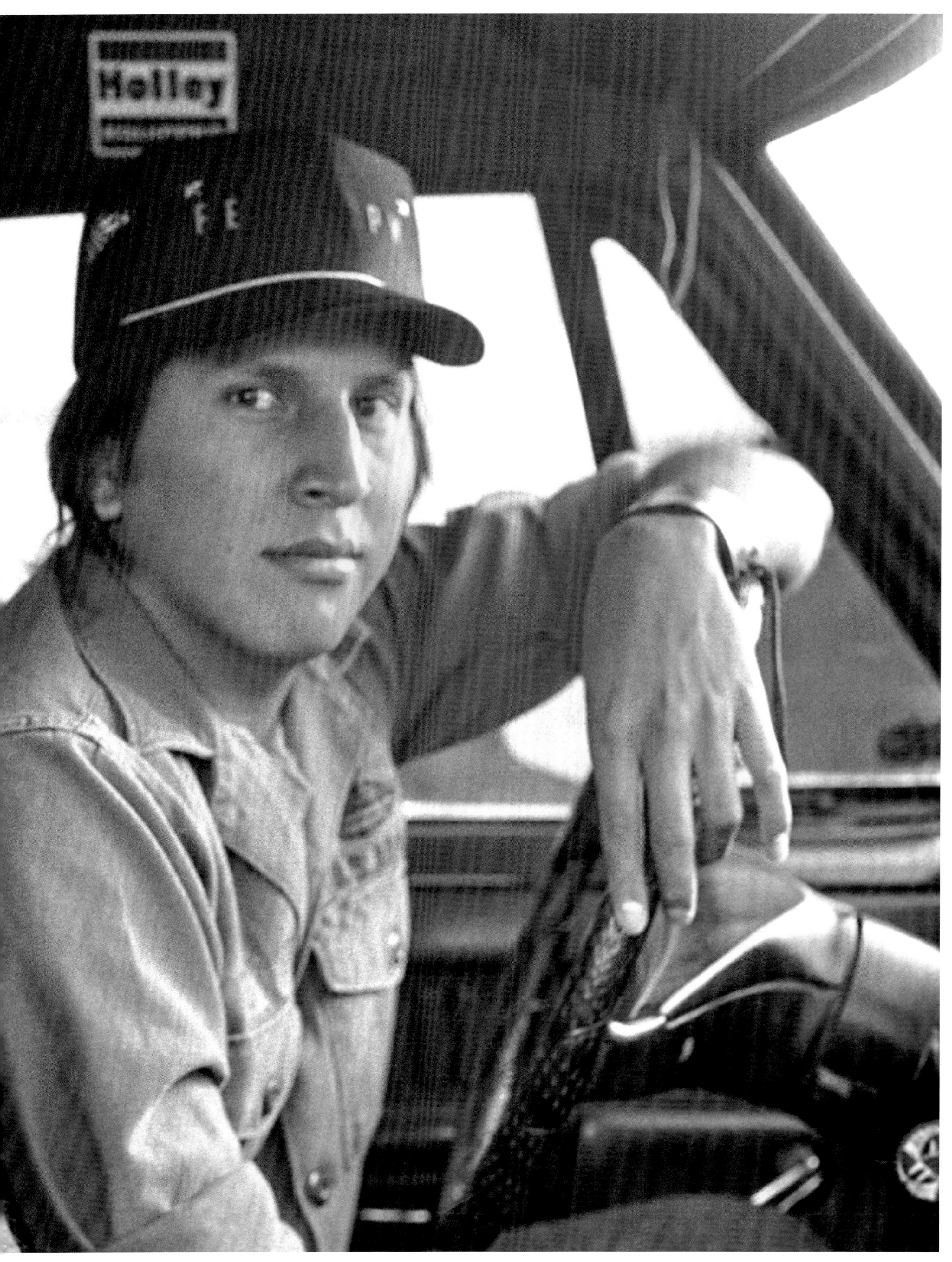

Marilyn Garcia and her brother Marvin, Santa Ana Pueblo, 1983.

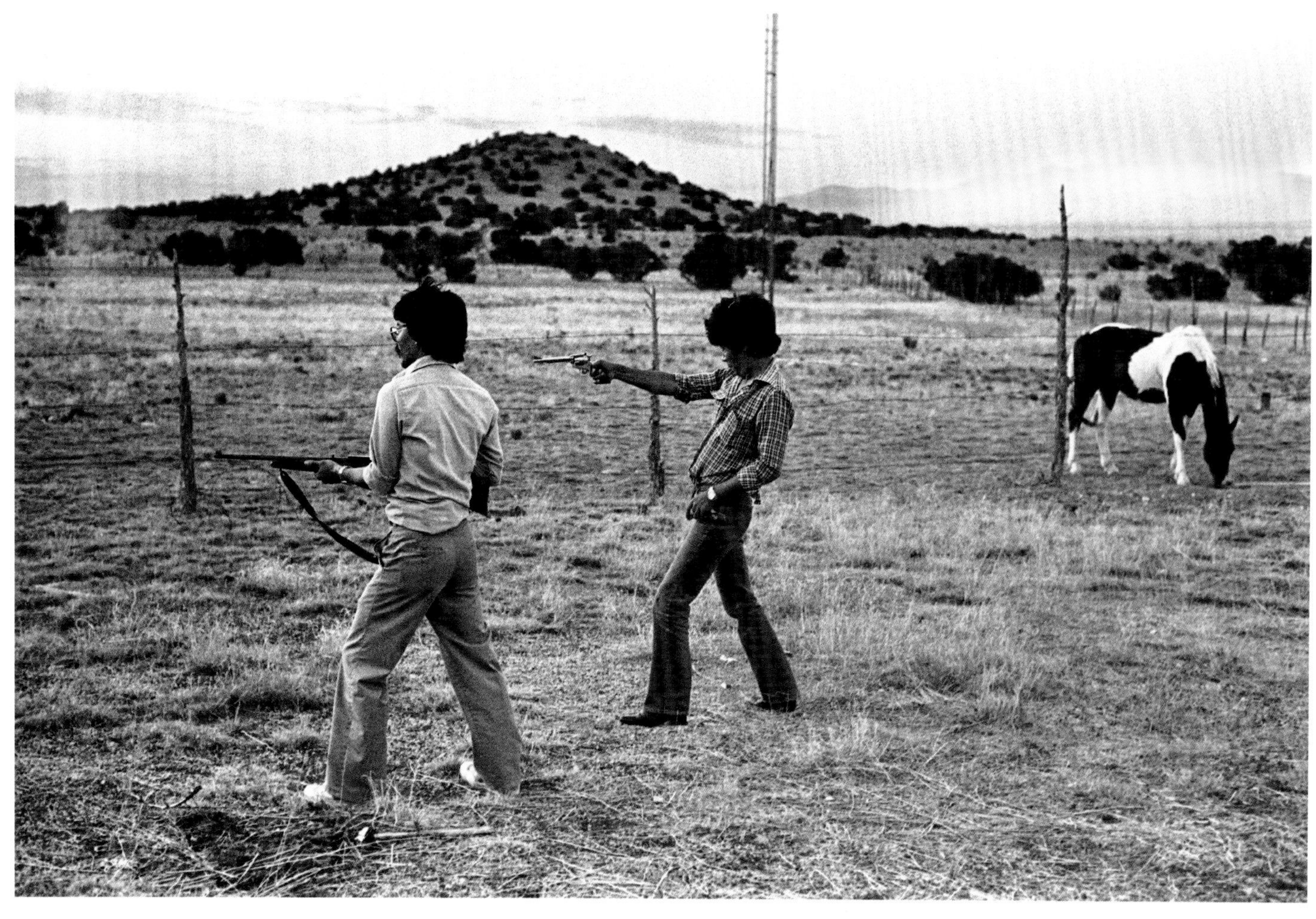

Pema Rabgay and Paljor Thondup, Synergia Ranch, Santa Fe, 1982.

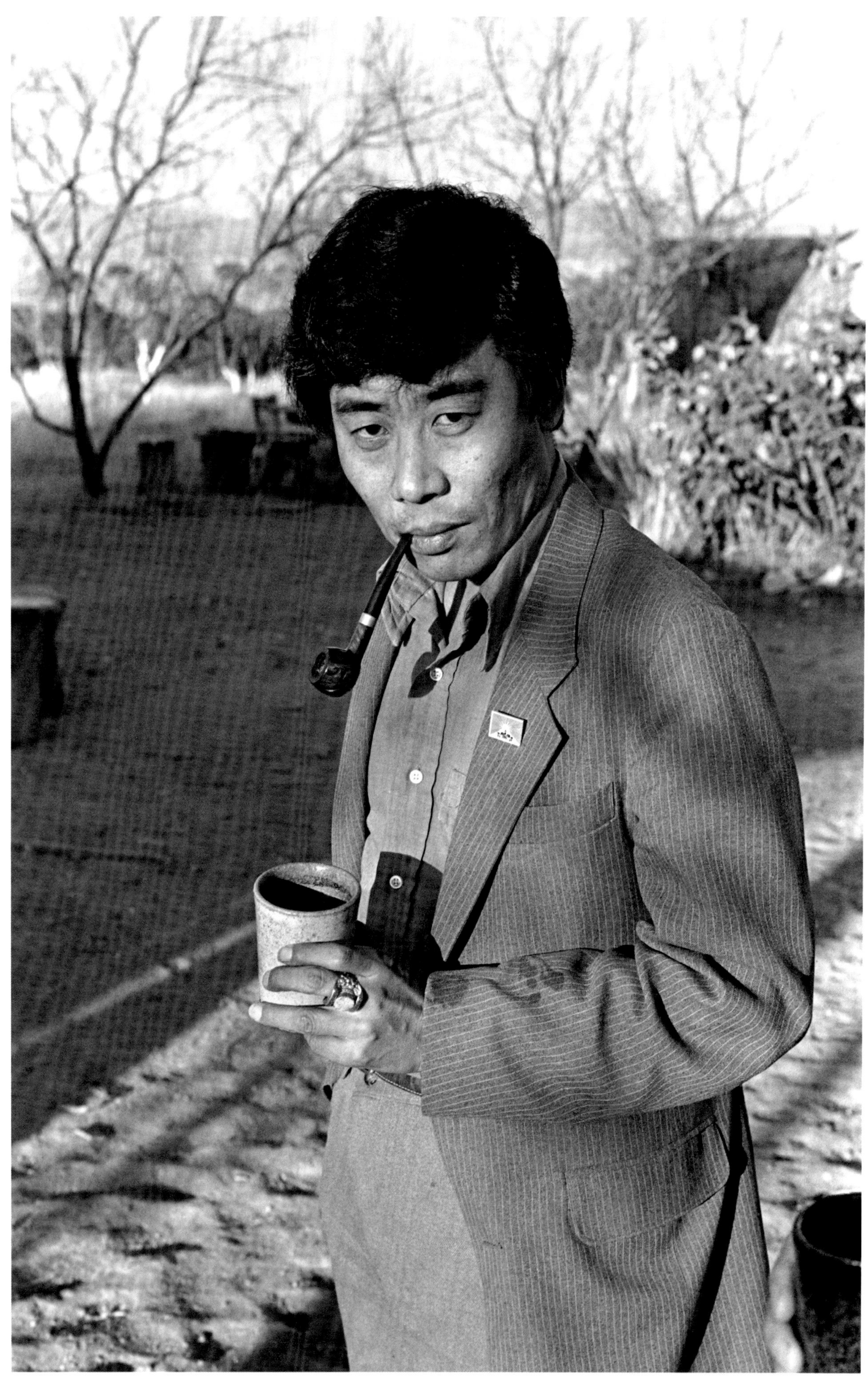

Paljor Thondup, Synergia Ranch, Santa Fe, 1982.

OVERLEAF: Puye Cliff Dwellings, Santa Clara Canyon, Santa Clara Pueblo, 1982.

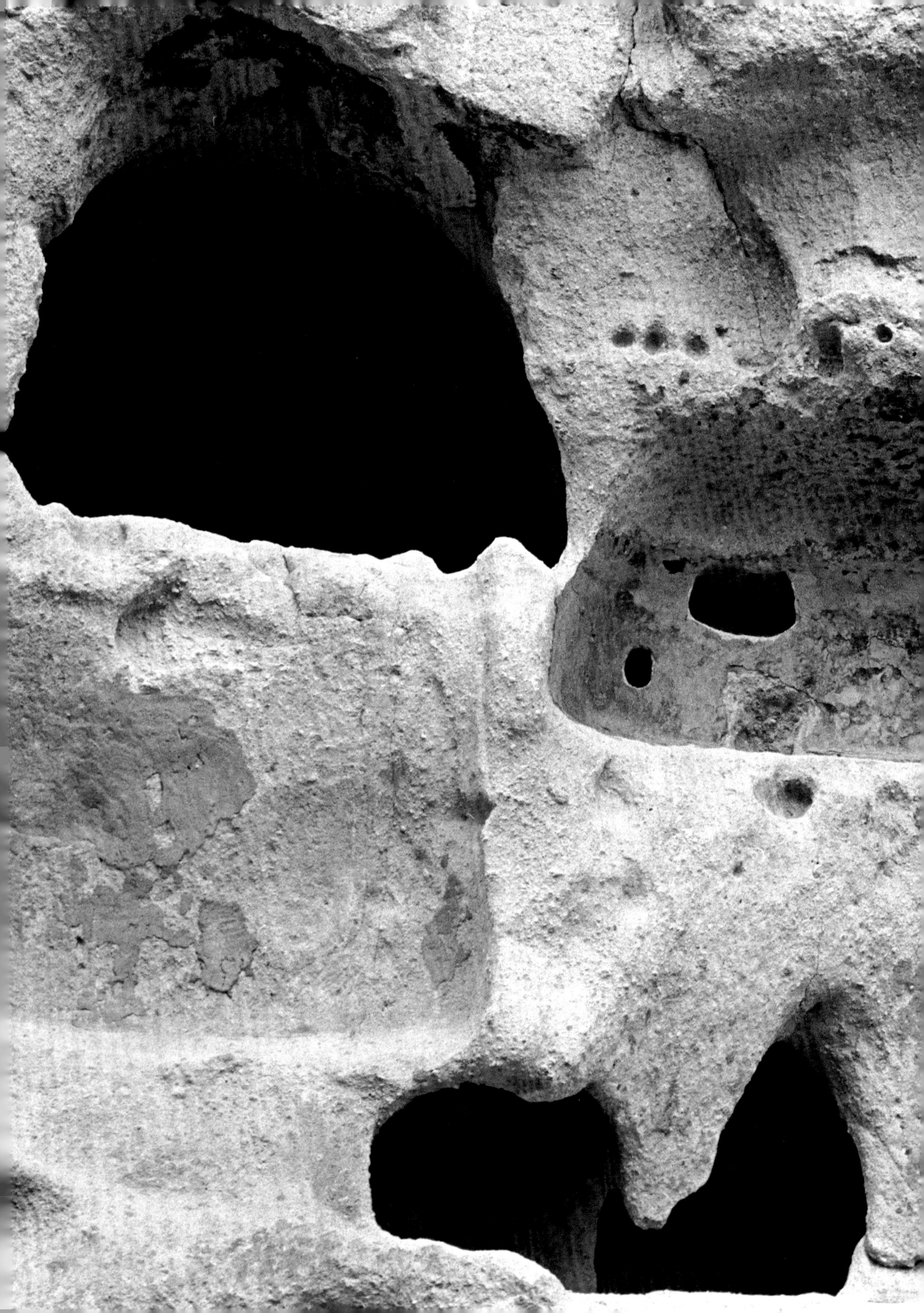

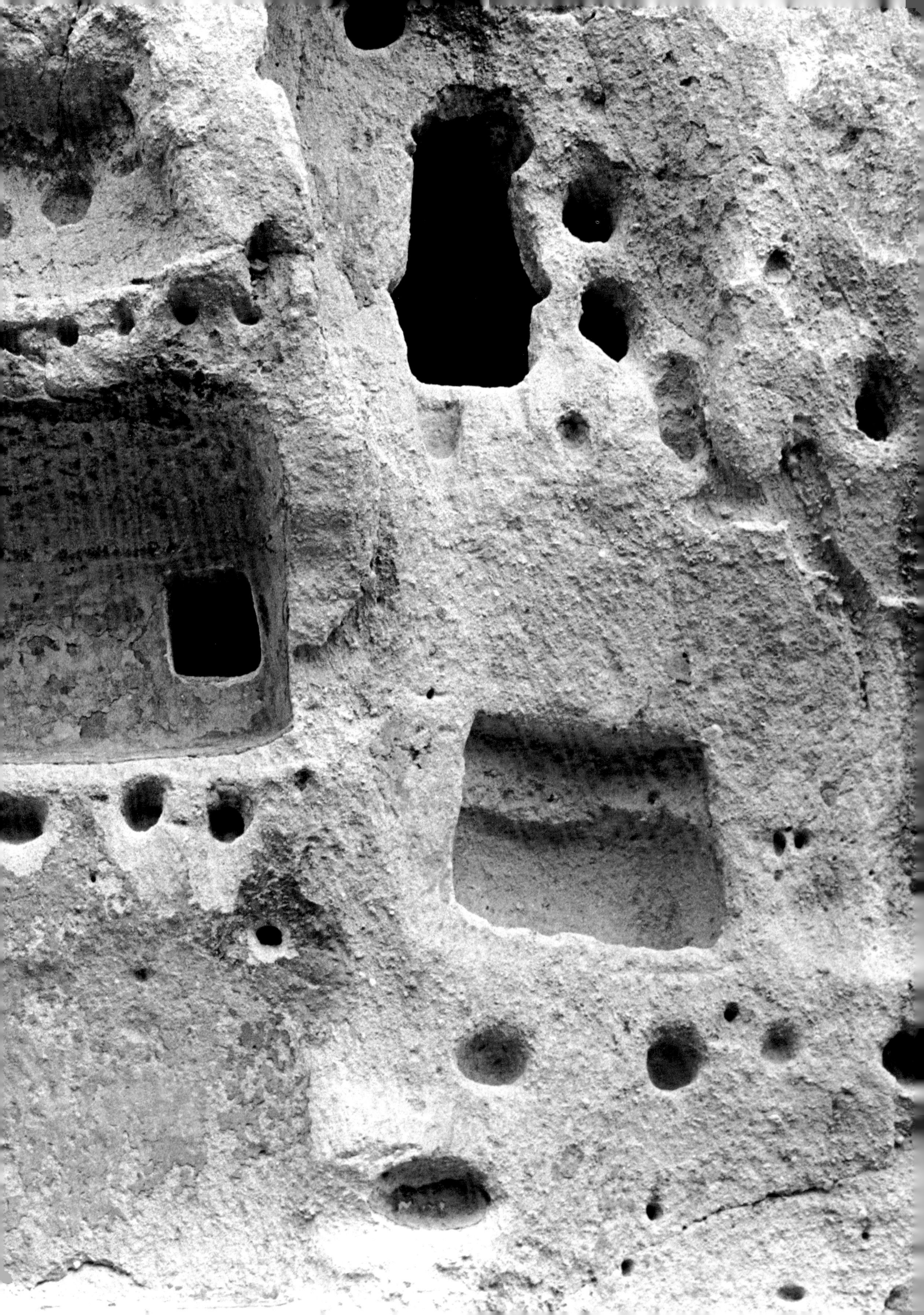

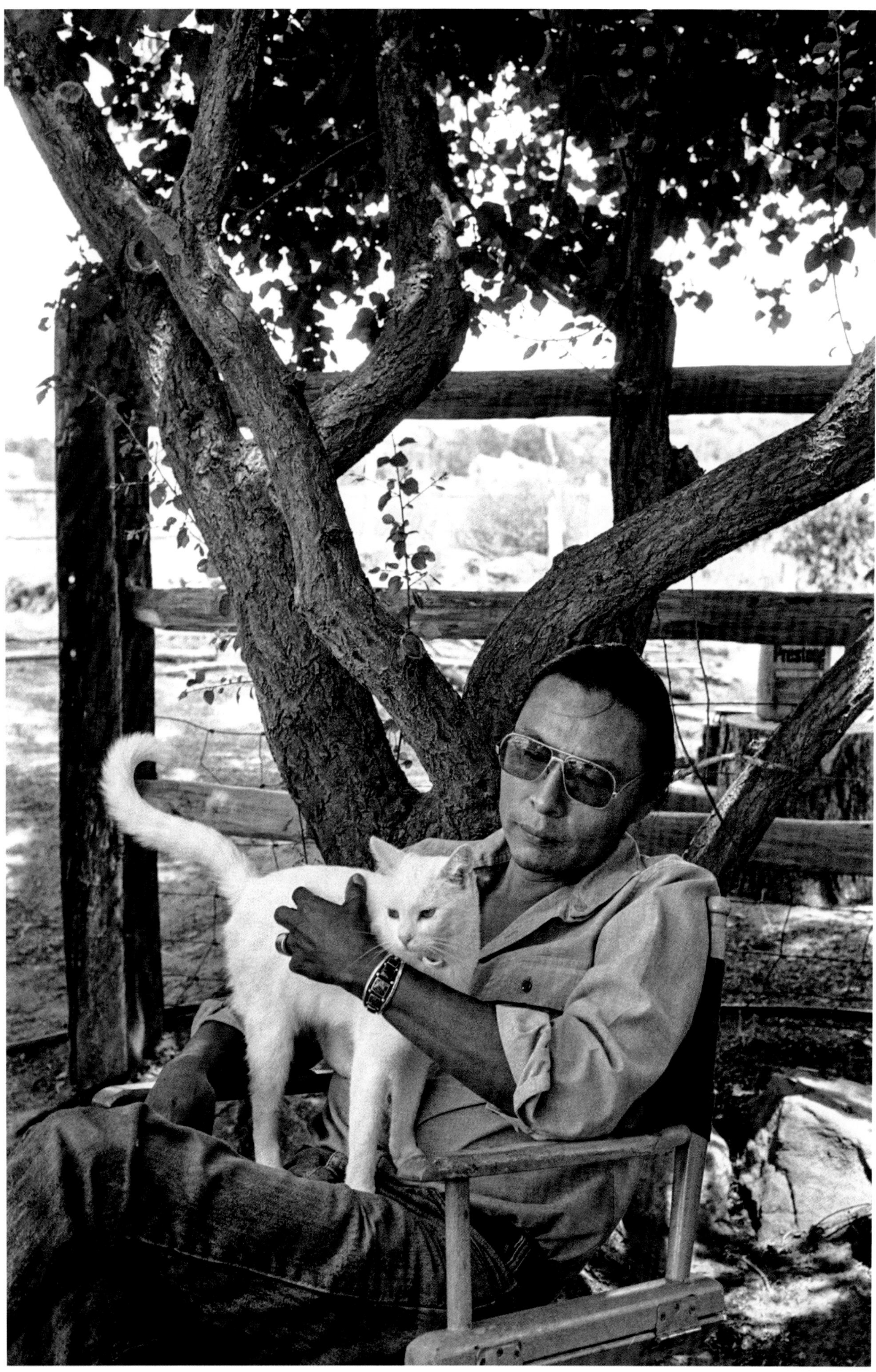

Diné jewelry artist Yazzie Johnson, Velarde, 1982.

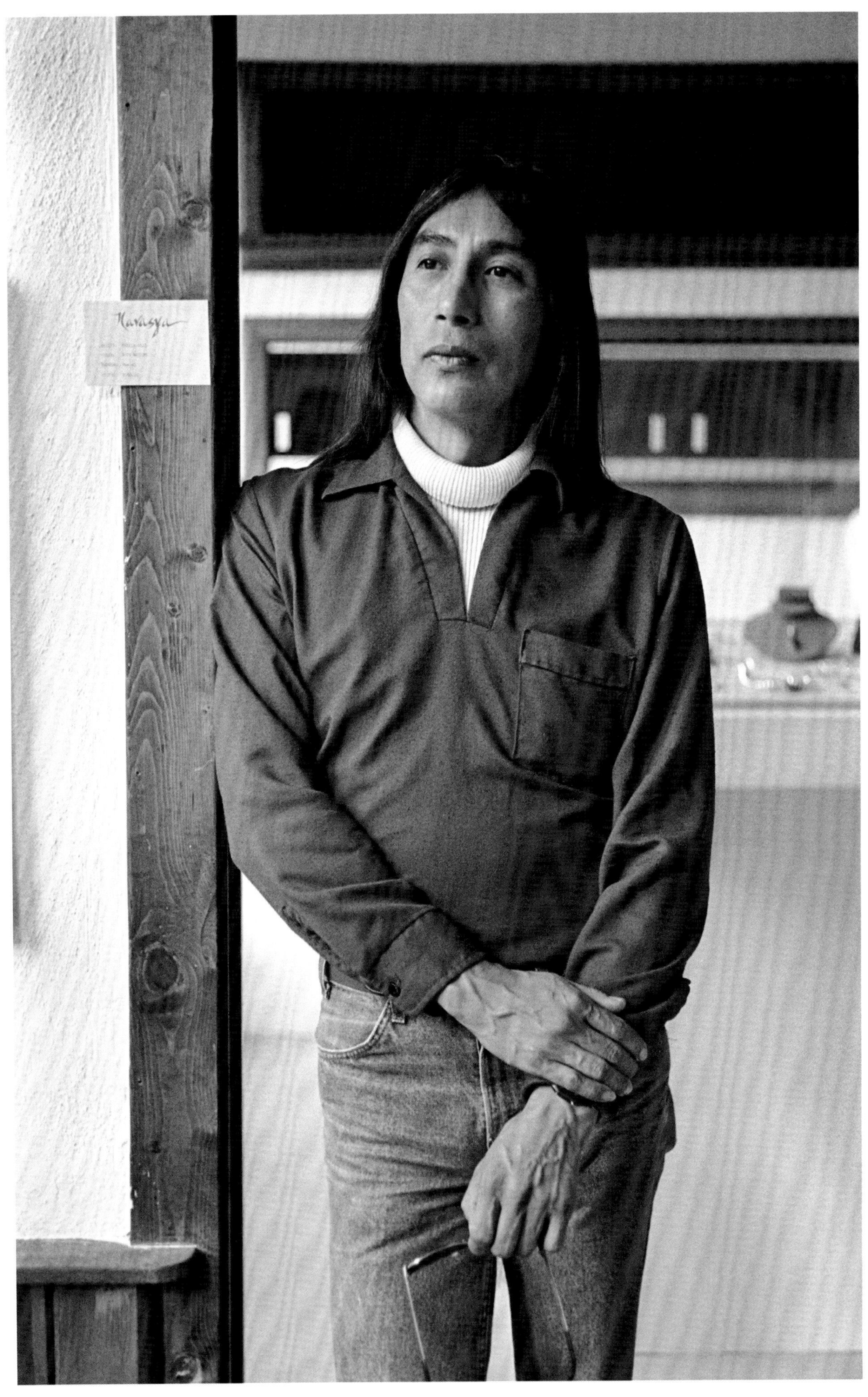

Hopi artist Phil Navasya, Santa Fe, 1982.

OVERLEAF: Chimayó, 1981.

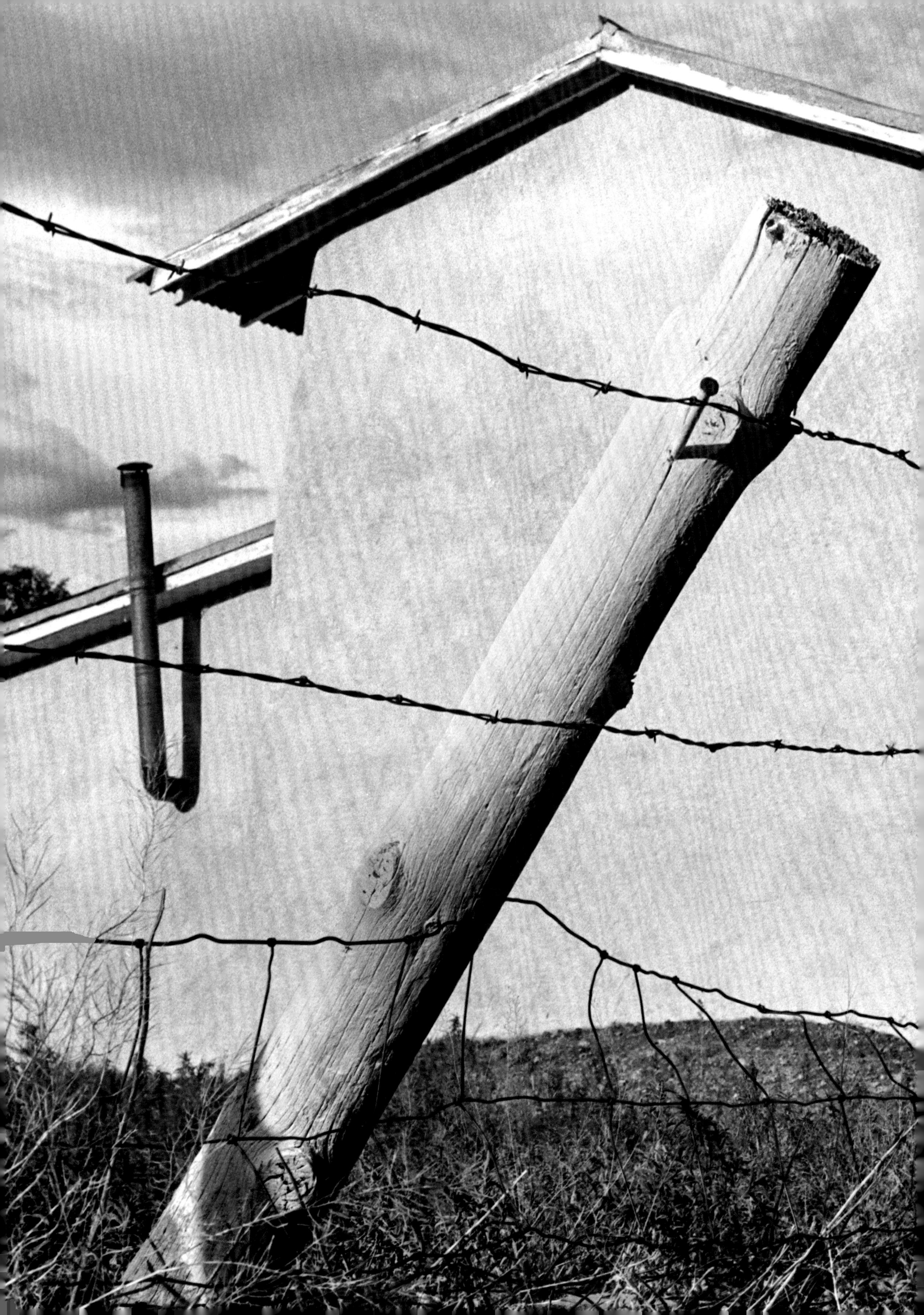

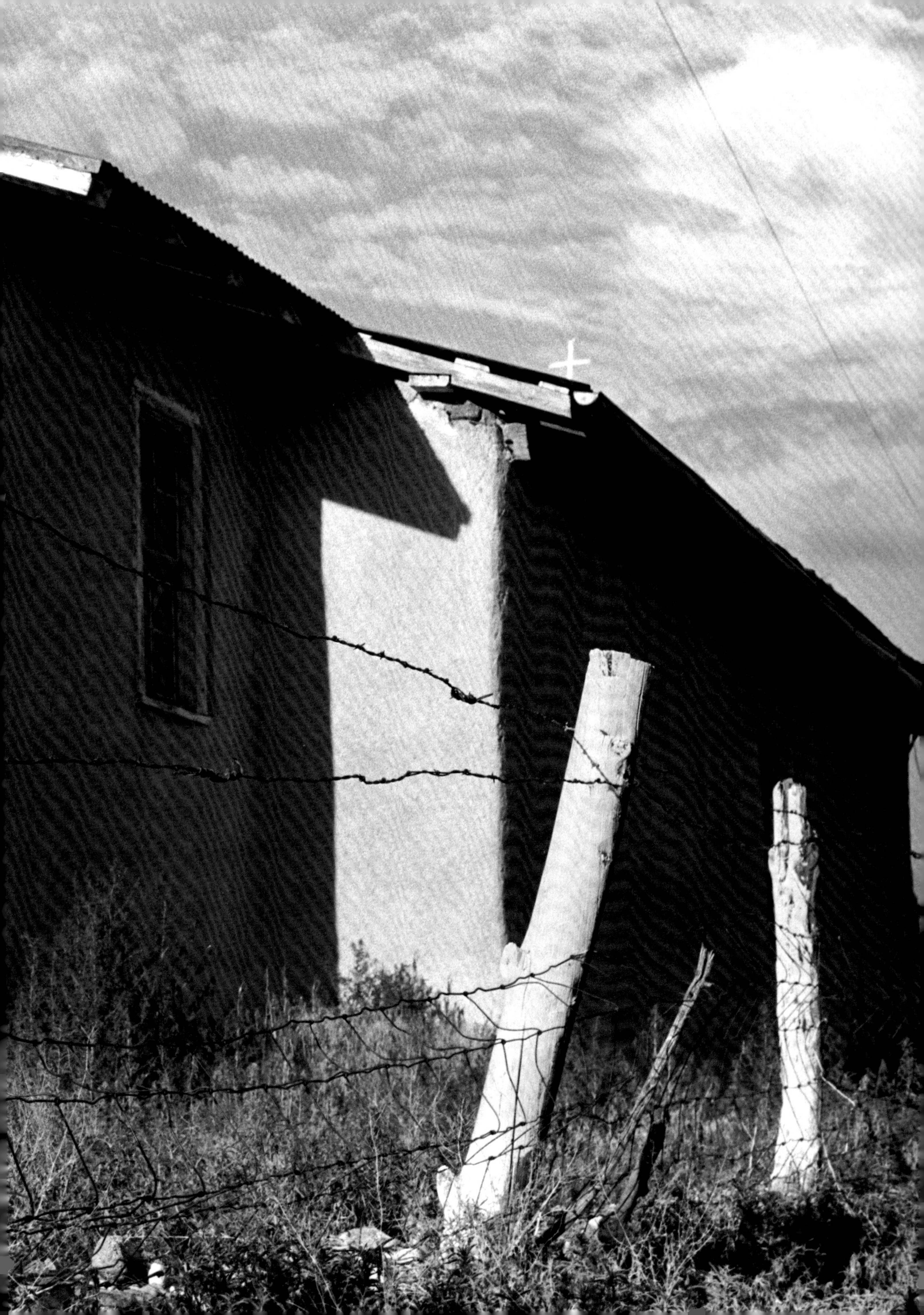

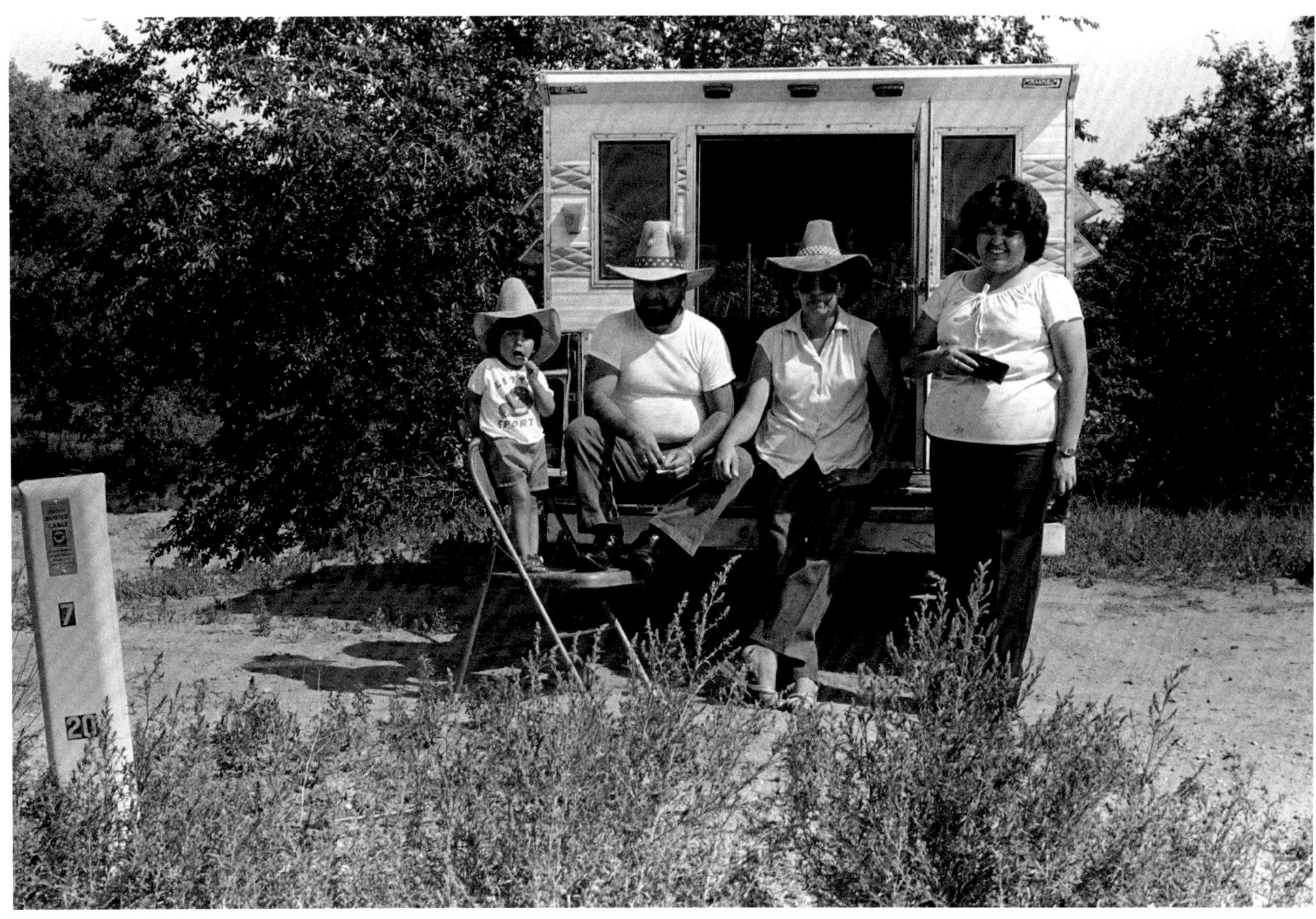

Fiesta de los Moros y Cristianos, Chimayó, 1981.

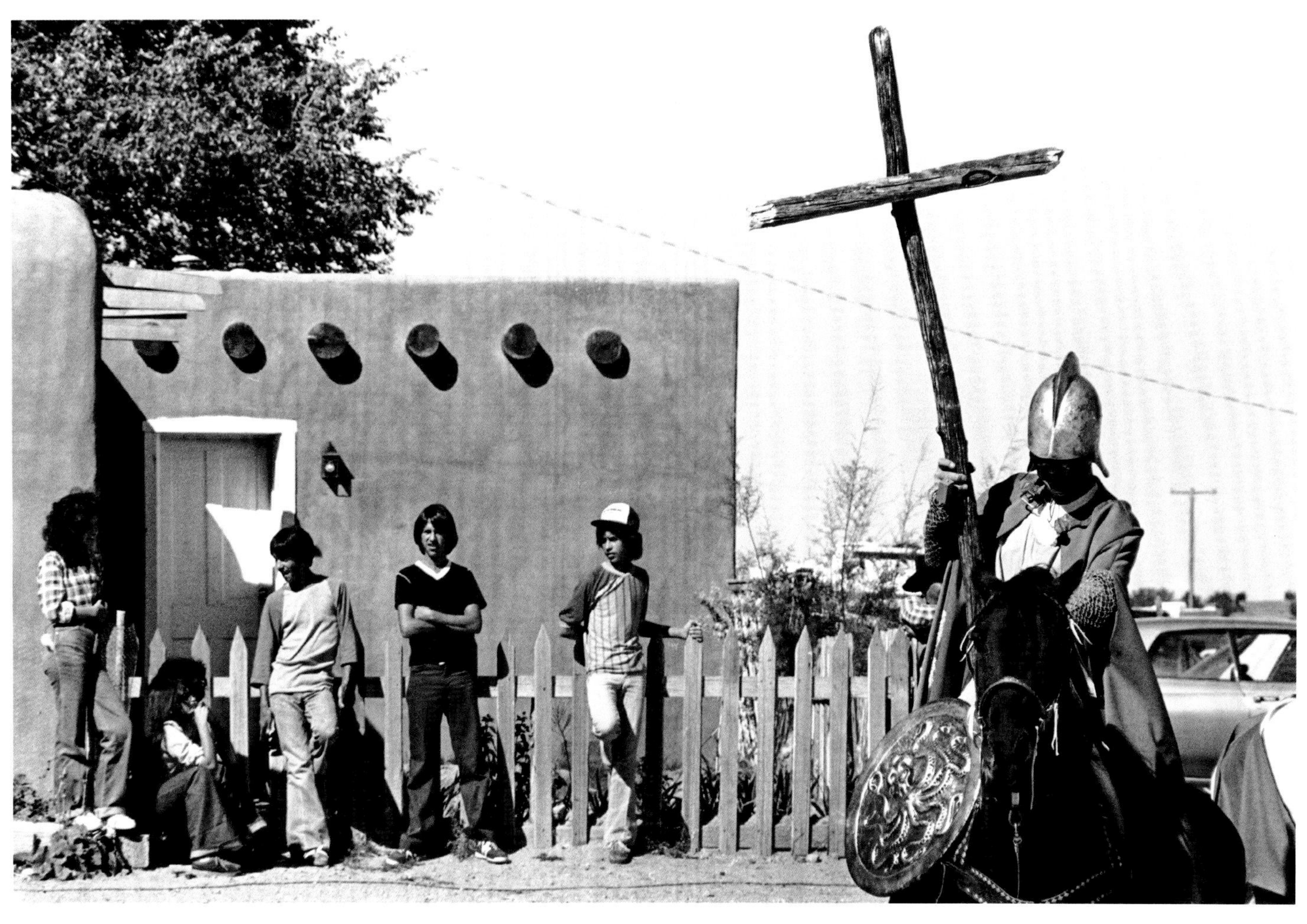

Fiesta de los Moros y Cristianos, Chimayó, 1981.

OVERLEAF: Percy Lujan preparing for Fiesta de los Moros y Cristianos, Chimayó, 1981.

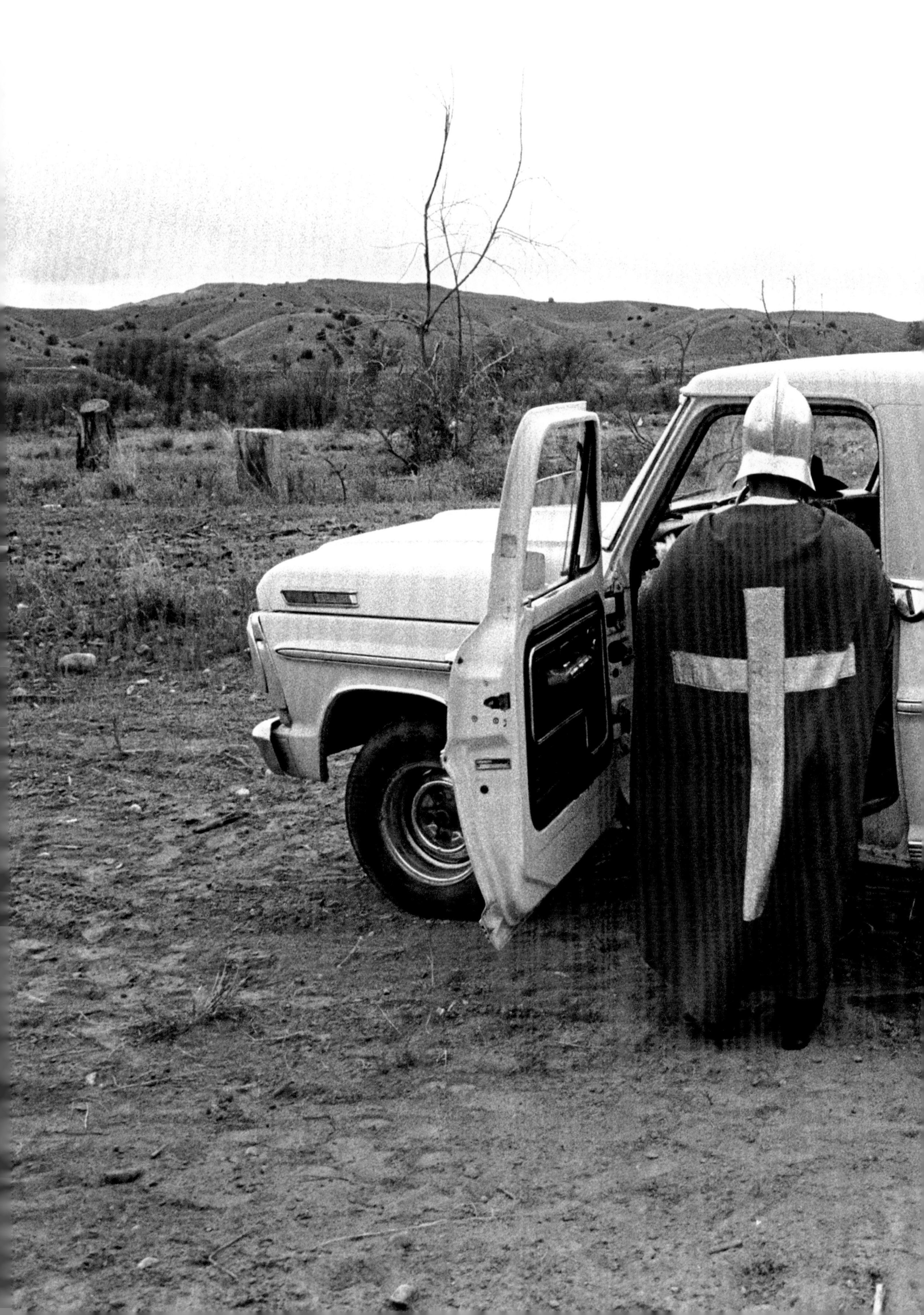

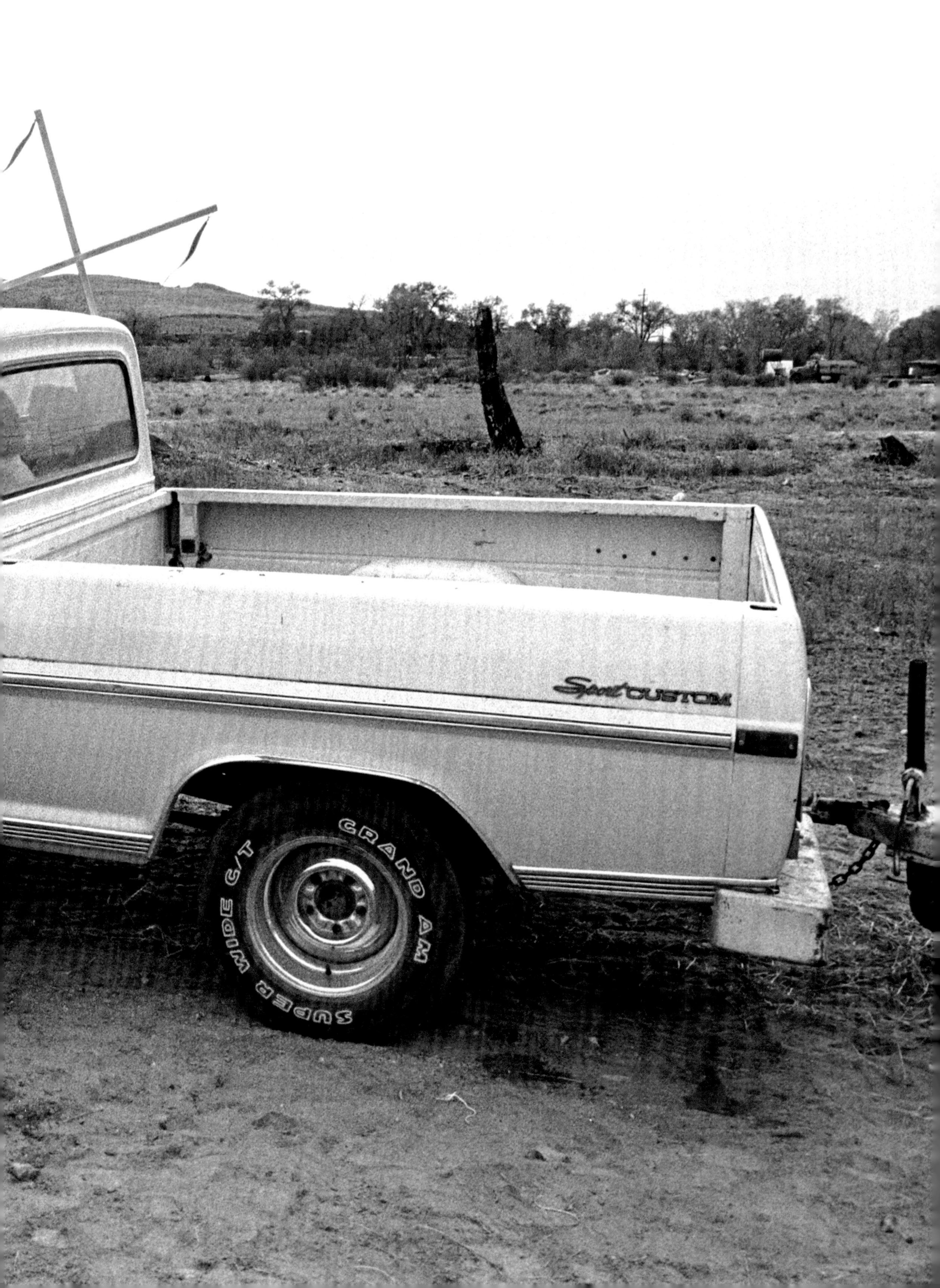
Sport CUSTOM
GRAND AM
SUPER WIDE G/T

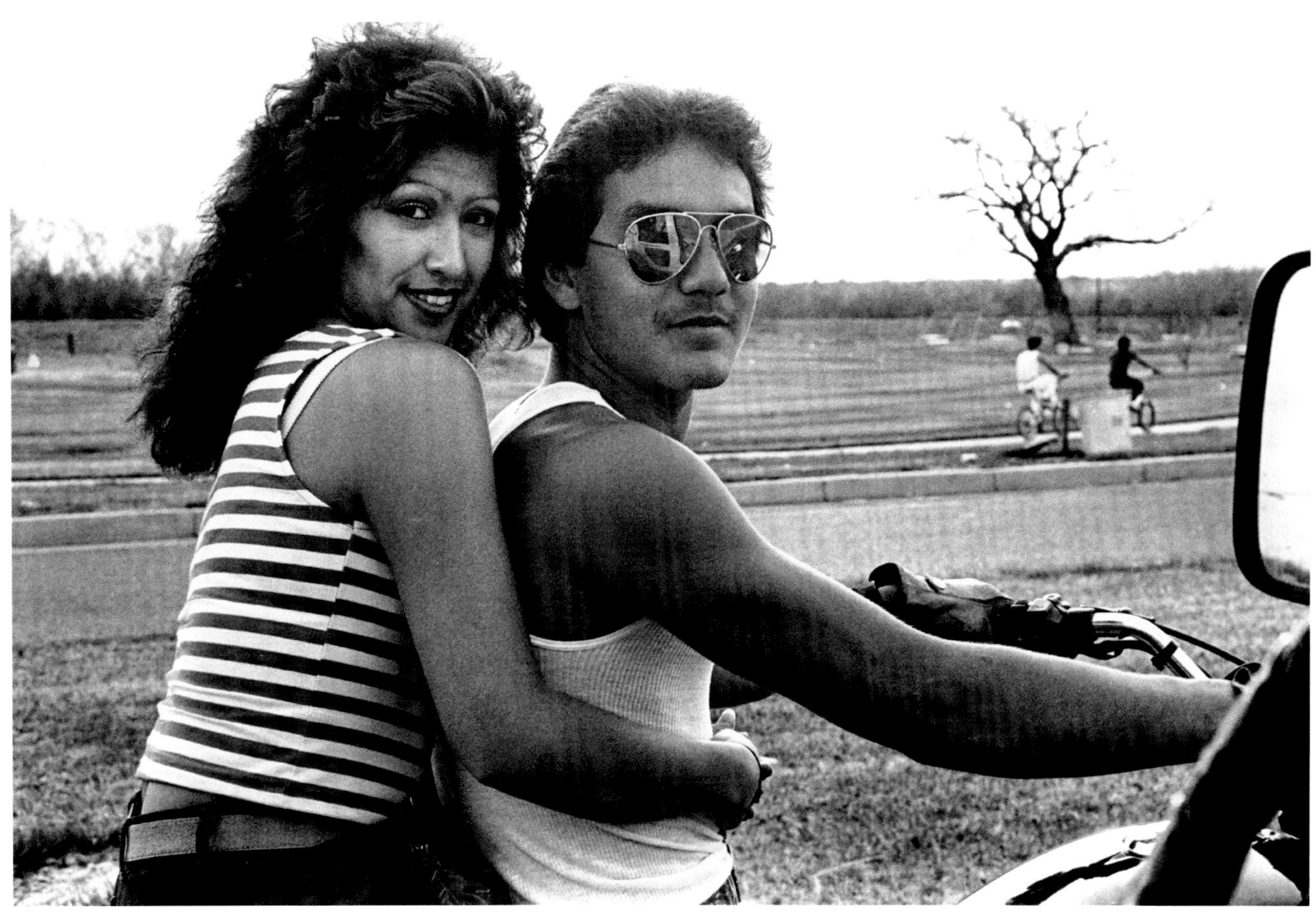

South Valley, Albuquerque, 1981.

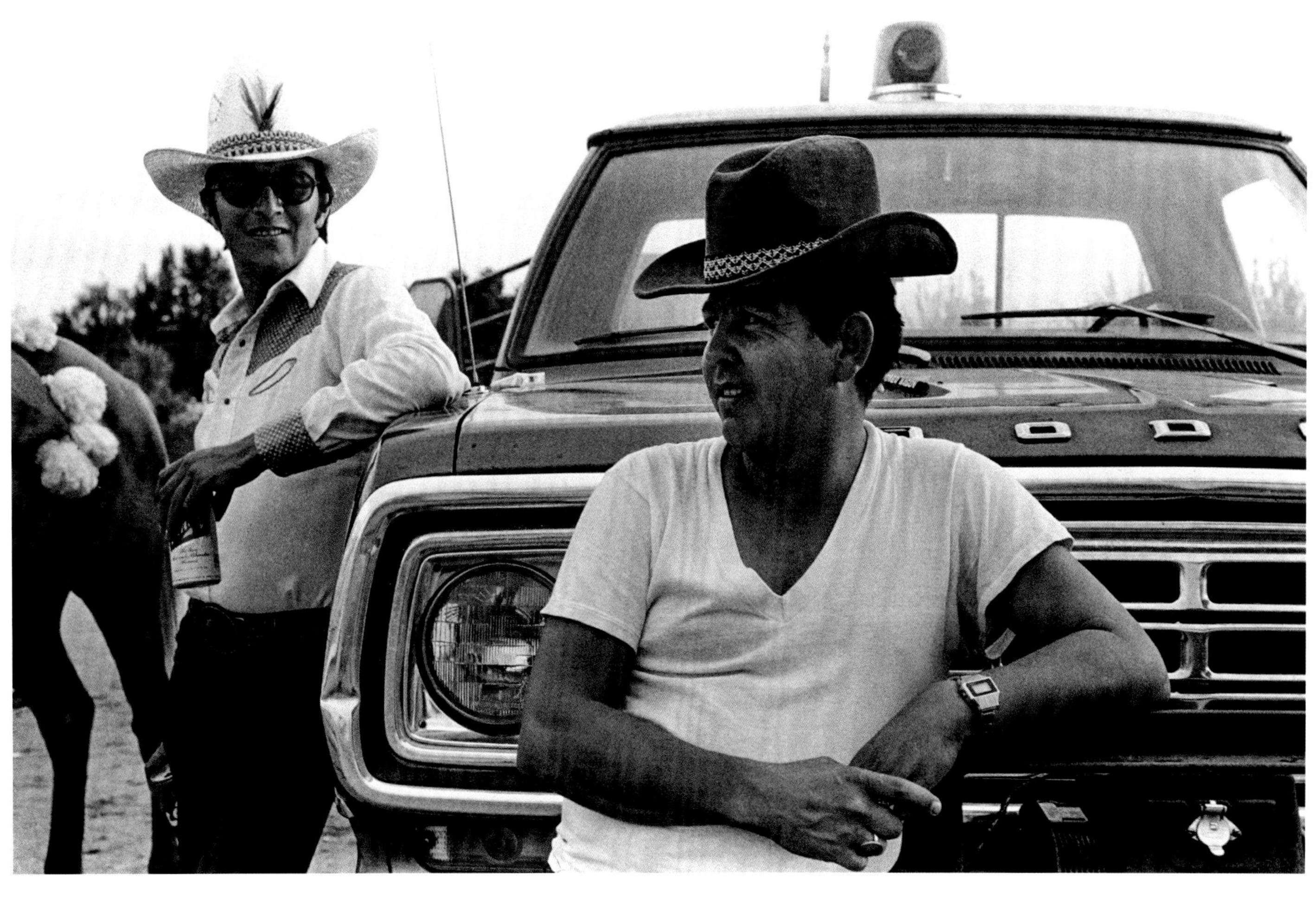

Chimayó, 1981.

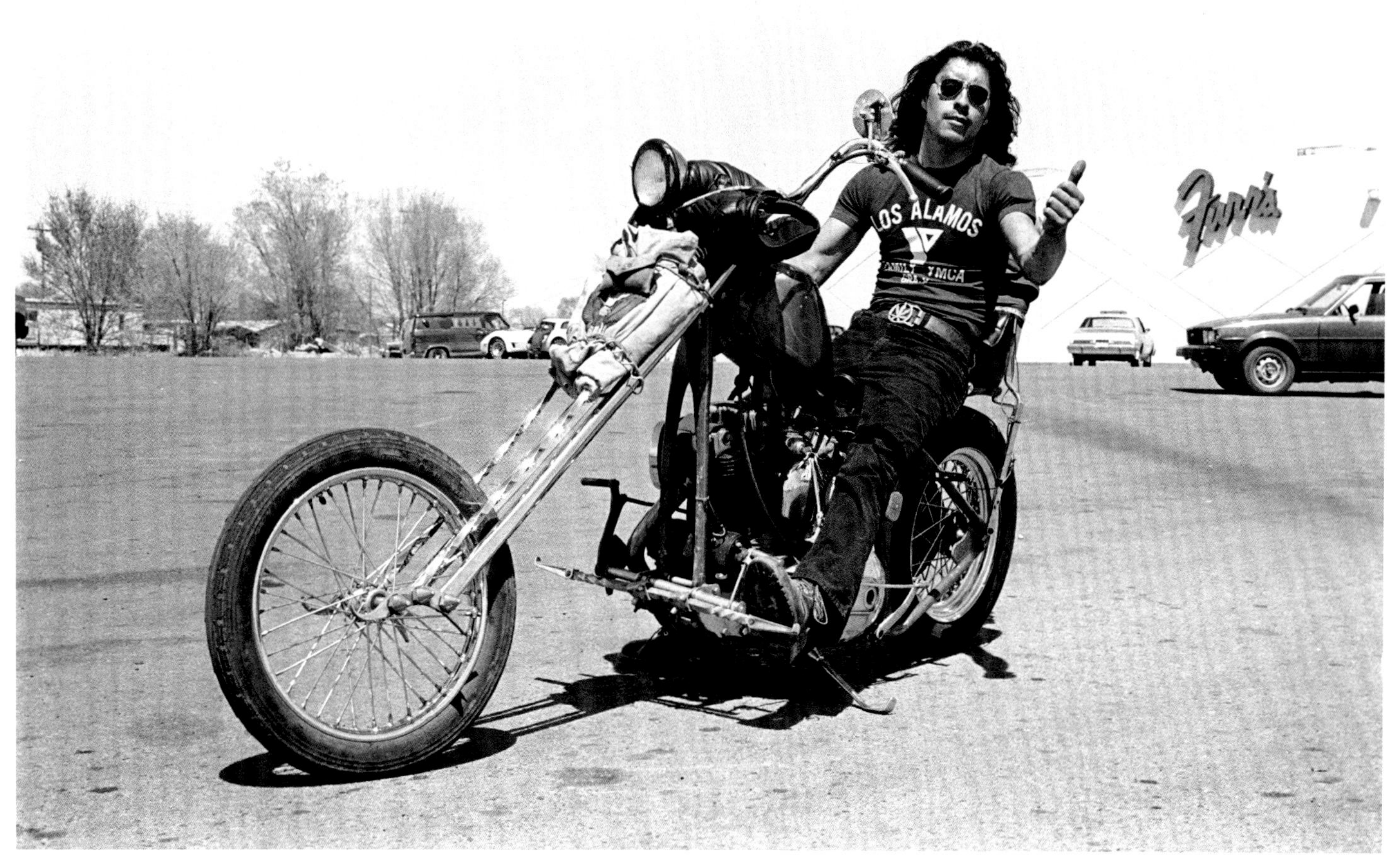

ABOVE AND OPPOSITE: Española, 1981.

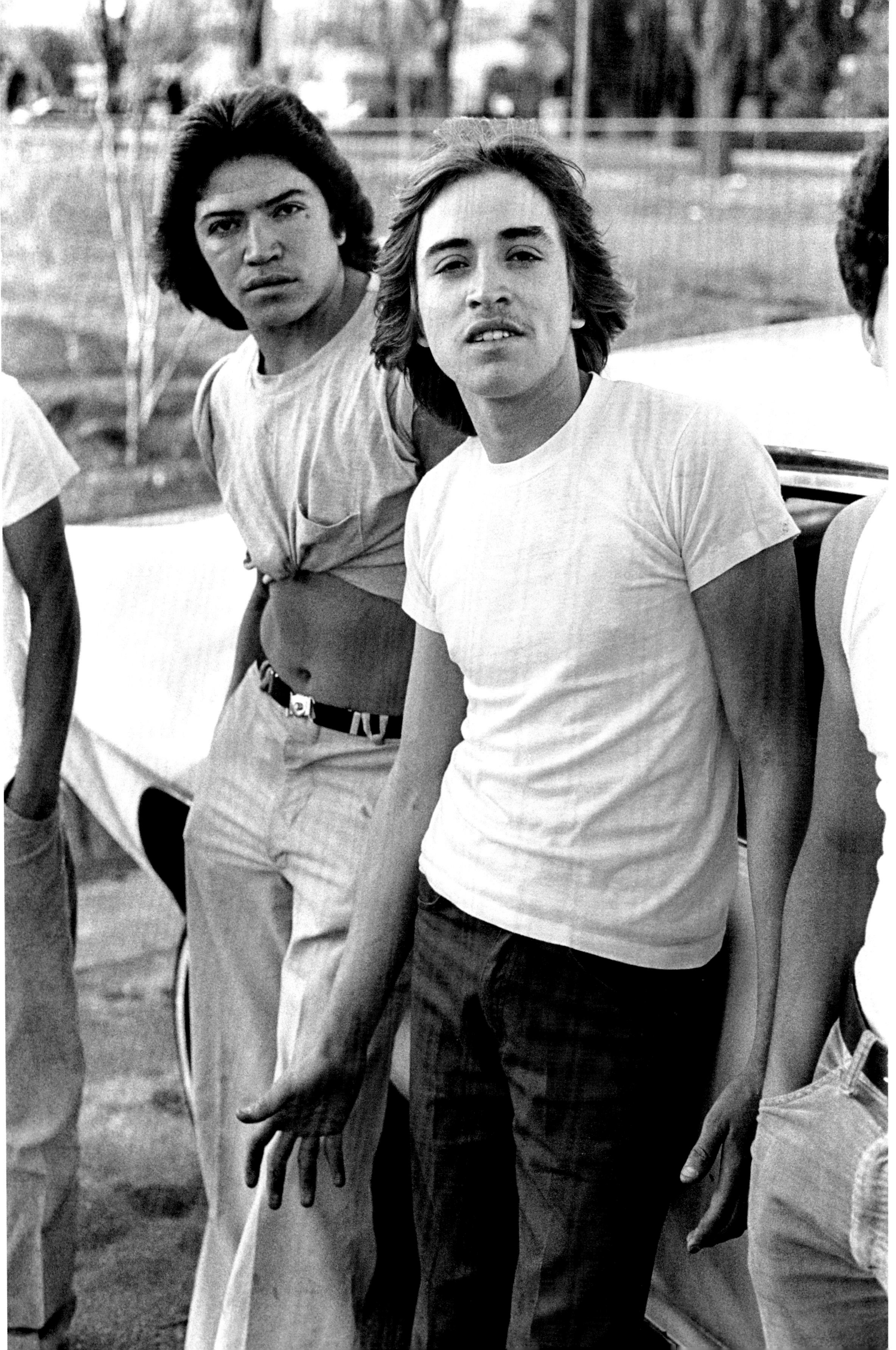

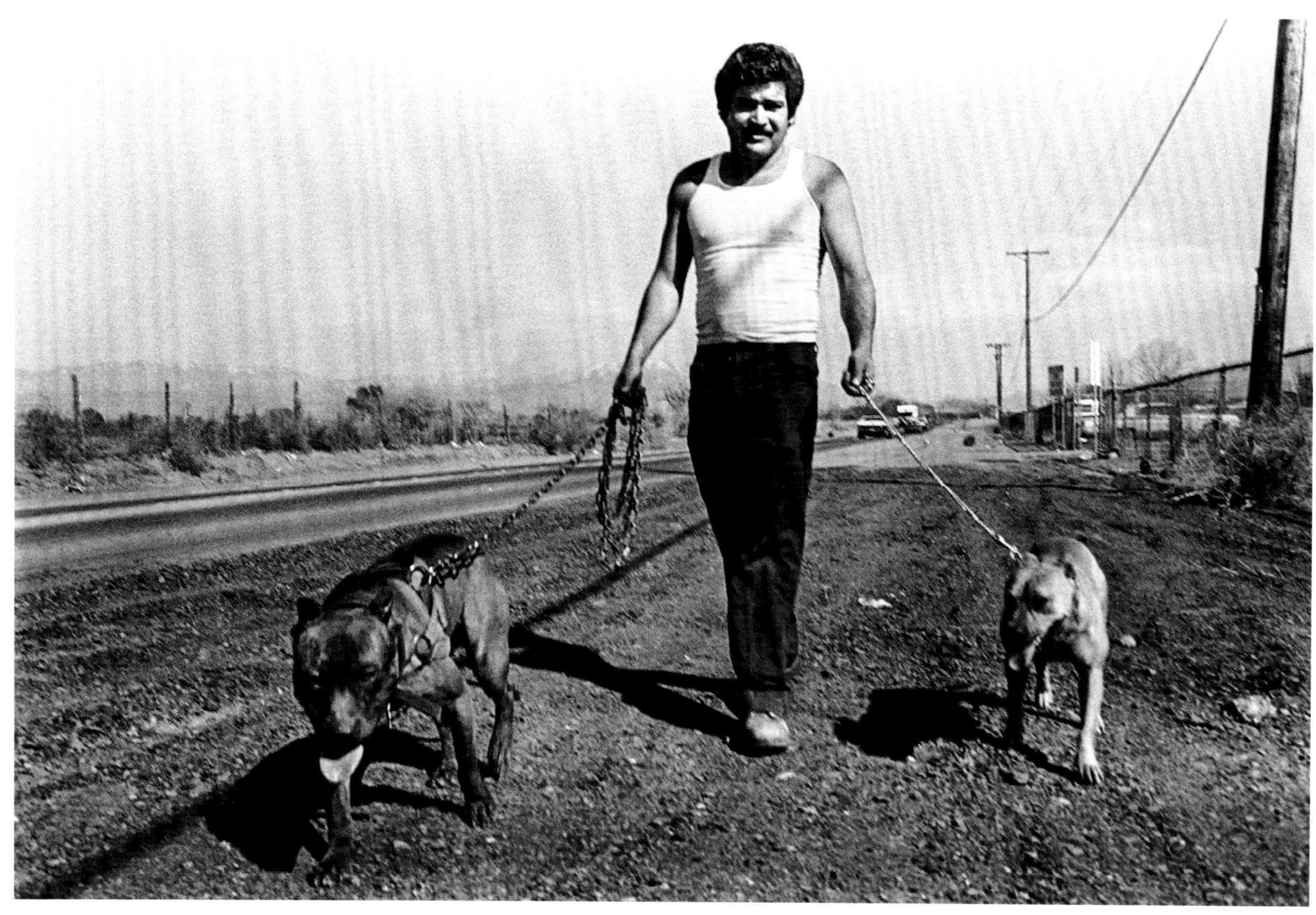

South Valley, Albuquerque, 1981.

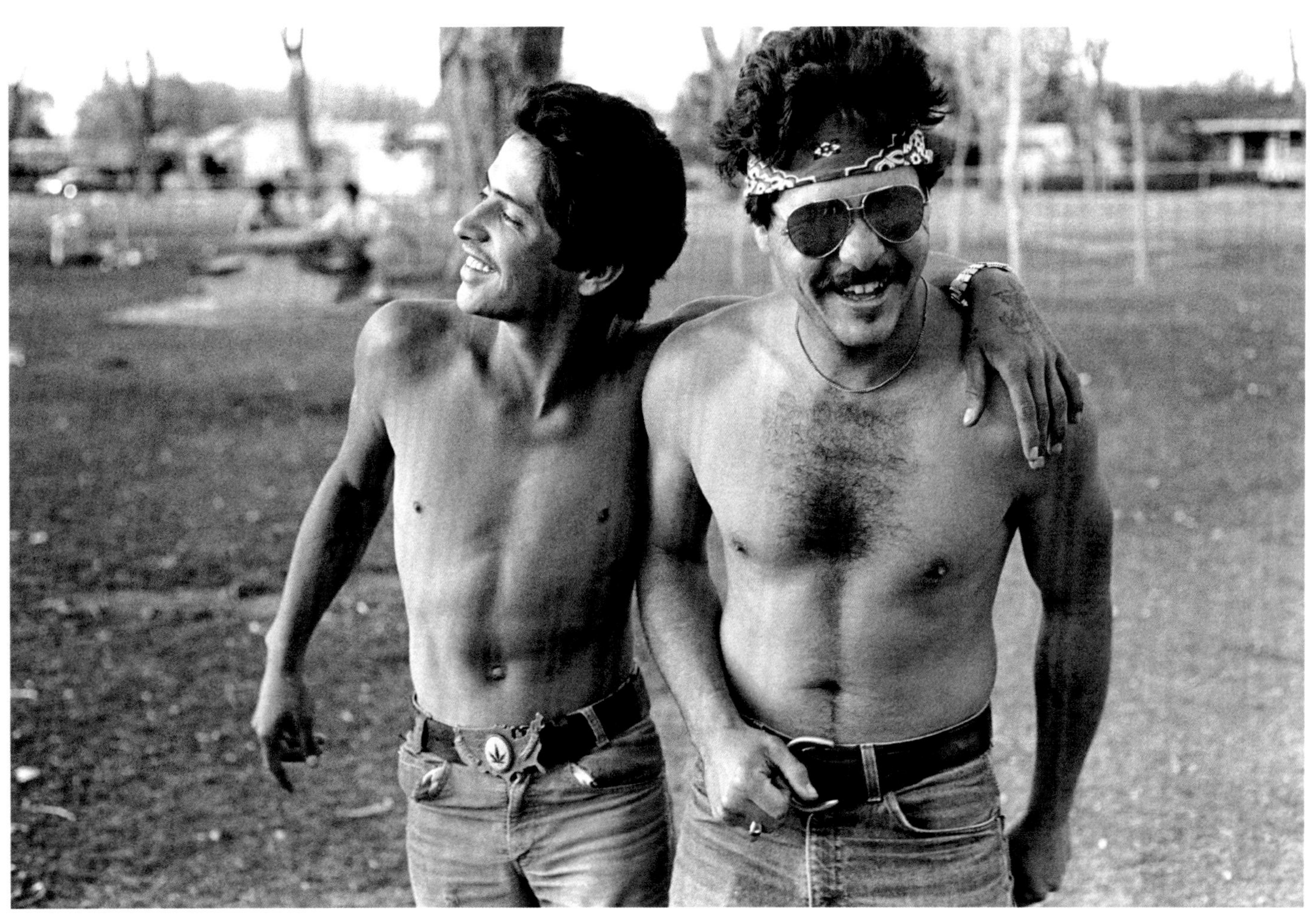

South Valley, Albuquerque, 1983.

OVERLEAF: Behind the Holy Cross Church, Santa Cruz.

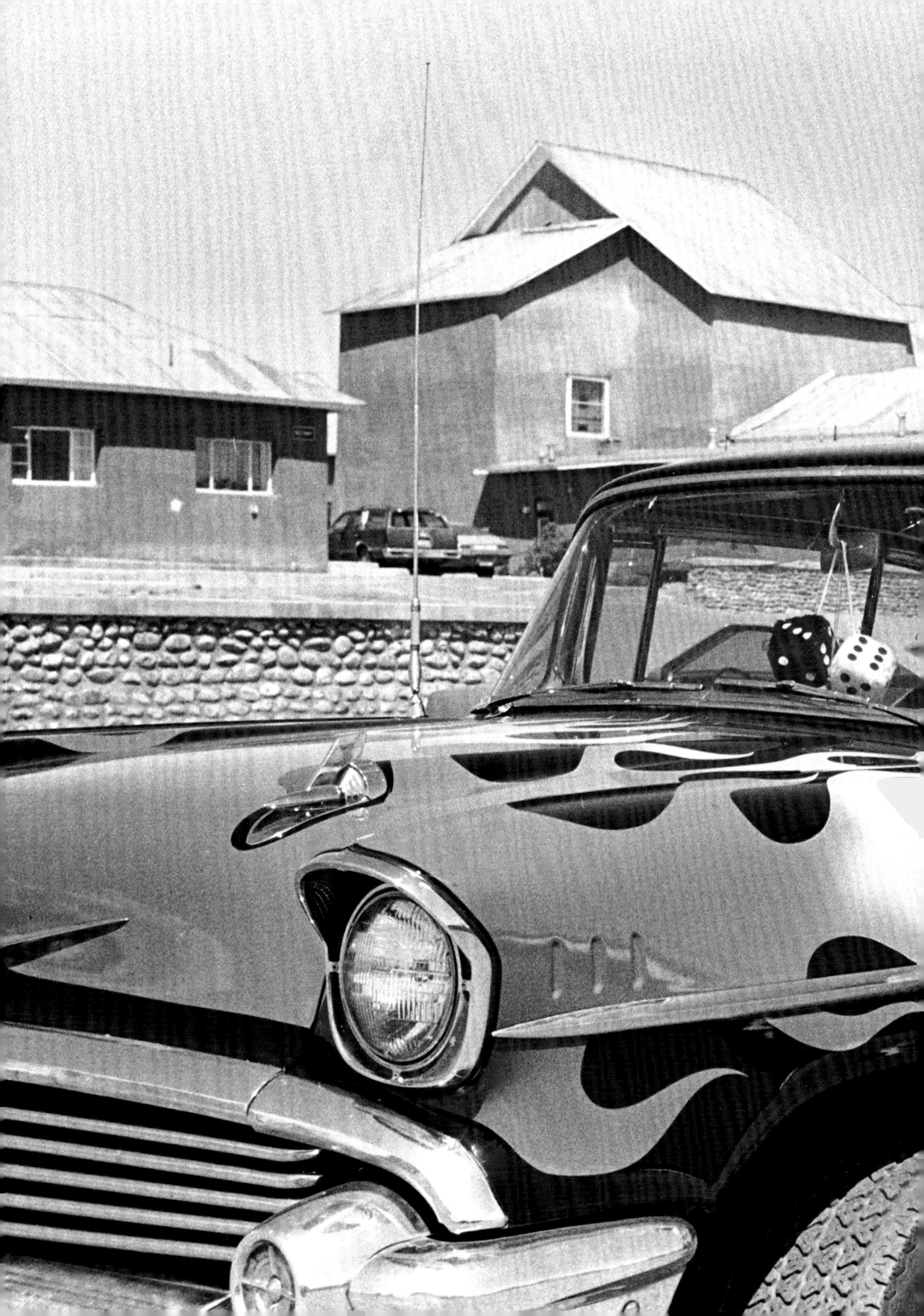

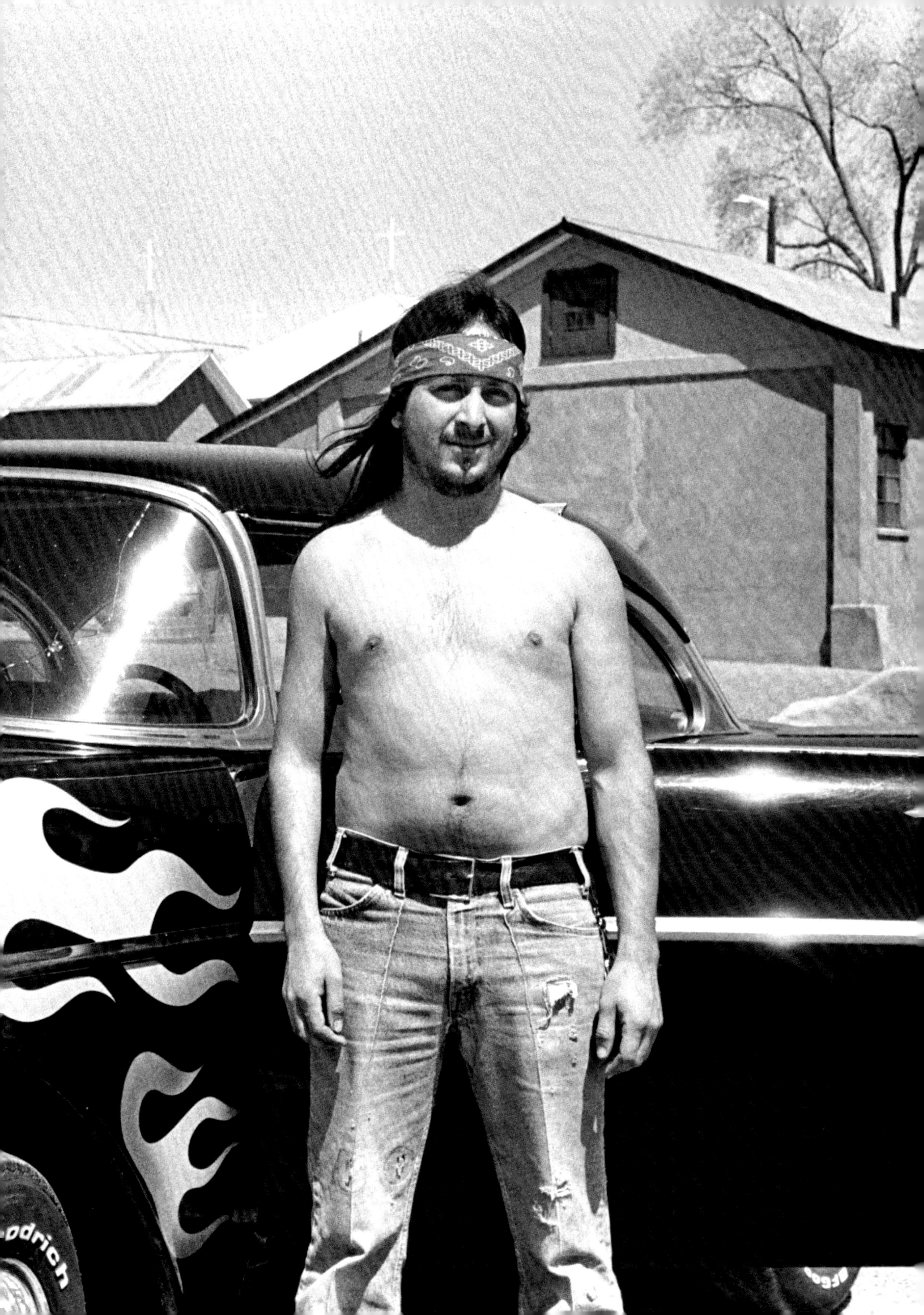

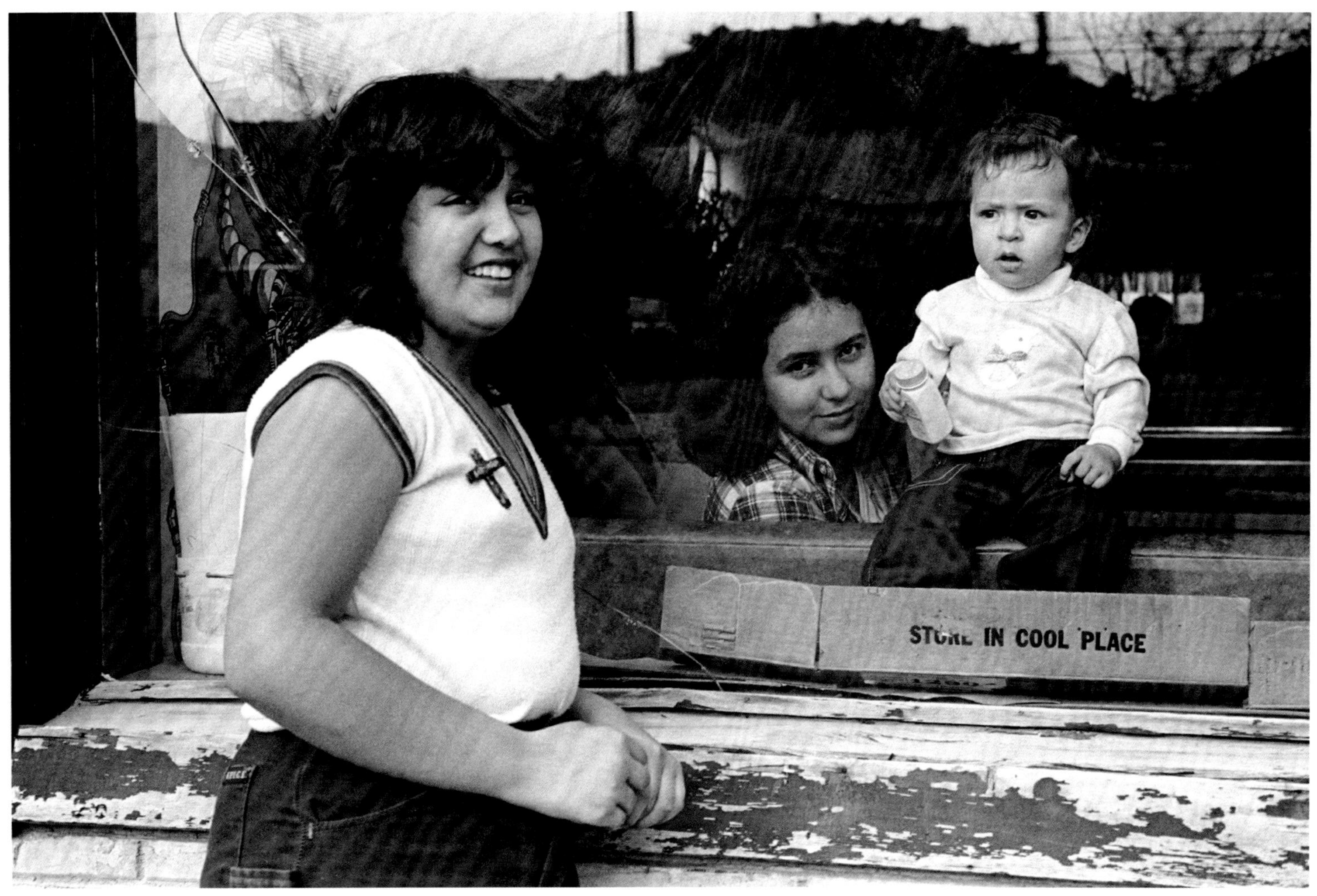

ABOVE AND OPPOSITE: Good Friday, Chimayó, 1982.

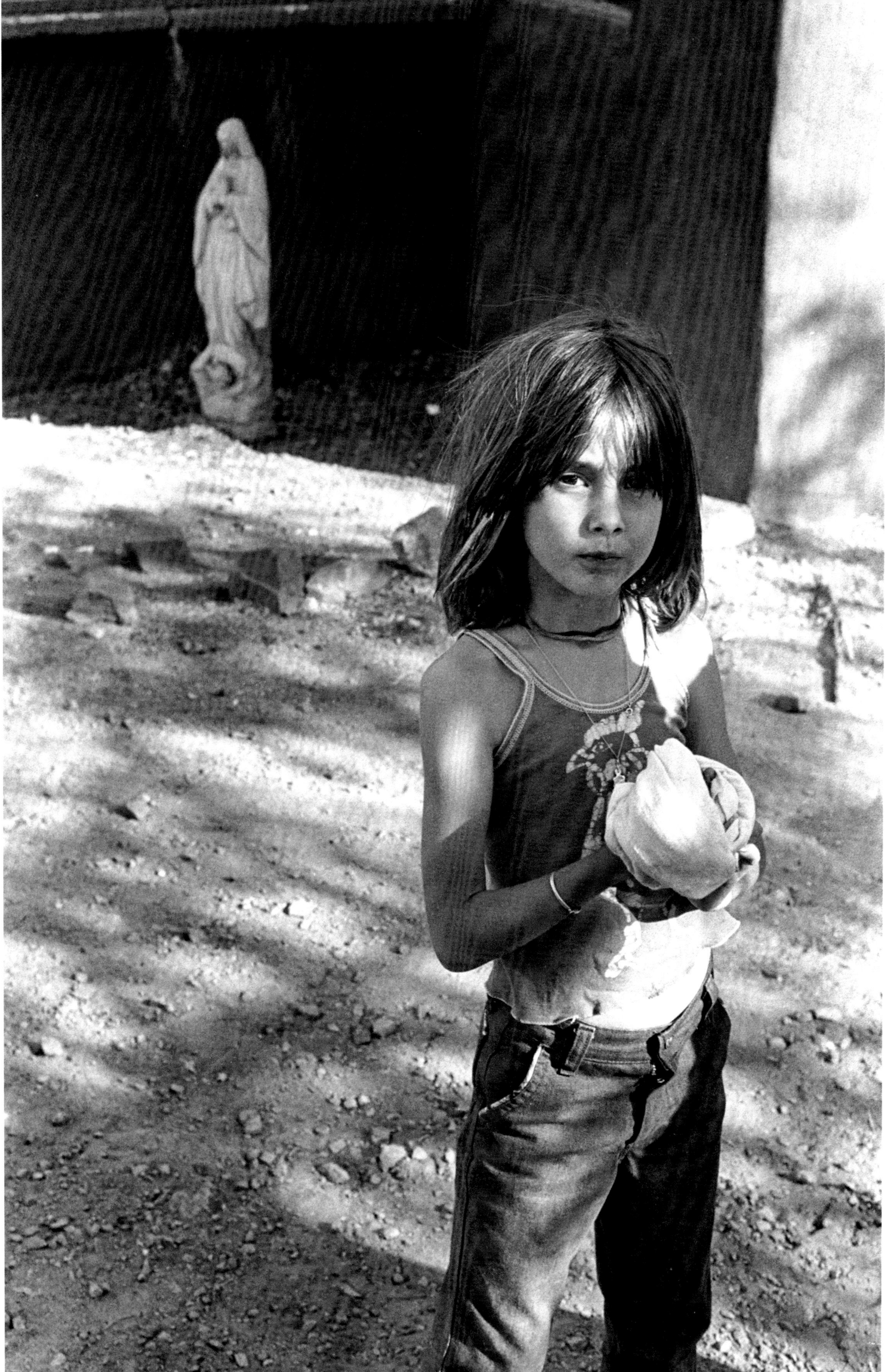

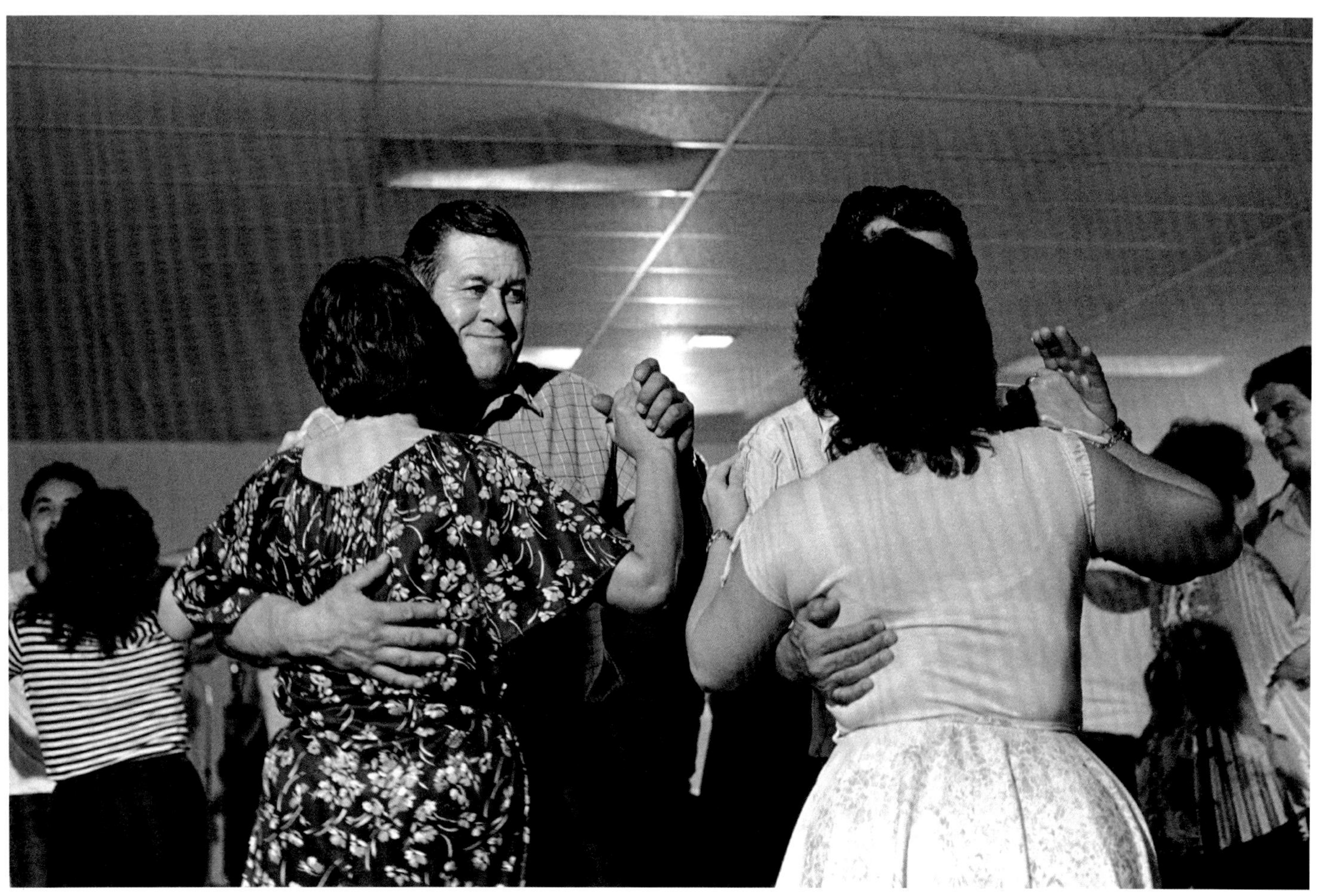

Leopoldo's Lounge, Chimayó, 1981.

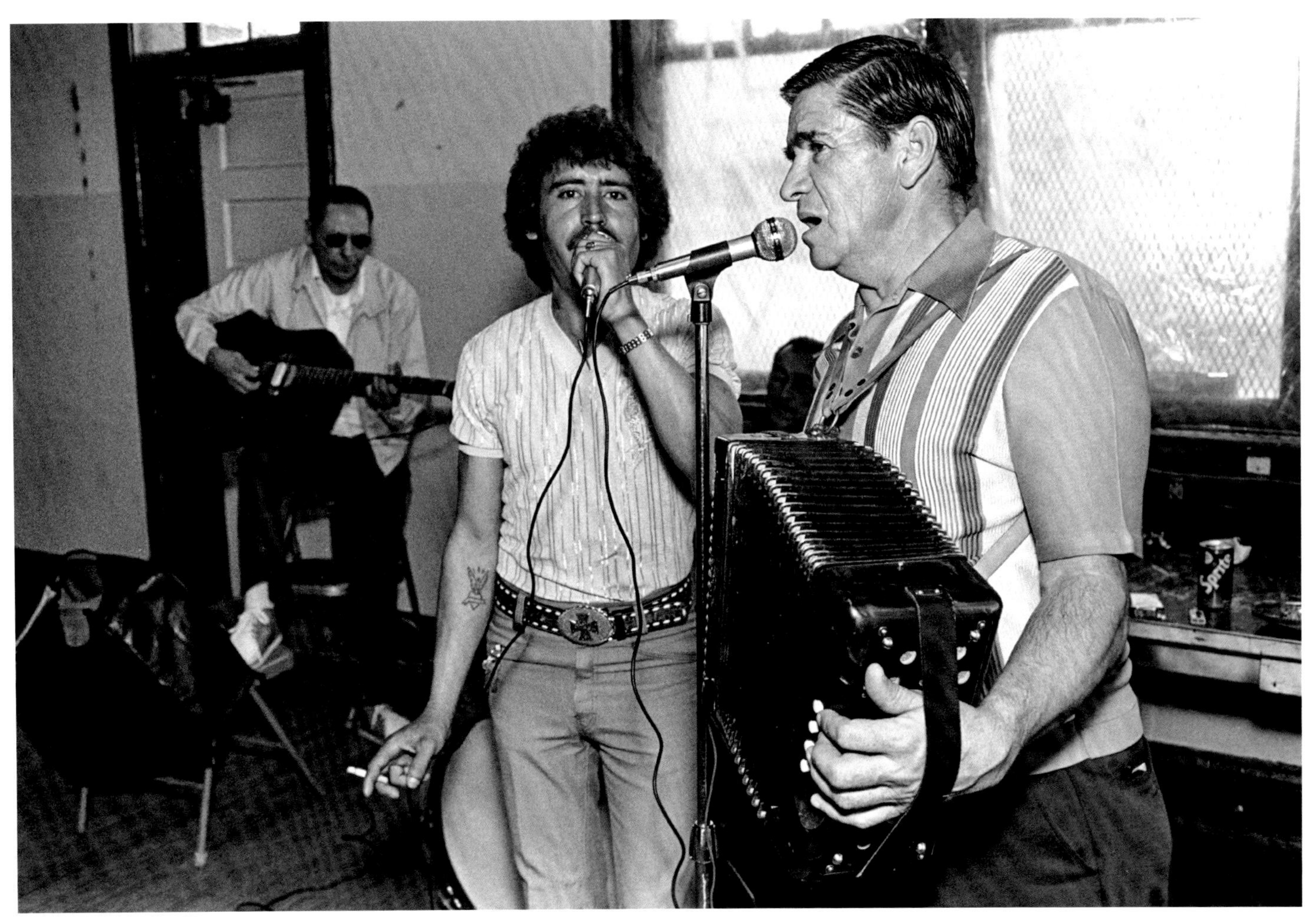

Casa Armijo, Albuquerque, 1983.

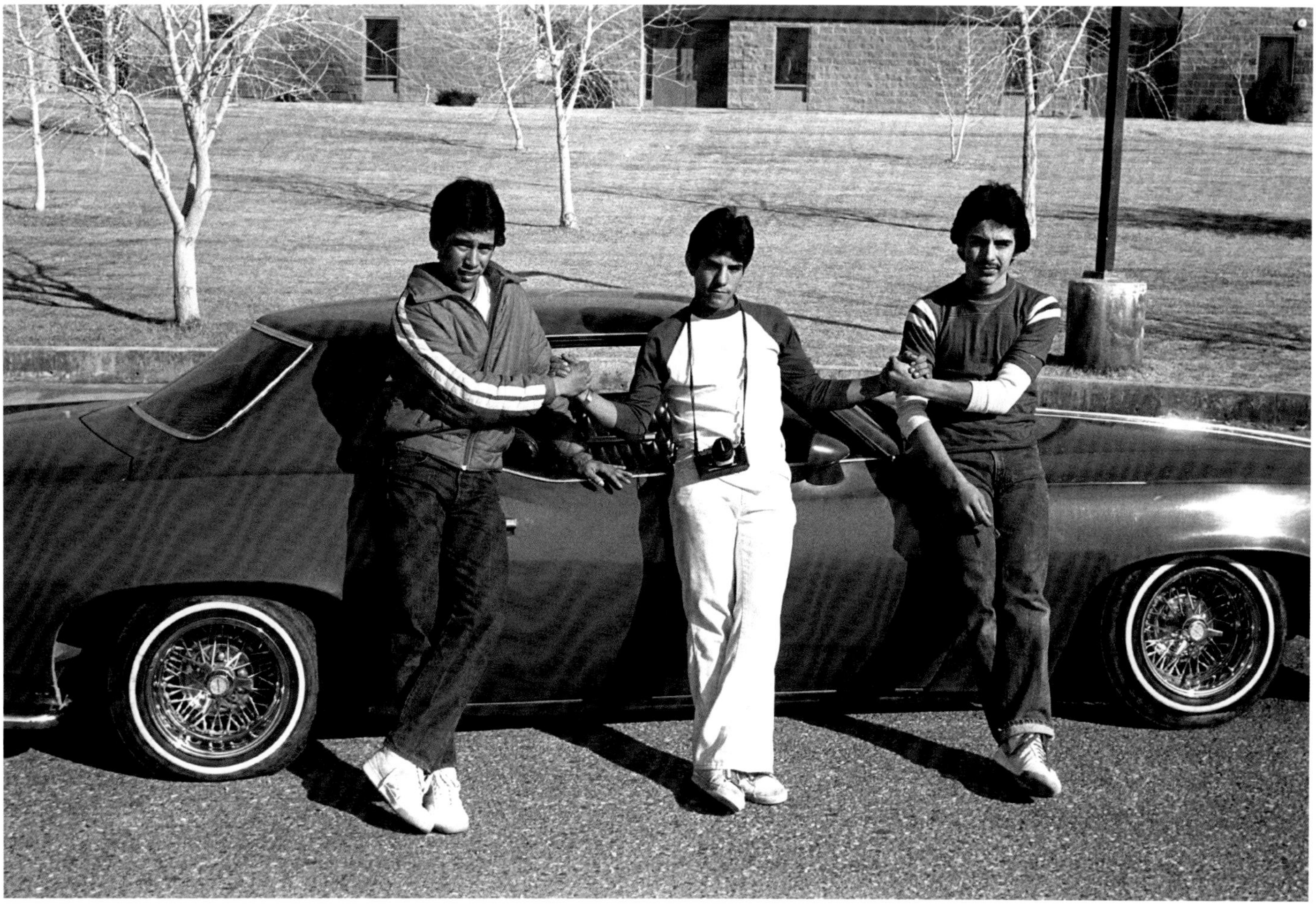

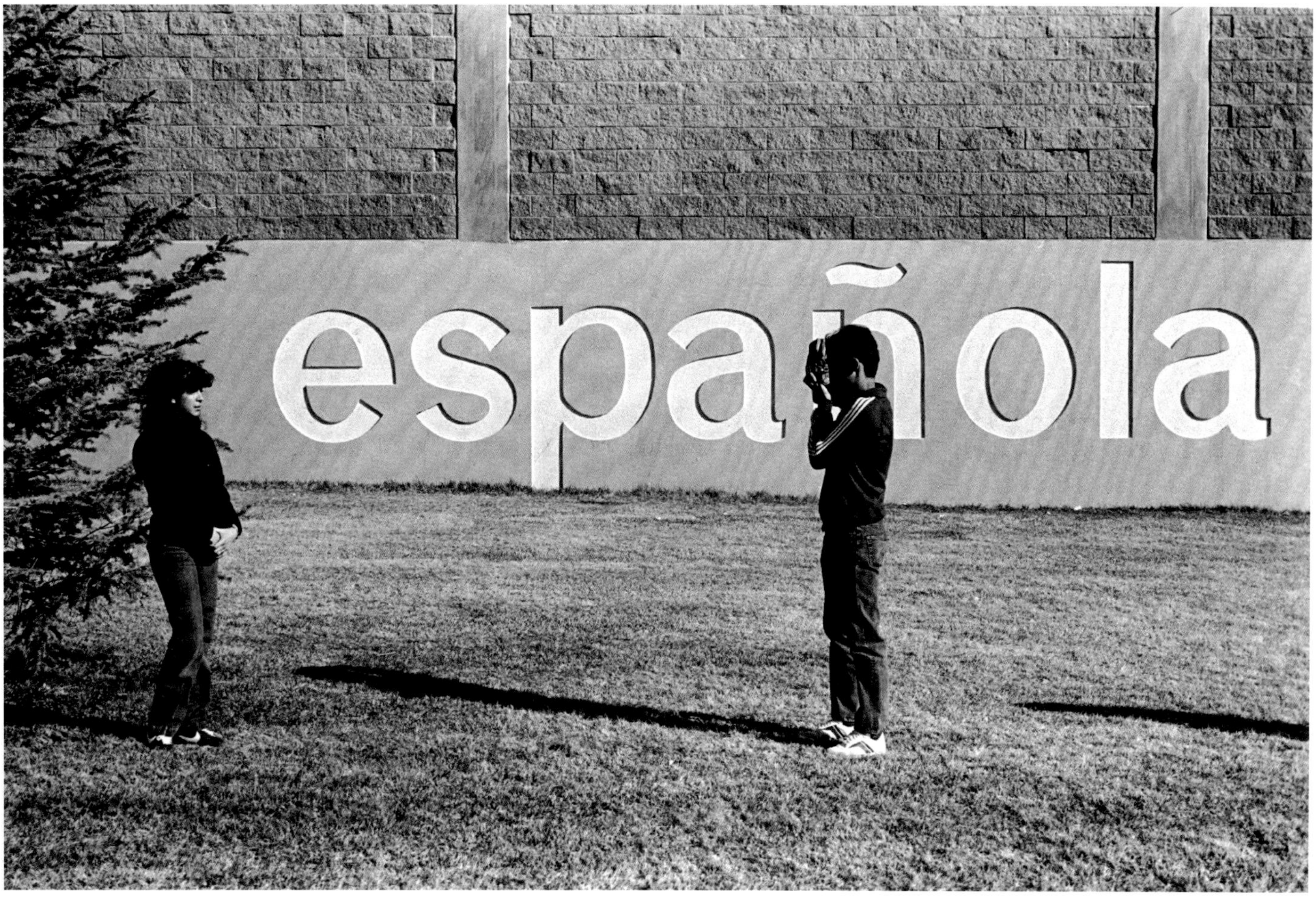

ABOVE AND OPPOSITE: Española Valley High School, Española, 1982.

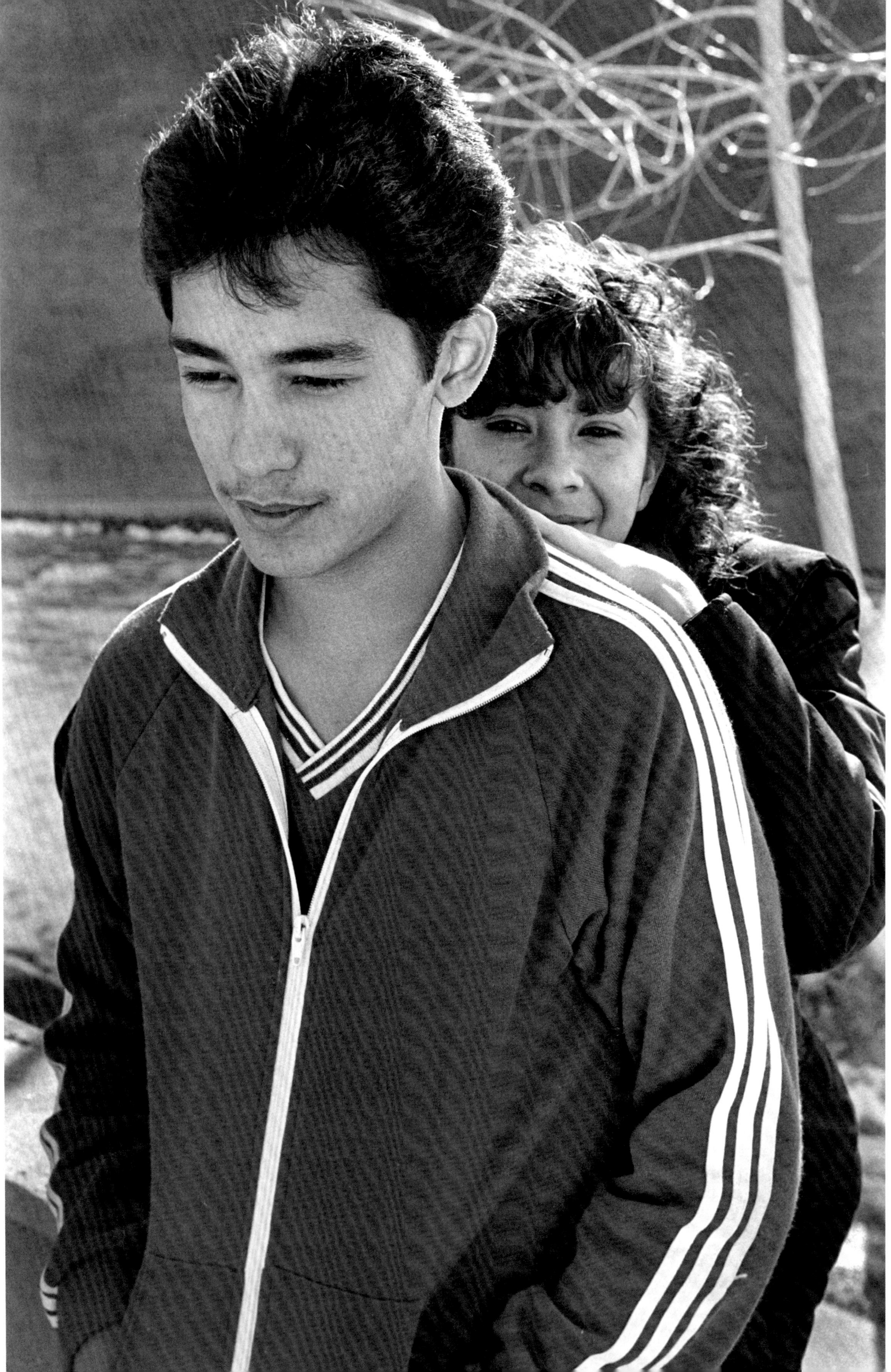

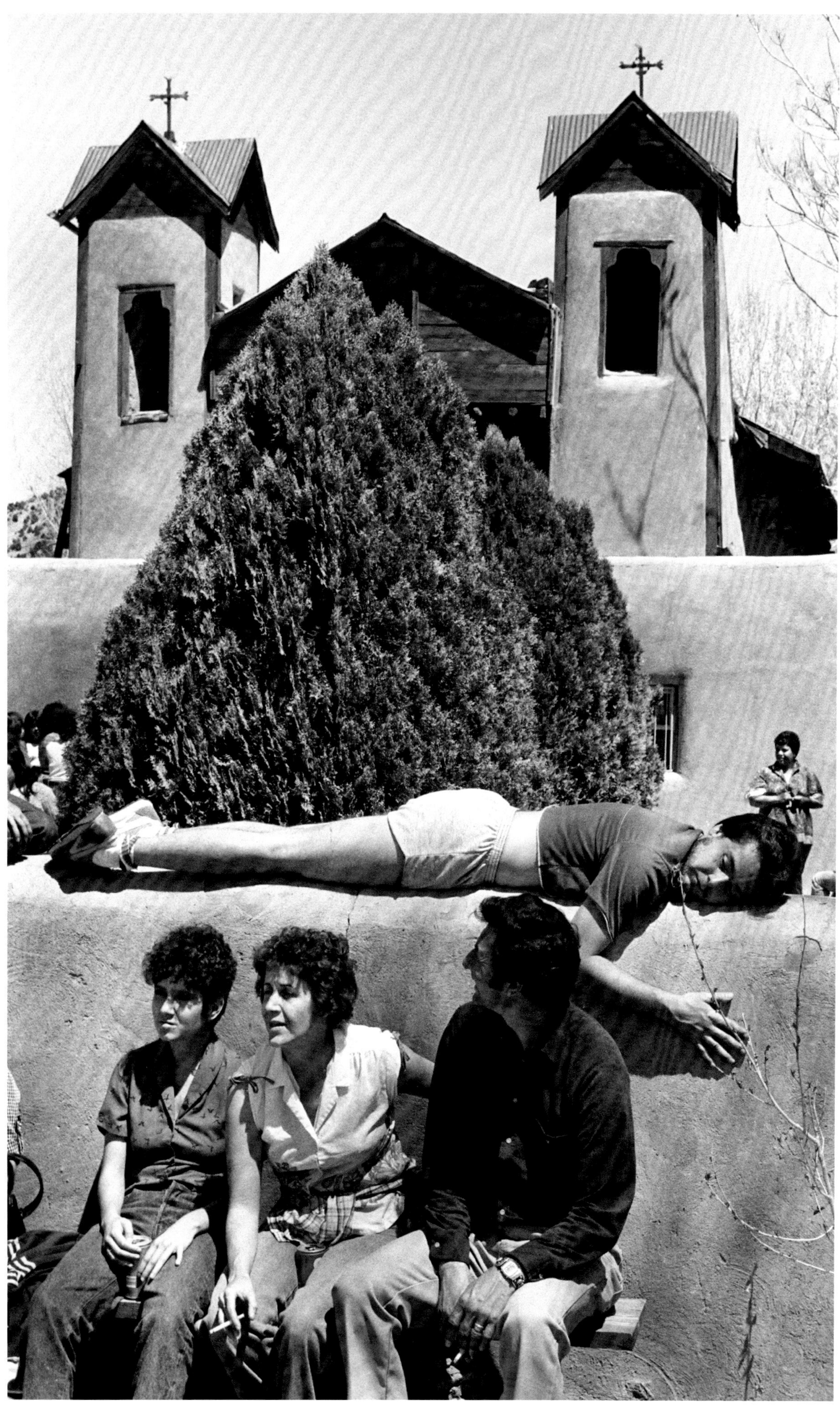

Good Friday, Chimayó, 1981.

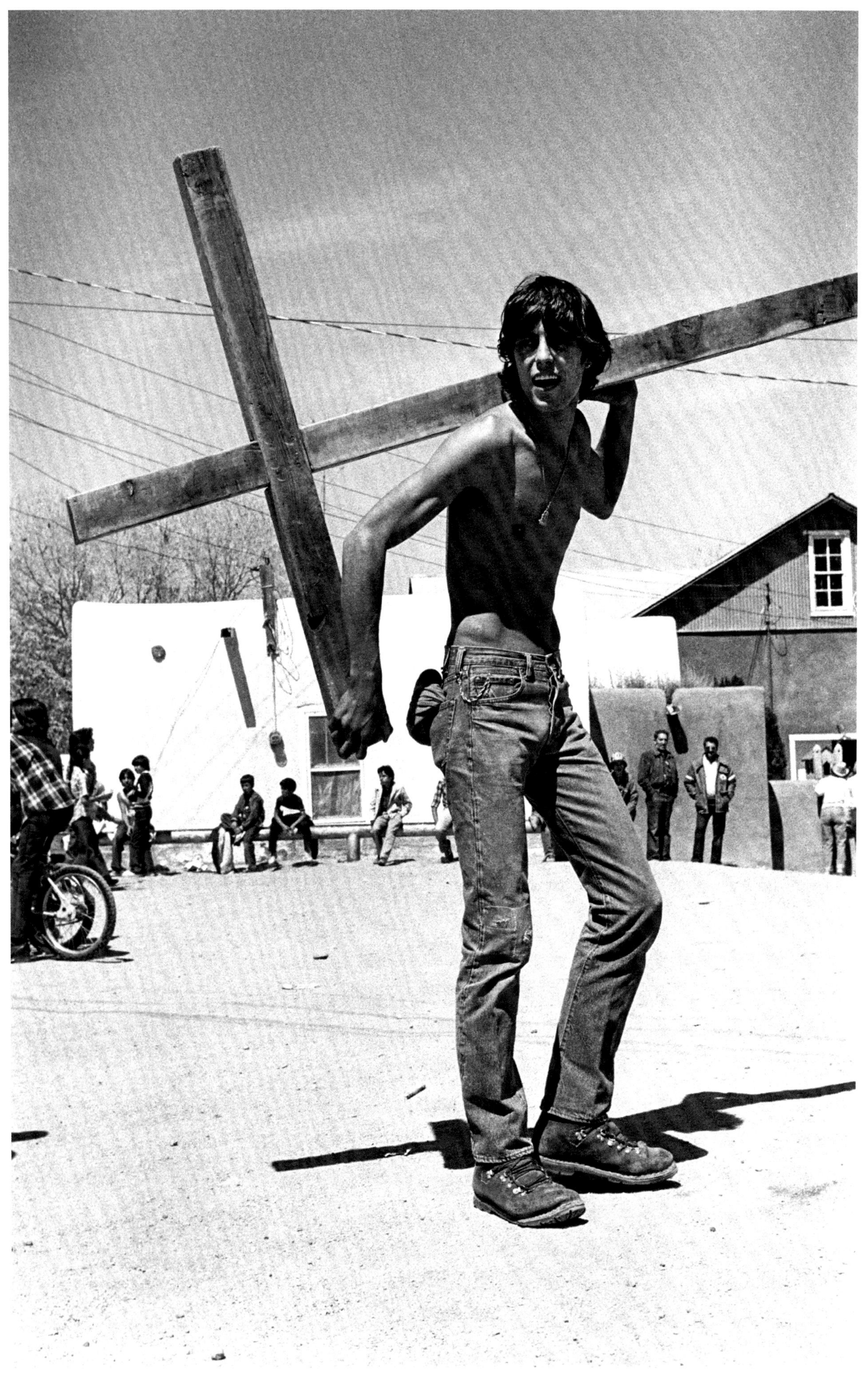

Good Friday, Chimayó, 1981.

OVERLEAF: Fiesta, Chimayó, 1981.

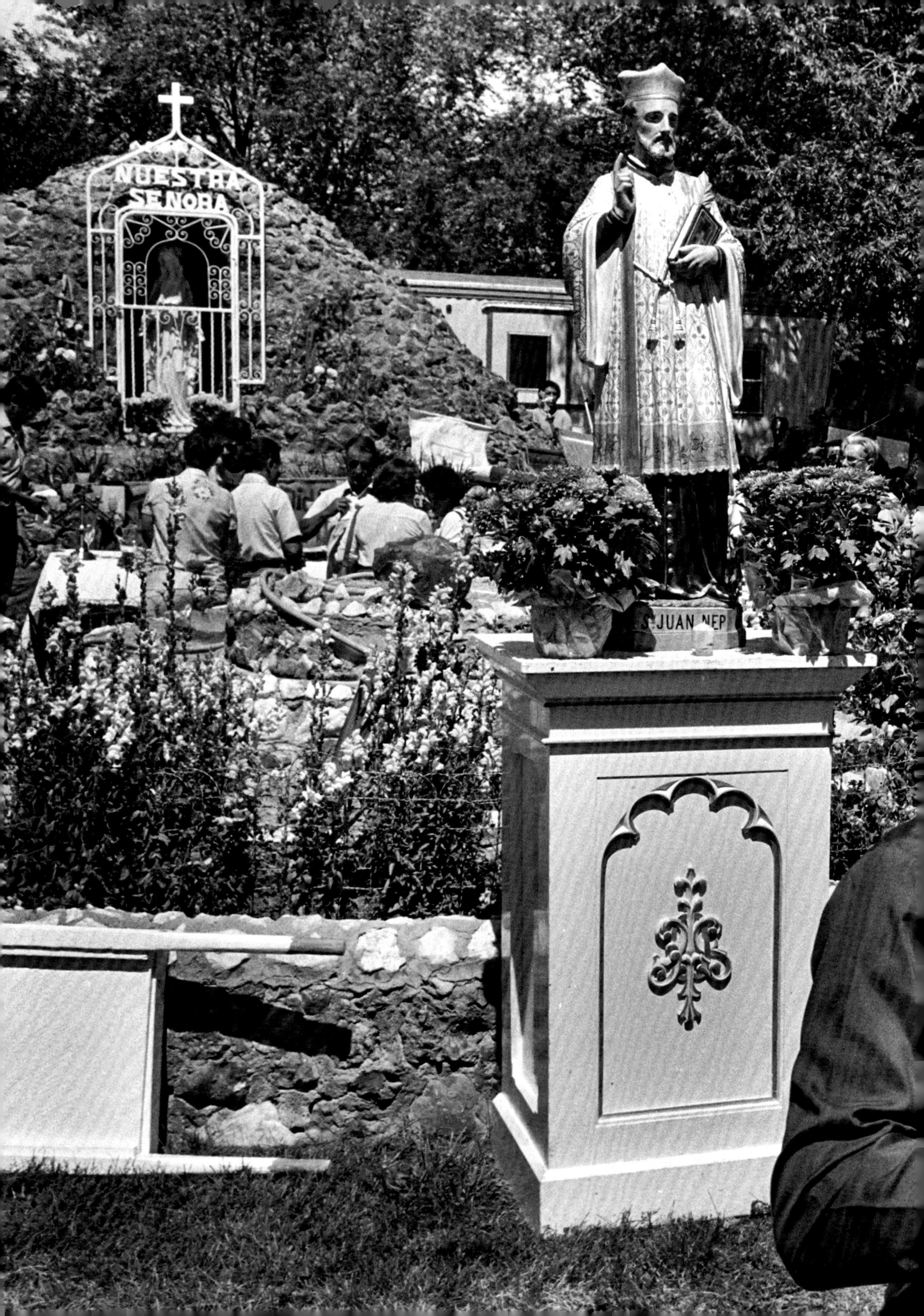
NUESTRA
SENORA
S. JUAN NEP

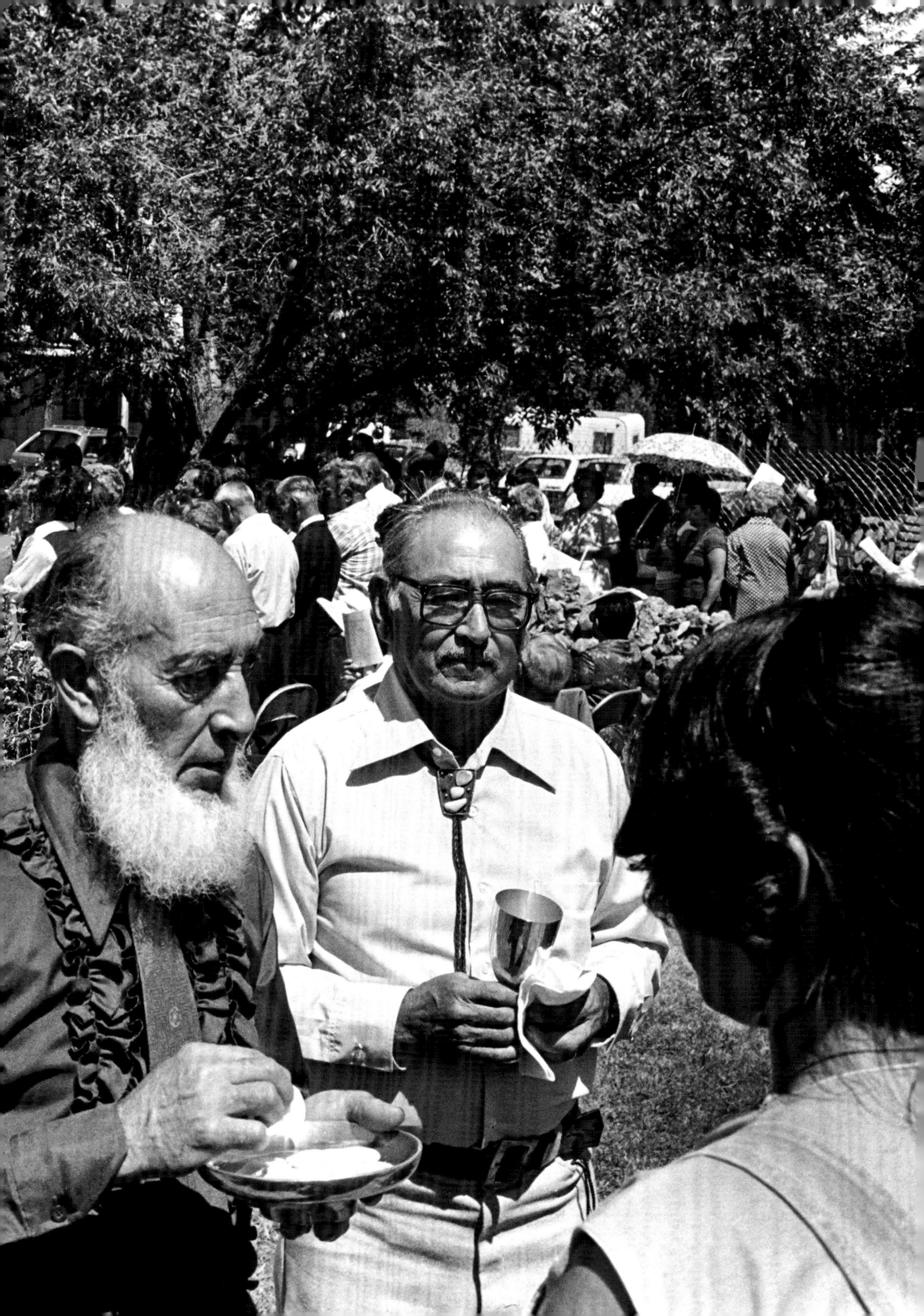

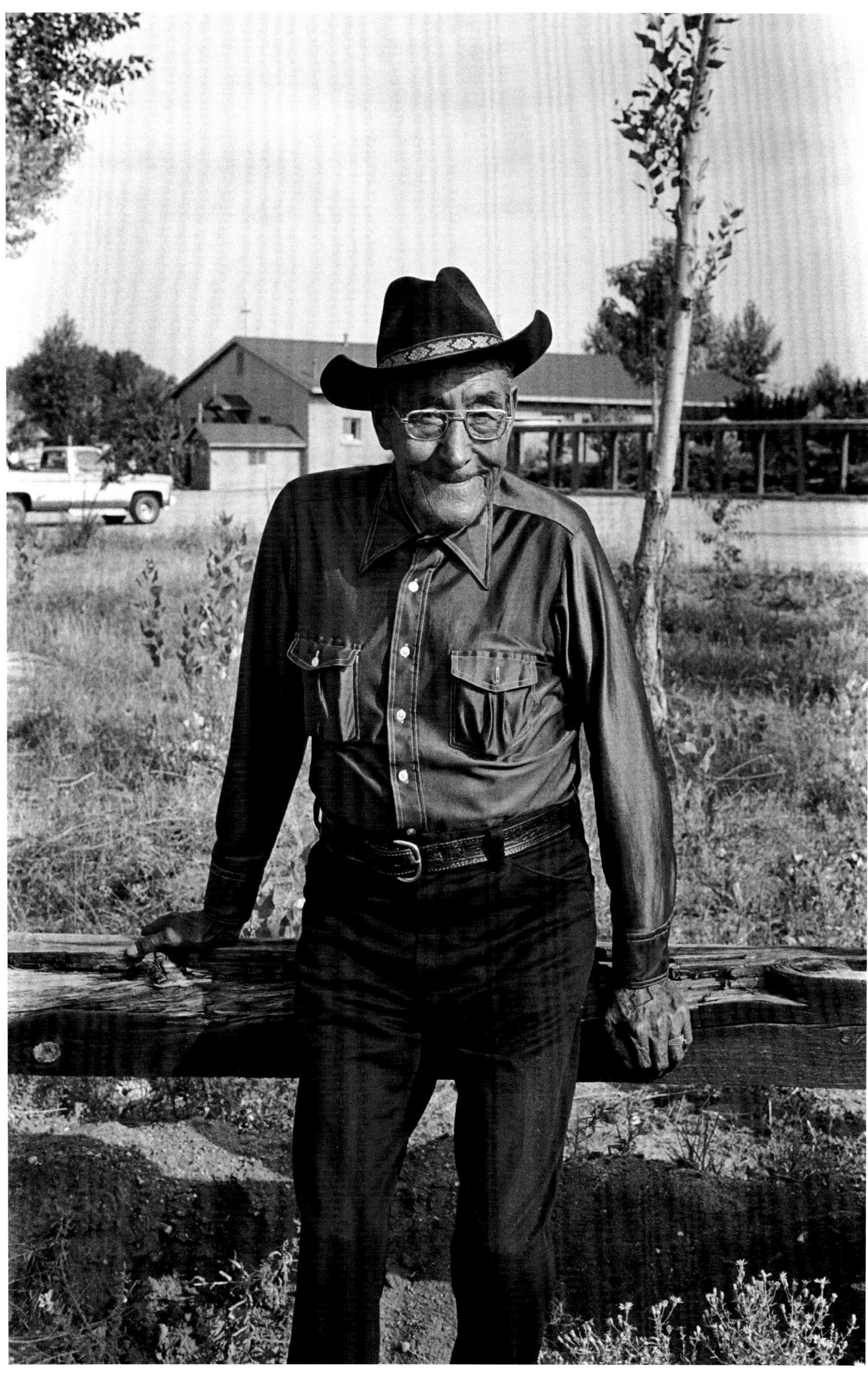

Fiesta, Chimayó, 1981.

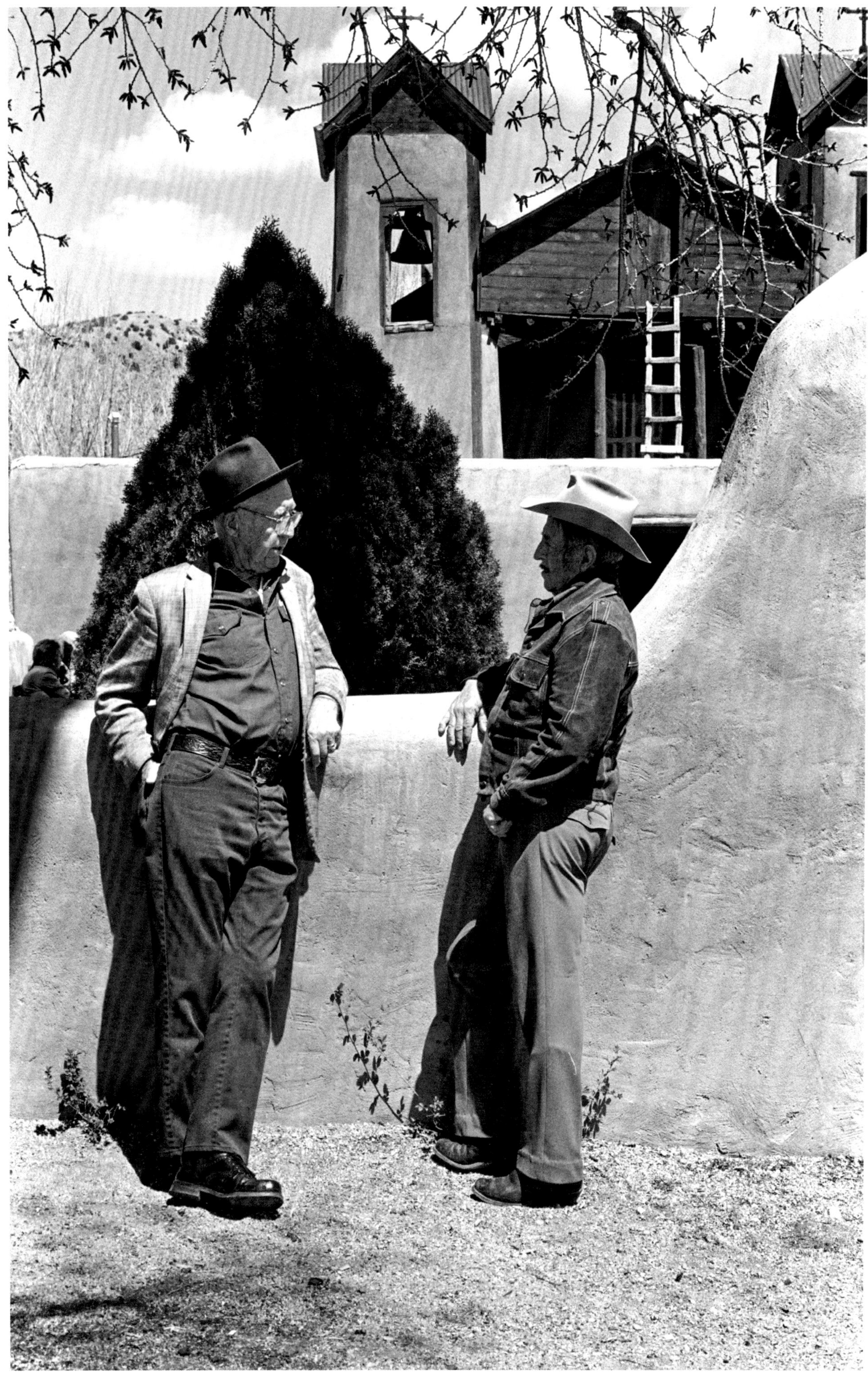

Fiesta, Chimayó, 1981.

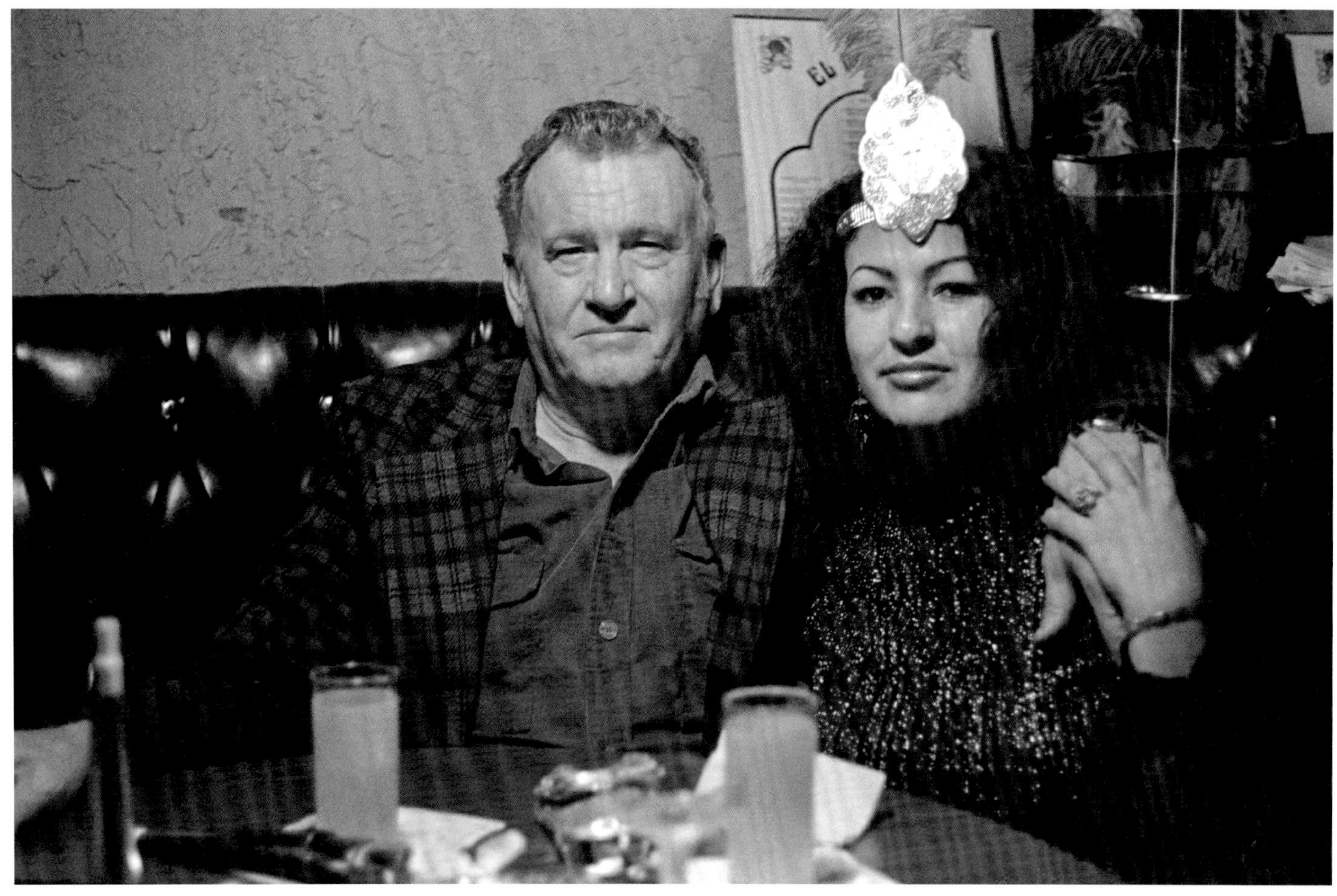

New Year's Eve, La Bamba Club, Albuquerque, 1983.

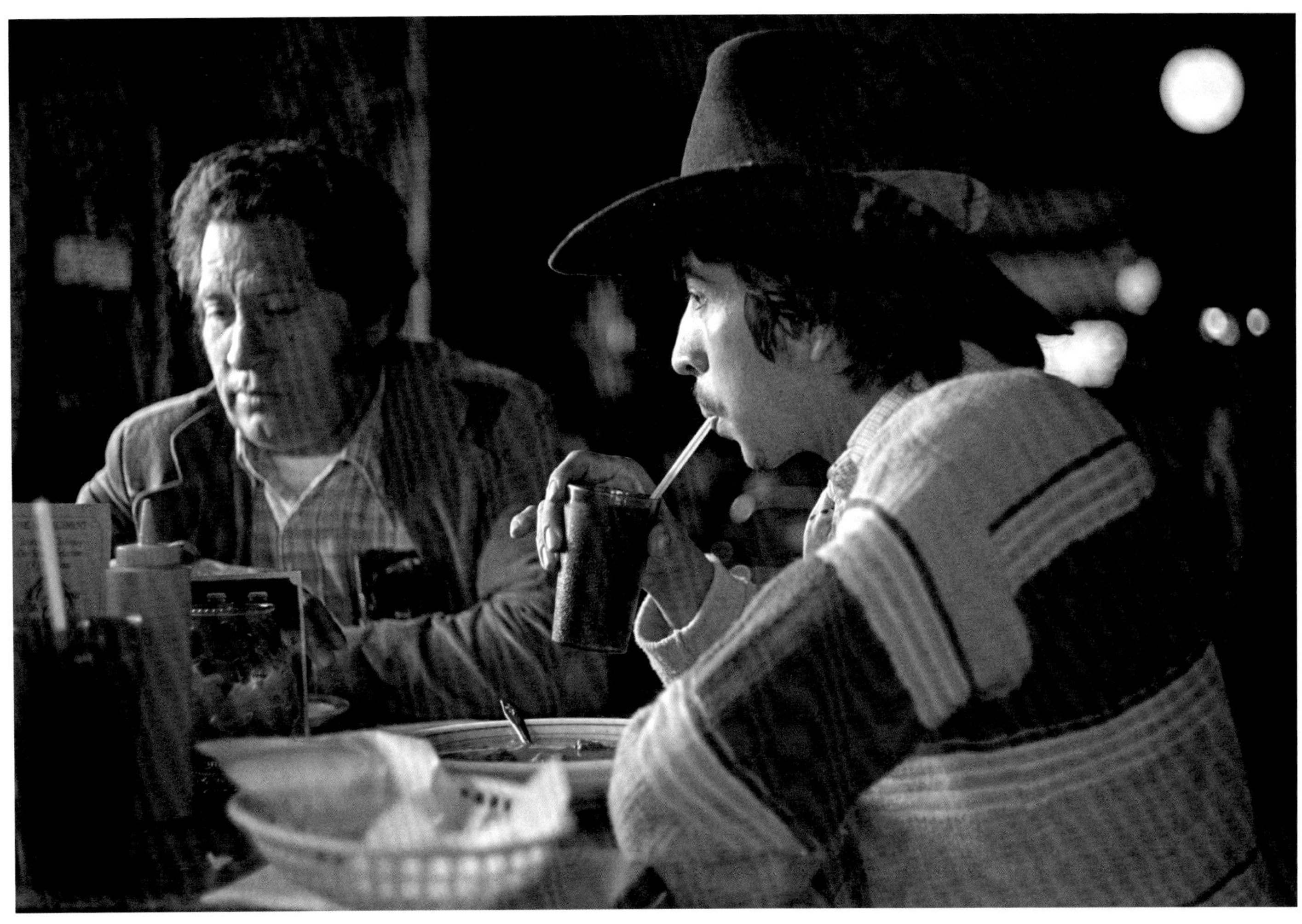

Restaurant in Cuba, 1982.

OVERLEAF: Flaco Jiménez, Santa Fe, 1981.

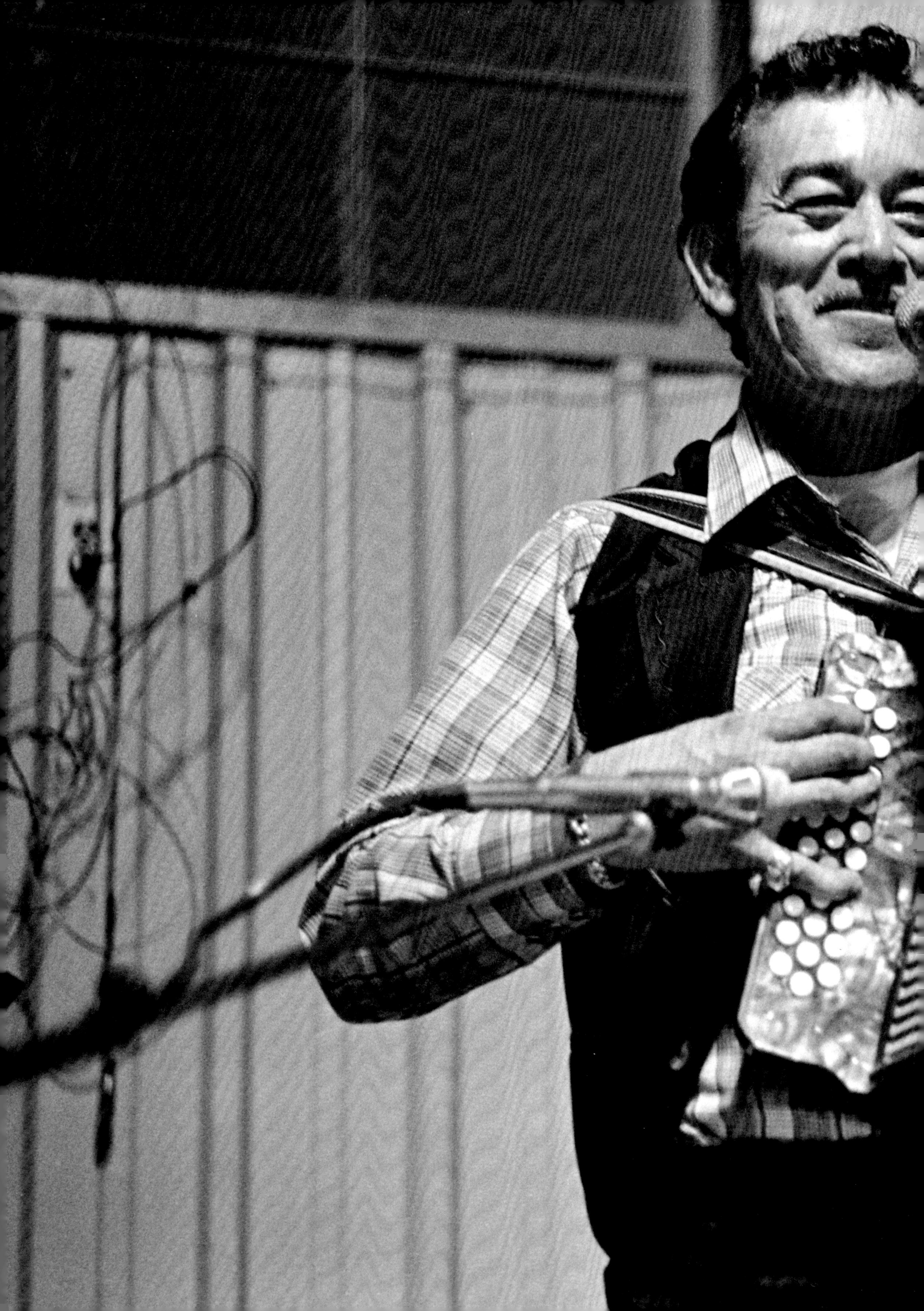

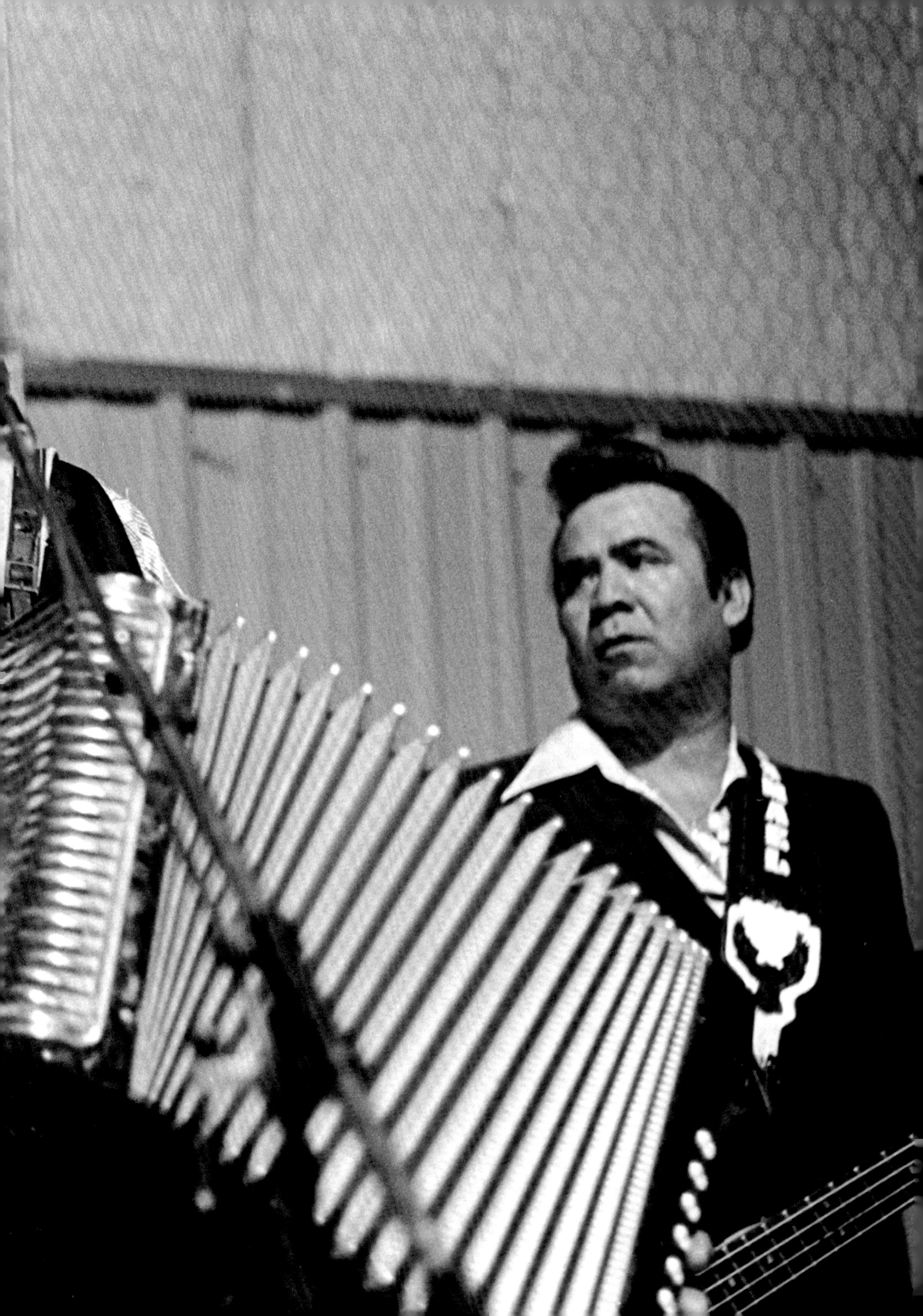

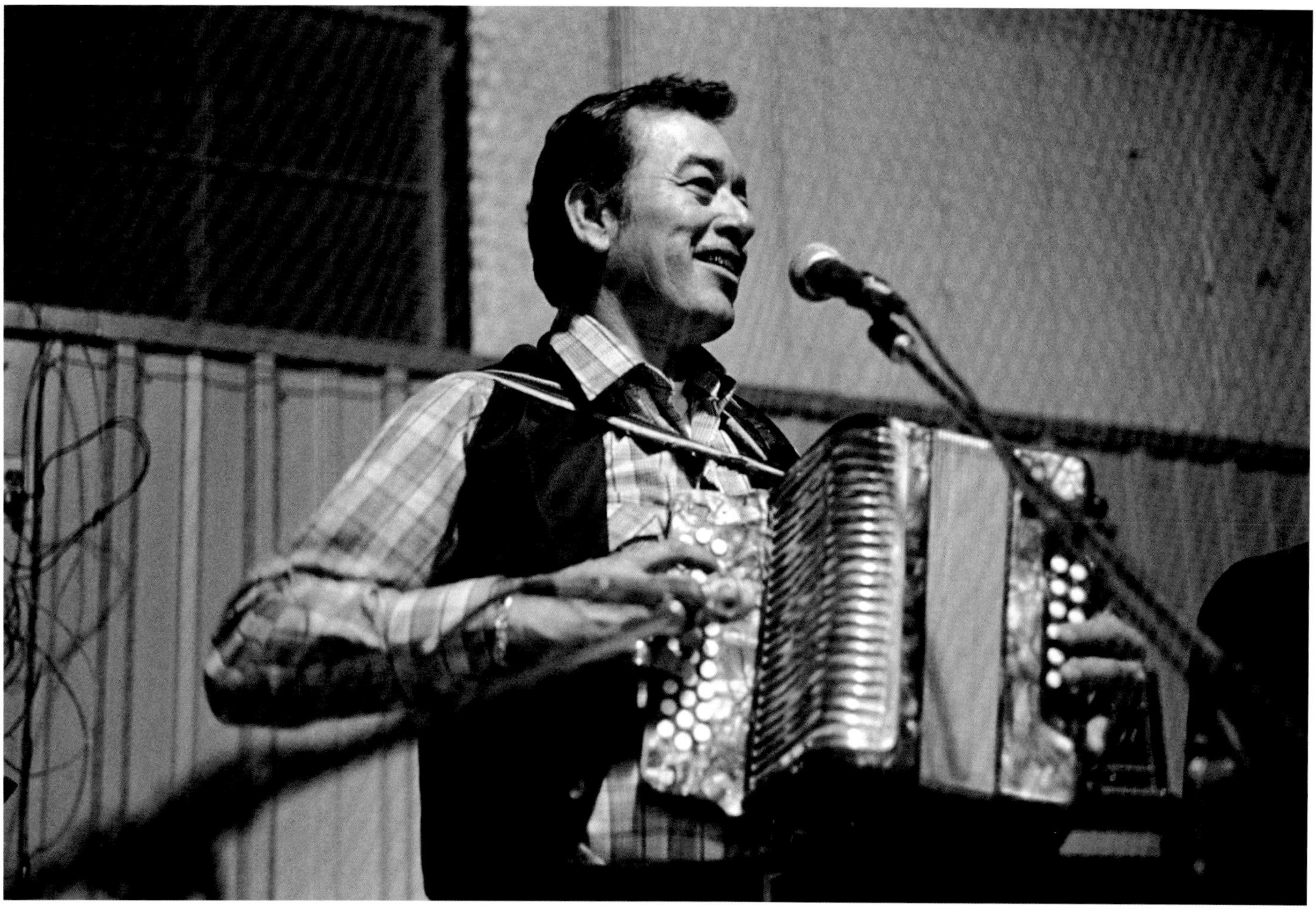

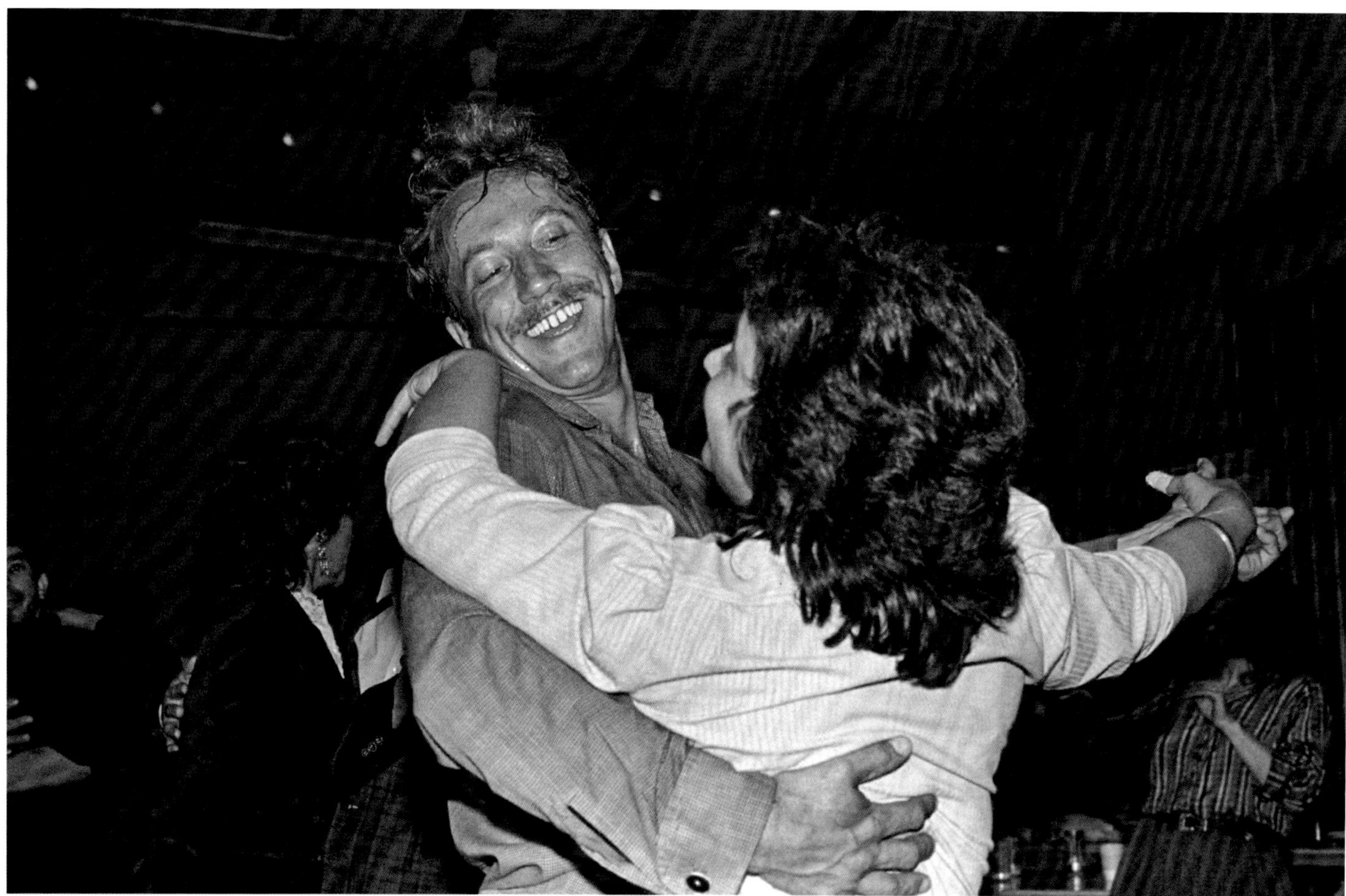

Flaco Jiménez concert, Santa Fe, 1981.

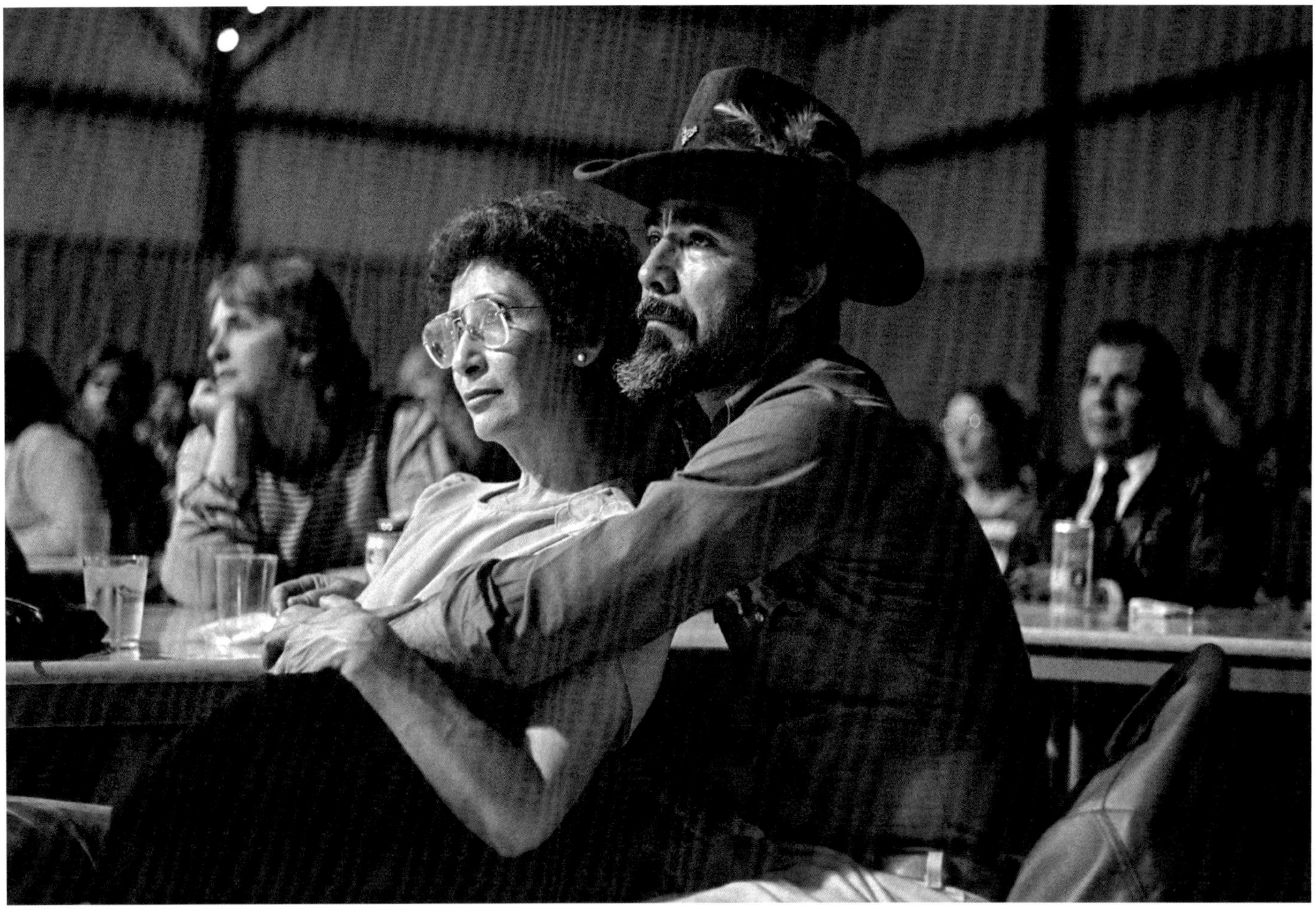

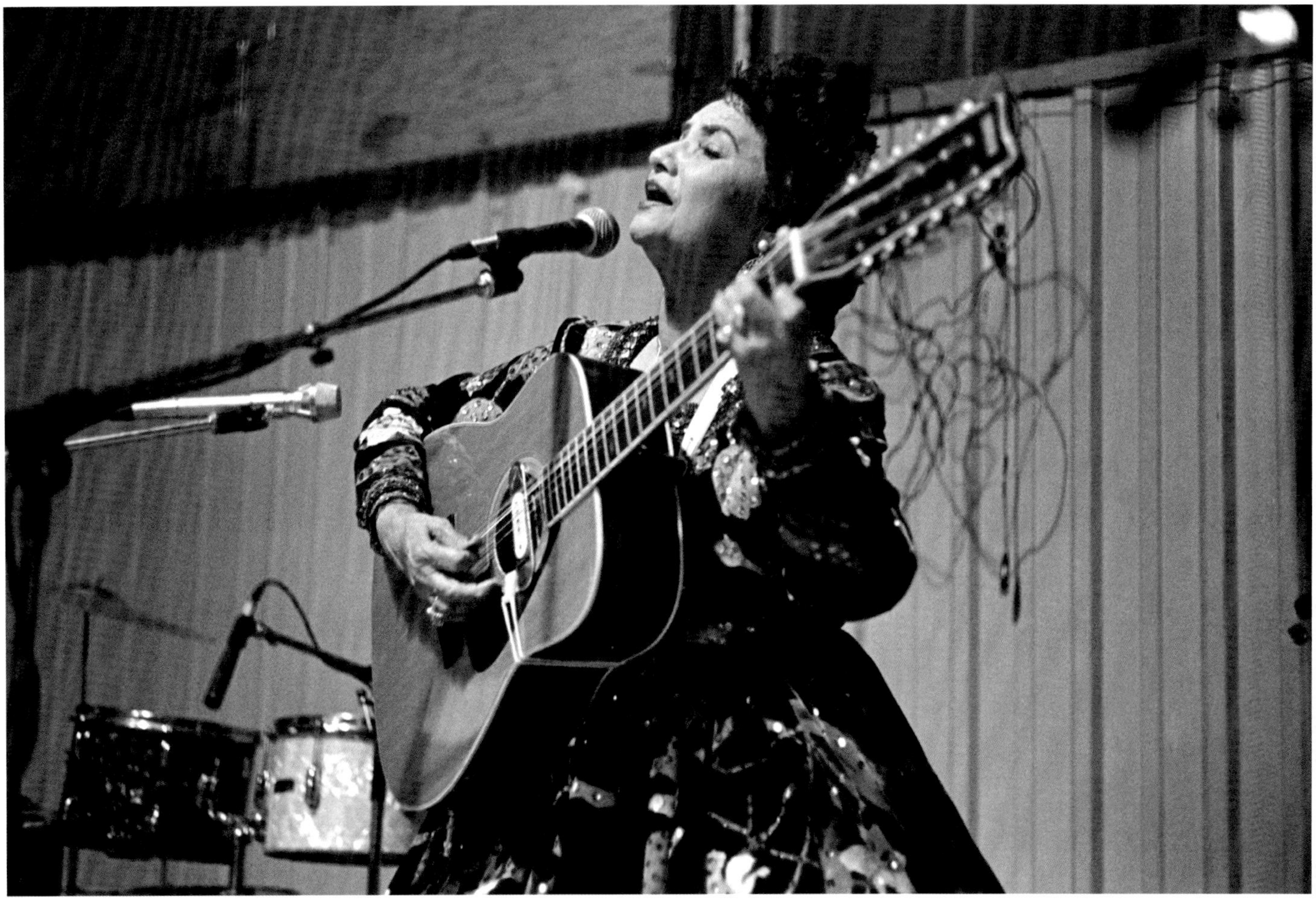

Flaco Jiménez concert, Santa Fe, 1981.

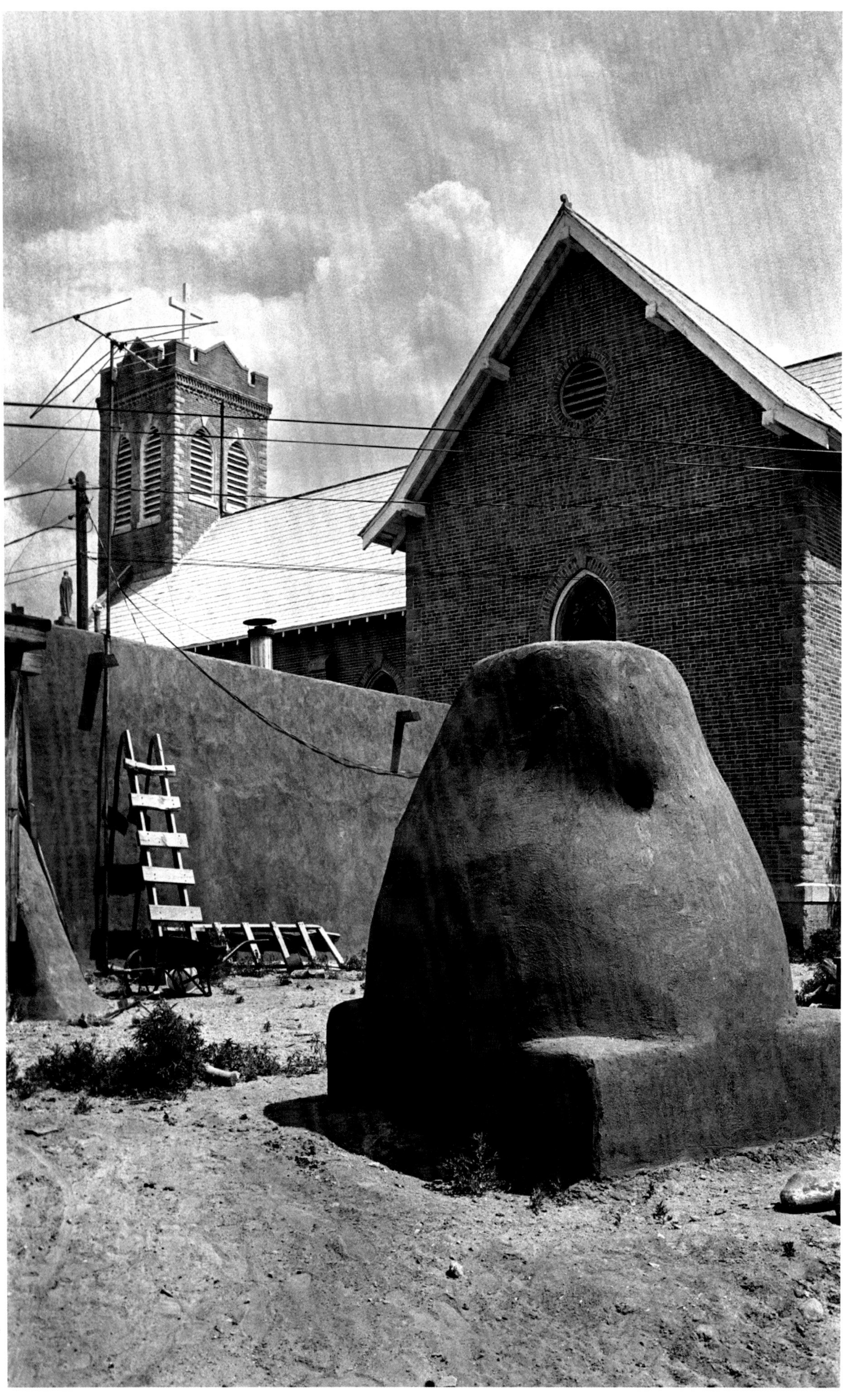

Horno (bread oven) and church, Ohkay Owingeh, 1981.

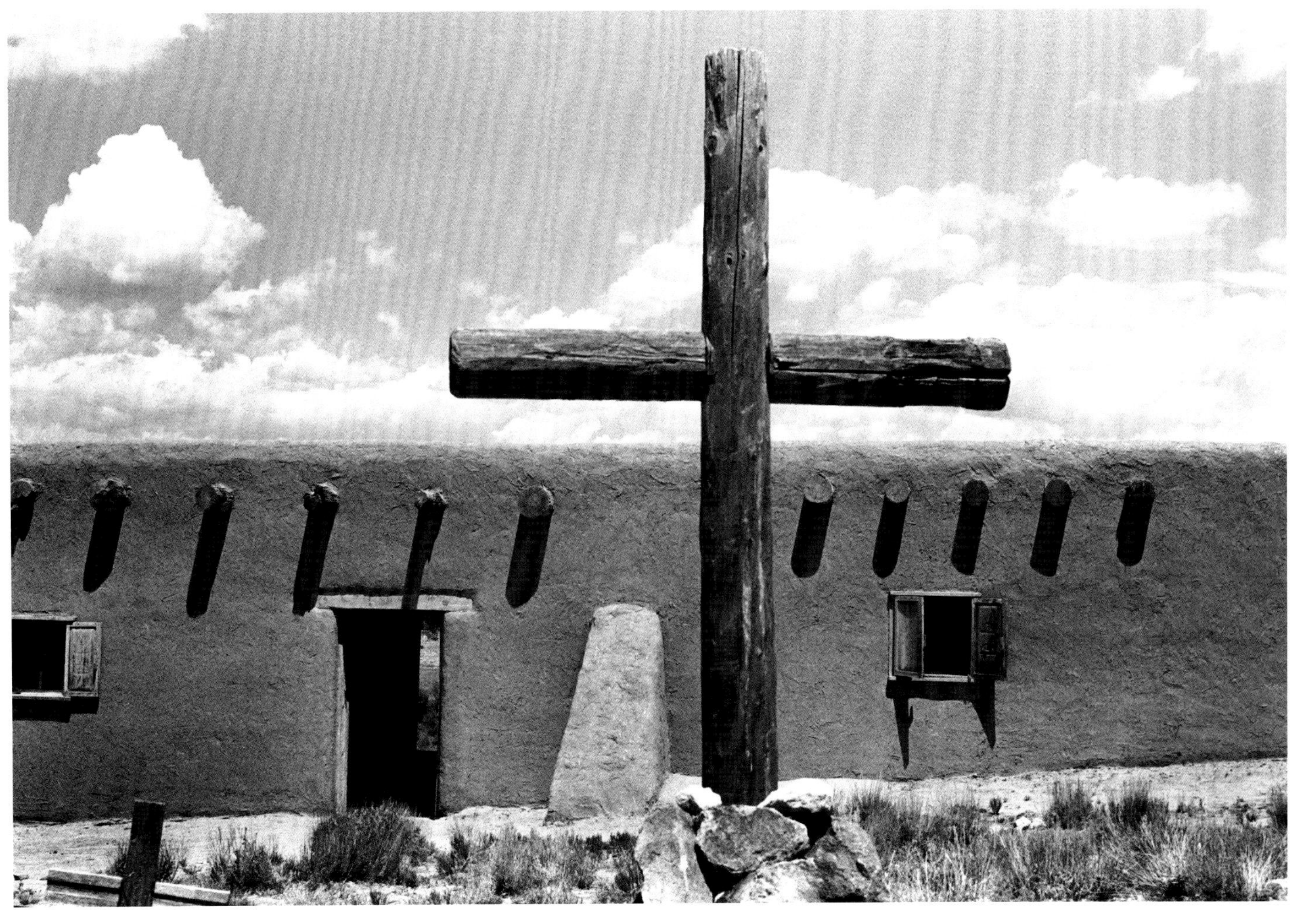

El Rancho de las Golondrinas, La Cienega, 1981.

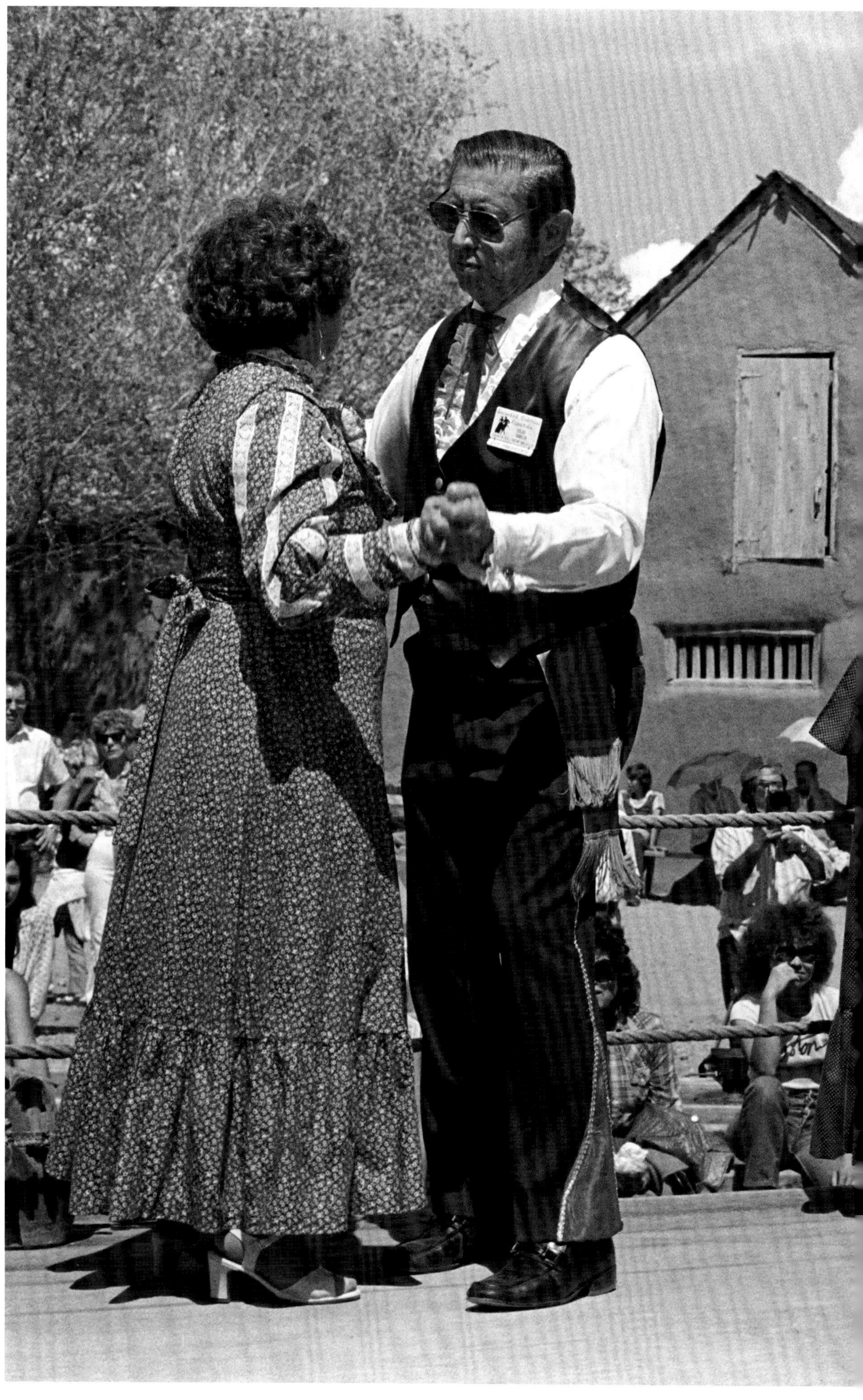

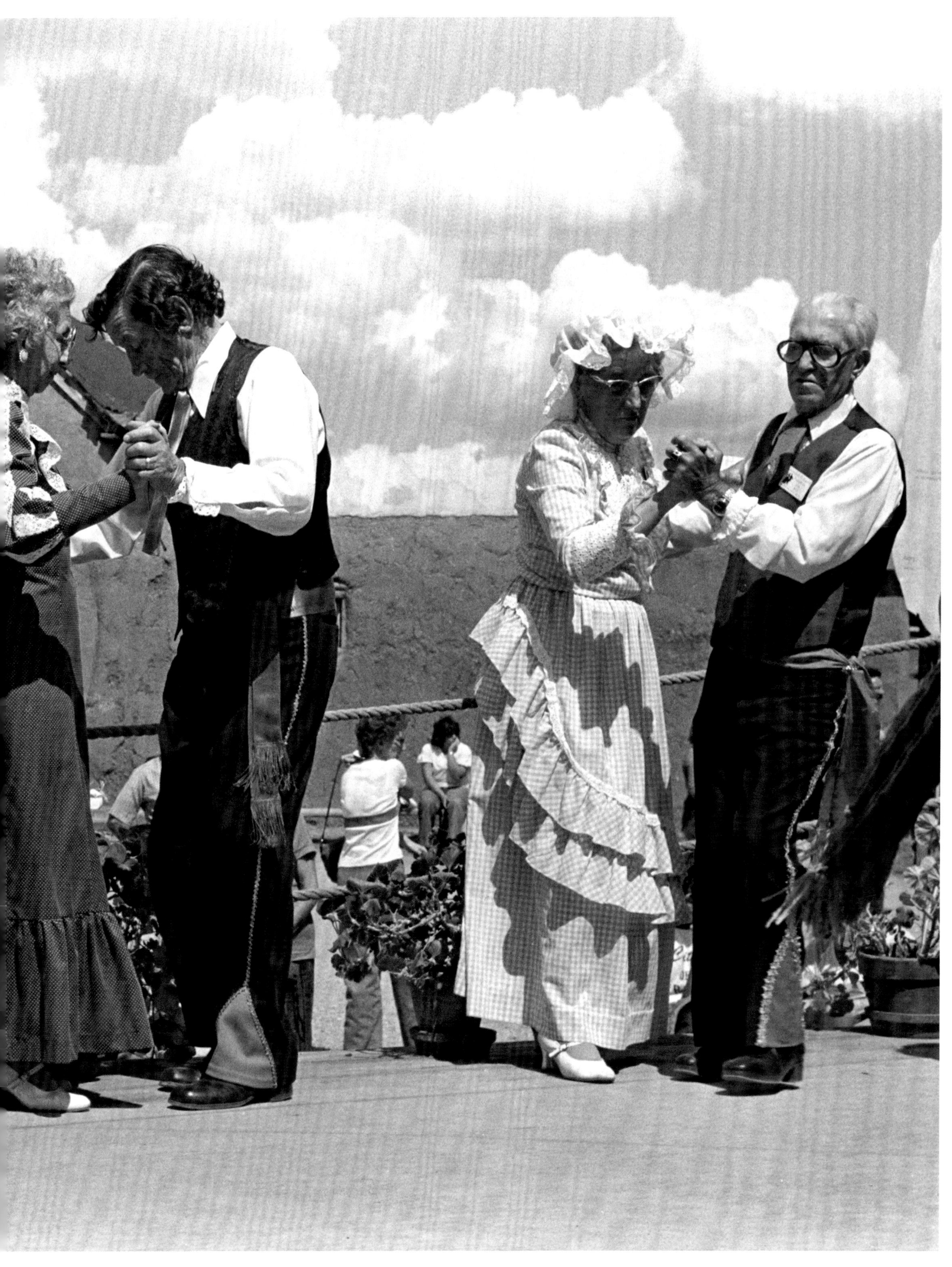

El Rancho de las Golondrinas, La Cienega, 1981.

OVERLEAF: Good Friday, Chimayó, 1982.

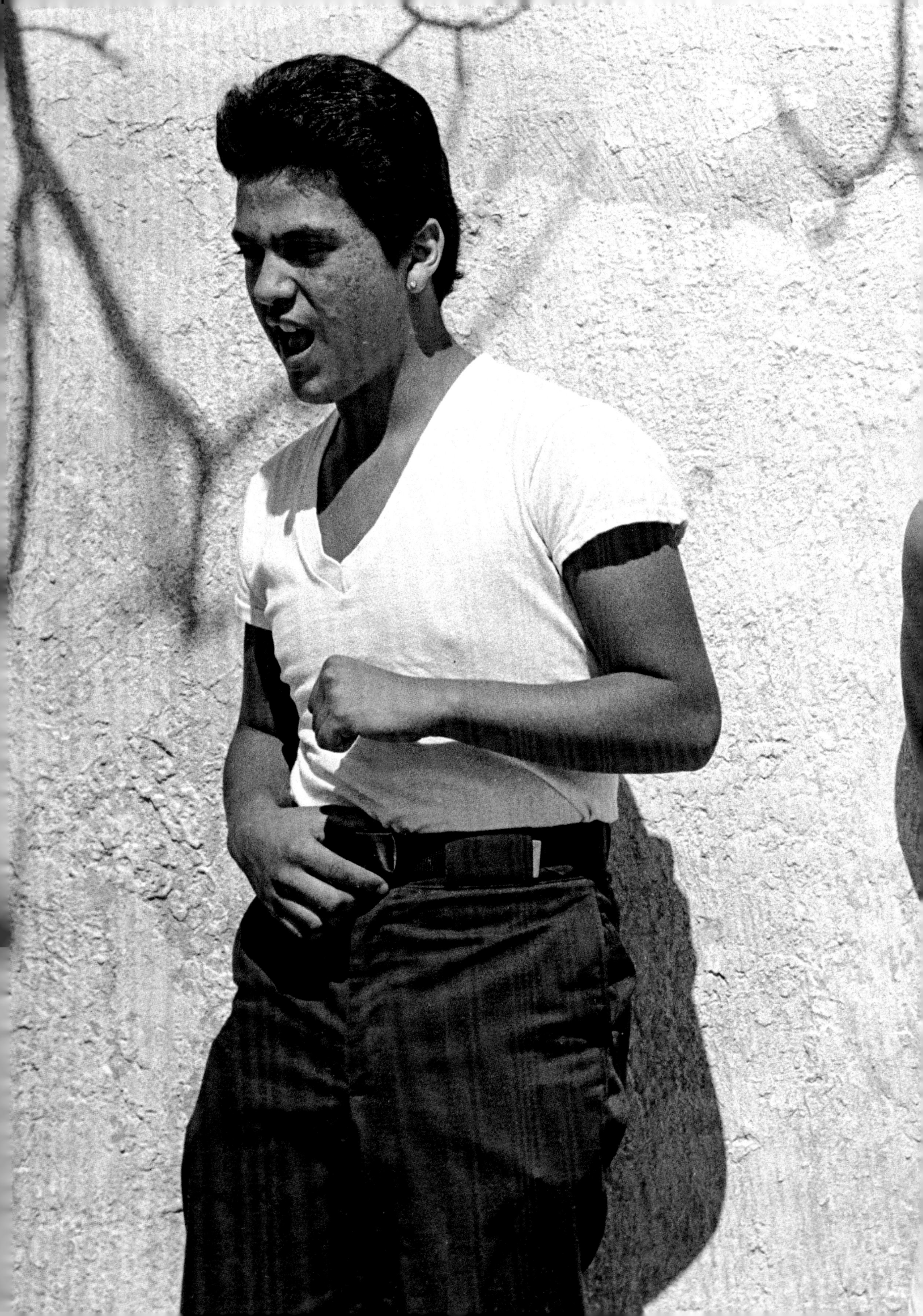

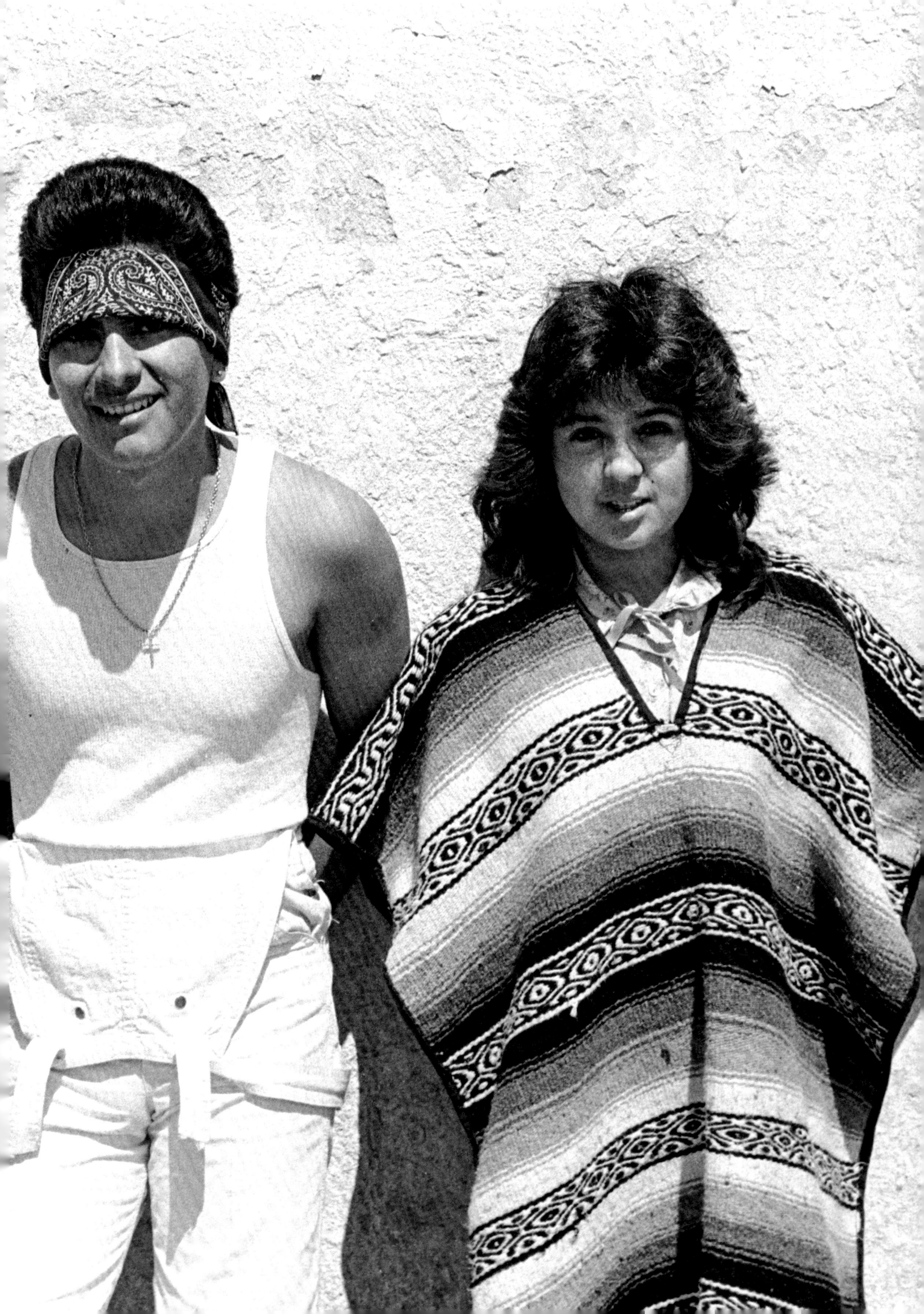

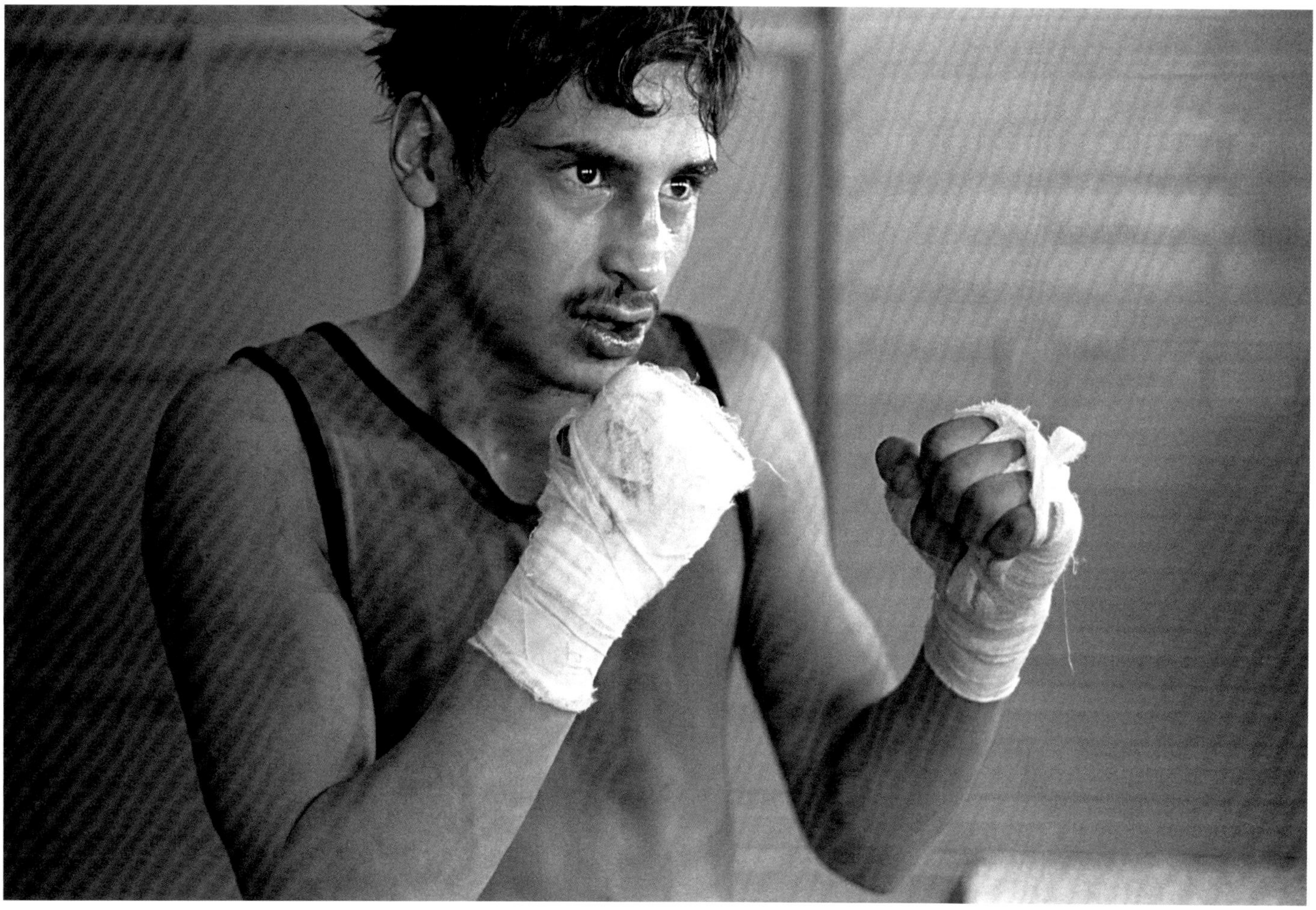

Police Athletic League boxer, Albuquerque, 1983.

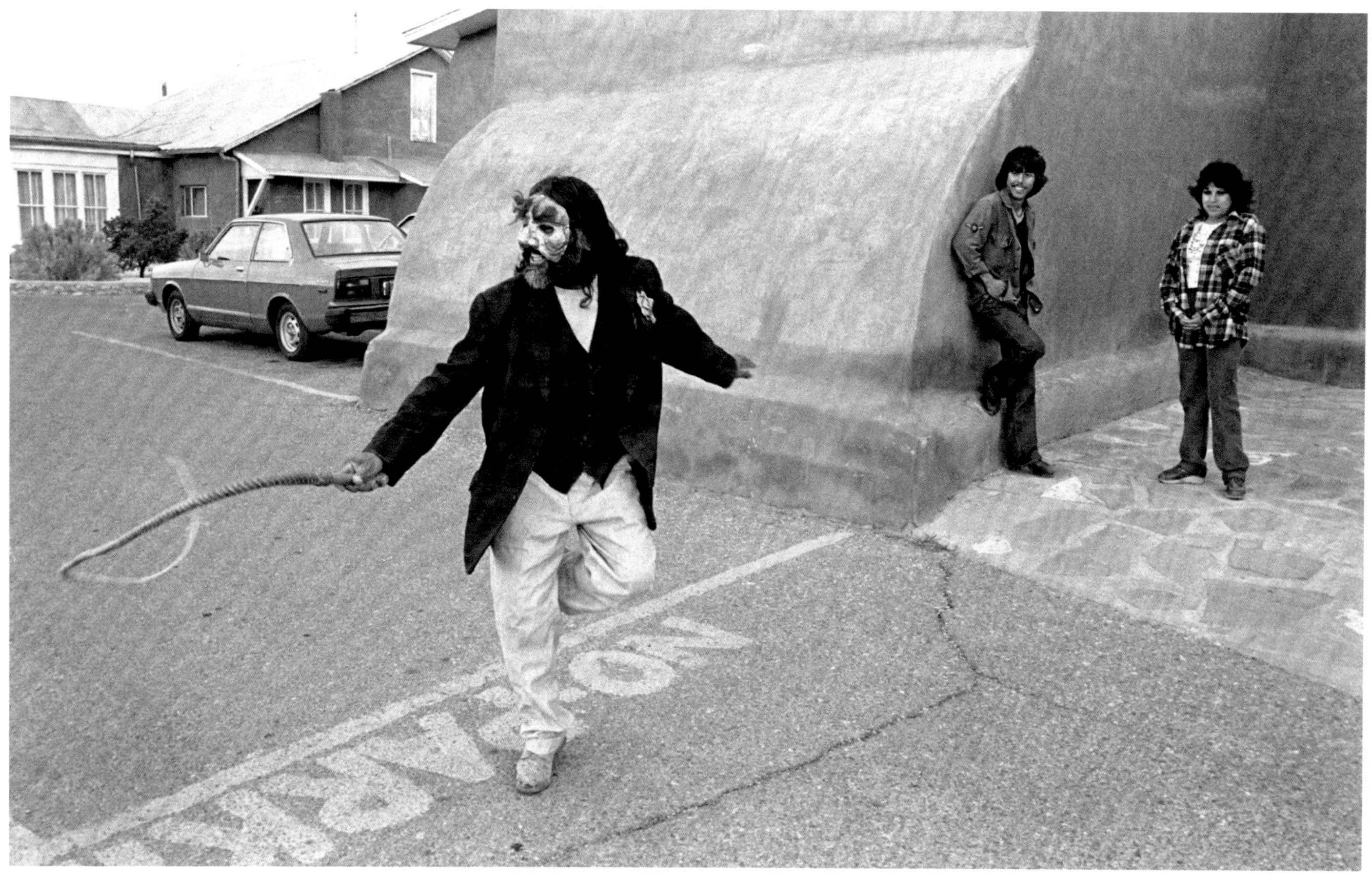

Rudy Herrera, El Abuelo for the El Rancho Matachines, Pojoaque, 1983.

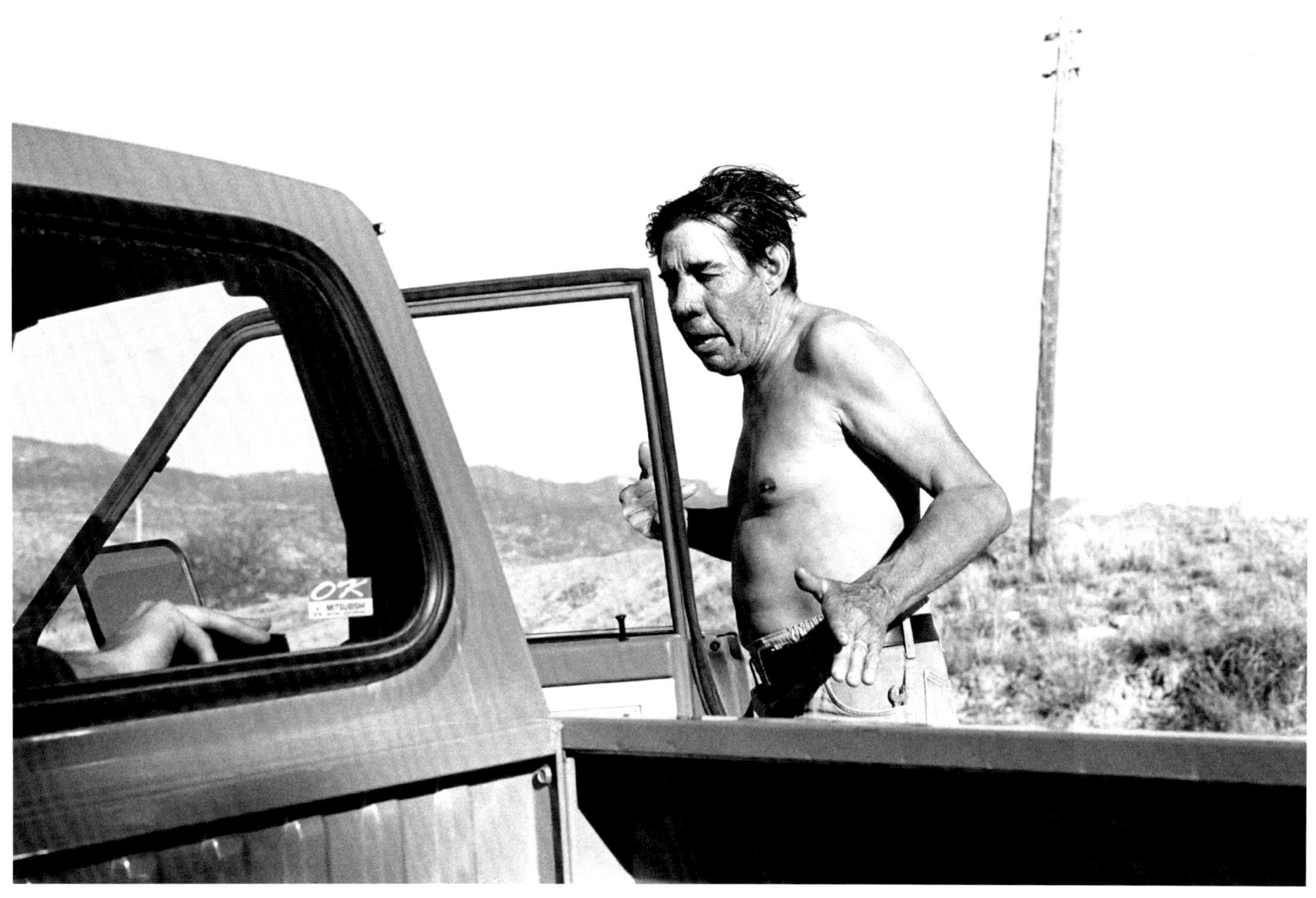

Nambé, 1981.

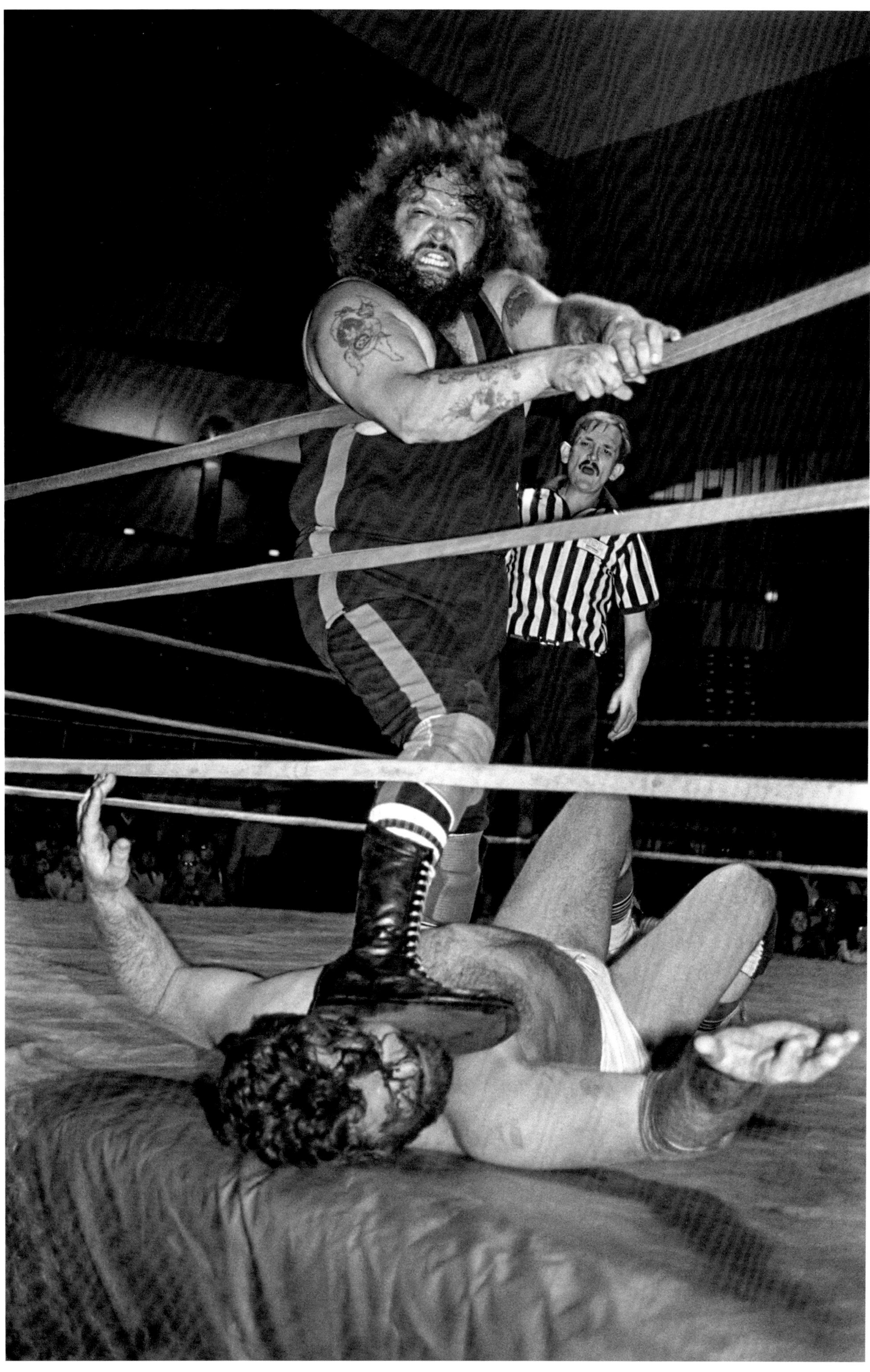

Professional wrestling, Albuquerque, 1983.

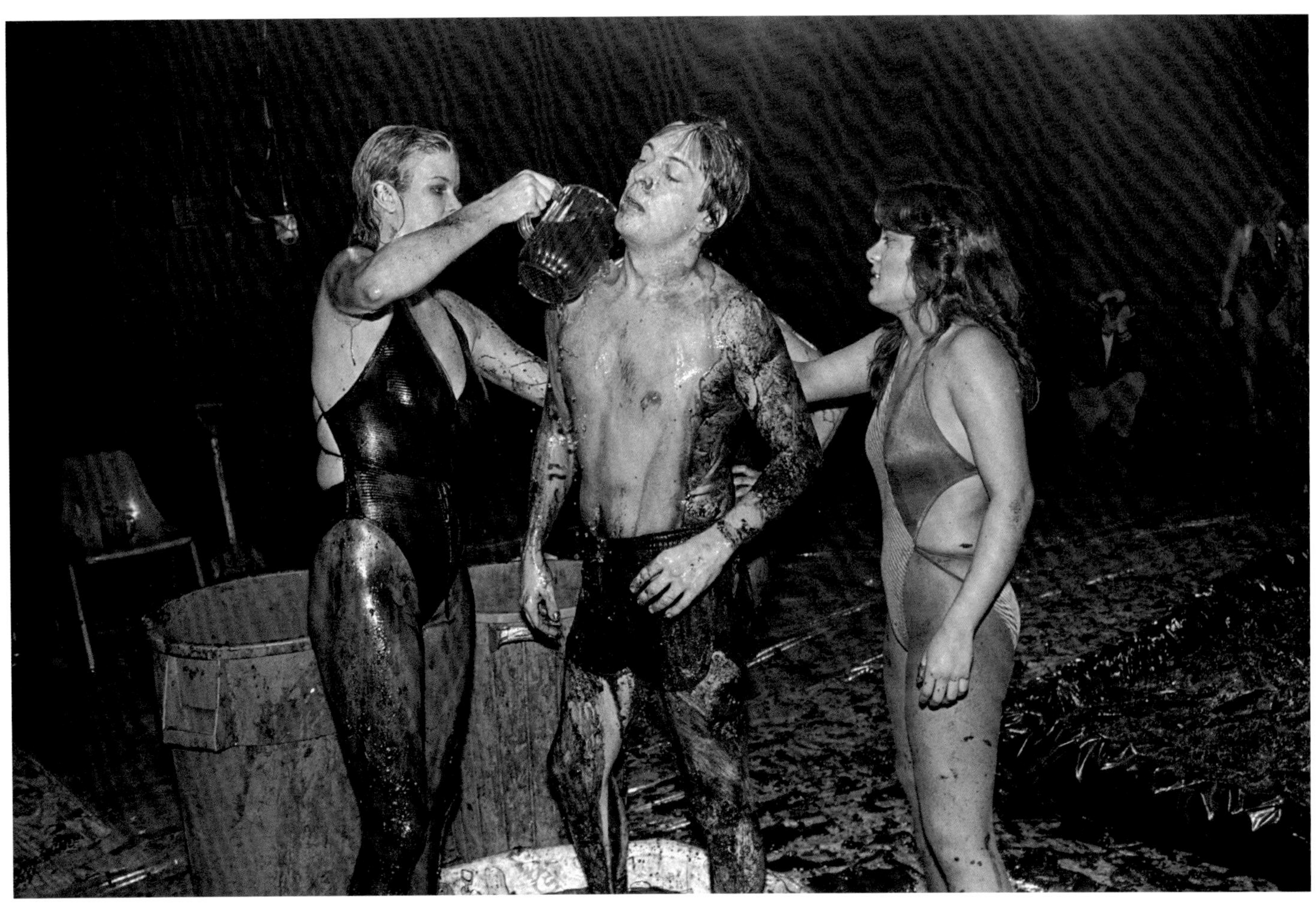

Mud wrestling, Albuquerque, 1983.

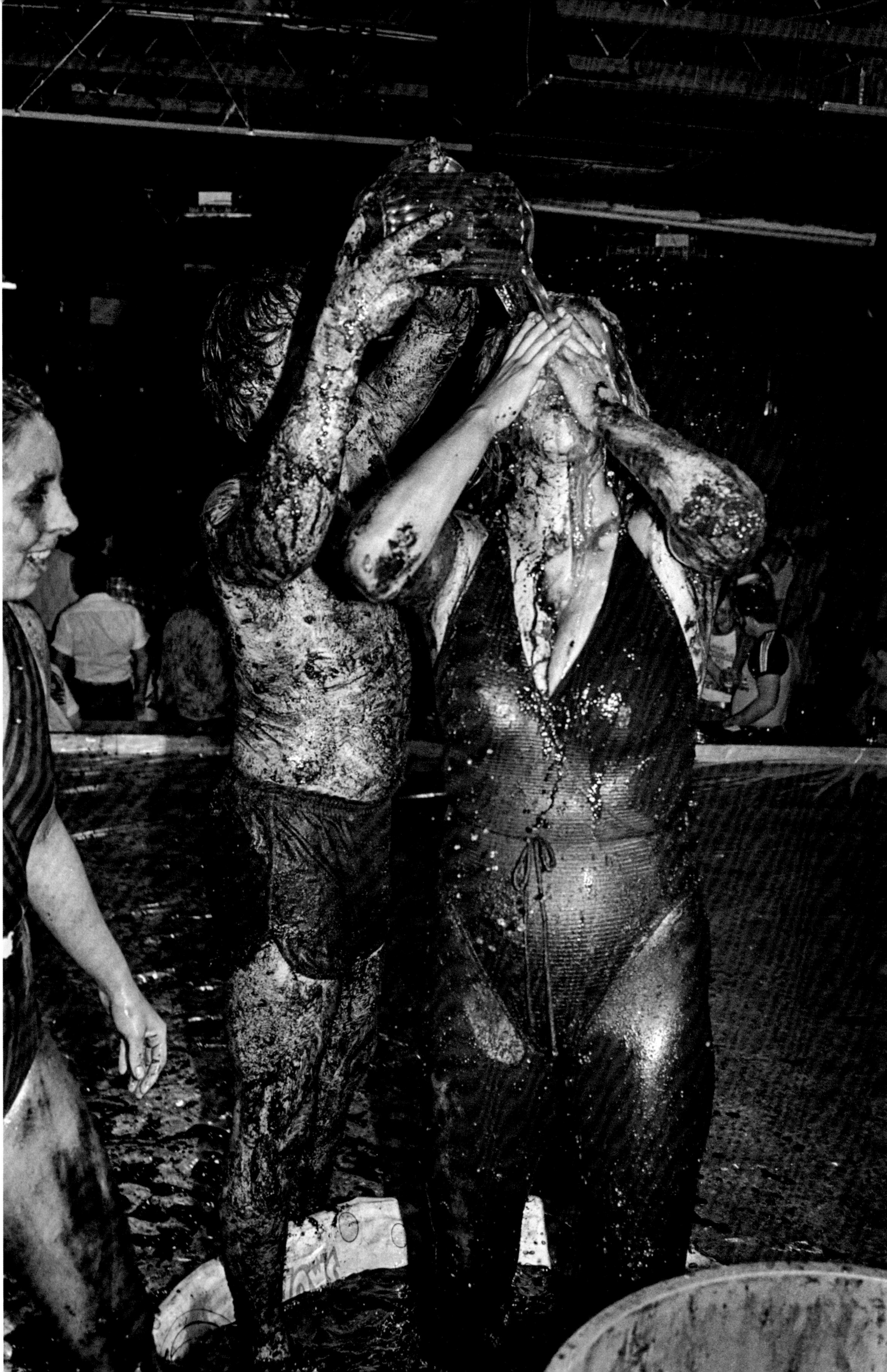

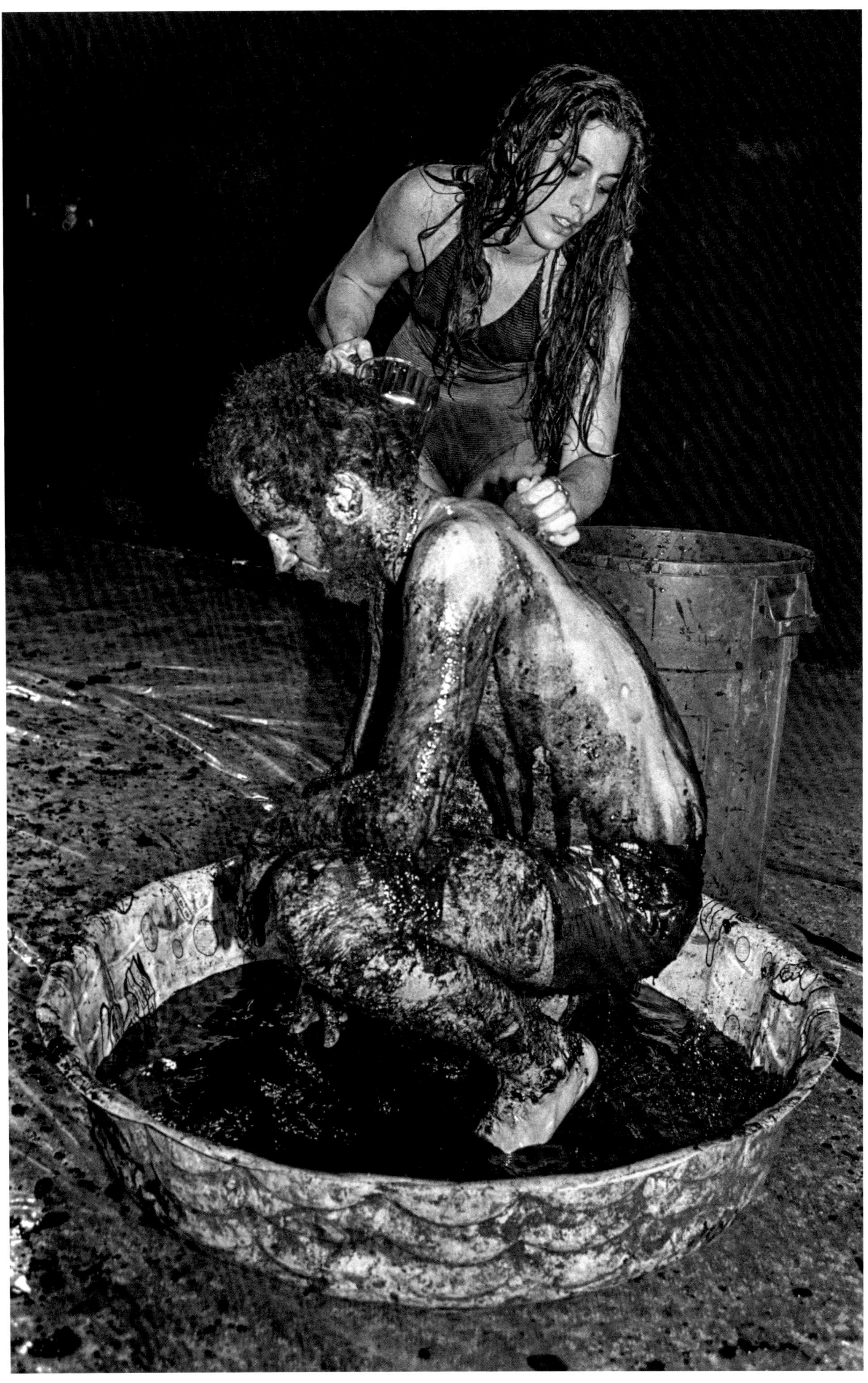

OPPOSITE, ABOVE, AND OVERLEAF: Mud wrestling, Albuquerque, 1983.

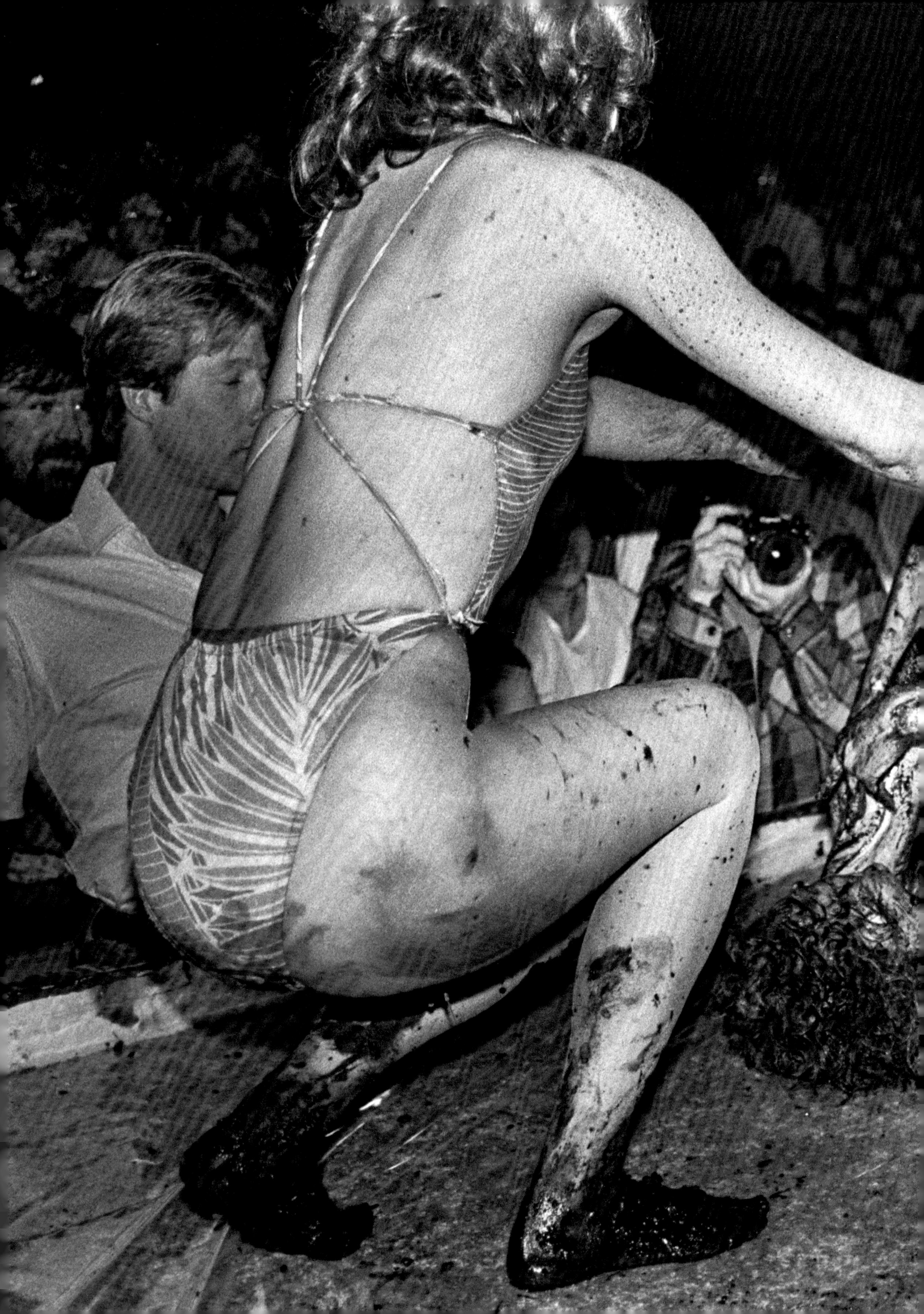

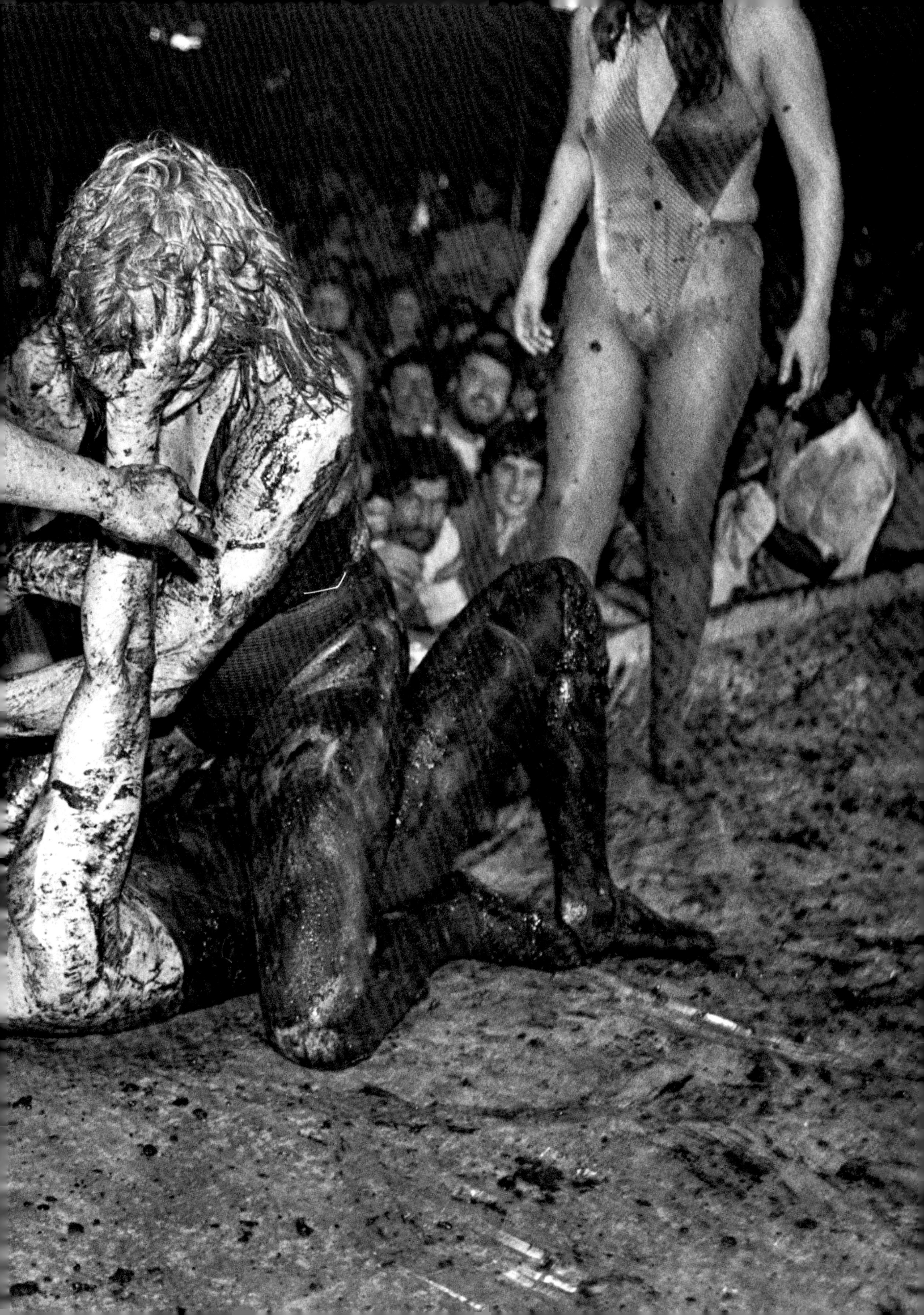

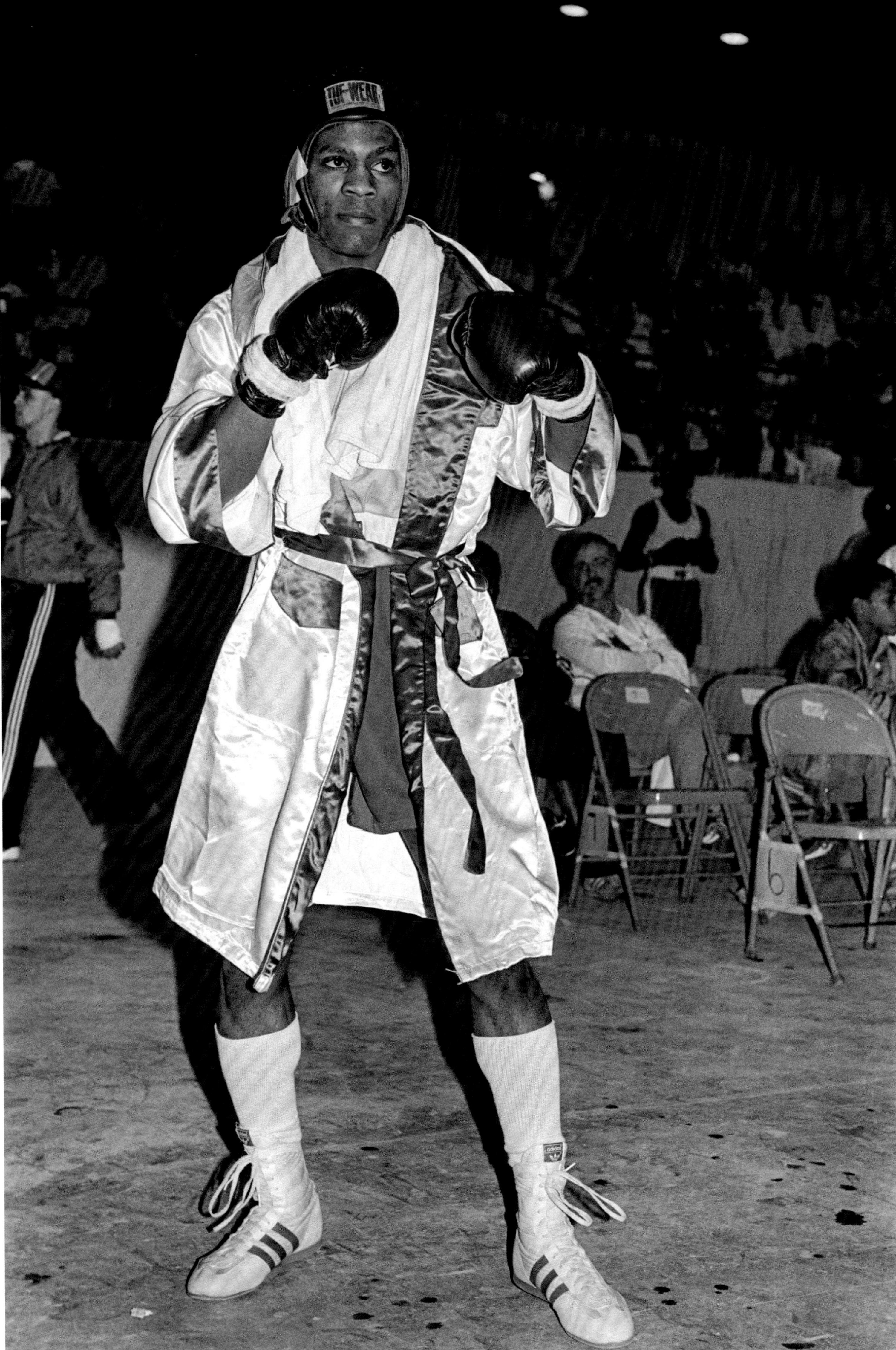
TUF-WEAR
6

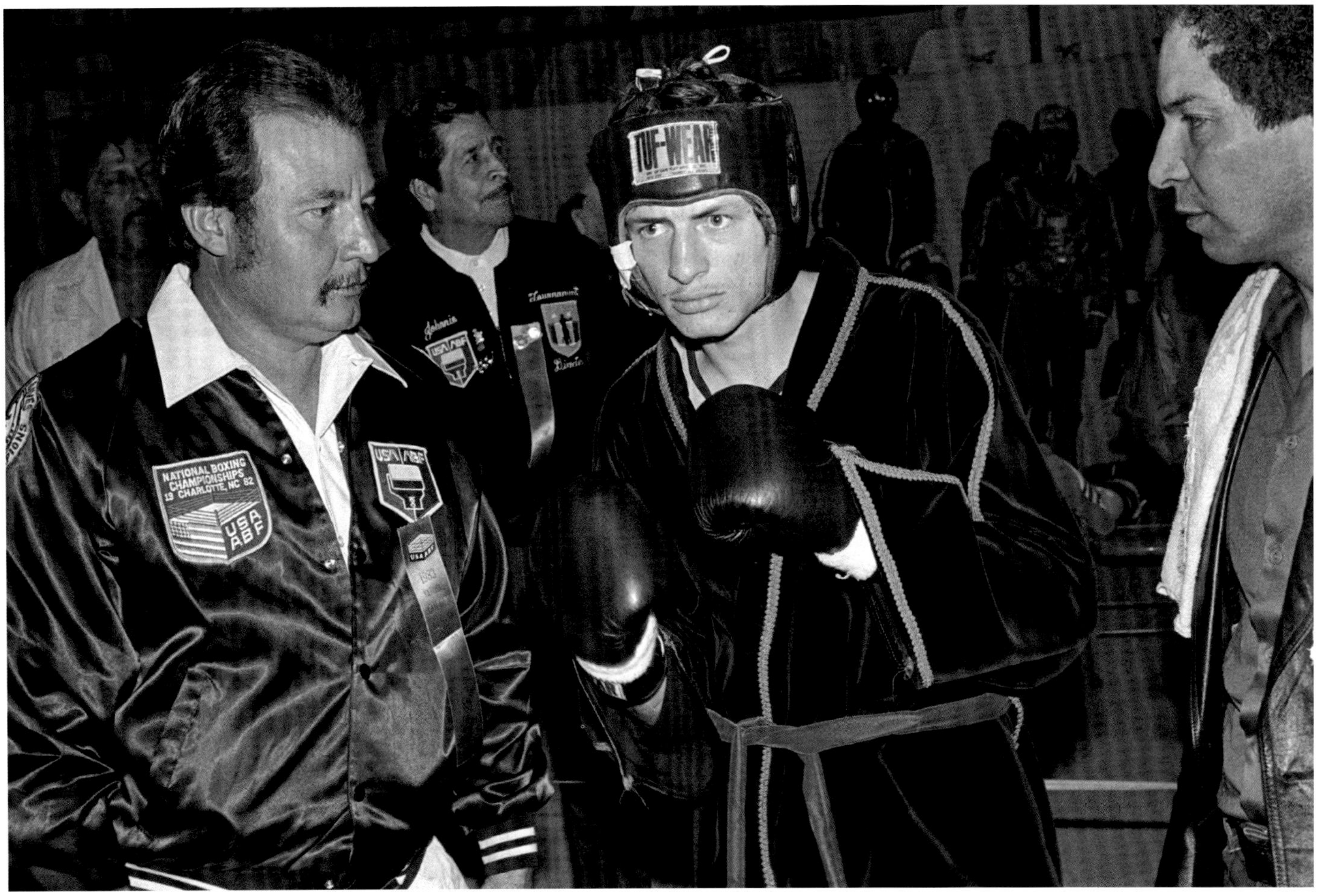

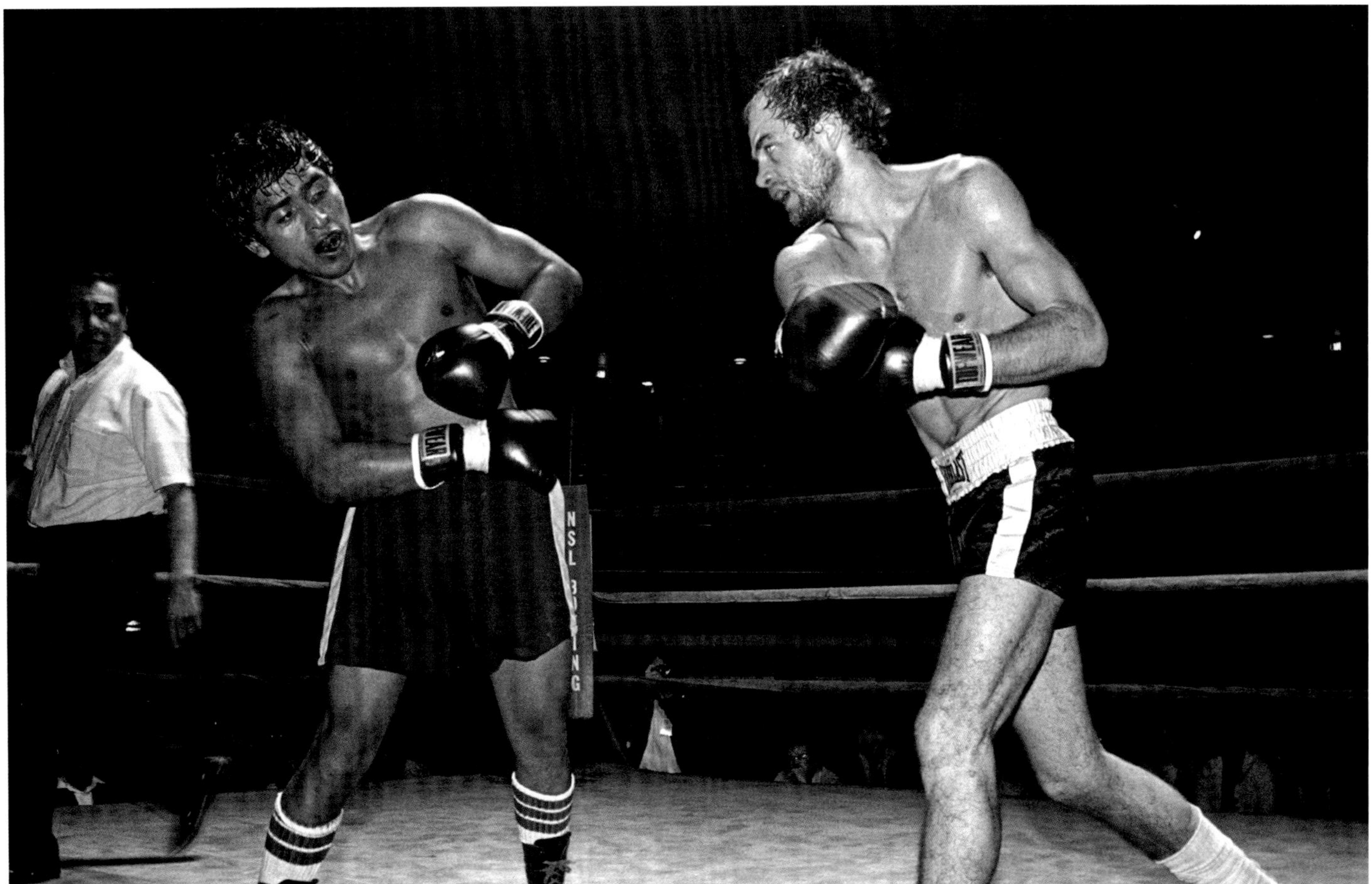

OPPOSITE, ABOVE, AND OVERLEAF: Police Athletic League and Golden Gloves boxing match, Albuquerque, 1982.

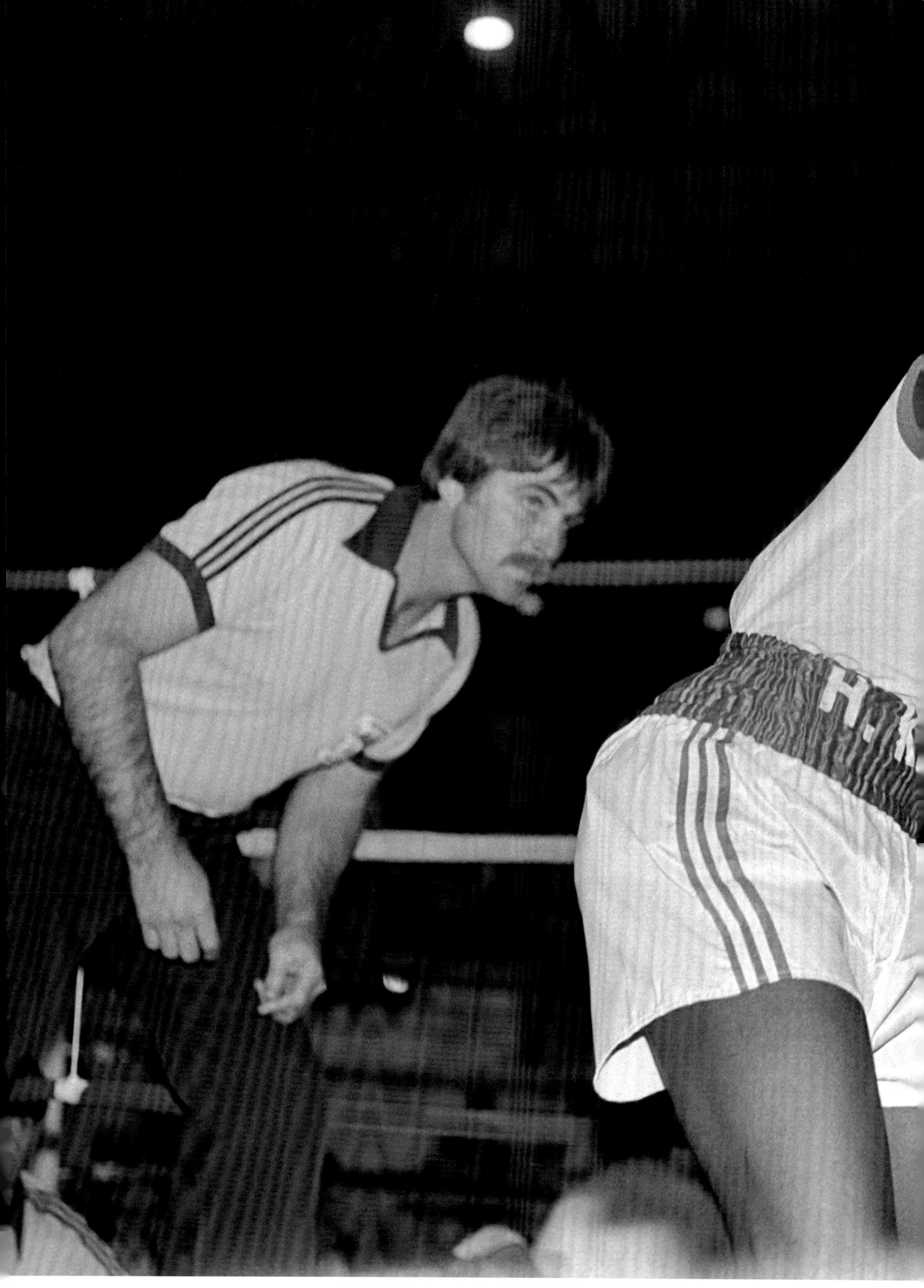

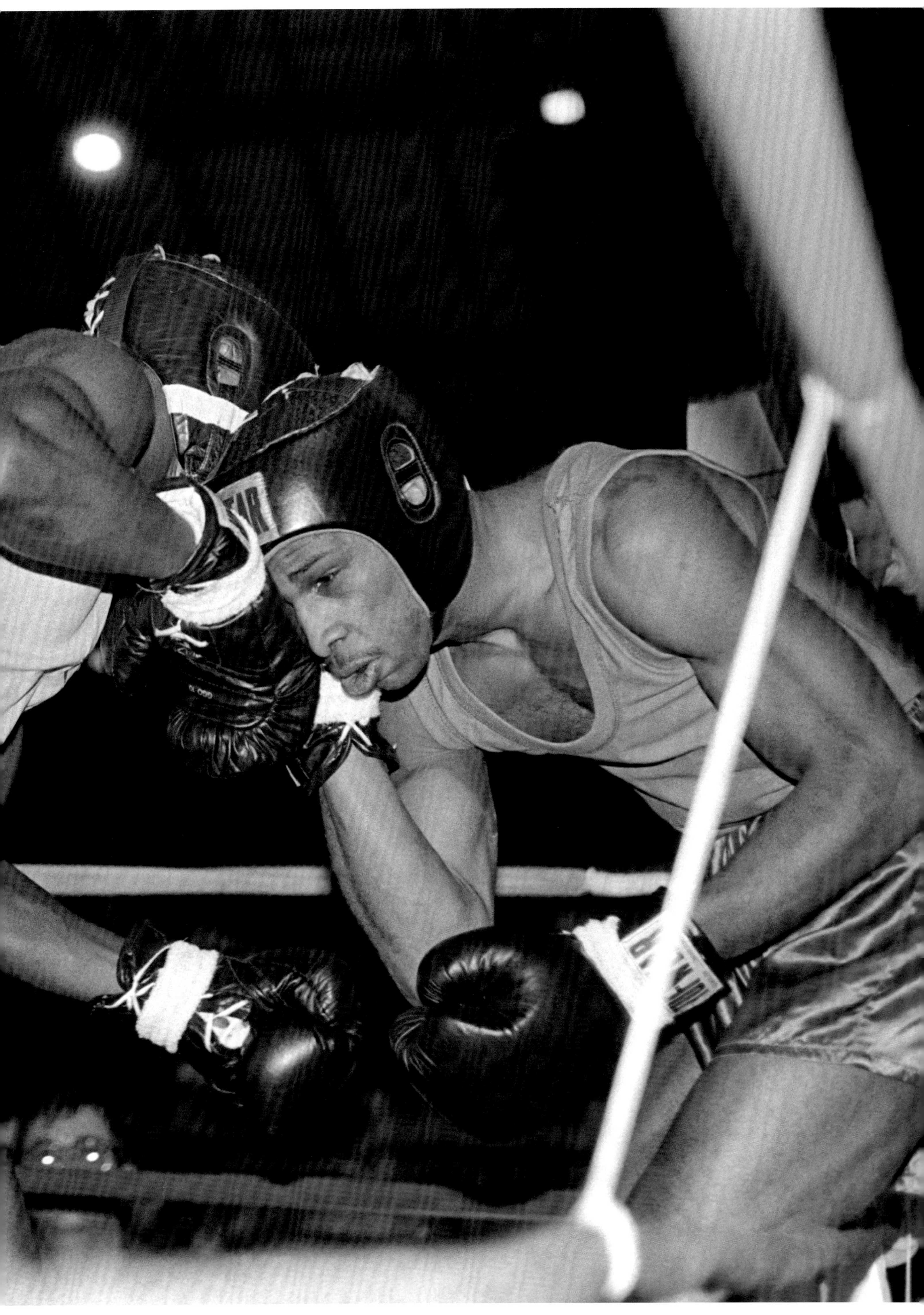

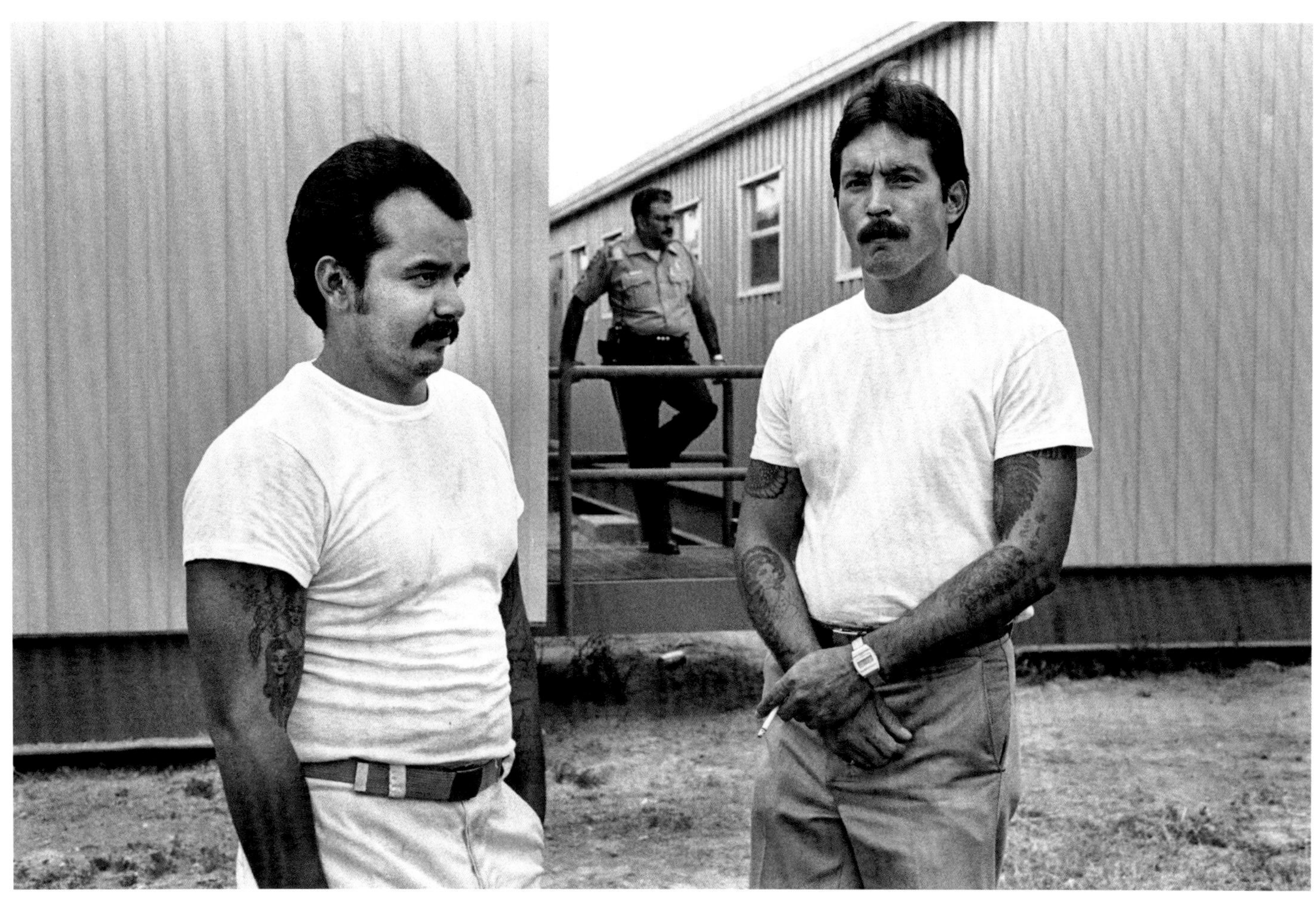

ABOVE, OPPOSITE, AND OVERLEAF: Weightlifting competition, Penitentiary of New Mexico, Santa Fe, 1983.

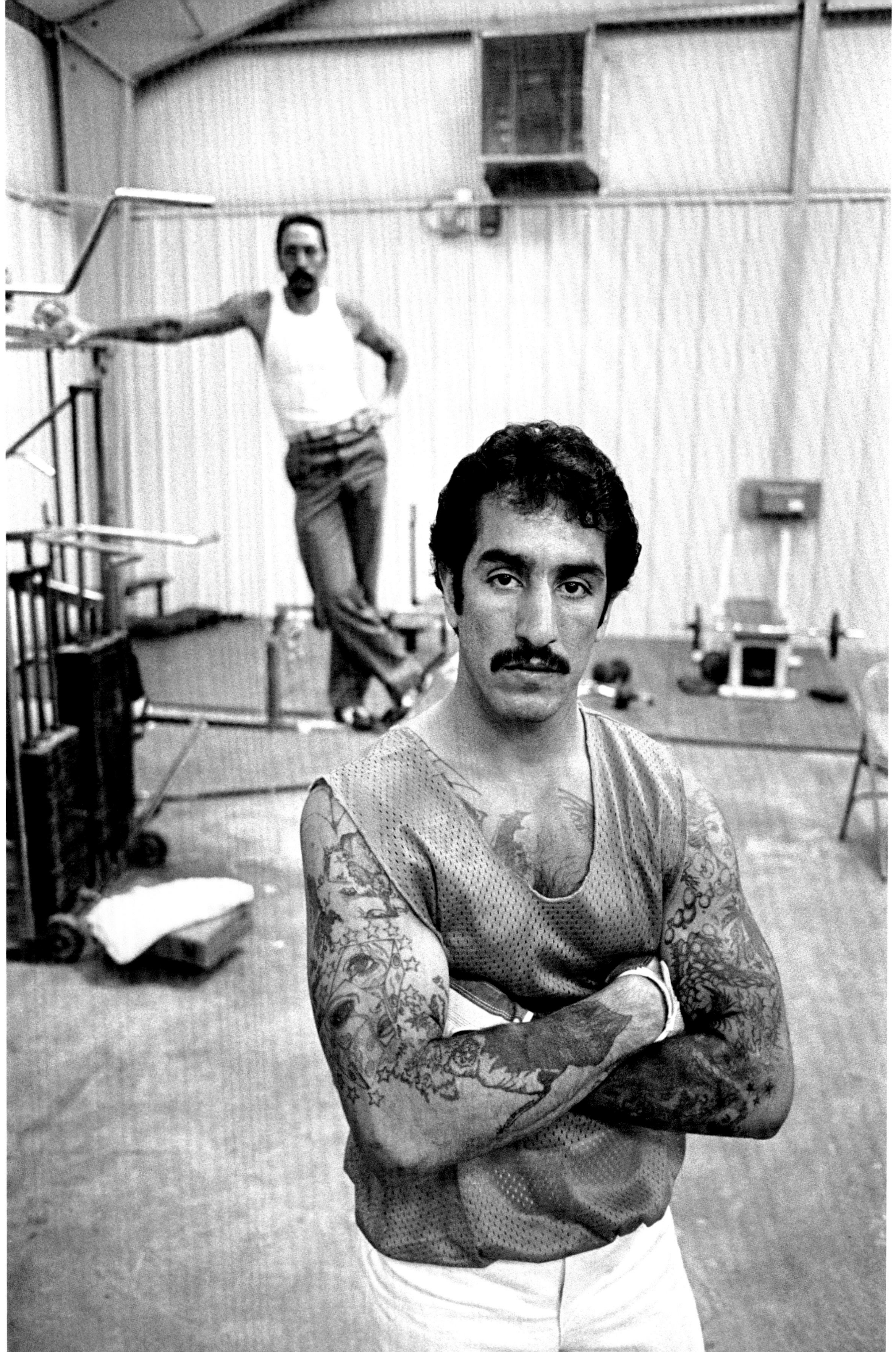

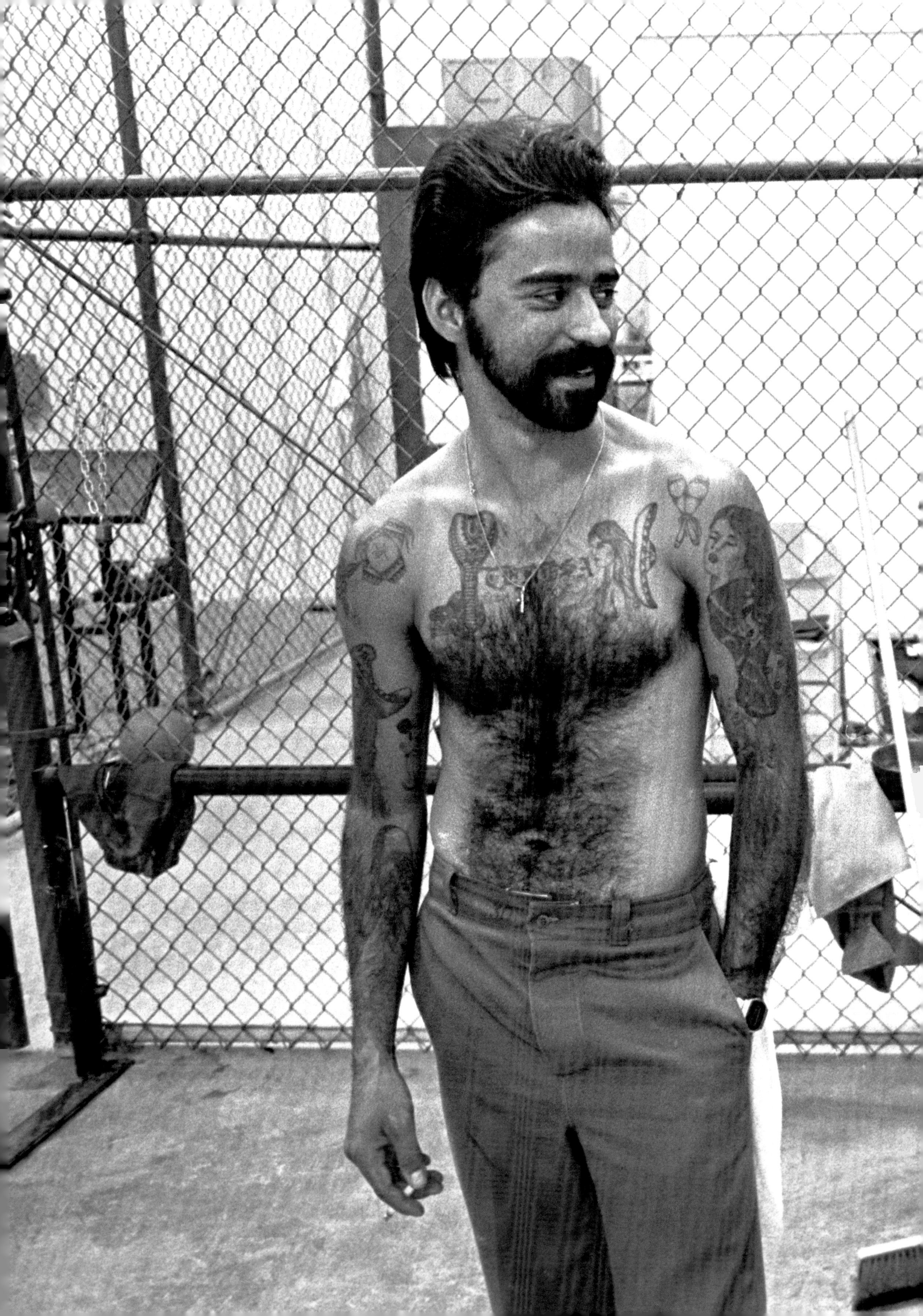

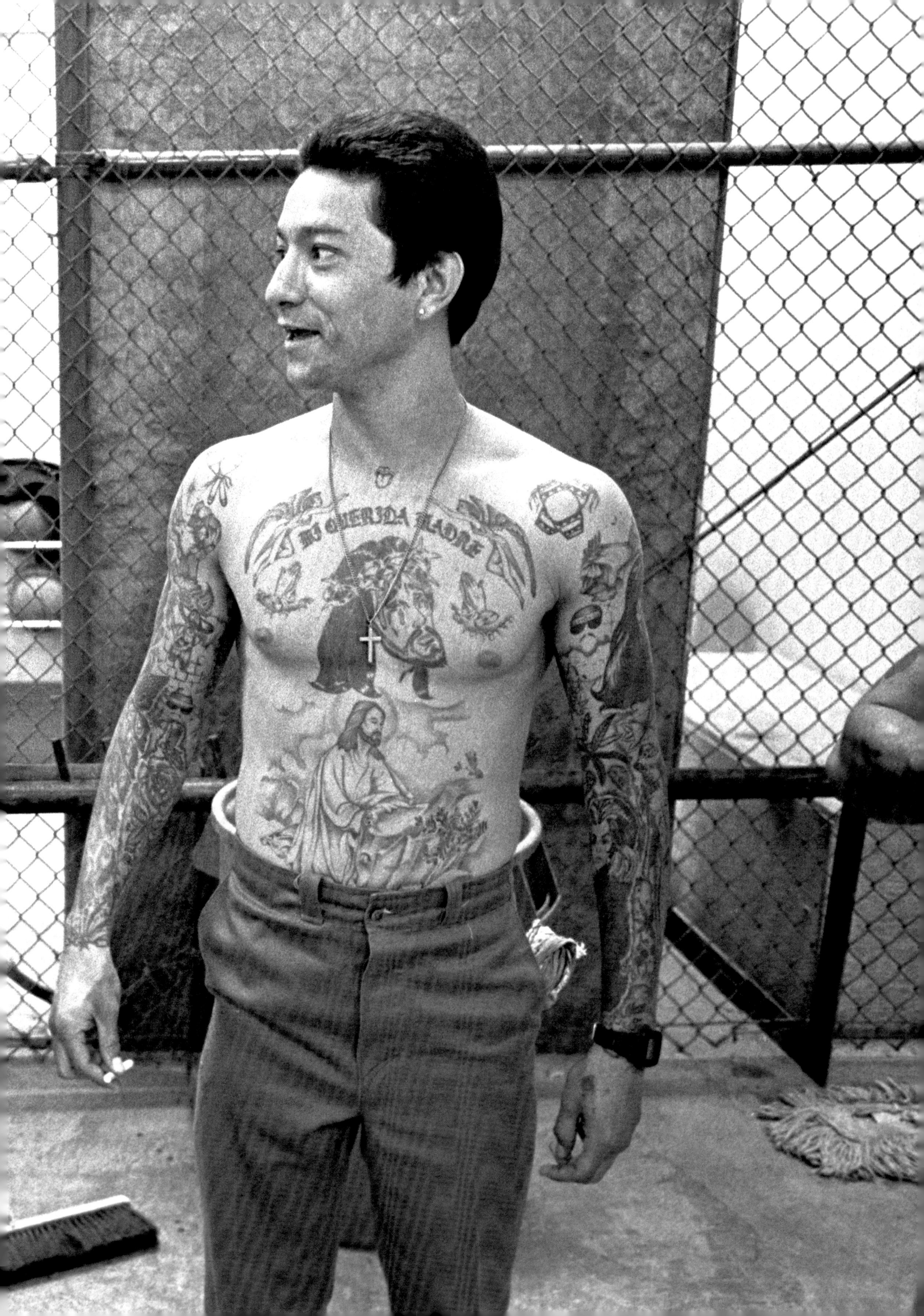

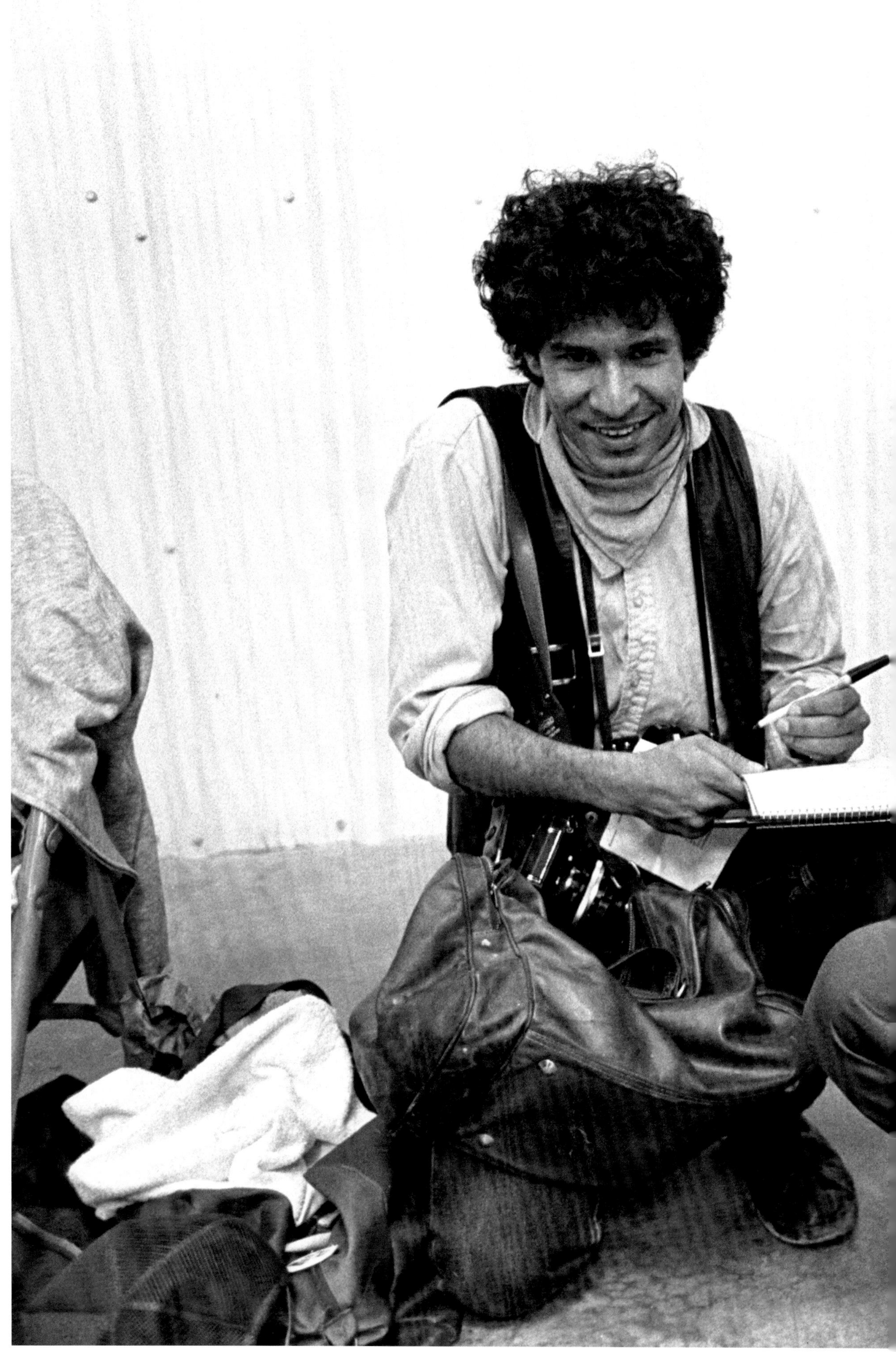

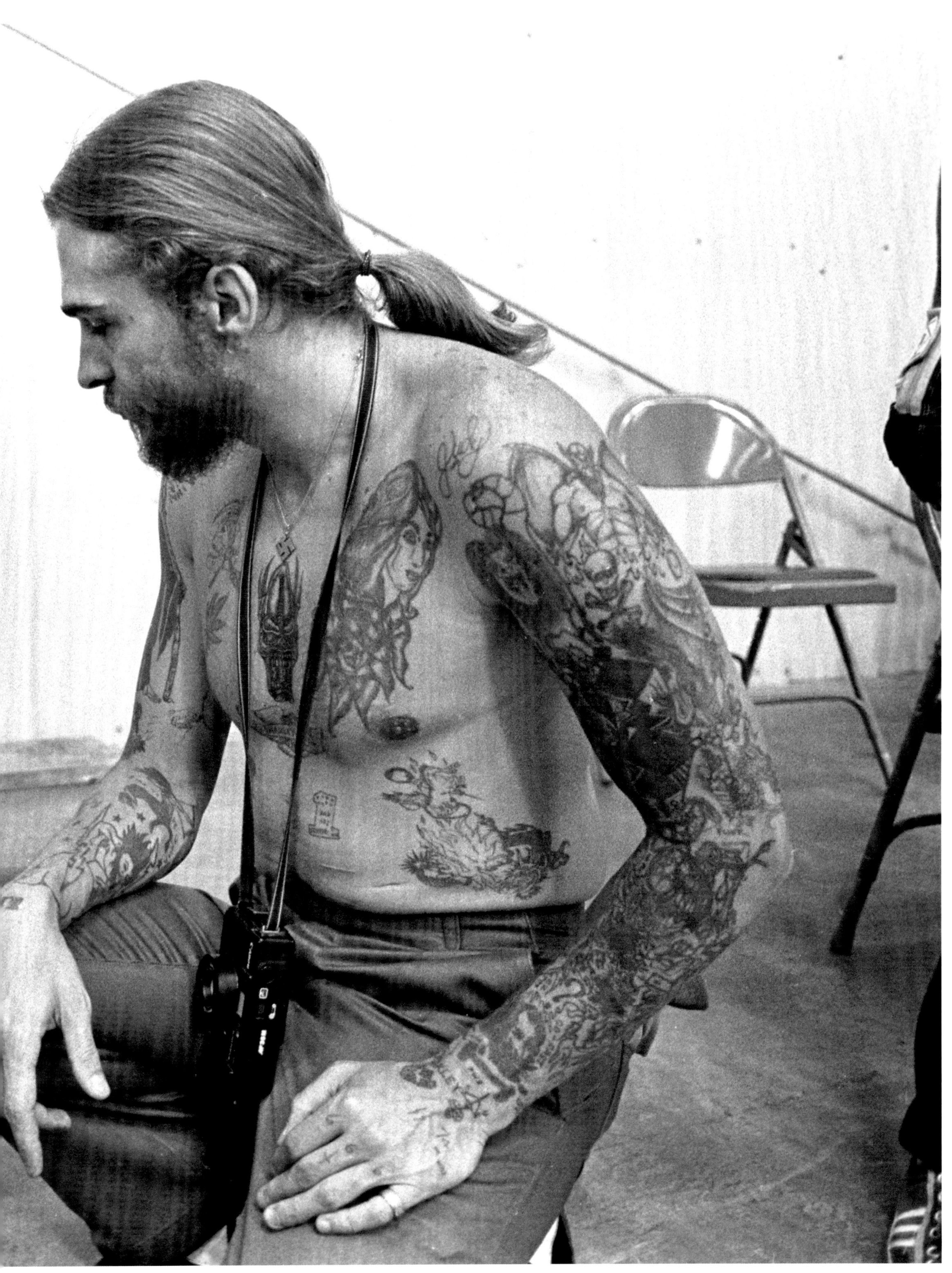

Photographer Rahoul Contractor with a competitor in the weightlifting competition, Penitentiary of New Mexico, Santa Fe, 1983.

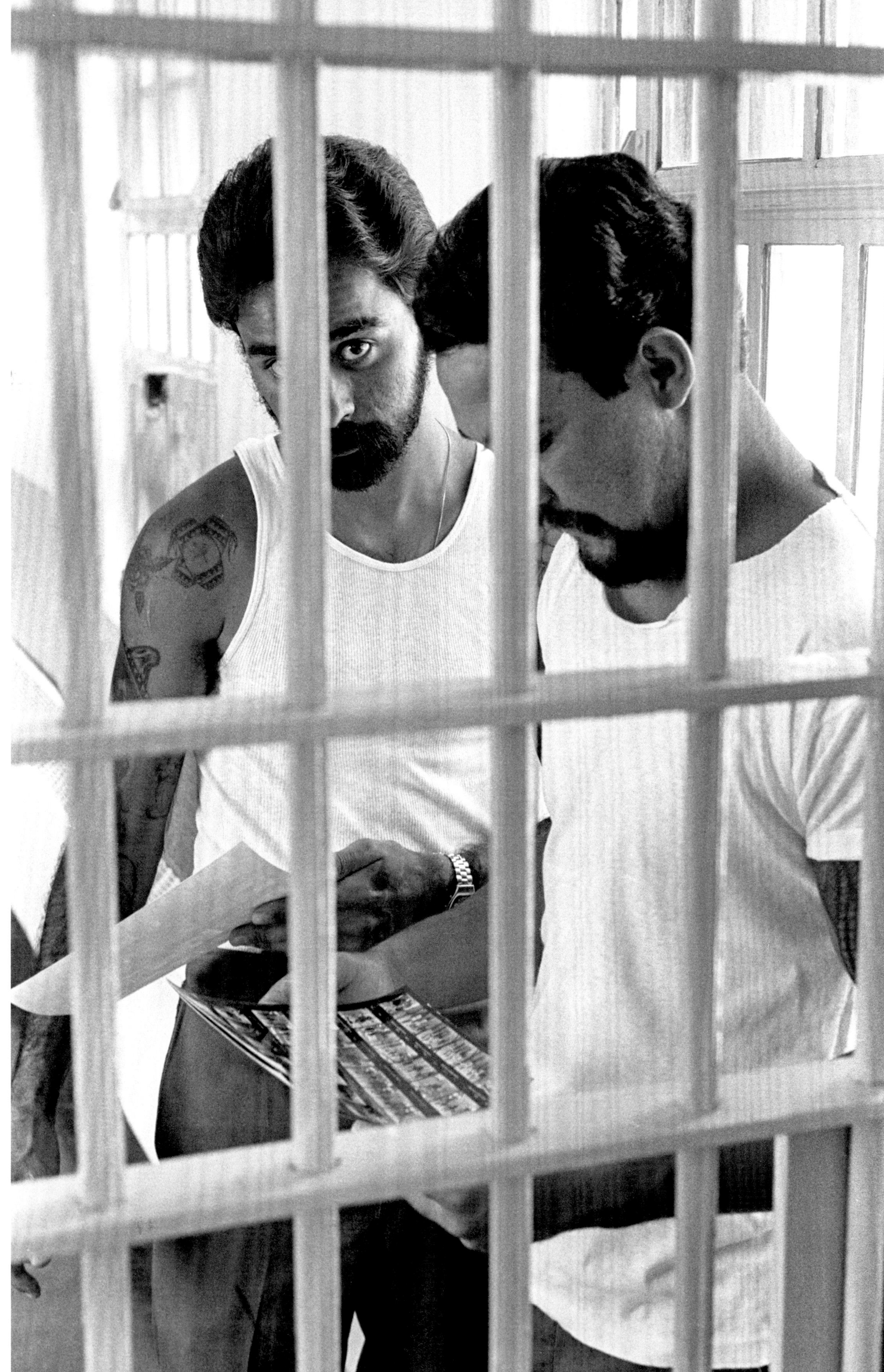

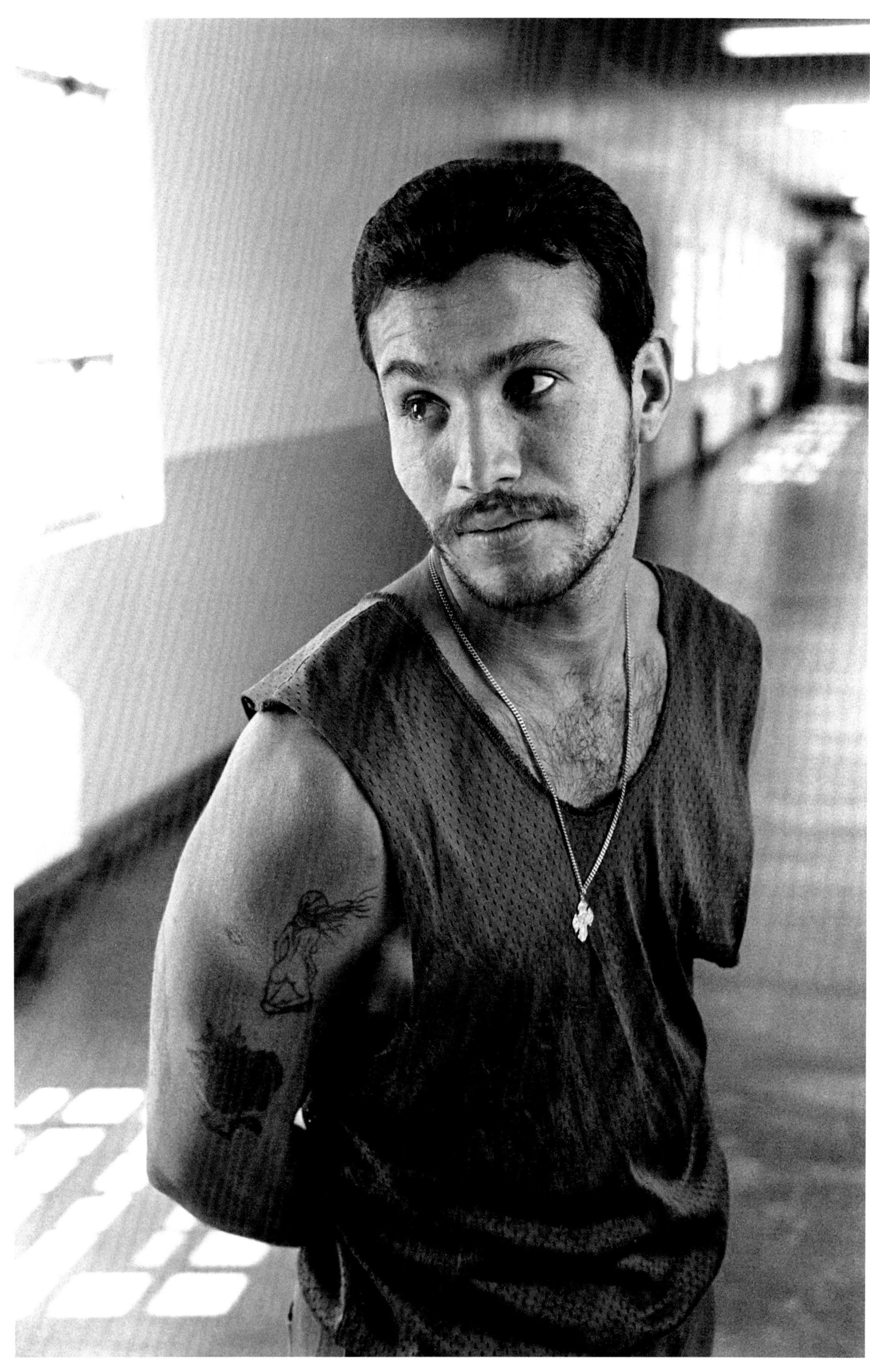

OPPOSITE AND ABOVE: Photography workshop, Penitentiary of New Mexico, Santa Fe, 1983.

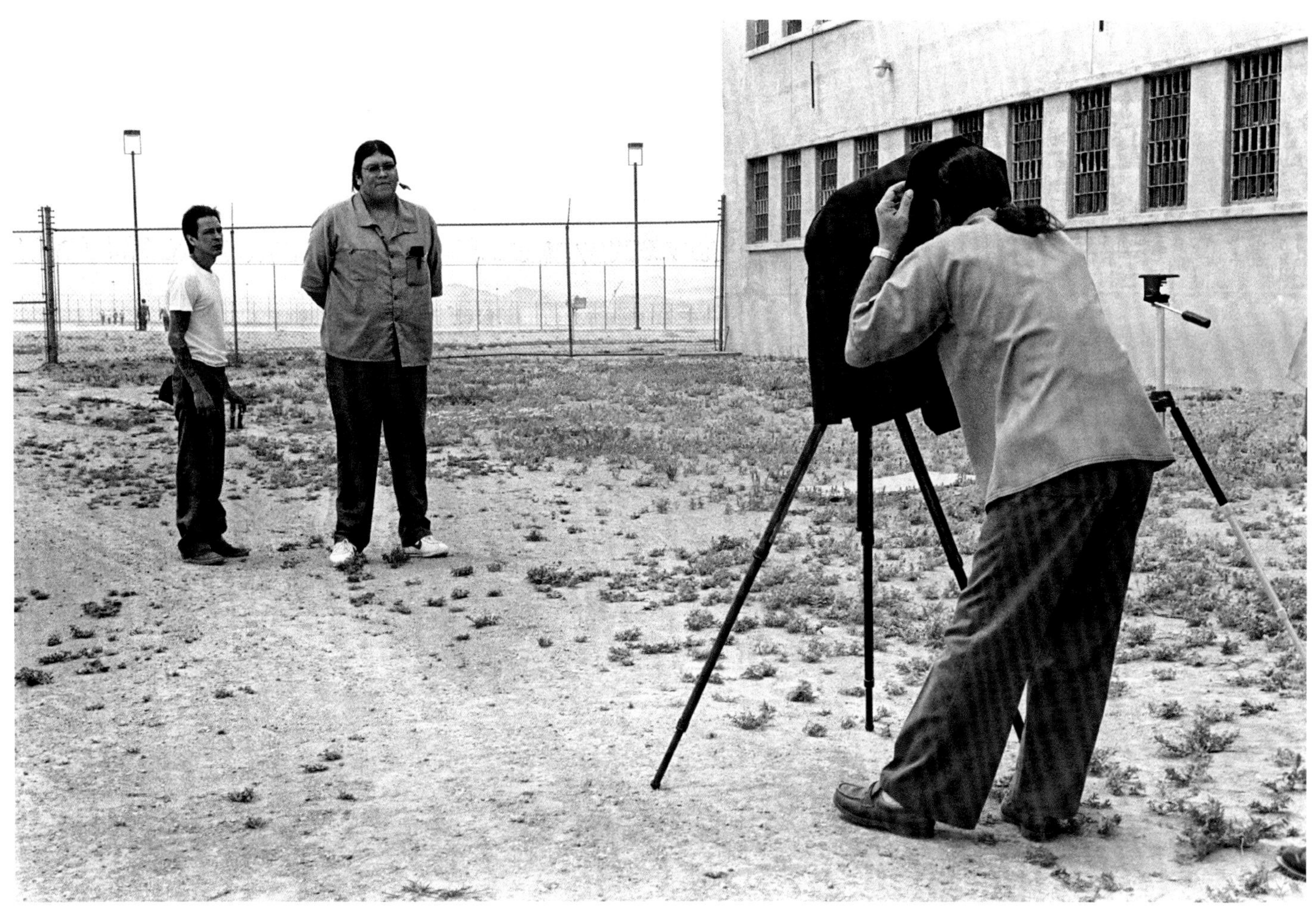

ABOVE, OPPOSITE, AND OVERLEAF: Photography workshop, Penitentiary of New Mexico, Santa Fe, 1983.

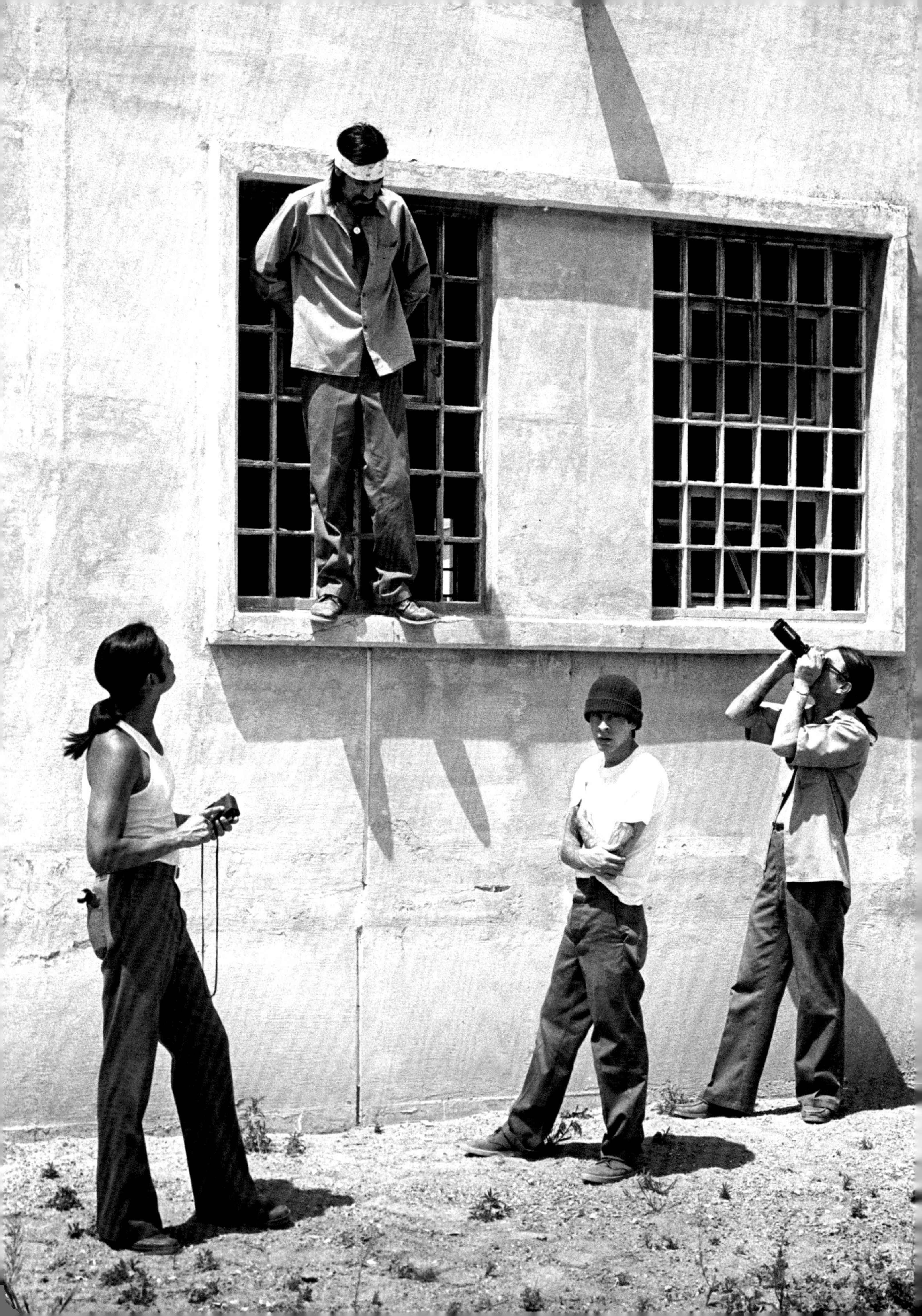

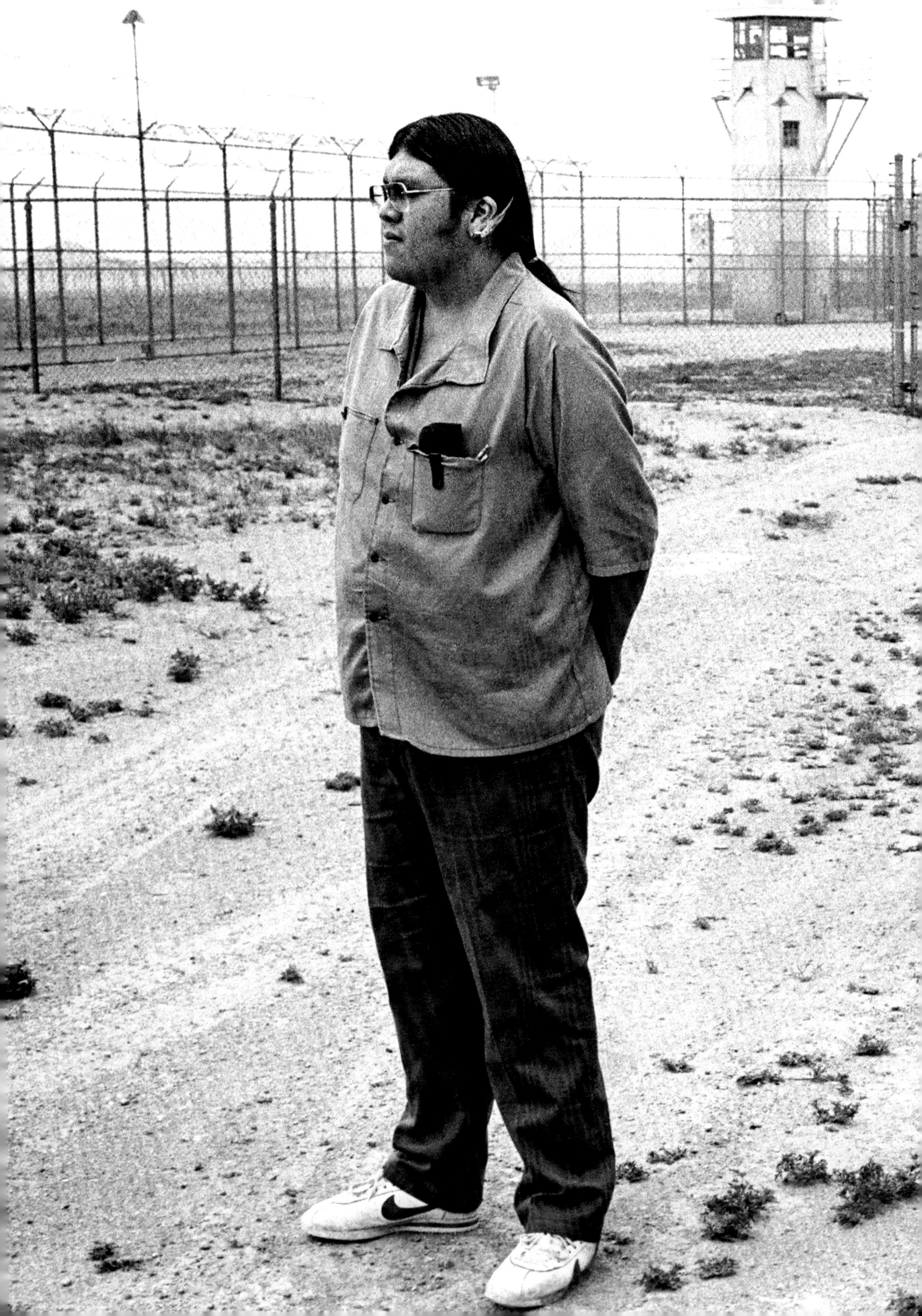

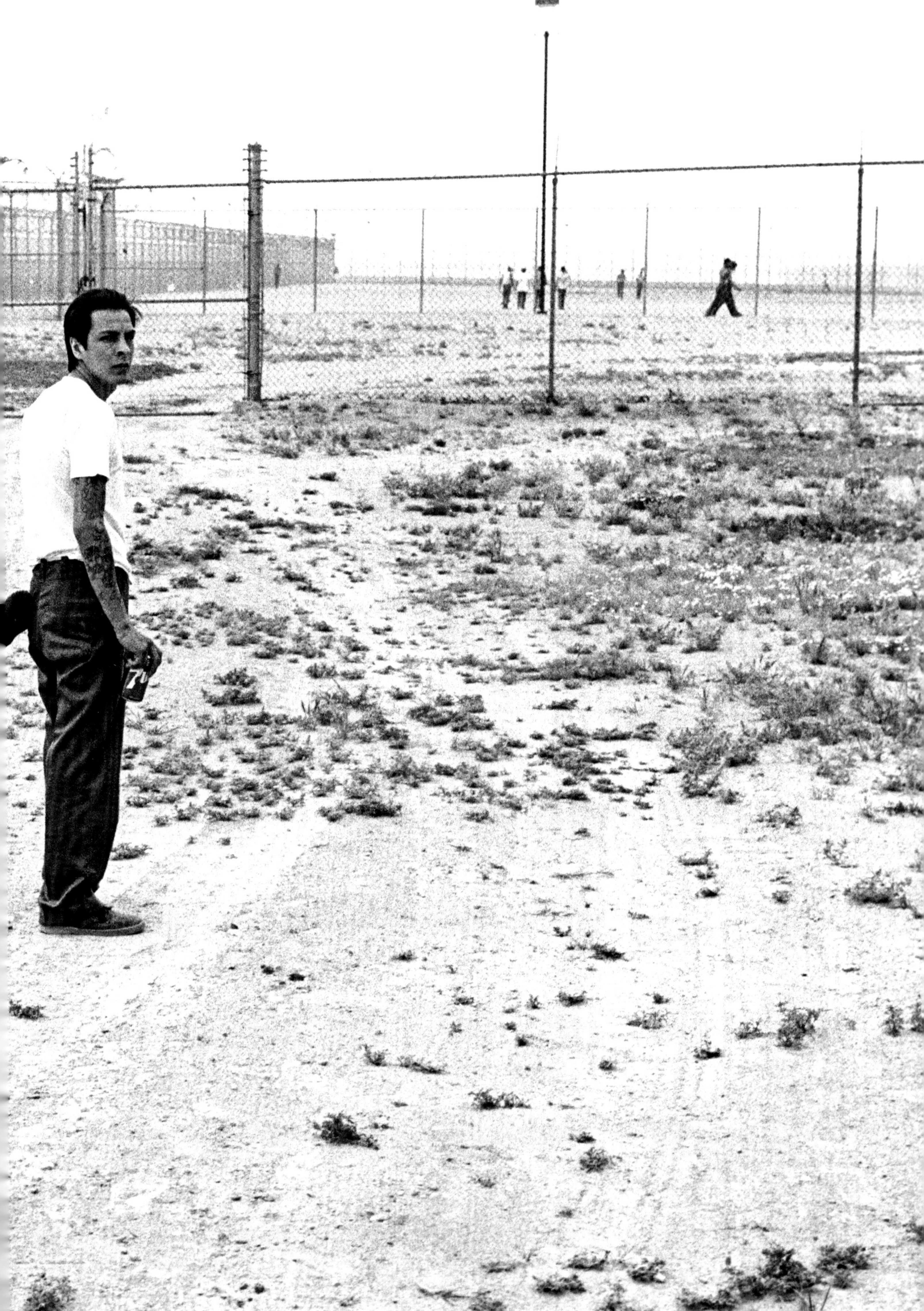

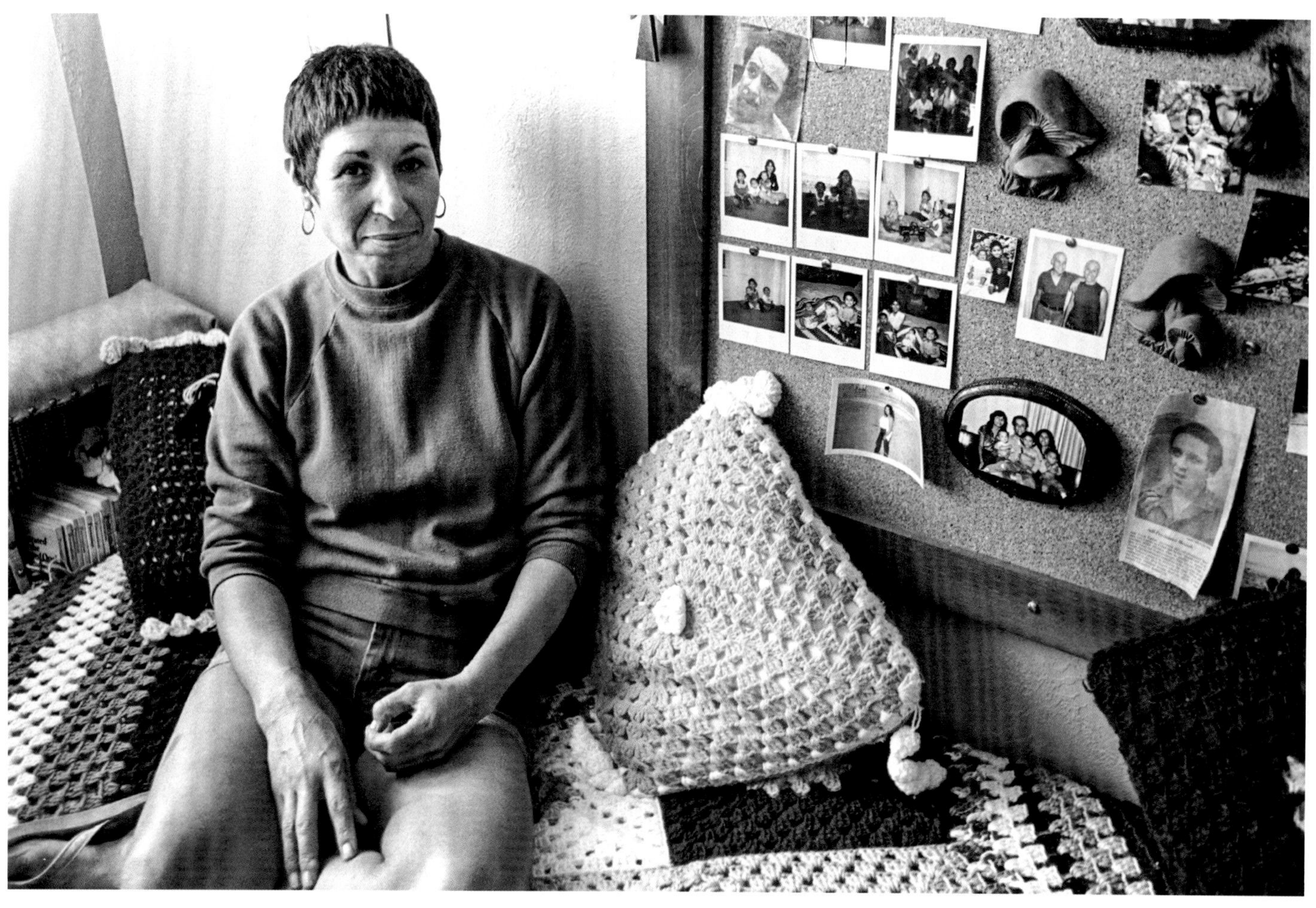

Women's Unit, Penitentiary of New Mexico, Santa Fe, 1983.

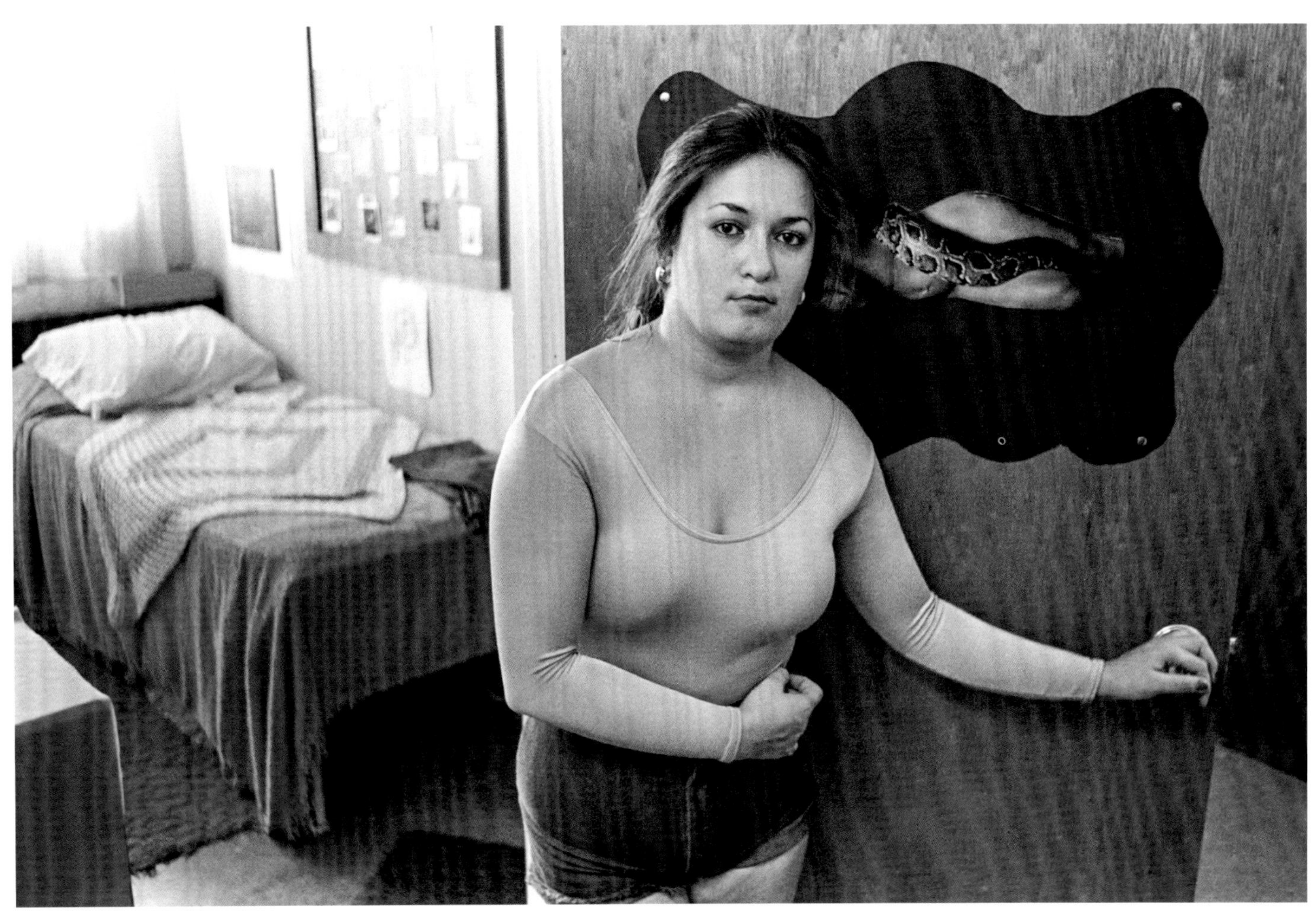

Women's Unit, Penitentiary of New Mexico, Santa Fe, 1983.

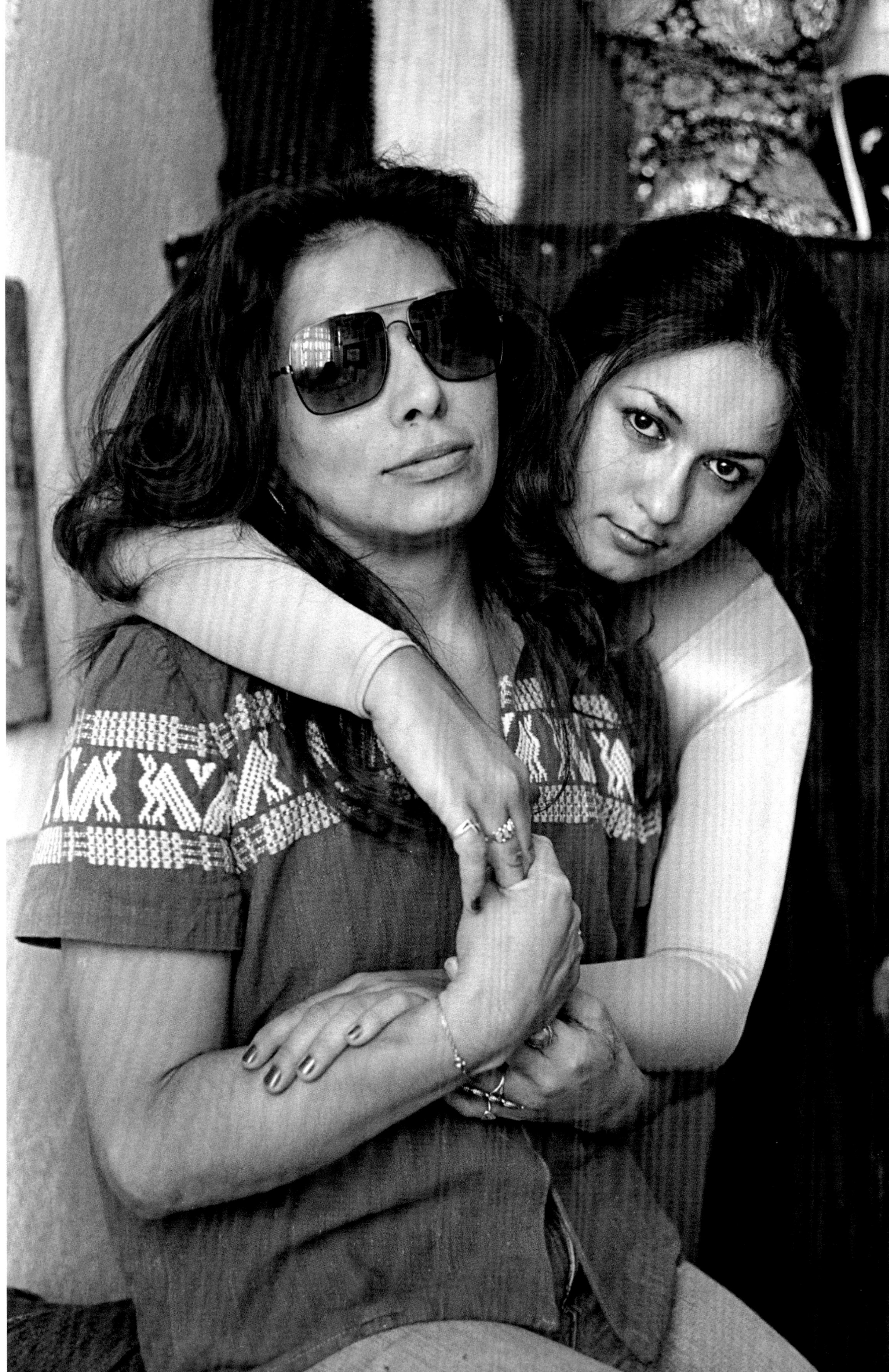

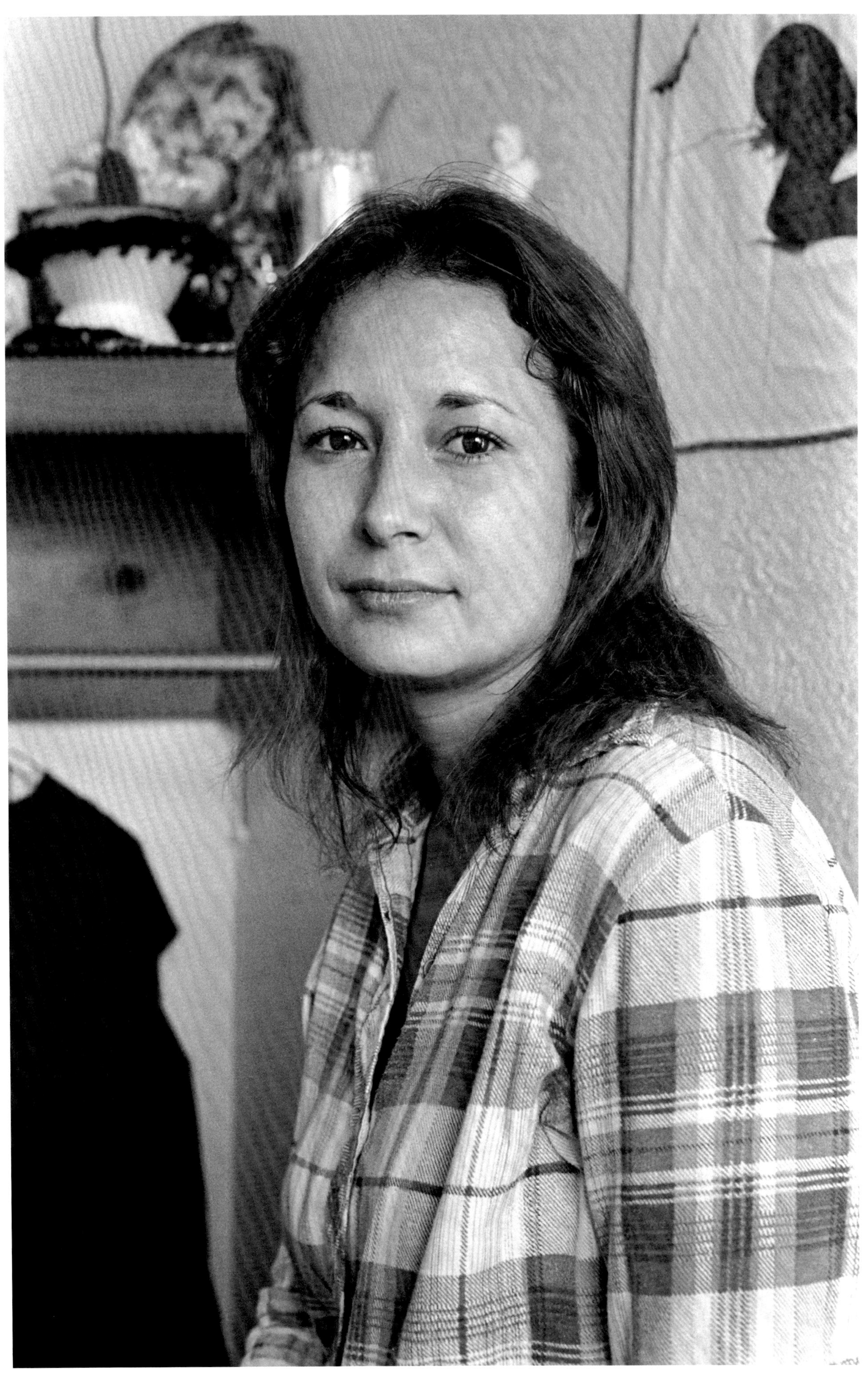

OPPOSITE AND ABOVE: Women's Unit, Penitentiary of New Mexico, Santa Fe, 1983.

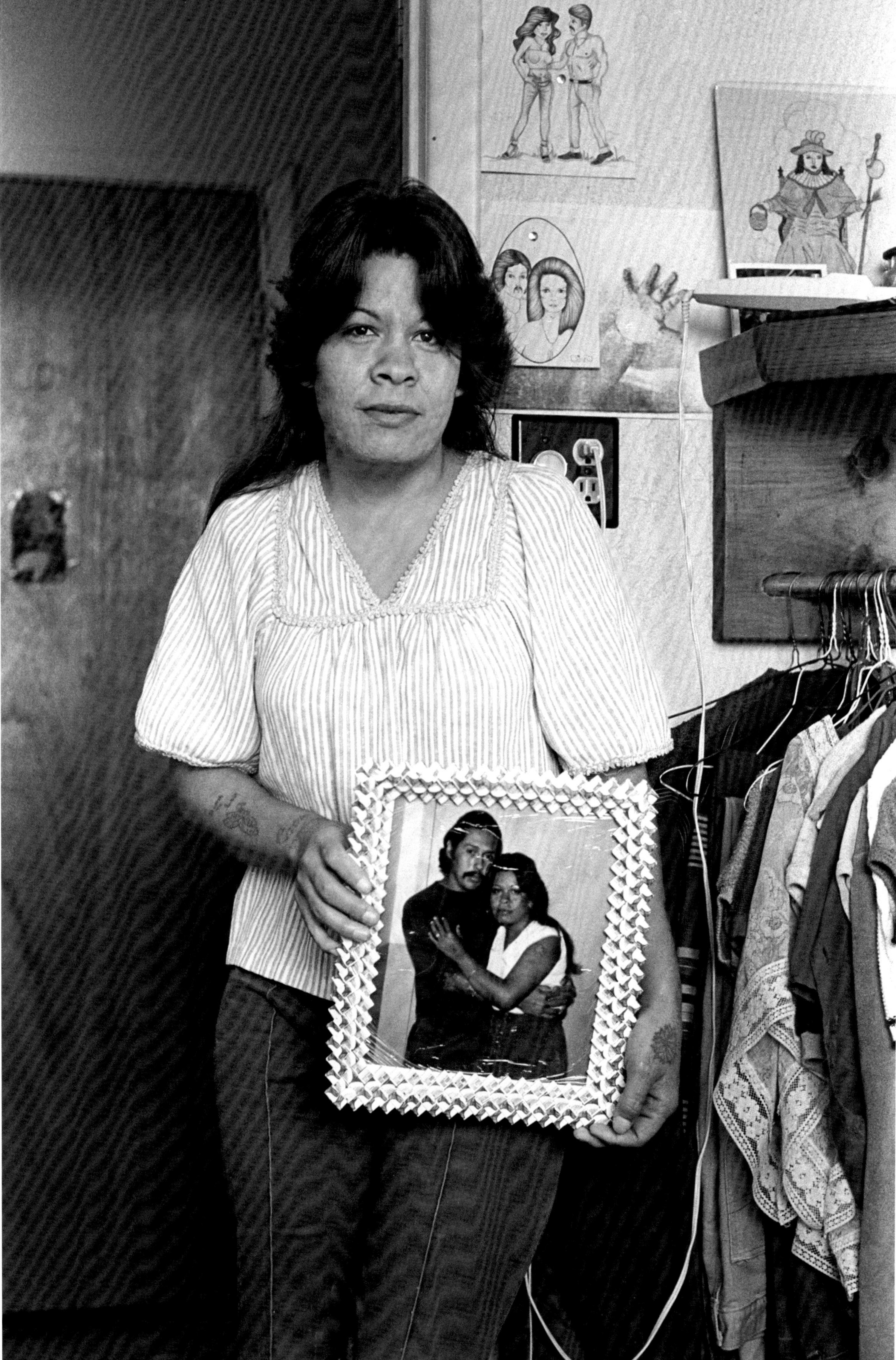

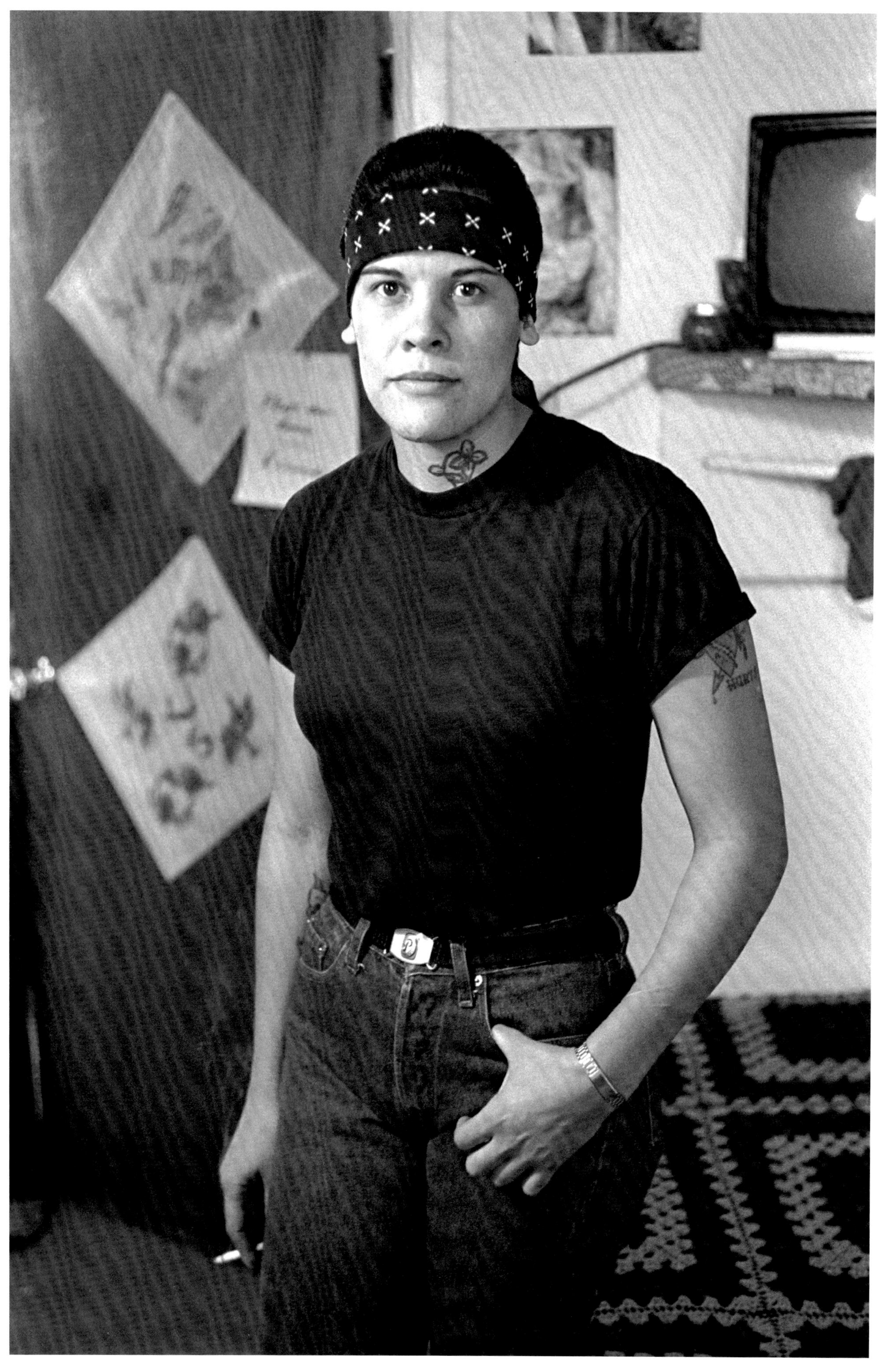

OPPOSITE AND ABOVE: Women's Unit, Penitentiary of New Mexico, Santa Fe, 1983.

OVERLEAF: Indian Powwow, Penitentiary of New Mexico, Santa Fe, 1982.

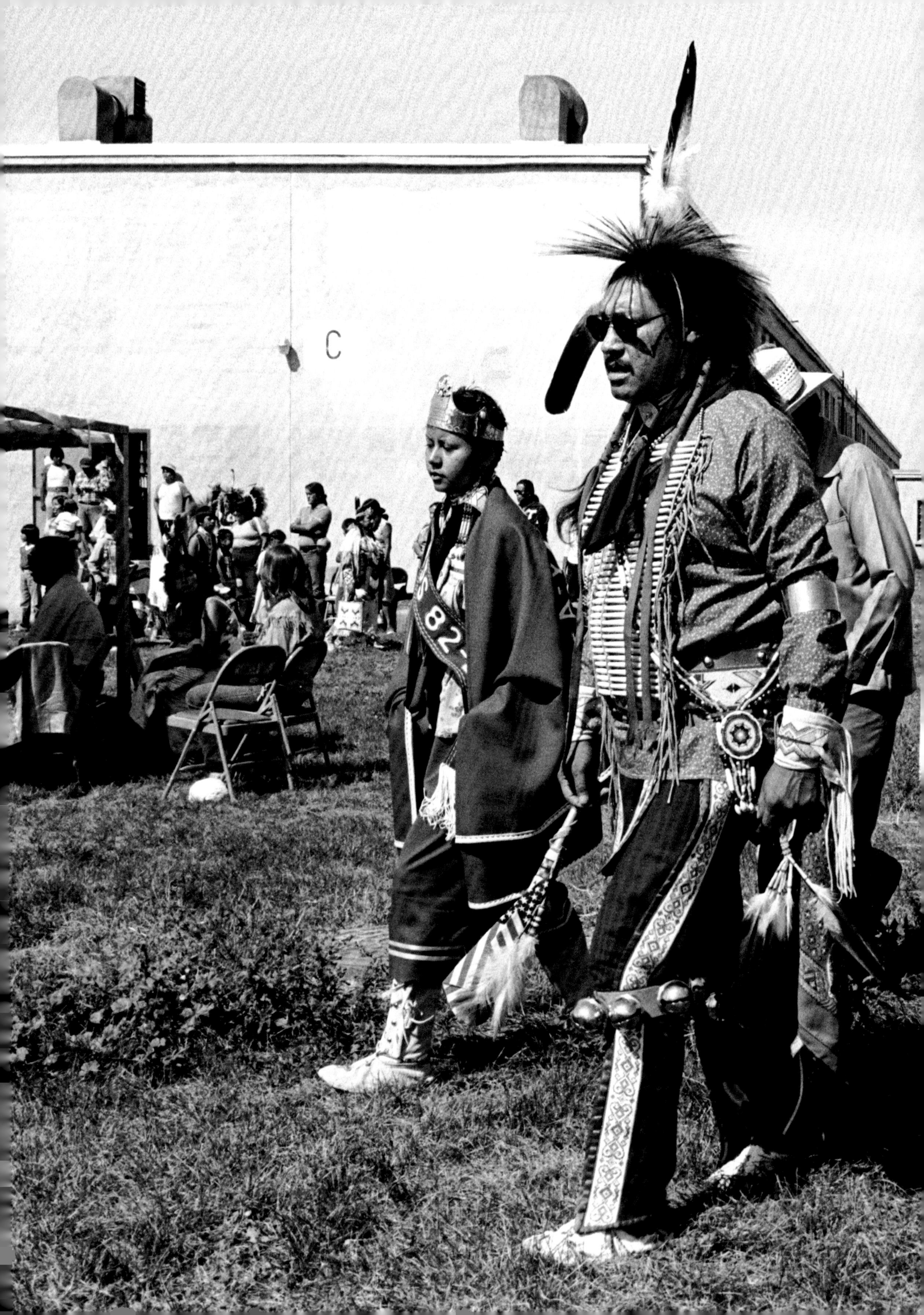
C
82

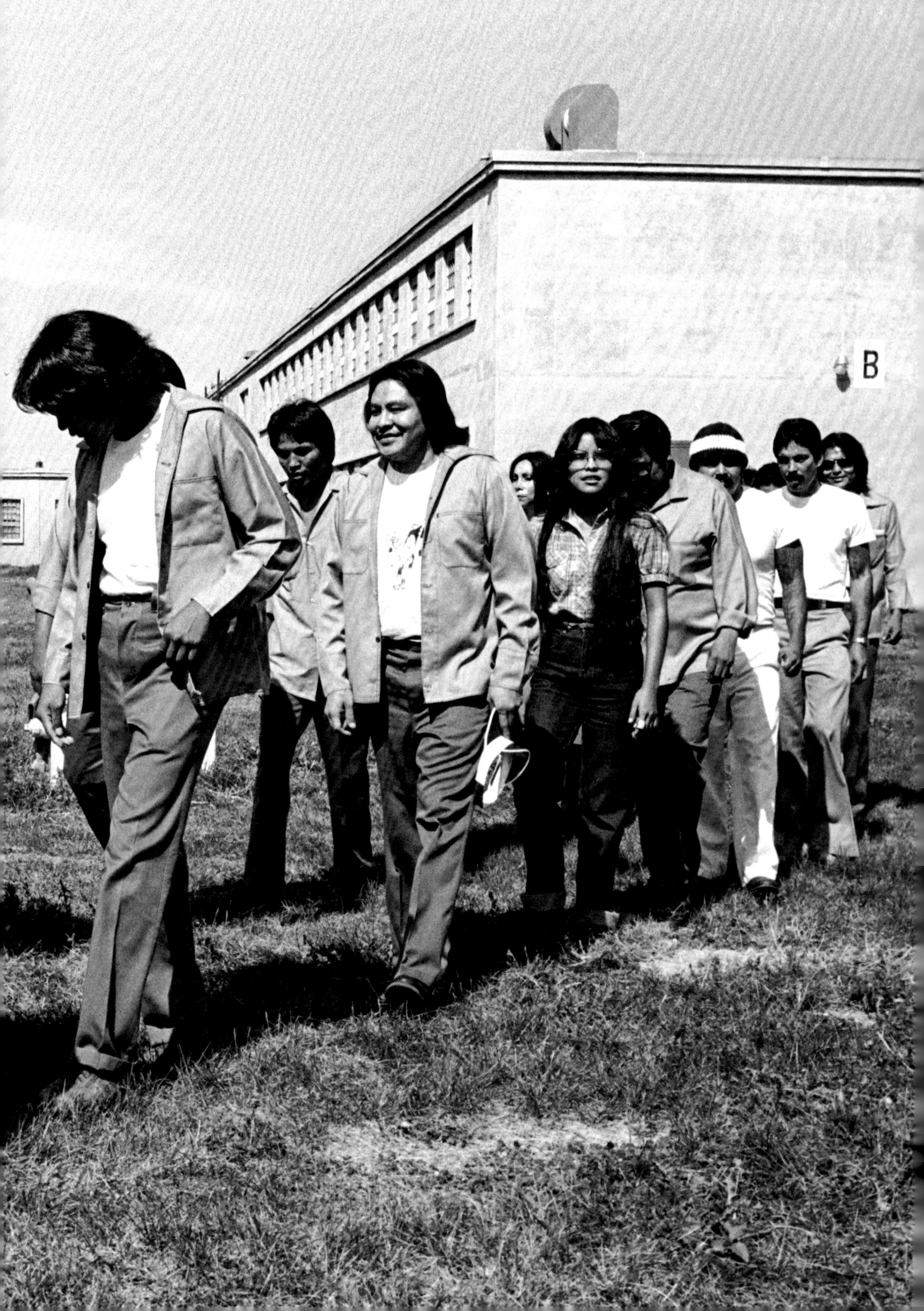
B

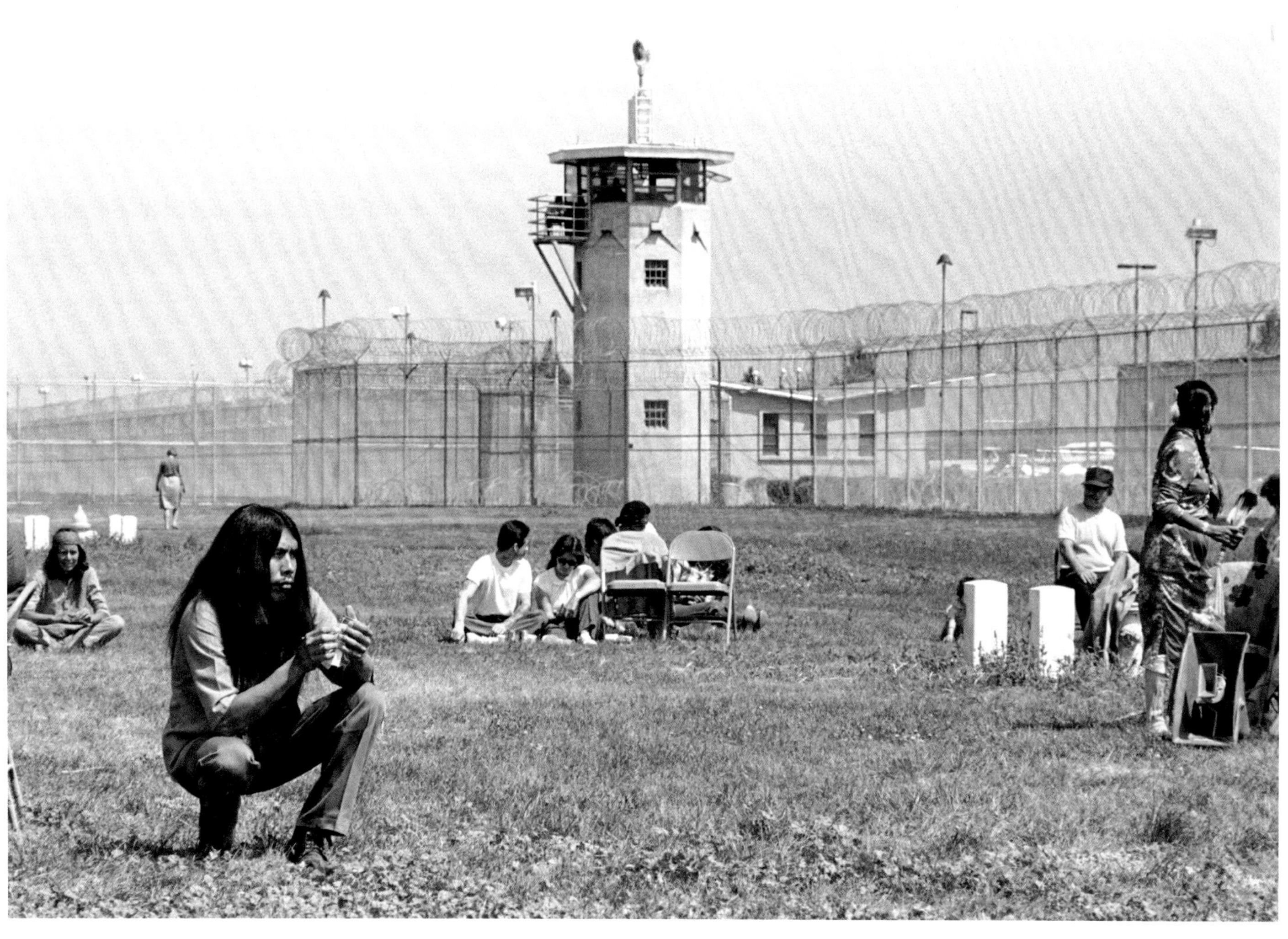

Indian Powwow, Penitentiary of New Mexico, Santa Fe, 1982.

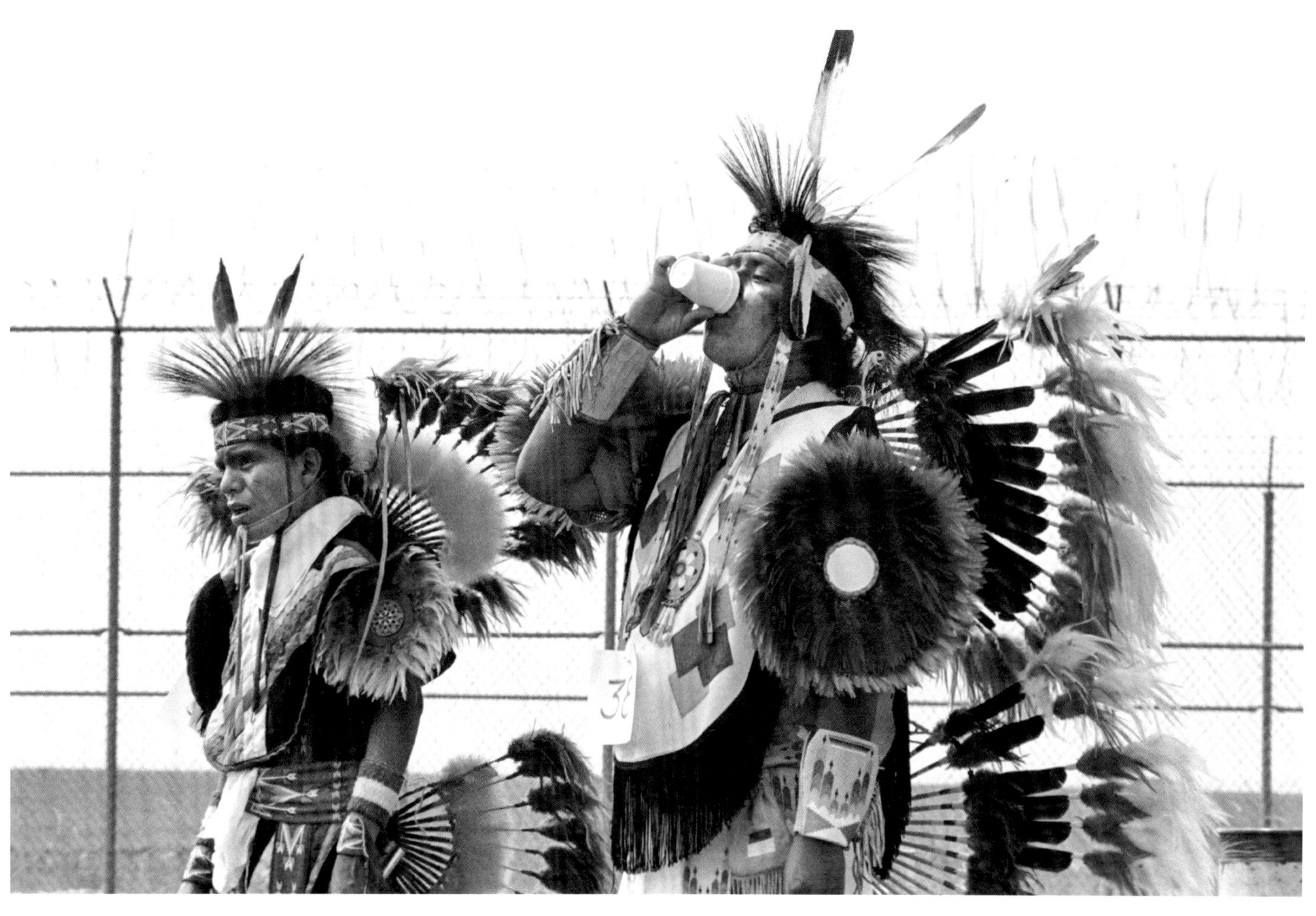

Indian Powwow, Penitentiary of New Mexico, Santa Fe, 1982.

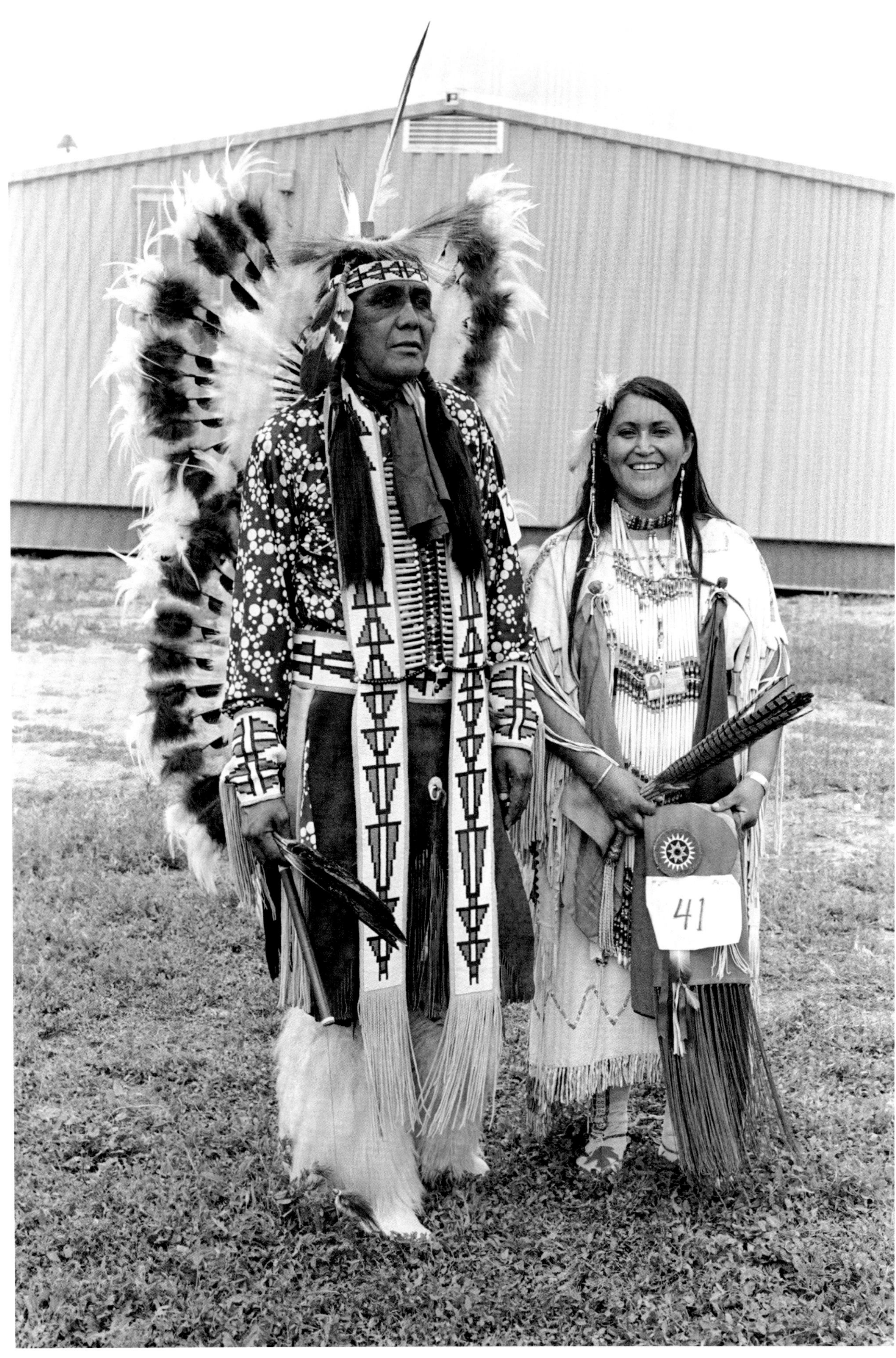

Indian Powwow, Penitentiary of New Mexico, Santa Fe, 1982.

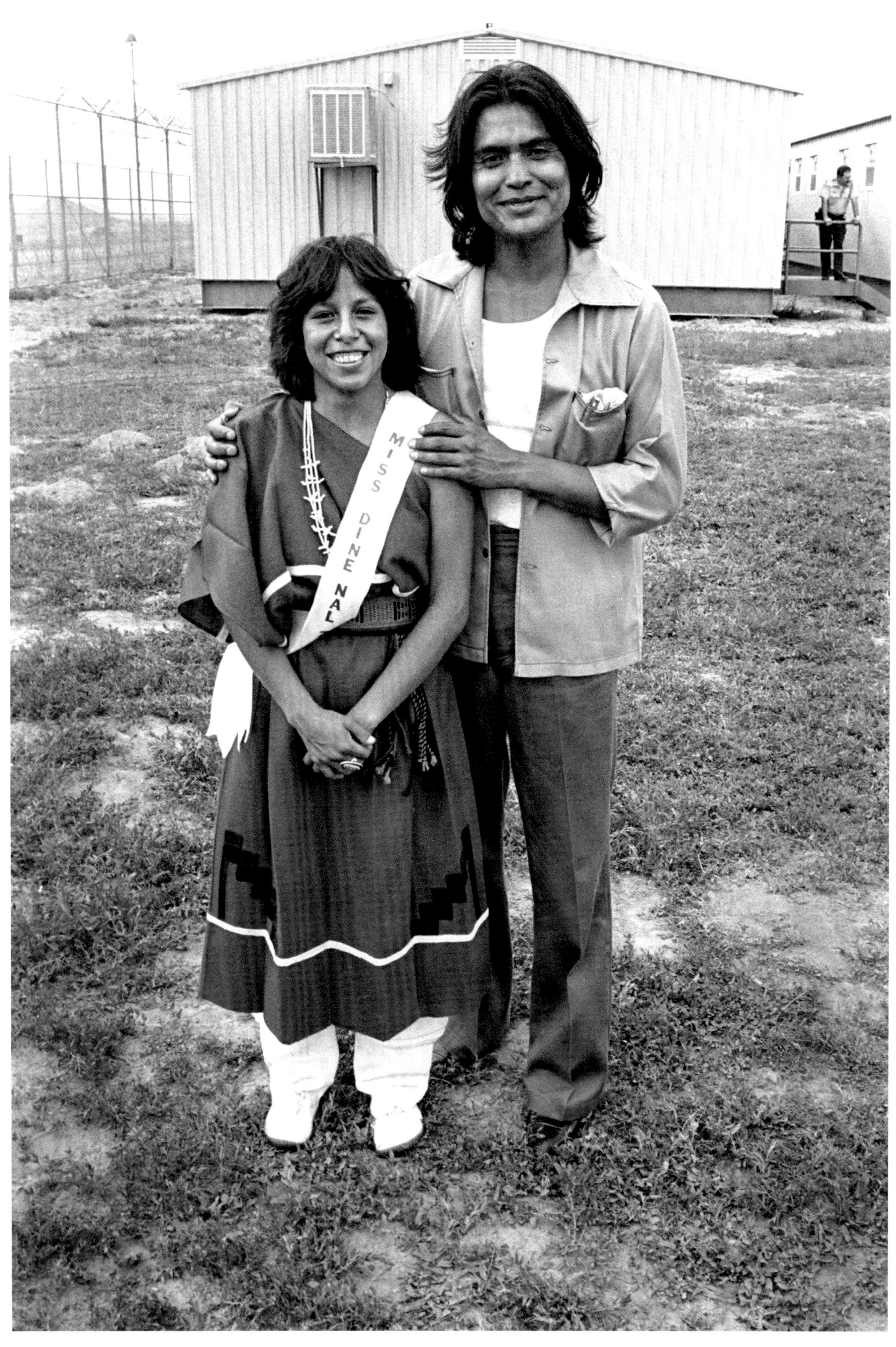

Indian Powwow, Penitentiary of New Mexico, Santa Fe, 1982.

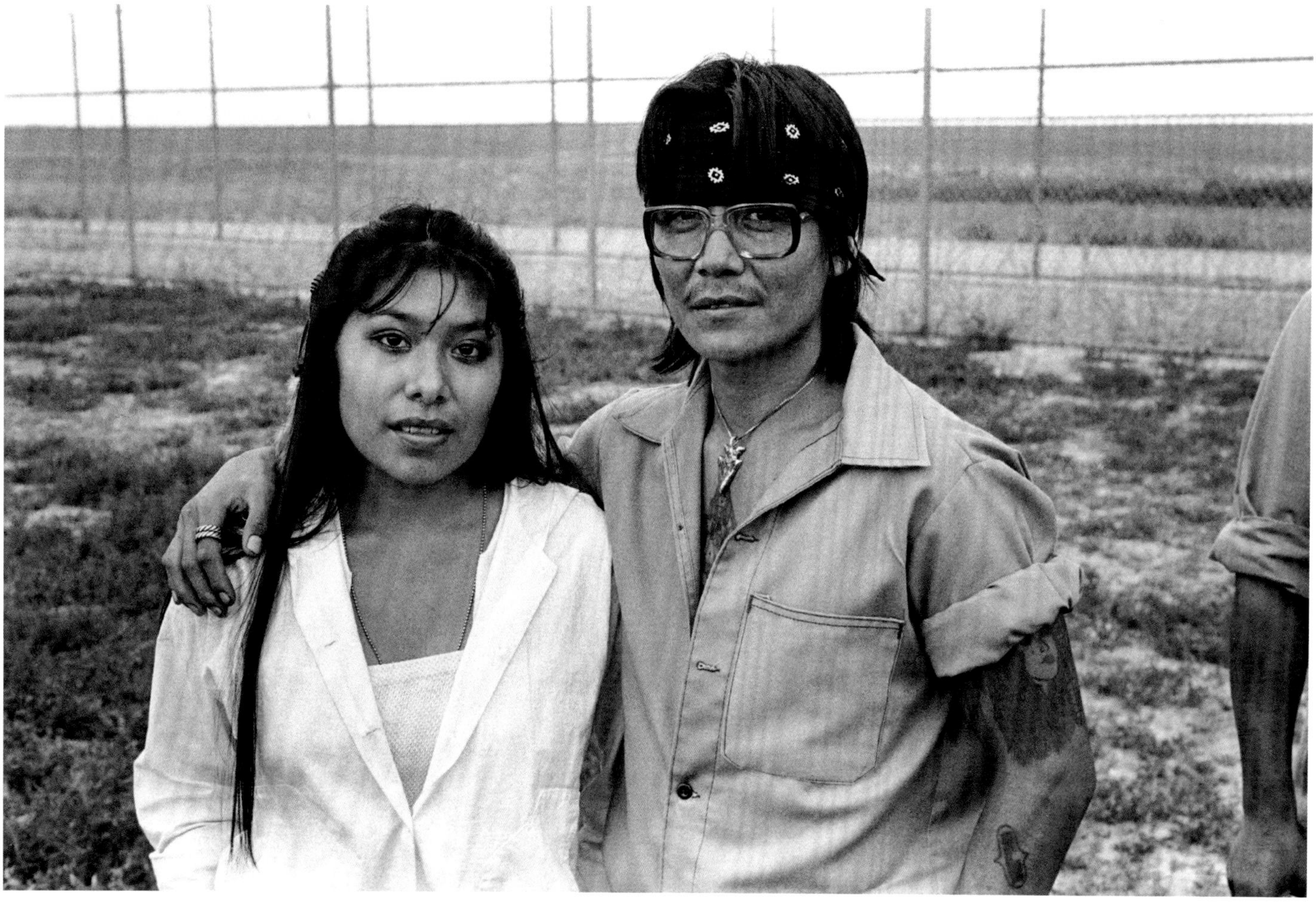

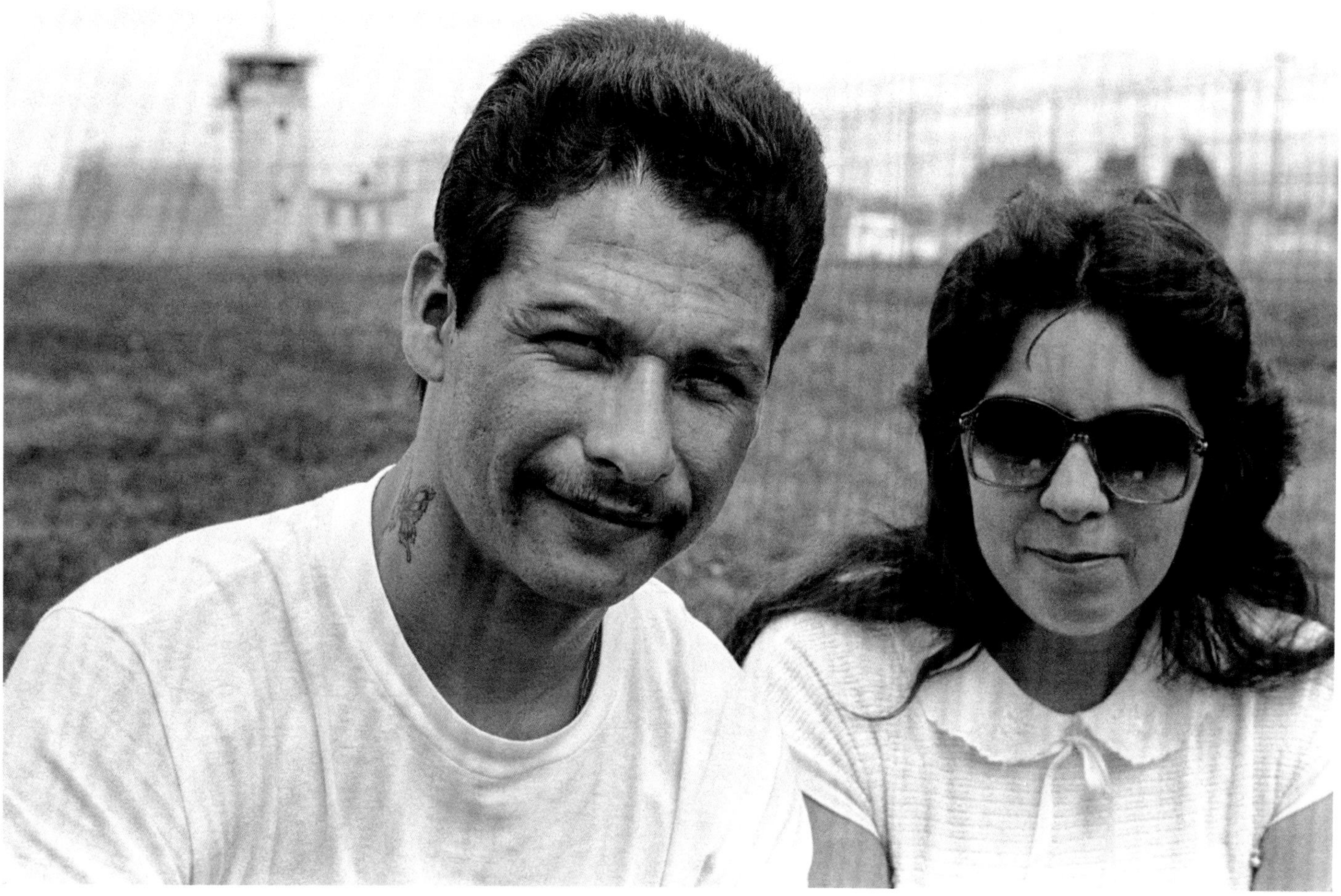

Indian Powwow, Penitentiary of New Mexico, Santa Fe, 1982.

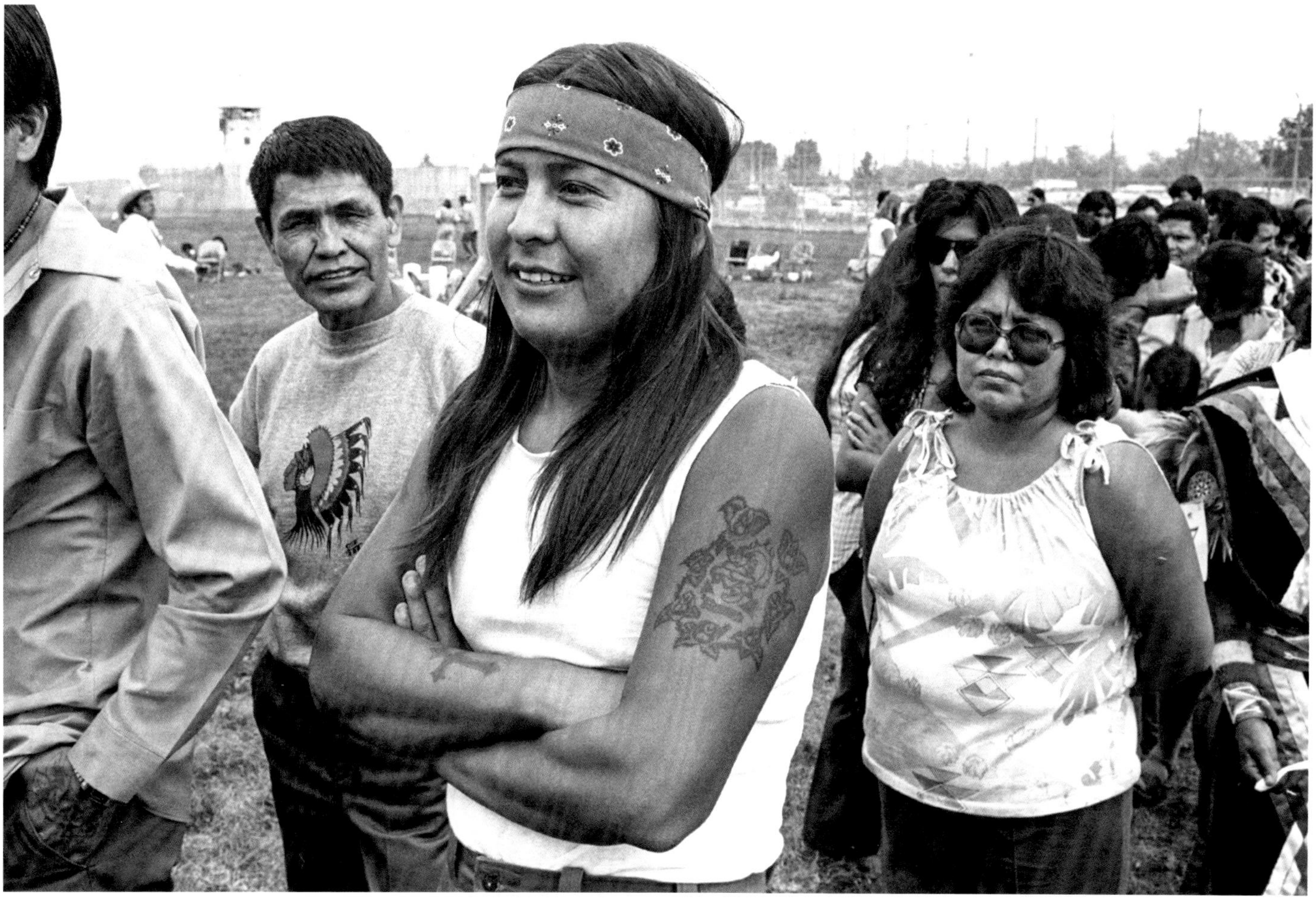

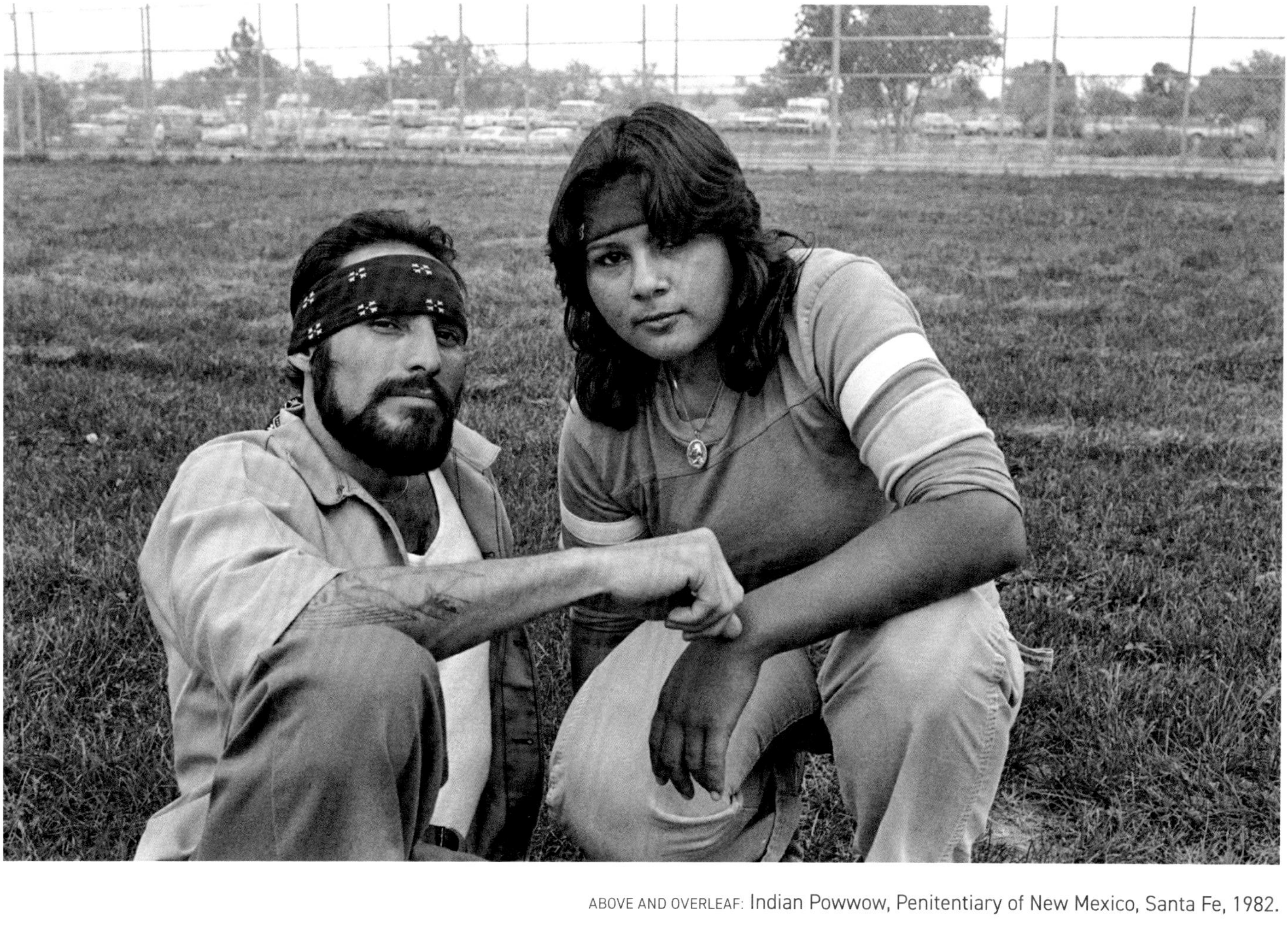

ABOVE AND OVERLEAF: Indian Powwow, Penitentiary of New Mexico, Santa Fe, 1982.

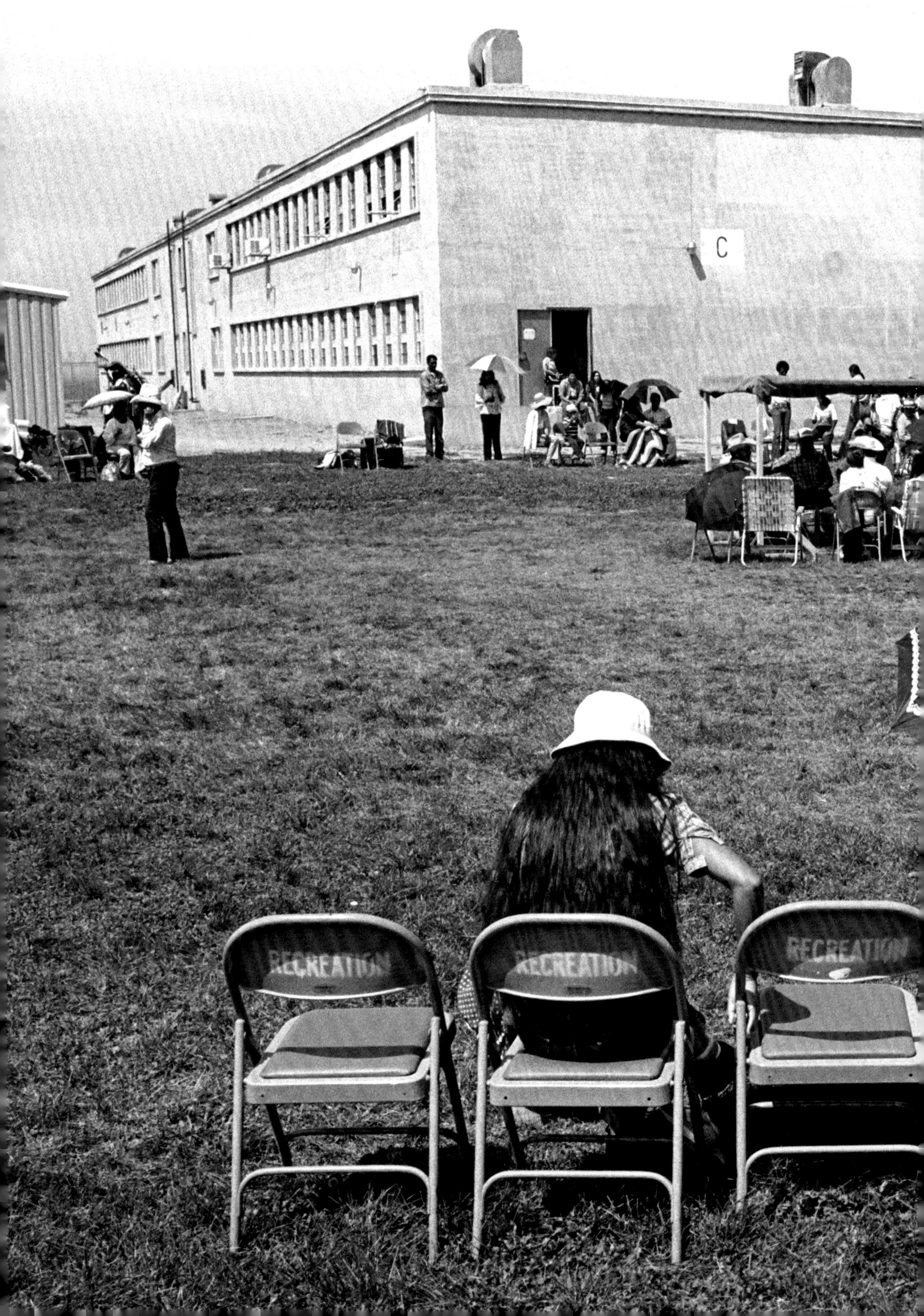
C
RECREATION
RECREATION
RECREATION

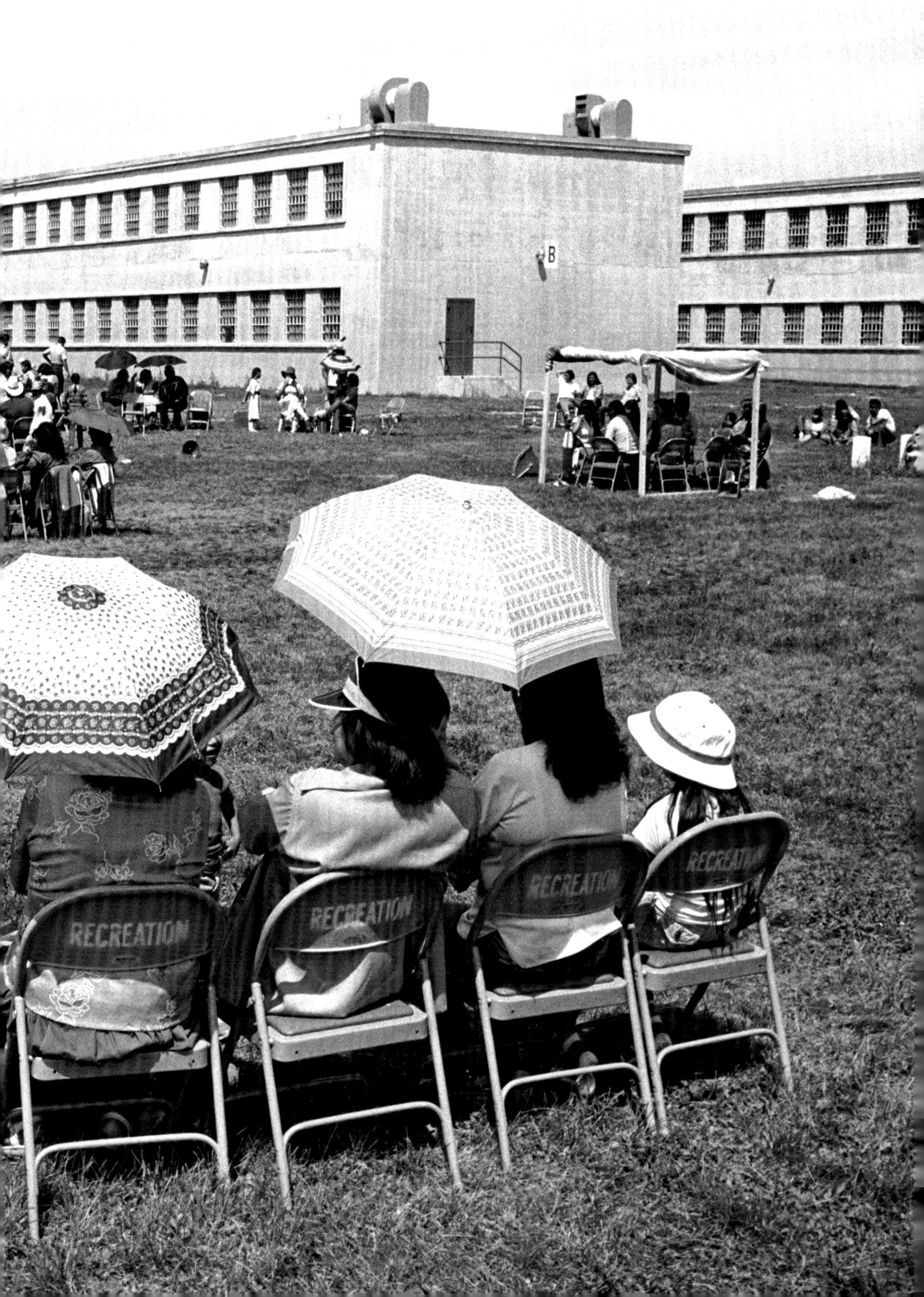
B
RECREATION
RECREATION
RECREATION
RECREATION

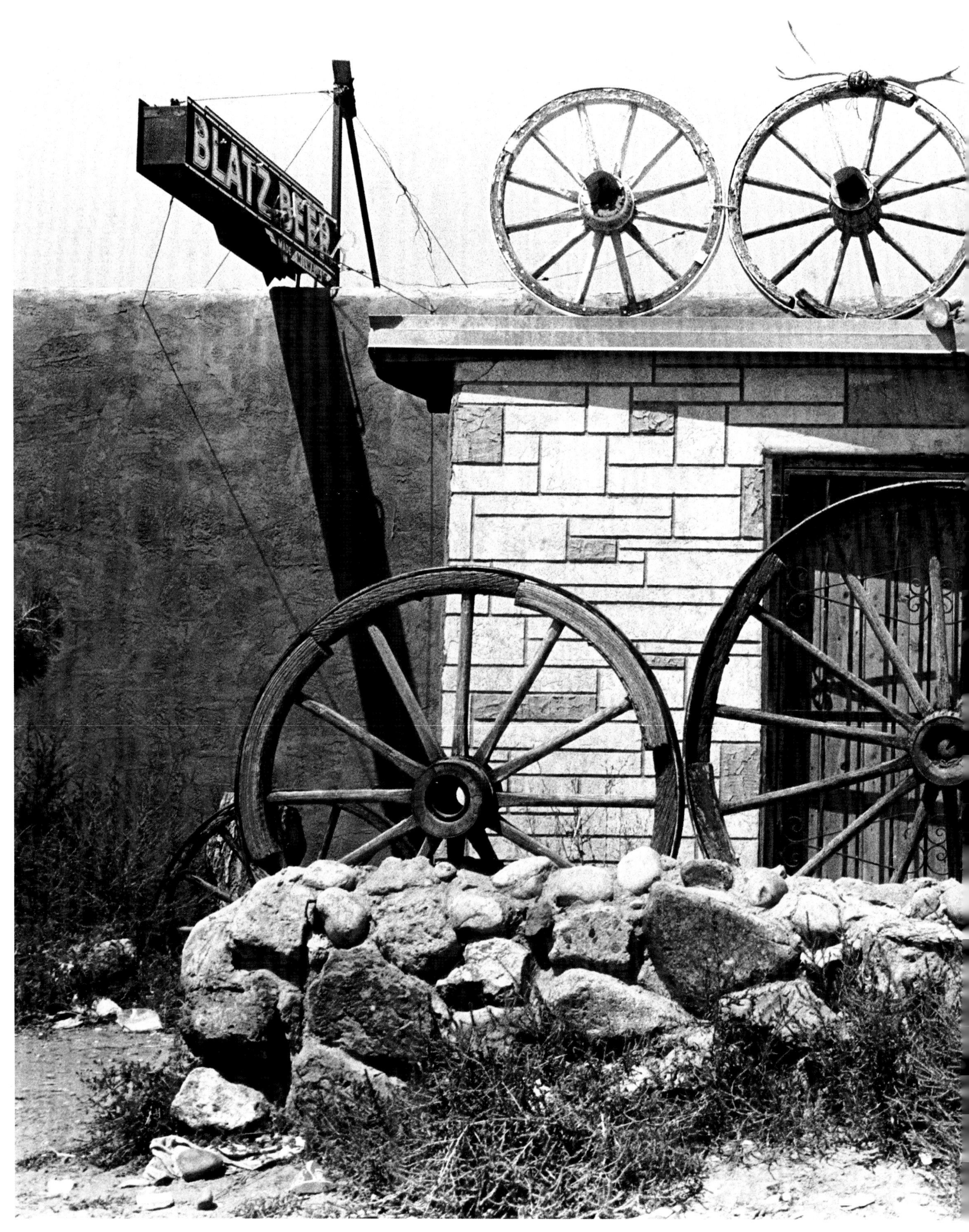

Madrid, 1982.

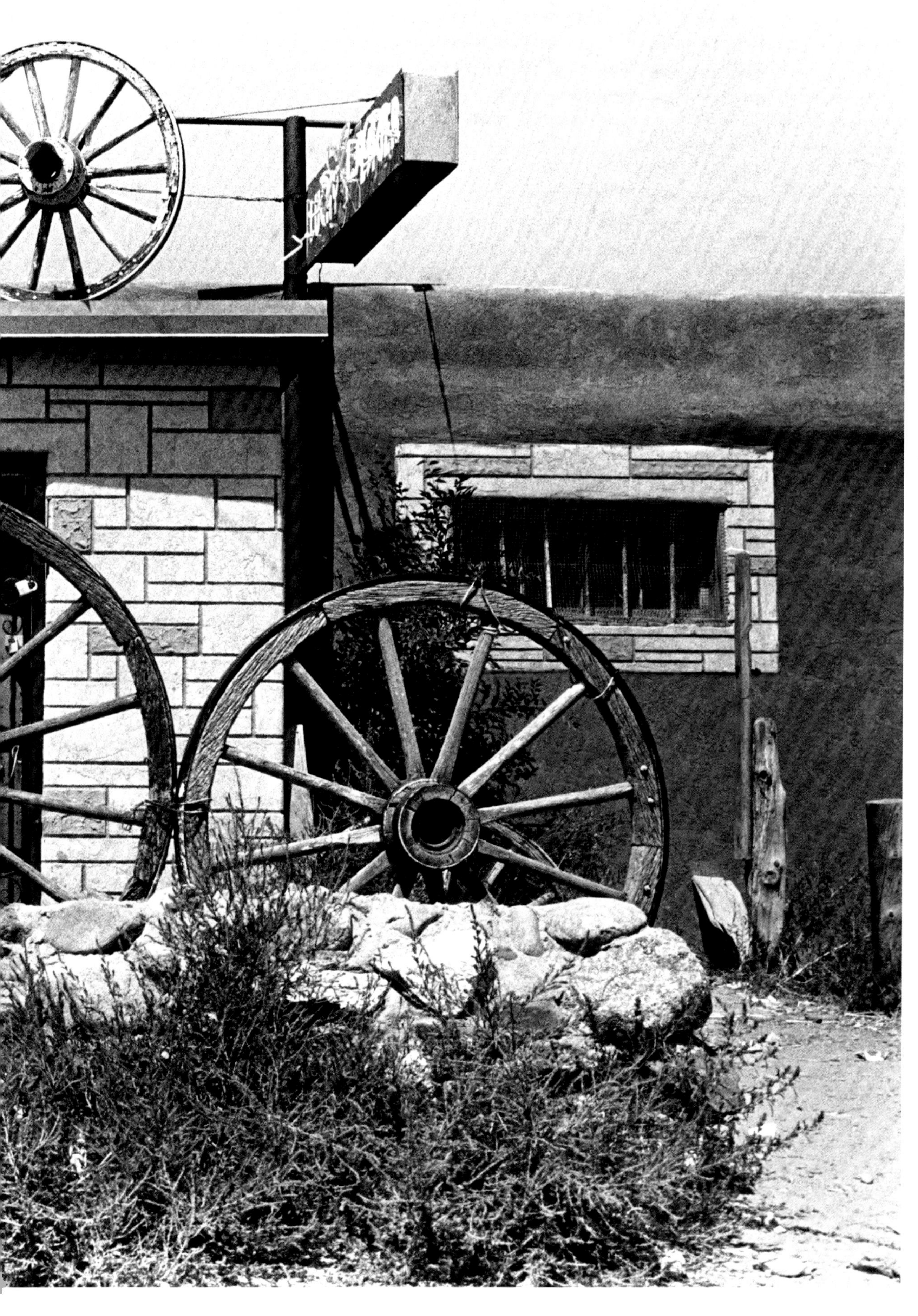

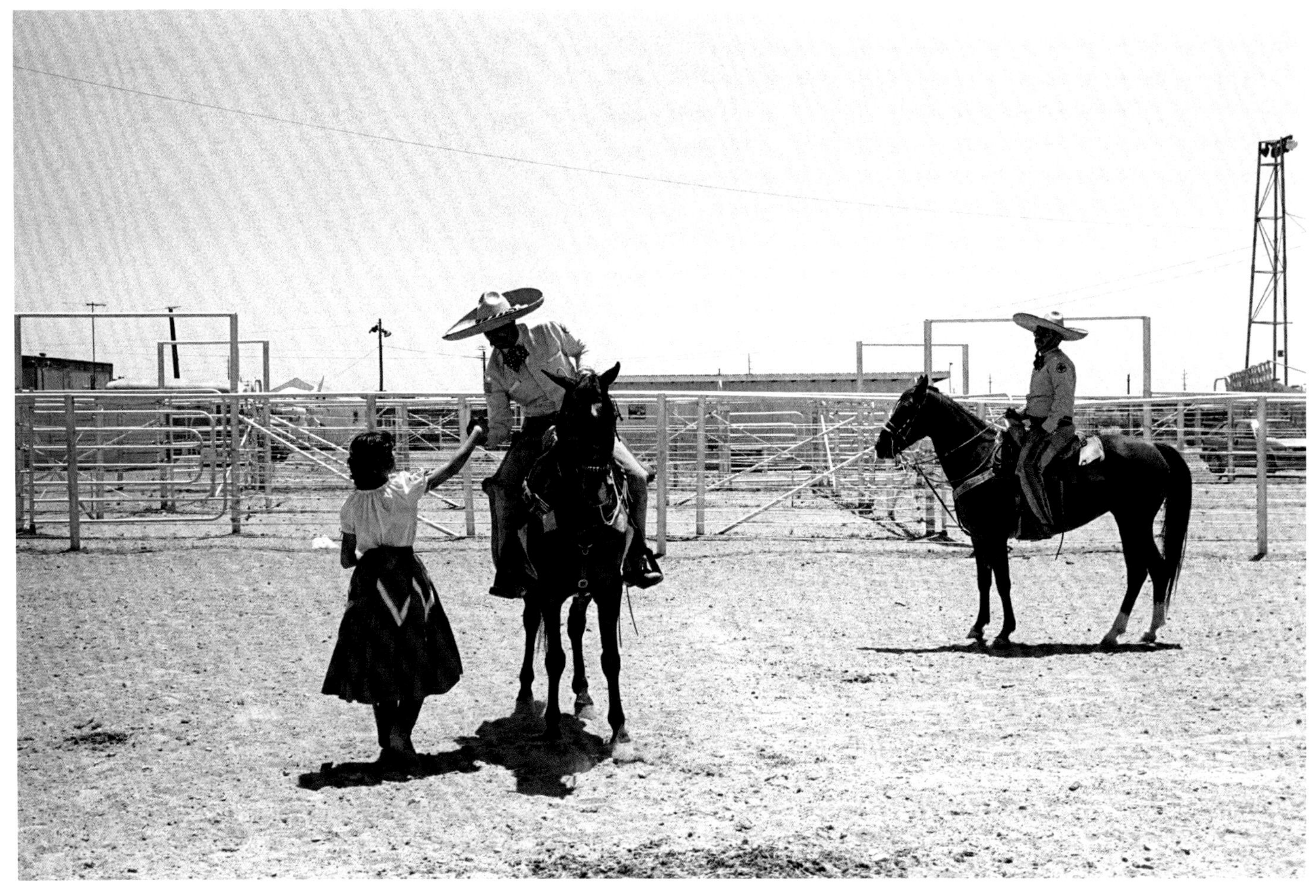

Rodeo de Santa Fe, 1982.

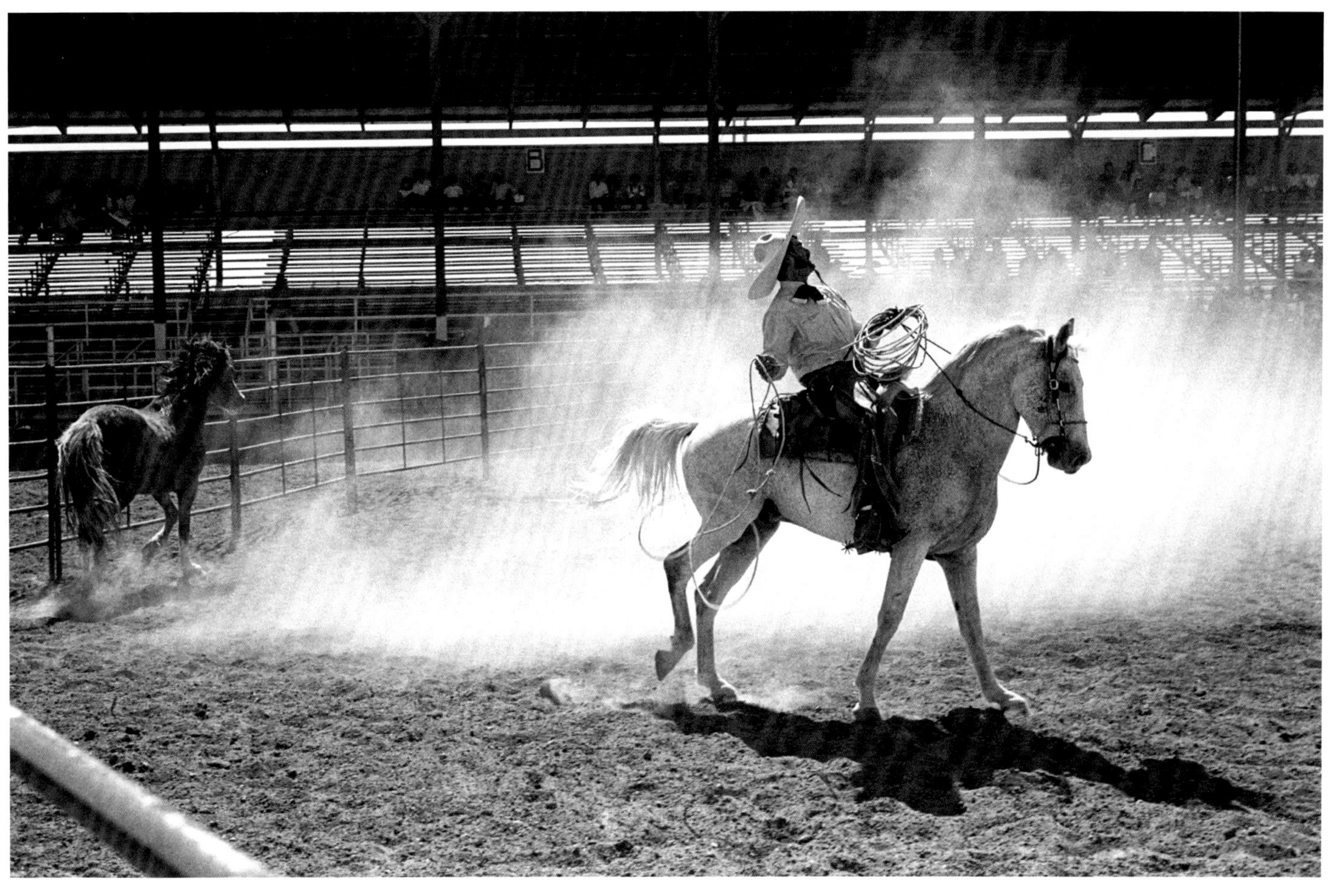

Rodeo de Santa Fe, 1982.

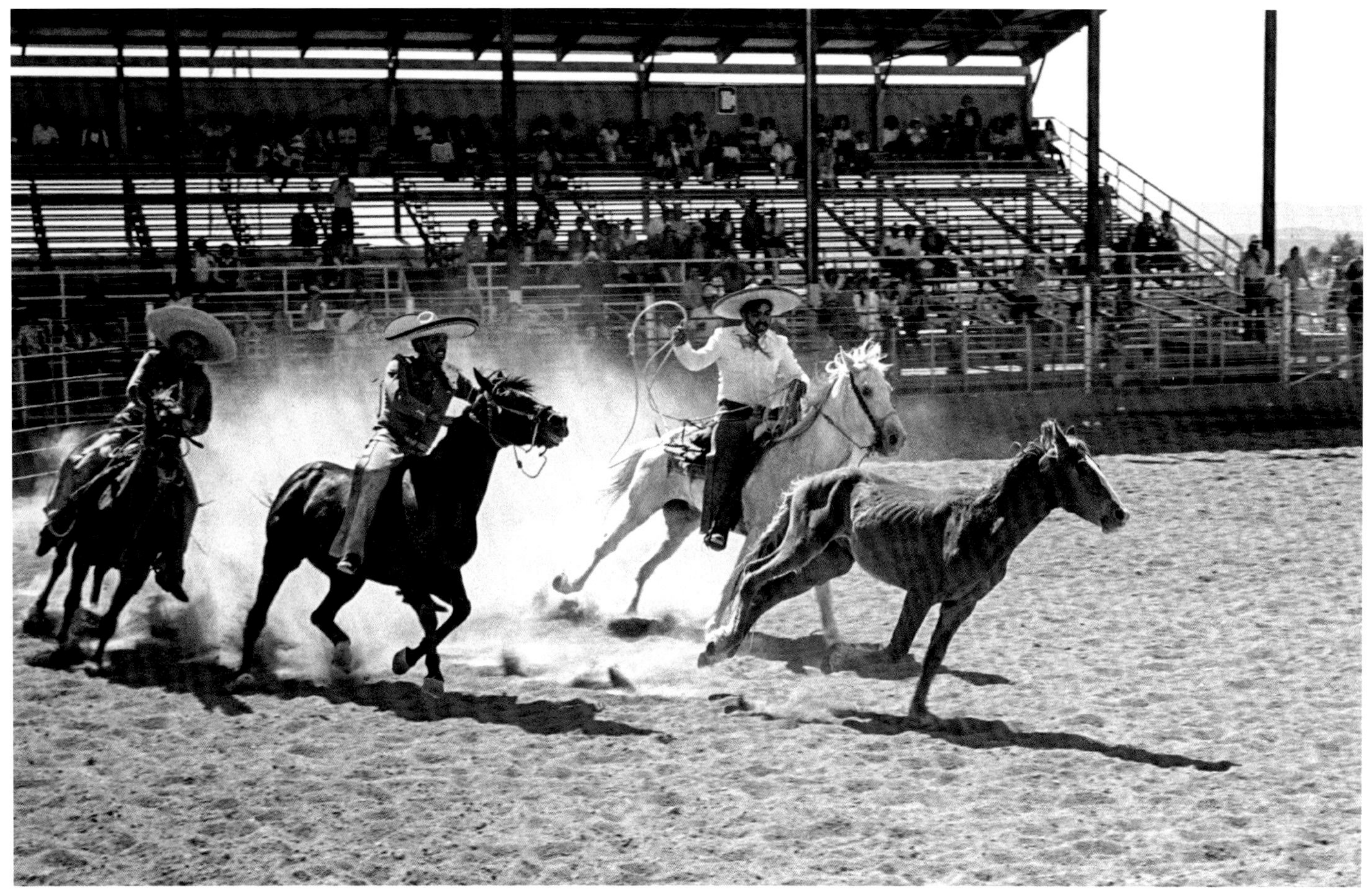

Rodeo de Santa Fe, 1982.

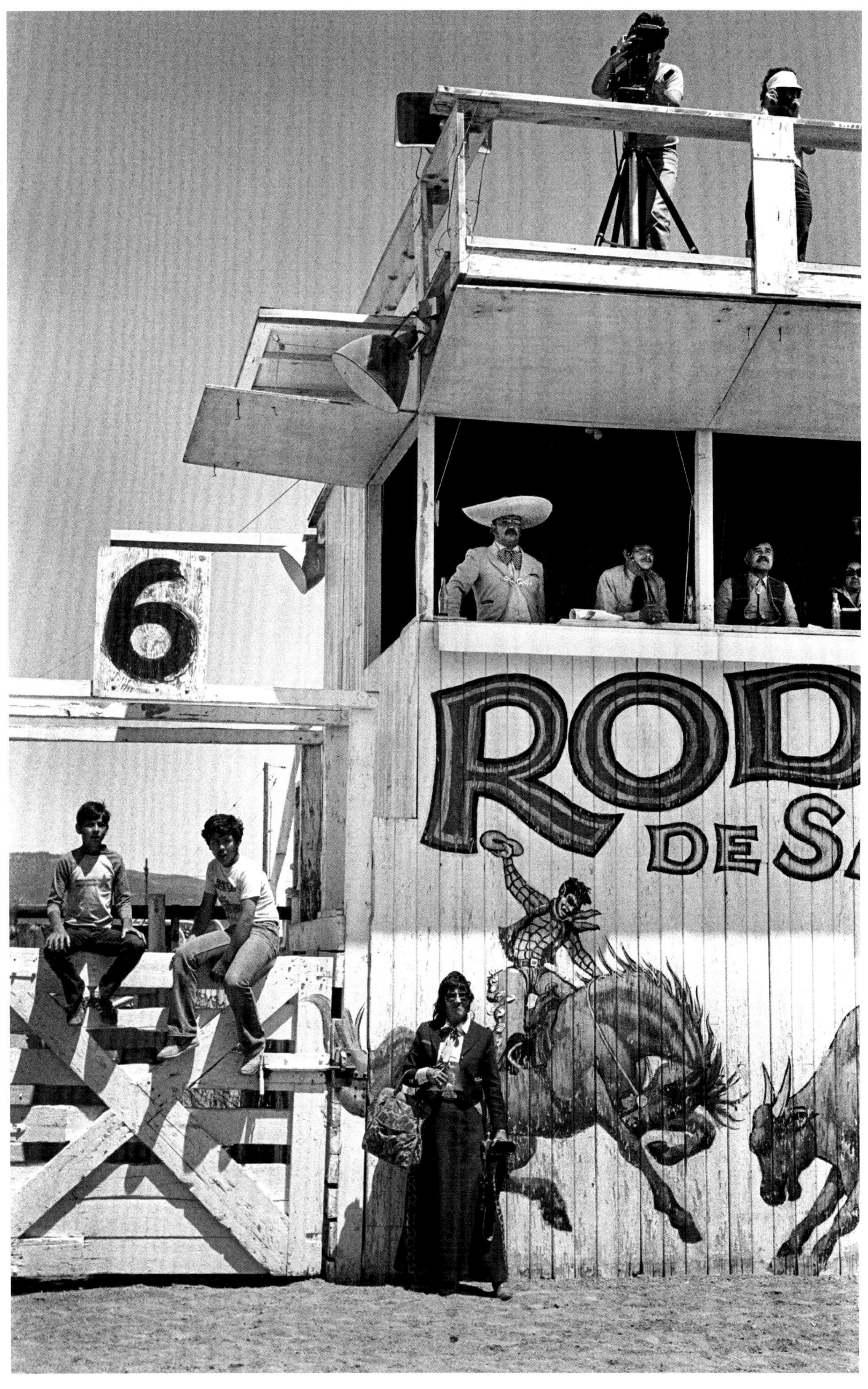

Rodeo de Santa Fe, 1982.

OVERLEAF: Albuquerque International Balloon Fiesta, 1981.

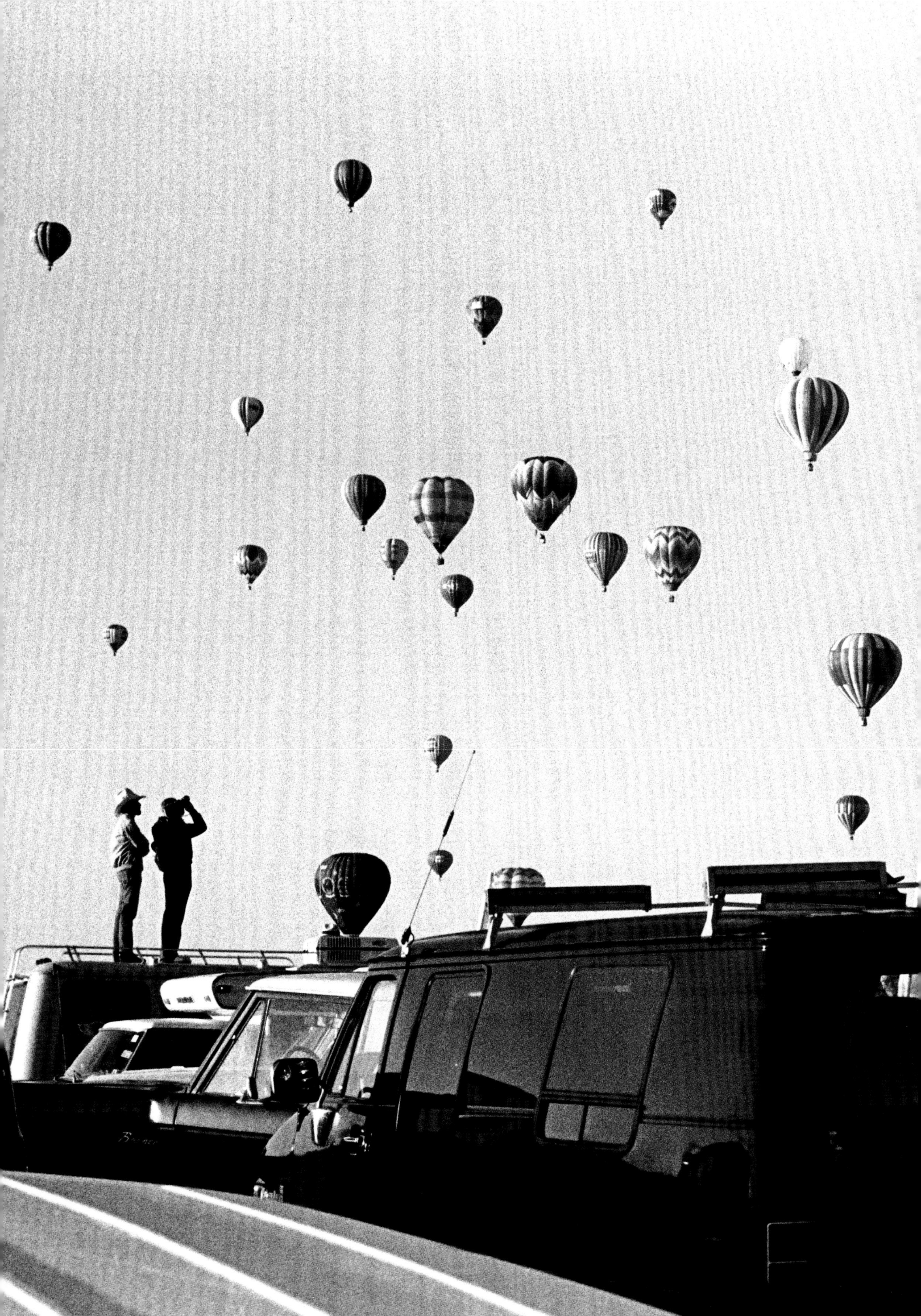

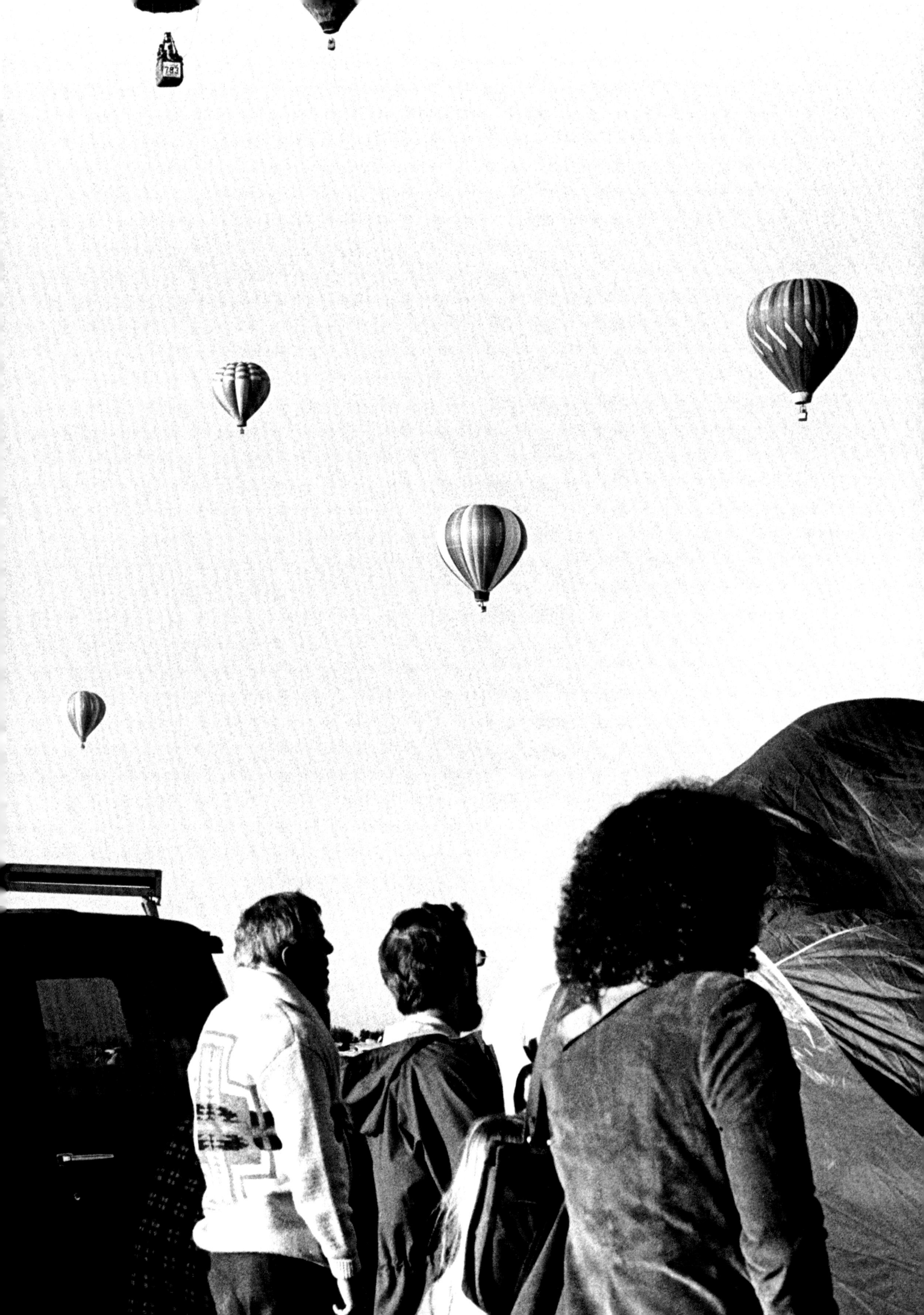

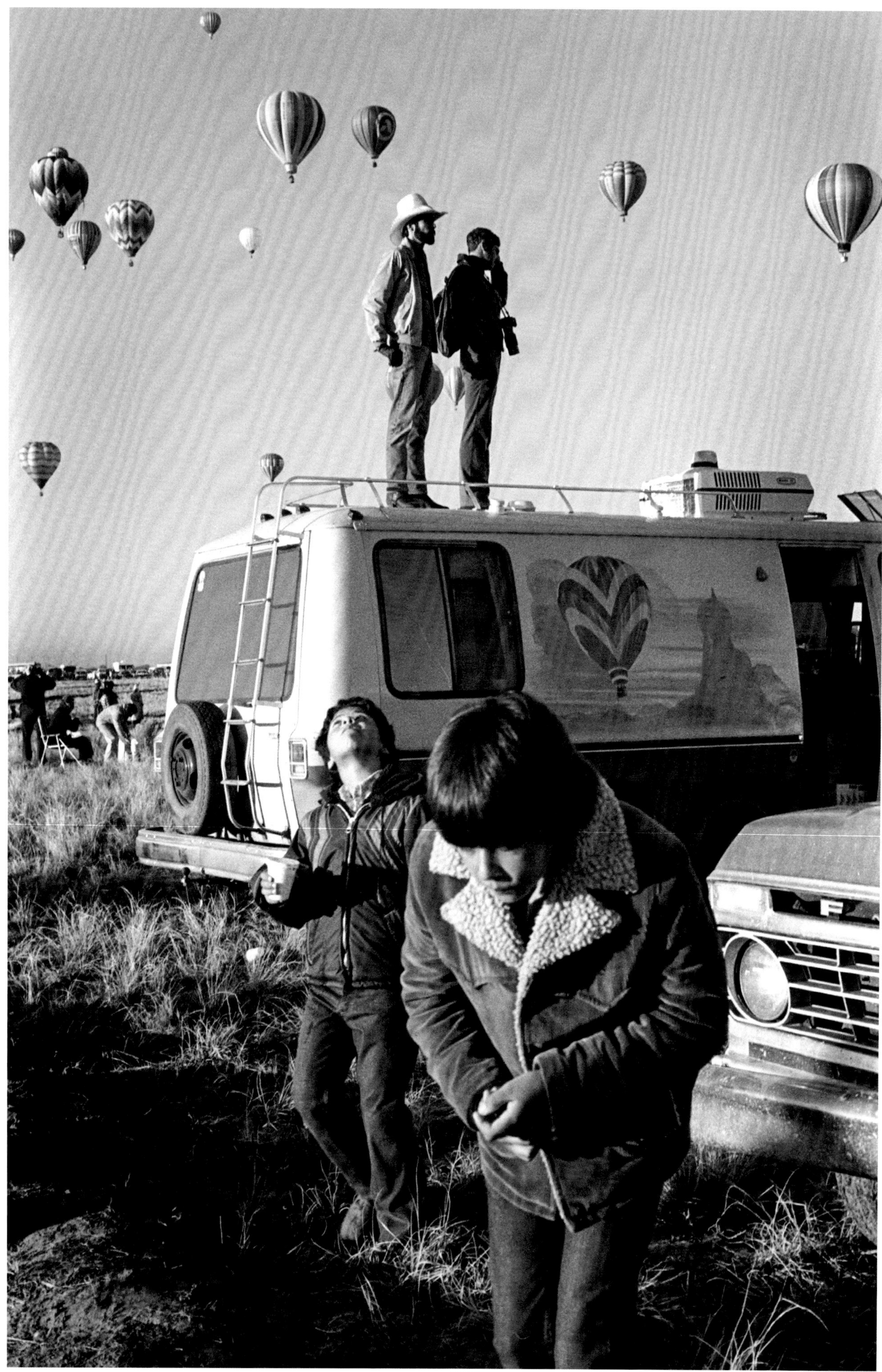

ABOVE AND OPPOSITE: Albuquerque International Balloon Fiesta, 1981.

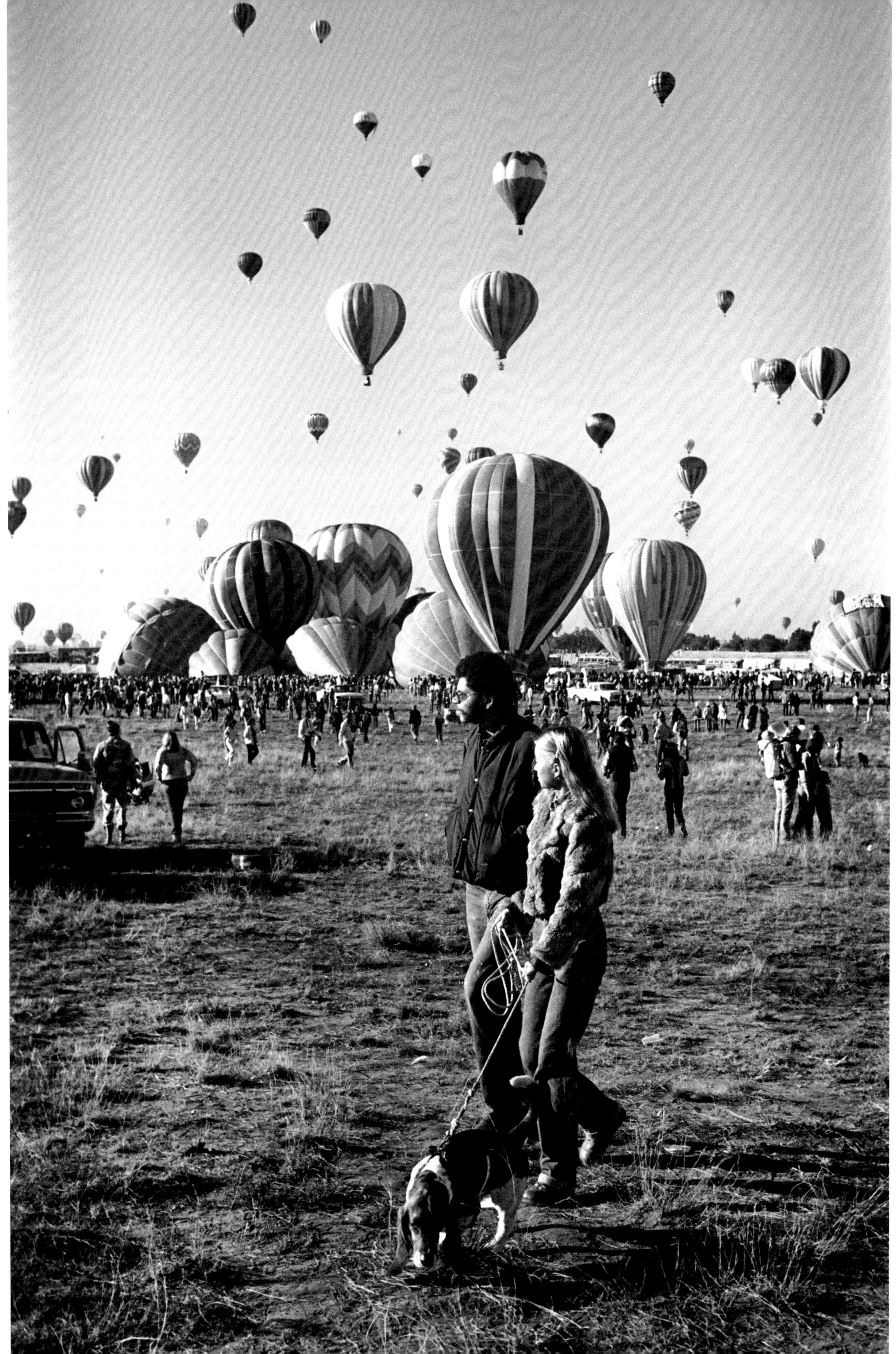

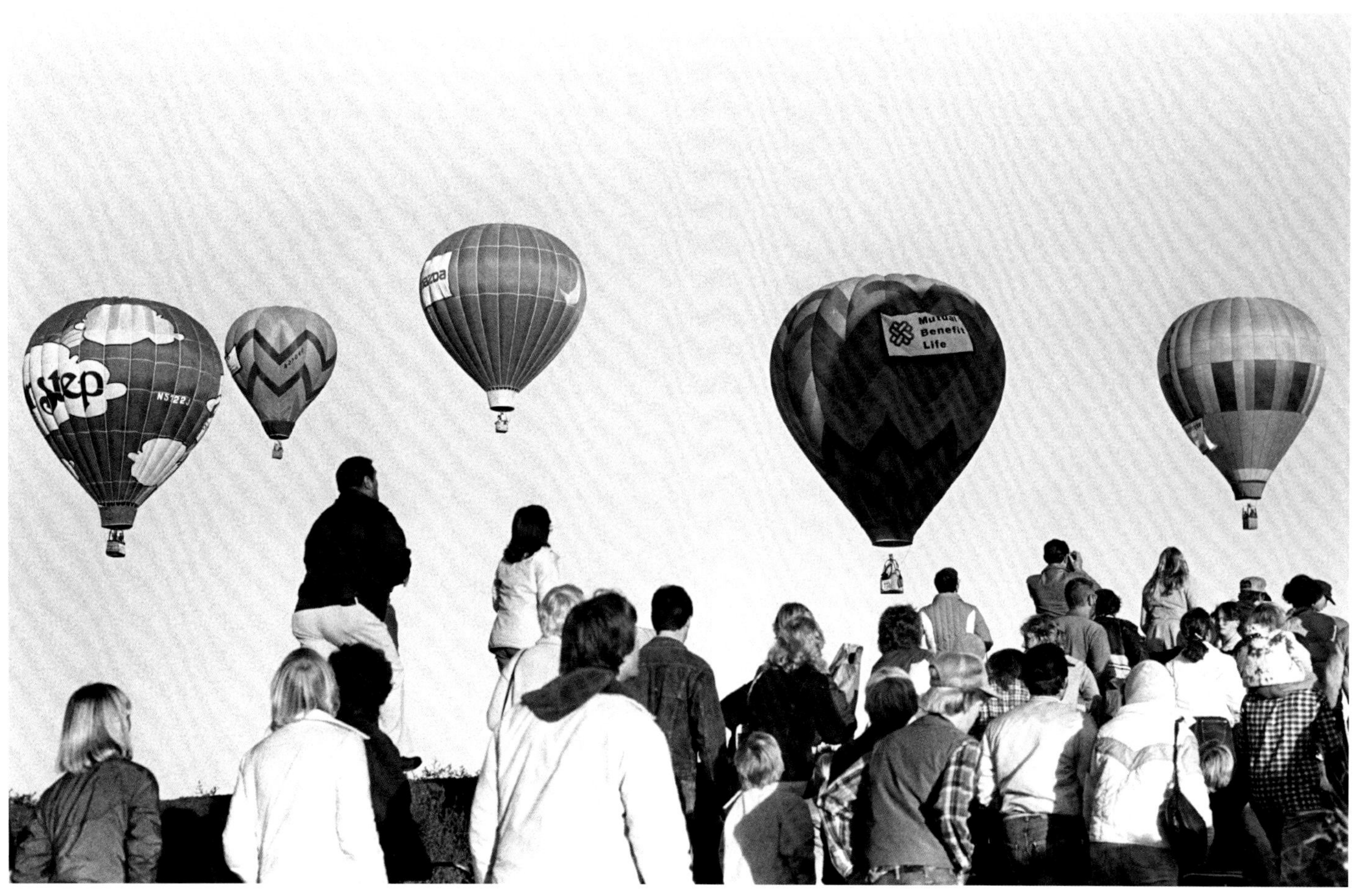

Albuquerque International Balloon Fiesta, 1981.

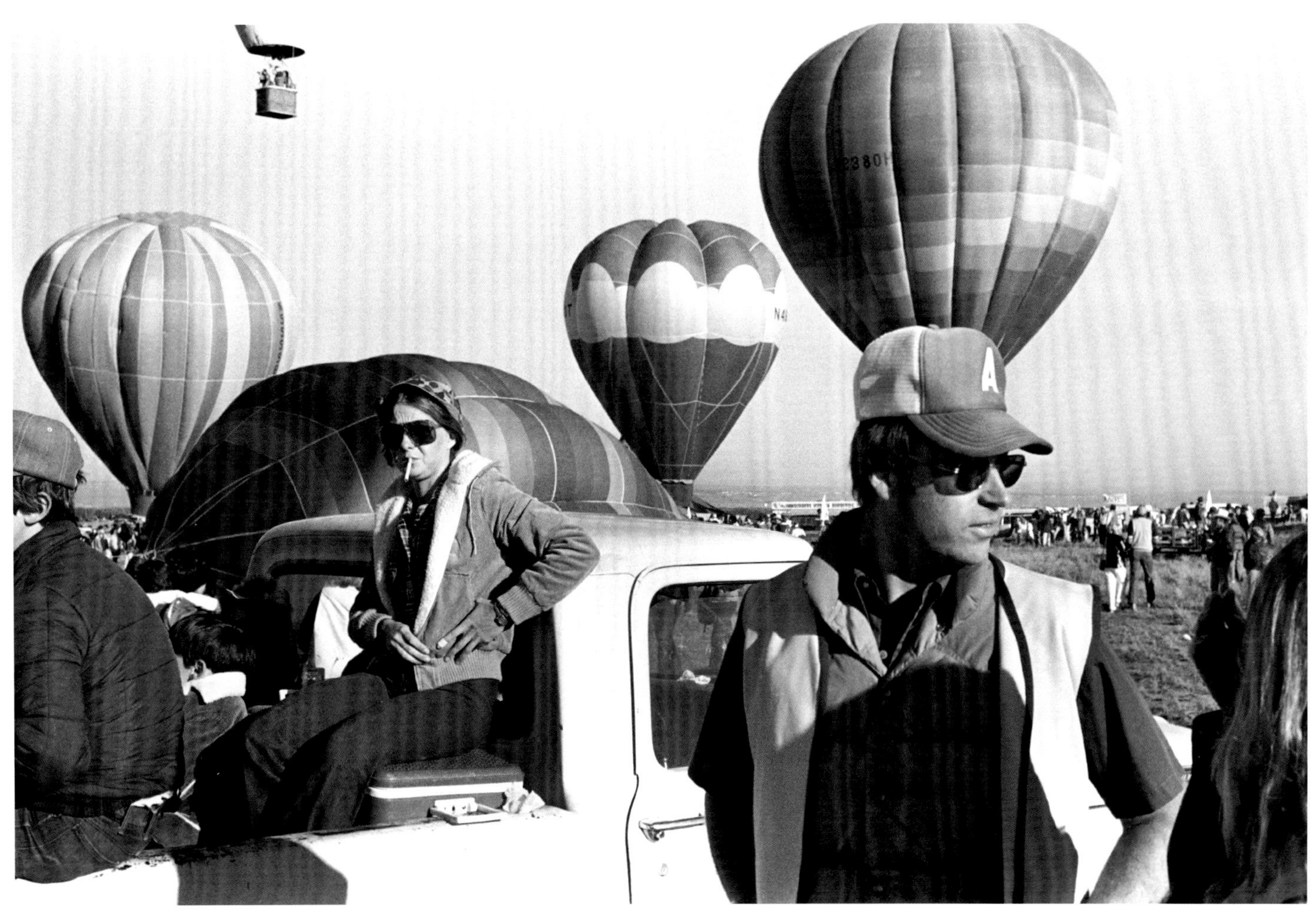

ABOVE AND OVERLEAF: Albuquerque International Balloon Fiesta, 1981.

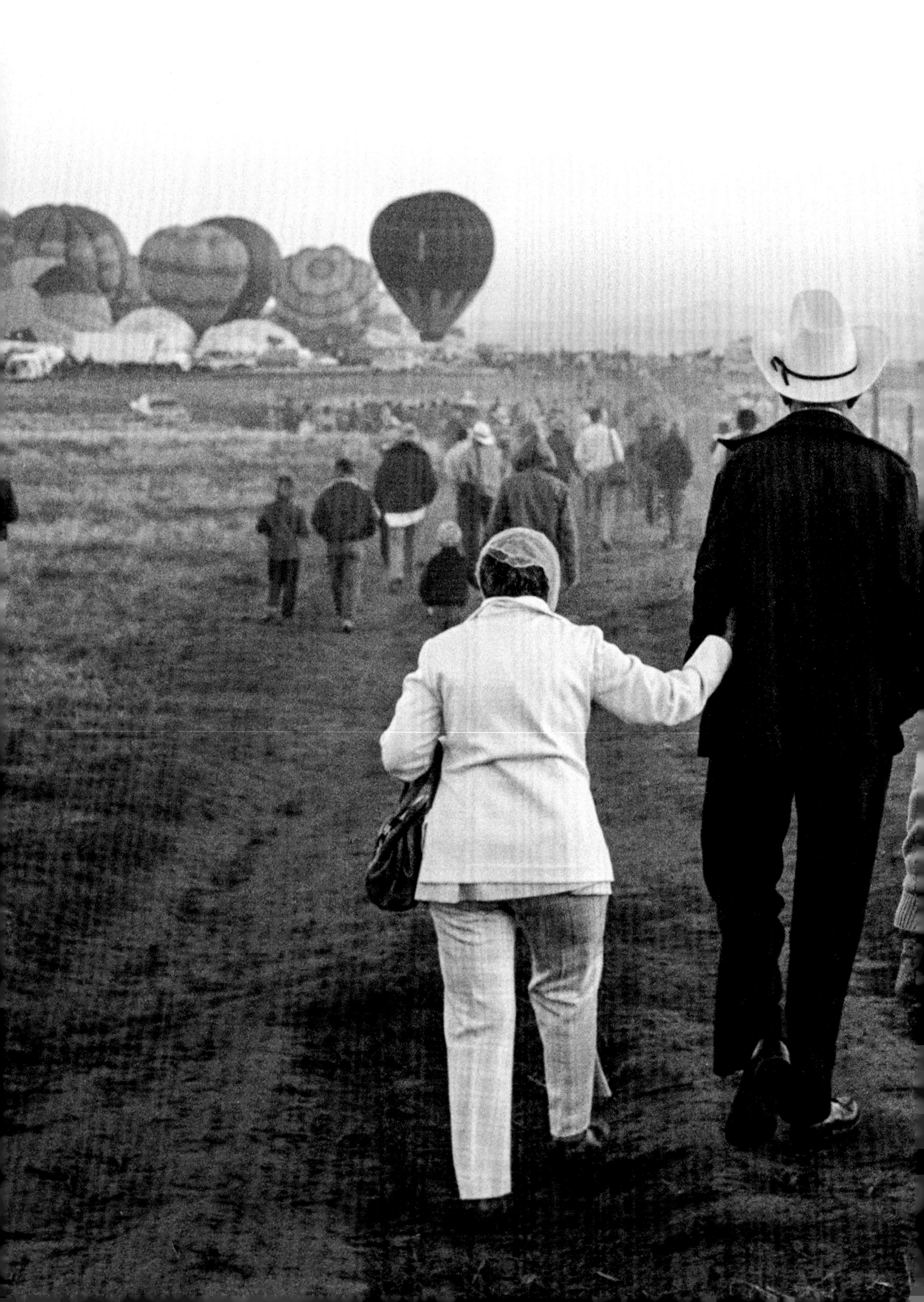

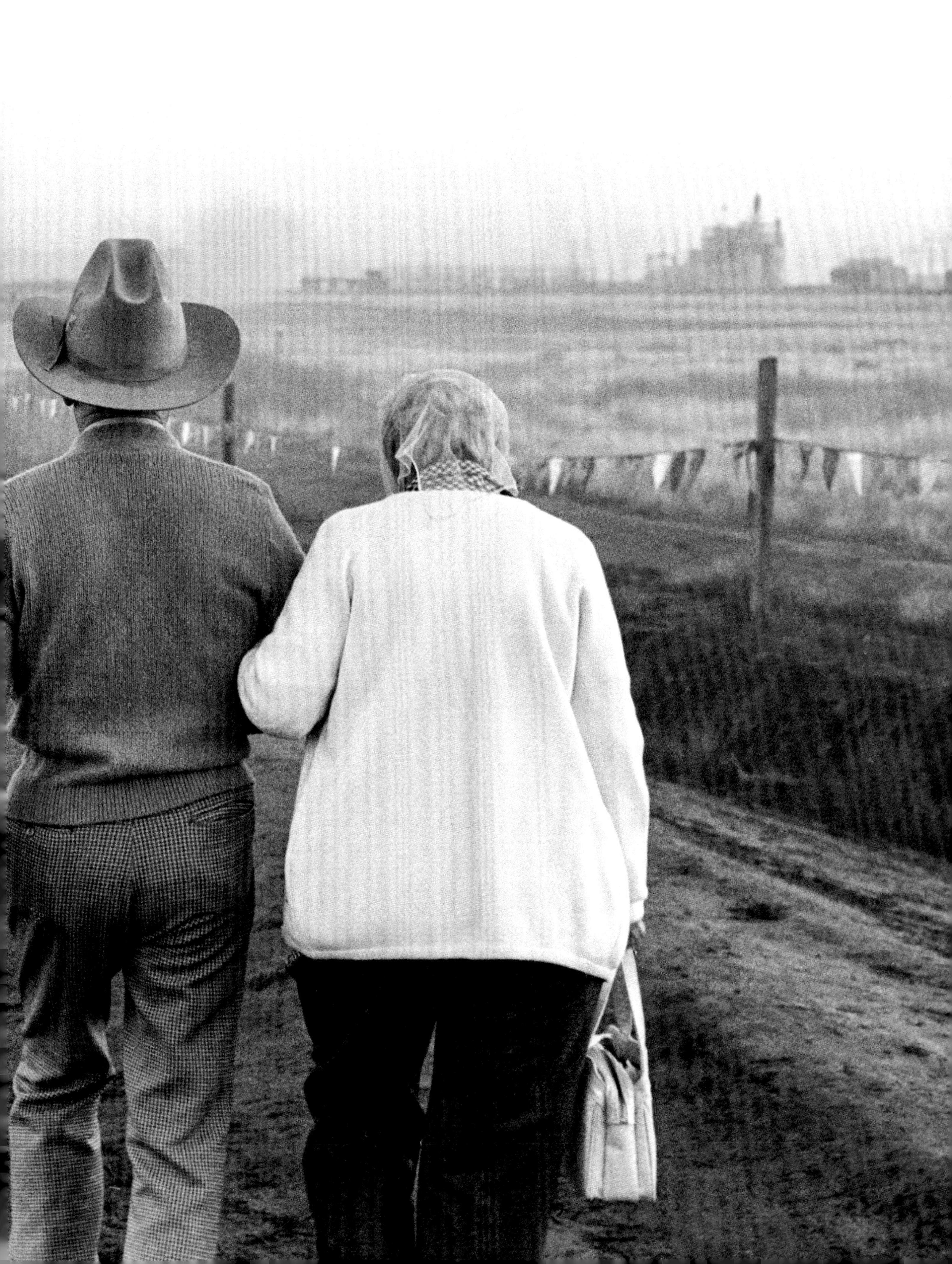

Acknowledgments

As ever, I am indebted first and foremost to my wife, Laura McKeon, who has always encouraged and supported my photographic work while keeping me grounded in our rich and loving family life. Ryan, Maria, Tara, Greg, and Ramona of our growing family have all contributed their suggestions about the images for the book.

My thanks to an extraordinary publishing team: Anna Gallegos, director of the Museum of New Mexico Press, for her enthusiastic interest in publishing this collection of photographs from forty years ago; art director and book designer David Skolkin, for his sensitive eye and careful attention to the final design and production management of the book; and Kate O'Donnell, for her superb editorial skills and for identifying several individuals and putting me in touch with Rahoul Contractor's family. Like so many who have pored over this snapshot of New Mexico in the early 1980s, Kate was there.

I also thank Nick Costantino for his fastidious and careful work on the scans of the hundreds of 35-mm negatives and for creating the excellent first draft of the book layout. Nick has worked with me for more than seven years, scanning several thousand negatives and transparencies and collaborating on the design of five of my books.

Bernard Plossu's Preface brings to us his enduring love for New Mexico and his energetic, fresh, and ever-curious perspective on photography. Matthew Martinez's essay provides a powerful lens through which to view and understand the photographs of Native people of Ohkay Owingeh and the other Northern Pueblos, and of incarcerated Native Americans at the Penitentiary of New Mexico. Don Usner, native New Mexican photographer and writer, reviewed an early layout of the book and gave his valuable seal of approval to the project. Thanks to Ian and Lois Alsop and to my brother Peter for reading through the early drafts of my narrative essay. My thanks to Kitty Leaken for her help with identifying many Santa Feans in the photos and to Nancy Sutor and Rahoul Contractor's siblings—Kirin, Maya, and Devendra—for sharing information on Rahoul. Sincere appreciation goes to Rexine Calvert at the Ohkay Owingeh Pueblo Library and Teresa Naranjo and Charles Suazo at the Santa Clara Pueblo Library, all of whom helped identify members of their communities who are pictured here.

My deepest gratitude extends to all the people of New Mexico who were voluntarily or inadvertently caught in front of my camera. My appreciation and thanks go to so many friends, acquaintances, and strangers encountered along the way. The list is long: the St. John's student-hitchhiker in Amarillo, Cheryl Brostrom, Stephen Cooper, Paul Hudock, Bruce "Pacho" Lane, Leroy Perea, Martin Eder, Michael Hausman, Edward James Olmos, Bernard Plossu, Nick Potter, Bill Clark, Ricky Stevens, Paljor Thondup, Pema Rabgay, Project Tibet, Synergia Ranch, Walter Nelson, Weston DeWalt, Lise Hosour, Terry Husebye, Ray Belcher, Siegfried Halus, Kitty Leaken, Steve Long, the staff and residents of the Penitentiary of New Mexico, *The Santa Fe New Mexican*, Doug and Martha Keats, Brad and Holly Bealmear, Kathy O'Neil, Wally Gordon, Linda Montoya, Jim Fisher, Robert Reck, Elray Deroin, Arturo Sandoval, and Marilyn Garcia, her mother Mary, and her brothers Mark, Michael, and Marvin. To name only a few.

If you were in Northern New Mexico in the early eighties and your name does not appear here, it probably should. I hold my time here and the people I met in great affection and boundless gratitude. Any errors, omissions, or lapses of memory are, of course, my own.

The Authors

Kevin Bubriski is a documentary photographer and Guggenheim Fellowship recipient whose photographs are in the permanent collections of the San Francisco Museum of Modern Art, the Museum of Modern Art, the Metropolitan Museum of Art, and Bibliothèque Nationale de France in Paris, among others. His numerous books include *The Uyghurs: Kashgar before the Catastrophe* (GTF Publishing), *Legacy in Stone: Syria before War* (powerHouse Books), *Nepal: 1975–2011* (Peabody Museum Press and Radius Books), *Look into My Eyes: Nuevomexicanos por Vida, '81–'83* (Museum of New Mexico Press), and *Portrait of Nepal* (Chronicle Books). He lives in Vermont.

World-renowned French photographer **Bernard Plossu** was born in Vietnam and grew up in Paris. His publications include *Le Voyage Mexicain: 1965–1966* (Contrejour), *Monet Intime* (Filigranes), *Avant l'Age de Raison* (Éditions Filigranes), *¡Vámonos! Bernard Plossu in México* (Aperture), *The Still Hour / La hora inmóvil* (La Fabrica), *Western Colors* (Thames and Hudson), and *En Dépliant les Montagnes* (Éditions Bressard). His work is widely exhibited in galleries and museums internationally and is in the permanent collections of the Albuquerque Museum, the Museum of Fine Arts, Houston, the Center for Creative Photography in Tucson, the San Francisco Museum of Modern Art, the Centre Pompidou in Paris, and the Institut Valencià d'Art Modern (IVAM) in Valencia, Spain. Plossu lives in La Ciotat, France.

Matthew J. Martinez, Ph.D., is a lifelong educator who has dedicated his career to the protection of and education about heritage sites. He has researched and published in the areas of Pueblo history, documentary filmmaking, and cultural production. Martinez previously served as First Lieutenant Governor at Ohkay Owingeh and is currently Executive Director of the Mesa Prieta Petroglyph Project, a nonprofit organization in northern New Mexico whose mission is focused on land stewardship and educational outreach.

 The Museum of New Mexico Press is a division of New Mexico Department of Cultural Affairs.

Director: Anna Gallegos
Art director and book designer: David Skolkin
Project editor: Joan Kathryn O'Donnell
Composition: Set in Dante and Din
Manufactured in China
10 9 8 7 6 5 4 3 2 1

Library of Congress Control Number: 2024934395
ISBN: 978-089013-685-0

Museum of New Mexico Press
PO Box 2087
Santa Fe, New Mexico 87504
mnmpress.org

JACKET: Anita Lujan and Juan Lujan, Deer Dance, Ohkay Owingeh, 1982.
COVER: Good Friday, Chimayó, 1982.